FIGHTING YEARS

OSWALD GARRISON VILLARD

FIGHTING YEARS

Memoirs of a Liberal Editor

BY OSWALD GARRISON VILLARD

Harcourt, Brace and Company   New York

first edition

E
664
V65
V5

Appleton 282 Ap '39

17683

TO

MY WIFE

AND TO OUR

DOROTHEA MARSHALL, HENRY HILGARD,

AND OSWALD GARRISON, JR.

ACKNOWLEDGMENT

To Lewis S. Gannett and Carl Van Doren for advice and encouragement; to my classmate W. DeLancey Howe for helpful criticism; to my secretary Maude L. Kimberley, who for twenty-five years has loyally suffered the vagaries of an editor.

CONTENTS

ILLUSTRATIONS

FIGHTING YEARS

Chapter I. The "Divergent Strains"

AS Mark Twain once remarked about someone else, I was born abroad "during the temporary absence" of my parents. As a boy I was proud of this because I liked Germany and my German relatives, and it seemed to give me a little distinction since my two brothers and my sister were American-born. I made no mistake in the selection of my father and mother, and was exceptionally lucky in becoming related to my father, for there were various times in his life before I became his son when I nearly lost my chance to be that. For example, on the seventh day of April, 1863, a Confederate teamster in all likelihood preserved my father's life, and put me under lasting obligation, by driving his team and wagon across a couple of wires laid upon the ground and severing them. For my father was on the Federal flagship *New Ironsides* and those wires ran from Fort Moultrie to a vertical boiler full of explosives placed in the center of the channel close to the Moultrie shore for the express purpose of destroying Admiral Dupont's heavy-draught vessel. It was not the fault of the *New Ironsides* that the Confederate plan did not succeed. So badly under-engined as scarcely to be able to stem the tide, she placed herself squarely on the boiler, hung there, was compelled to anchor, never got any further, and was thus unable to take part in the attack on Fort Sumter which resulted in the defeat of the rest of the fleet. All that the *New Ironsides* could do was to engage Fort Moultrie at close range. Officers in the fort again and again pressed the key of their new-fangled galvanic battery, but the teamster had saved the flagship and the men on her.[1]

[1] Cf. Lieutenant Colonel Freemantle (of the British army), *Three Months in the Southern States*, New York, 1864, pp. 198-99. See also, Loyal Legion Commandery of the State of Illinois, *Military Essays and Recollections*, Chicago, 1891, p. 195.

My father was the only one of the war correspondents with the fleet who obtained permission to participate in the battle rather than remain in safety on a transport beyond the Charleston bar. When the engagement was on, he forgot that he was a non-combatant, volunteered his services, and acted as aide to Captain C. R. P. Rodgers, which brought him a letter from that officer saying, "your personal gallantry and unhesitating devotion in the exercise of your professional duty won for you the respect and confidence of us all." Six days later my father personally delivered his long account of the Federal defeat to his employer, the New York *Tribune*, which issued it in full in an extra edition. This remarkable journalistic exploit won for him what was his second leave of absence since his reporting of the Battle of Bull Run in 1861. On the advice of the managing editor, he spent it in Boston where he passed two fateful weeks, for there he met Fanny Garrison, the only daughter of William Lloyd Garrison. In 1866, as soon as it was financially possible for them after the close of the war, their marriage took place.

A magazine writer, who has written of the "curiously divergent strains" within Oswald Villard, thought that there must needs be something "unusual and contradictory" about the product of those strains, and seemed to think that he found in them the explanation of my failure in life. In fact, the strains were extraordinarily similar. Henry Villard and his father-in-law were alike in their fundamental beliefs and ideals, and approached life from the same point of view, although they could hardly have had more dissimilar upbringings. Mr. Garrison had staked his life for many years on liberty for the Negro slaves; for this same cause Henry Villard had just risked his existence, and he continued to risk it as a war correspondent until the end of the horrible slaughter in the Wilderness and before Richmond. Both men were republicans to their finger tips, could conceive of no other defensible form of government, and passionately believed that it was possible to build the edifice of a perfect State upon American soil. Both held to the same social idealism, were complete liberals, were ardent internationalists in that they abhorred war, were devoted free traders, and

believed in the brotherhood of man. Both were steeped in the doctrines of the Manchester school of British liberalism, and both
personally knew and admired John Bright and Richard Cobden.
True, there were a few divergencies between my father and my
grandsire. To Garrison the use of wine was a crime second only to
justification of slavery. My father never gave it up. Furthermore,
it took some time to win one who was reared in Germany to
woman suffrage. But the two men lived together for months, yes,
years at a time—Mr. Garrison died under my father's roof—in
complete sympathy and deep affection, for both sought to serve
their generation and their time with all the means at their command.

William Lloyd Garrison was not, as he has so often been described, a "fire-eater" in the usual sense, nor was he in his own
home "uncomfortable," but one of the most lovable, kindly, and
generous of men. It was difficult then to reconcile him with the
grim, determined crusader who, in his editorial chair and on the
platform, poured forth the strongest language he could frame to
arouse his countrymen and overwhelm his adversaries. John Jay
Chapman, one of the Garrison biographers, wrote that he doubted
"if any man ever knew the Bible so well, or could produce a text
to fit a political emergency with such startling felicity as Garrison."
In proof of this, Mr. Chapman adduced the text provided by Garrison for Wendell Phillips's speech on the Sunday following Lincoln's call for troops in 1861: "Therefore thus saith the Lord: Ye
have not hearkened unto me in proclaiming liberty everyone to his
brother, and every man to his neighbor: behold I proclaim a liberty for you, saith the Lord, to the sword, to the pestilence, and
to the famine." "I doubt," Mr. Chapman continues, "whether
Cromwell or Milton could have rivaled Garrison in this field of
quotation; and the power of quotation is as dreadful a weapon as
any which the human intellect can forge." [2]

Mr. Garrison's face in repose was strikingly benevolent; in action remarkably mobile. The slightest smile, his daughter wrote,
"gave him the kindliest and sunniest of expressions." He had a

[2] John Jay Chapman, *William Lloyd Garrison*, New York, 1913, p. 165.

winning voice, a heart overflowing with good will. But when he said he would be "as harsh as truth and as uncompromising as justice" he meant it, and he lived up to it. The torrent of denunciation of slavery that came from his lips he never felt to be inconsistent with his own inborn kindliness, or his devotion to Biblical precepts and the teachings of the Savior. When it came to attacking wrong, his face was rigid, his eyes steely; he was of the iron of the Covenanter, crystal-clear, slashing, indomitable, unyielding, overwhelming, Niagara-like in the vigor and magnificence of his vocabulary—he who had never had schooling after his twelfth year. He was no polished orator—just a human being possessed of the tremendous sense of wrong that completely mastered him. As Chapman puts it: "The young Garrison, the man of twenty-four, when he discovered Immediate Emancipation, was the vortex of an unseen whirlpool. Through his brain spun the turbillion. Something was to break forth; for the power was bursting its envelope. The flood issued in the form in which we know it,—with purposed vilification, with excoriating harshness, with calculated ferocity. Only in this manner could it issue: the dam could hold the flood no longer, nor live it into poetic expression." [3]

It is the fashion of a new school of historians to say that this man and others brought on the Civil War by the violence of their language, that the Abolition cause would have progressed far faster had they been calm and moderate in their utterances. But Garrison's language was dictated by the monstrous evil which he sought to challenge, which, when he first defied it, was not only established in our fundamental laws but dominated the political, financial, and economic life of the nation, was entrenched in privilege, was favored by the church, the press, the learned professions, the universities, by all the elect and the well-to-do. Assault these citadels with gentle, unoffending words? Impossible. The verbal violence of Garrison did shock and horrify the possessing classes who, as always, wished to let well enough alone, did not propose to have the serenity of their lives disturbed by firebrand agitators, and above all would do nothing to interfere with making money

[3] John Jay Chapman, *William Lloyd Garrison*, New York, 1913, p. 193.

by trade with the South.[4] The truth is that Wendell Phillips and Garrison were so constituted that they were never unaware of the endless personal suffering caused by slavery. They felt the lashes upon their own backs, the brandings upon their own limbs. Their eyes never failed to see broken and tortured families, mothers torn from their offspring, the numberless ravished women who bore their masters' children only to see those children "sold South" if the master died or lost his means. They never forgot by day or by night the demoralization by slavery of the slaveholders themselves. Given their natures, it was impossible for them not to appeal to high heaven with all the vehemence of which they were capable, determined that no man or woman rest in peace if they could but reach them with their spoken or written word.

What could you do with a man like this Garrison? He had no social position to lose. He was in debt to nobody. No one had any hold upon him with which to padlock his utterances. He had no sacrifices to make. Furthermore, he insisted upon living an absolutely blameless private life, which was a great vexation to his enemies. You threw him into jail, and he liked it immensely, and utilized the opportunity to strike off his best bit of verse. You put a price upon his head and he gloried in it. You threatened him with death, and dragged him through the streets with a rope around his waist, and he showed his courage by failing even to be excited, and went home to utilize your outbreak against him in a most effective sermon against the thing that you were seeking to uphold. You tried to reach him through his bank account, or his social affiliations, or his desire for power, and you found that he had none of these.

You ridiculed him as a nobody. He calmly admitted it and went on preaching his gospel of liberty. You tried to close the mails to him, to undermine his influence, his reputation, his judgment, and his sanity, and he went on pounding you, convicting you out of your own mouth, and printing in his column in *The Liberator*, headed "The Refuge of Oppression," telltale happenings

[4] Garrison's imprisonment in Baltimore was due to his denunciation of a ship captain from his home town of Newburyport who took part in the slave trade.

in the South, taken chiefly from Southern newspapers, which portrayed at its worst the institution which you were seeking to defend or to let alone. You called him an effeminate fanatic because he would stand up for the cause of woman in a day when there were fewer suffragists than Abolitionists and, in spite of this, he continued to insist that his platform was not occupied unless women stood upon it. How could you keep your patience with a man like this—one who would not only "let loose the savage Negro" upon the Southern communities, but believed that every walk of life, every sphere of intellectual activity, should be opened to the despised sex, and actually preached that women, not men, should decide what place women should occupy in modern society? And always he insisted upon being happy, no matter what you said or did to him.

My earliest memories have to do with this grandfather in his home in Roxbury, then a pleasant suburb of Boston, to which came every member of the family, with complete love and devotion, to round out a circle unmarred by discord of any kind. There was something in those mild eyes behind the gold spectacles, and in those wonderfully firm lines around the generous mouth of the head of the house, which gave the little grandson concern if he strayed from the straight and narrow path. One of his clearest recollections is of the nonresistant grandfather [5] leading a terrified, and therefore decidedly nonresistant, grandson into durance vile for having wickedly and malevolently assailed other urchins with what the Abolitionists were wont, in their Biblical language, to call "carnal weapons." The transformation which came over the kindly eyes and the firm mouth of the Liberator, then turned jailer, made it easy for that little boy in later years to picture his grandfather in the heat of uncompromising attacks upon the powers of evil; to see him, in his mind's eye, facing the Rynders's mob in New York City, or writing that ringing declaration that he would not "retreat a single inch" and that he *would* "be heard."

[5] Tolstoy repeatedly expressed his indebtedness to Garrison for his confirming him in nonresistance, just as Gandhi has expressed his indebtedness to Tolstoy for his policy of nonviolence.

WILLIAM LLOYD
GARRISON

HELEN BENSON
GARRISON

As for Henry Villard, Romance watched by his cradle as well as the fairies who were so generous in their benefactions to him. They endowed him primarily with a superb physical presence and personal beauty—he stood a straight six feet, with a great frame crowned by a magnificent head that made men invariably turn to look at him when he entered a room or an assembly. Born Heinrich Hilgard in the old Kaiser city of Speyer on the Rhine, in 1848, when but thirteen, he broke up the school he was attending at Zweibruecken, in the Palatinate, by refusing to lead his class in prayer for "his consecrated majesty," the King of Bavaria. That royal personage having just been deposed in the Palatinate by this boy-rebel's uncle, Friedrich Hilgard, who was the head of the provisional revolutionary government, my father insisted that it would be illegal to pray for the king and not for his uncle's government. It was the last straw for the harassed teachers and the school was closed—never again to open its doors for my father. When the pitiful little revolutionary army was dispersed by a few volleys from the Prussian Guards, kindly loaned by the King of Prussia to the endangered monarch of Bavaria, the city authorities decreed that Heinrich Hilgard could never again attend any school in Zweibruecken. His father, who had remained loyal to the king, being a judge and on his way to the Supreme Court of Bavaria, emerged from hiding and exiled his only son for a year, sending him to a military school in Pfalzbourg in Alsace, then French territory.

The rift thus begun between father and son was widened during my father's university years. He revolted at the University of Munich against his father's decree that he must study law. Transferred to the University of Würzburg, he lived not wisely, nor too well, and, seeing that a second day of reckoning was at hand, embarked on a sailing vessel for New York. His father's threat to put him in the ranks of the army in the event of further difficulty was the reason both for his immigration and his taking, in fear lest his father have him returned to Germany, the name of a schoolmate in Pfalzbourg, Henri Villard. On October 18, 1853, when only eighteen and one-half years of age, he landed in

New York, without knowing a word of English, with no relatives and friends nearer than St. Louis, with only twenty dollars in his pockets and these borrowed on the ship. Under existing immigrant laws he would have been turned back. Life then became a desperate struggle for bare existence, and for such a battle this boy was hardly equipped. But the dauntless courage, the faith in himself, the unbending determination to succeed, which the fairies had vouchsafed to him, carried him—with his luck in finding a haven with a former servant of his father's—even through the panic of 1857 when many similar adventurers literally died of starvation, there being no public relief then for the destitute and the unemployed.

In 1858 the tide turned. Always having desired to be a writer above all else, this child of destiny reported in that year, in German, the Lincoln-Douglas debates for the New York *Staats-Zeitung* and began a friendship with Abraham Lincoln. Some of the incidents of their association have found their way into various books about the Emancipator and are recorded in my father's Memoirs.[6] Early the next year found him in Indianapolis rejoicing in being in the service of the Cincinnati *Commercial* as its Indiana legislative correspondent. Henry Villard had thus found his way into English language journalism in a little more than five years after landing at Castle Garden. But hardly had he entered upon his work in Indianapolis than he was expelled from the Senate press gallery because of some just strictures he had written upon one of the Democratic State Senators. He returned crestfallen to Cincinnati, to be received warmly by Murat Halstead, the distinguished editor of the *Commercial,* who not only upheld him editorially but gave him a thrilling assignment—to proceed to the new settlements in the wilds of Colorado to ascertain if the reported discovery of gold there was based on fact.

In the spring of 1859 my father had the distinction of being the only passenger in the first stagecoach run from Leavenworth

[6] See Carl Sandburg's *Abraham Lincoln, the Prairie Years,* New York, 1926; see also Emil Ludwig's *Lincoln,* Boston, 1930, and *Memoirs of Henry Villard,* Boston, 1904.

to Denver, a trip that took seven and one-half days. Later he interviewed the original discoverer of gold, and a widely published statement that Colorado gold *was* a reality, signed by Horace Greeley of the New York *Tribune*, Albert D. Richardson of the Boston *Journal*, and Henry Villard of the Cincinnati *Commercial*, had a marked effect in stimulating the great trek to Colorado in the summer and fall of 1859 and the spring of 1860. My father spent six months riding over a good portion of Colorado and then decided to return to the East in order to publish a book about Colorado and the gold region to be of use to emigrants. As he was nearing St. Joseph, Missouri, in November, 1859, driving a wagon which, with two horses, a gold watch, a rifle, and $1,200 in cash, was the price paid to him for some town lots he had acquired in the very center of modern Denver, he met two shivering men in a buggy. One of them was Abraham Lincoln, to whom he loaned a much appreciated, but never returned, buffalo robe.

With his book off the press in the spring of 1860,[7] my father plunged at once into the Presidential campaign, first of all reporting the Chicago convention which nominated Abraham Lincoln. This assembly always seemed to him unsurpassed for "intelligence, character, earnestness and enthusiasm." That campaign was a stirring and highly educational experience for this reporter twenty-five years of age. He covered Illinois, Indiana, Ohio, and Michigan, with occasional trips into Kentucky, Wisconsin, and Missouri, for the Cincinnati *Commercial*, the St. Louis *Missouri-Democrat*, and the New York *Tribune*, whose correspondence he readily obtained because of his friendship with Horace Greeley. He was in Chicago when the election took place and when it was over the New York *Herald* stationed him at Springfield, Illinois, to report for it, and through it for all the members of the New York Associated Press of that period, the day-by-day actions of the President-elect. Thus multitudes of Americans received their news

[7] My father's book on Colorado, published in Cincinnati in June, 1860, *The Past and Present of the Pike's Peak Gold Regions,* was reissued as a vital historical document by the Colorado Historical Society through the Princeton University Press in 1932.

of Abraham Lincoln from December until March from the pen
of this immigrant youth whose mastery of English dated back
scarcely three years. Those stirring months of daily contact with
one of the greatest figures in history terminated for my father
when he, too, took the historic train that bore Abraham Lincoln
to Washington. Immediately upon starting, my father helped to
preserve the pathetic farewell to his friends and neighbors, which
Lincoln had just uttered, by inducing the President-elect to write
it out for him on a pad, so that it could be telegraphed, a priceless
document which my father unfortunately lost in the exigencies of
the war so close at hand.

Next came the Civil War; to few men was it given to see
more of this struggle. Bull Run; Shiloh; the desperate battle at
Perryville, Kentucky; Fredericksburg; the attack on Charleston;
Murfreesboro; Chattanooga; Missionary Ridge; the Wilderness
and Petersburg, these were my father's major battles, none so terrible, he felt, as the horrible slaughter in the successive conflicts
in the Wilderness. He missed only the Appomattox campaign,
having returned to Germany for a happy and lasting reconciliation
with his father during the lull in the fighting. He arrived in
Boston early in April, 1865, expecting to be in at the death of the
Confederacy, only to hear of Lee's surrender and of the assassination of Lincoln. These four years of war left him a convinced
pacifist, a conviction intensified in 1866 by his observation of the
abominable wreckage of war which he found still on the fields of
battle of the Austro-German struggle, where he arrived just too
late to report the fighting.

For several years after my father's marriage an unkind fate
seemed to control his life, bringing ill health, even an apoplectic
stroke, to make the doctors prophesy that never again would he
be able to accomplish hard mental labor—a dreadful blow to a
man who lived by his pen. Presto change! There began an
entirely new and a marvelous phase of this man's career. The illness that had seemed all but fatal brought him, by the accident
of his recuperating in Heidelberg and his meeting one of a group
of German holders of defaulted Oregon and California Railroad

Company bonds, to the opening of a business career which, within eight years, made him the most talked-of figure in the American financial world. He was at once invited to join a bondholders' protective committee set up in Frankfurt and to give it the benefit of his knowledge of American conditions. In April, 1874, he sailed for New York as the official representative of the committee, at which time I first arrived in the United States. My father soon discovered that one of the railway lines, against which $3,000,000 of seven per cent bonds had been sold to German investors, had never been built at all. His first trip to Oregon soon after his return filled him with enthusiasm for the Pacific Northwest, and resulted in a lengthy printed report to the Frankfurt committee. This report favorably impressed another committee, which my father had also been asked to join, formed for the protection of the bondholders of the Kansas Pacific Railroad Company.

This straightening out of the affairs of these and still other companies, notably the Oregon Steamship Company running between Portland and San Francisco, the only regular connection that Oregon then had with the rest of the world, resulted in my father's having to assume the management of these companies because the bondholders' committees demanded that he work out the reorganization plans which he had devised and submitted after further study in Oregon. In a very short time, by the end of April, 1876, he was elected president of the Oregon and California Railroad and the Oregon Steamship Company, and later in the year he was appointed by the United States District Court for Eastern Kansas one of the two receivers of the Kansas Pacific Railroad Company. Seventeen years after leaving Denver, driving his two-horse wagon, he returned to that city on a special Kansas Pacific train, to find a fine city of thirty to forty thousand inhabitants in place of the hundred frame shanties and log houses he had left in 1859. Thereafter his rise in the railroad world was spectacular. Vision plus character, plus brains, plus unflagging energy, plus the belief that he could thus repay his debt to his adopted country, lifted him in the briefest of periods out of the role of a struggling press correspondent to that of a railroad organizer and builder. He became successively the creator and president of the Oregon Railway and Navigation Company, the creator of the Oregon Improvement Company, founded to develop the material and natural resources of Oregon, of the Oregon Transcontinental Company, and other corporations.

Few would believe in the possibility of so amazing a career were it to be set forth in a novel, or in the likelihood of such an incident as the Blind Pool of February, 1881. My father one day called upon his friends to loan him $8,000,000 for a certain enterprise which he had in mind, with no other explanation of what the money was to be used for except the simple statement that he would account for it in the following May—which accounting was, in fact, subsequently postponed until June. Nothing like this had happened in Wall Street before and nothing like it has happened since. There was a mad rush for participation, so that within twenty-four hours more than twice the amount my father had asked for was subscribed. Indeed, subscriptions commanded at once a 25 per cent premium and then jumped to 40 and 50 per cent! For their money the subscribers received nothing except a simple nontransferable receipt to which was signed the name of Henry Villard. With the money thus given him he founded the Oregon and Transcontinental Company and purchased a controlling interest in the Northern Pacific Railway Company, to the presidency of which my father was elected in September, 1881, thus assuming the burden of completing the first Northwestern transcontinental line. But nothing in this amazing rise to fame and fortune was more astounding than the brevity of his eminence. Only two and one-half years after the Blind Pool, Fate definitely turned against him. He found out what it was to be deserted by friends and sycophants. The railroad he had completed collapsed and so did others of his companies. There came a lapse of years and then an insistent demand that he again become the dominating personality in the Northern Pacific Railroad. He accepted, but the resumption of his railroad career brought him nothing but disappointments, bitterness, more unjust attacks upon his motives and his character.

Nothing could, however, satiate Henry Villard's creative instinct, nor dim his vision of what might be done nor his glimpsing of the future. At the very end of his life, in 1900, when sixty-five years old, he sensed the marvelous future of the then just appearing automobile. Thomas A. Edison once wrote that he could never have achieved what he did without the complete faith and the aid of Henry Villard, because the latter alone, of all the financiers of the 80's and 90's, could visualize the unlimited possibility of the electric current and light. My father built and equipped the first steamship, the *Columbia*, ever to be electrically lighted, only to find that no insurance company would insure a steamer which, they said, was certain to burn up before it reached Cape Horn; the original generator is carefully preserved in the Ford Museum at Dearborn. He was the first railroad president to experiment, years before any other, with the application of electrical power to the trains of a great railroad. He was the originator of the horizontal holding company when it was impossible to obtain money to finance electric light in local communities because of the lack of faith in such enterprises, a holding company device outrageously abused and distorted in the get-rich-quick years from 1924 to 1929 by the policy of piling one holding company on top of another. His keen interest in political life never abated. There was never a time when he did not regularly read the London *Times*, one or two German dailies, and often a French journal. With sinking heart he foresaw the changing character of American life, the nation's plunge into imperialism foreshadowed by the needless war with Spain. He never lost the international viewpoint which made him the journalist that he was and kept him at all times informed as to what was going on in the whole world.

If Henry Villard's face was stern in action—immediate subordinates stood greatly in awe of him—his countenance was extraordinarily winning when it was at ease or smiling. Then his blue eyes were kindliness itself, his large and firm mouth, with its heavy mustache, revealing perfect teeth. His persuasiveness was proverbial. Men of high importance preferred to write to him when they had to disagree with him. "I won't go to see him," said the most prominent New York banker once. "I don't want to go on with him, but if I see him he'll twist me around his little finger." Many others testified to his irresistible charm, enthusiasm, ability, forcefulness of statement. The impression he made upon others is best illustrated by the warmth of the friendships which he began during the Civil War, notably with General Sherman, when he was comparatively new to this country, which friendships continued for life. His temperament was usually sanguine to a degree; but when his spirits drooped they went down far indeed, and the rebound was slower as the years passed. It was this sanguineness and his ability to look so far ahead which were responsible for many of his mistakes and weakened his judgments. Many men who knew him and worked with him have said to me that his only trouble was that he was always far ahead of his times and built too rapidly, being too optimistic that the new field would at once support his enterprises. Again, his judgment of men was often faulty. He assumed that those around him were as sincere and as loyal as himself—a trait unhappily inherited by both of his sons.

Above all else my father was a most devoted American. I once asked him if it would please him to have me join a German club in New York. He startled me by the warmth of his reply. "Under no circumstances; you are an American and nothing else. Stick to your American clubs." Indeed, I believe that no other group of immigrants ever brought to the United States such passionate loyalty, such absolute devotion, as those Germans like my father who came here after their revolutionary efforts in 1848 to establish a German Republic. Although they were conscious of the social and intellectual backwardness of the America of the 1850's, it was still the realization of their democratic dreams, and they ever voiced their gratitude to our institutions which the native-born take as a matter of course. They sided at once with the North in the anti-slavery struggle and were among the very first to volunteer when war itself came—Sigel, Blenker, Willich, Schurz, Hecker—the list is long and impressive. My father declined a captain's commission that Lincoln offered him in the regular army only because he felt that he could be of greater service as a reporter in the field, though there he often had to take more chances than most officers. Some of these German-Americans had spent years in prison wearing heavy chains, and others, like Schurz, had preserved their lives as by a miracle. Their gratitude to the country that gave them asylum and citizenship was ever vibrant and alive; they were never without a profound interest in its political affairs and an abiding sense of public duty and civic responsibility.

My adoption of a journalistic career and my being his only child at home during his last years brought my father and me close together in a tie that endures. The inspiration of his ideals and of his character cannot be properly, or with sufficient modesty, described by a son who can never be grateful enough for an idealistic father who held his wealth to be merely a trusteeship. Henry Villard's greatest aim was to repay the country of his choice in return for, as he put it himself, "the incomparable advantages arising from the free play of the human faculties enjoyed in this country." To which he added that he never forgot that he was "himself a living illustration of the benefits of these conditions," and he never failed to acknowledge indebtedness to them. But this son of Henry Villard may perhaps be permitted to say that in all those precious years he never heard from his father's lips one selfish or self-seeking word, nor any expression of opinion that could be described as else than high-minded and liberal.

If the task of describing this parent is so profoundly difficult, that of conveying an adequate and just picture of my mother is still harder. Fanny Garrison Villard lived three lives. Her girlhood was wrapped up in the Abolition cause. To her father's modest home came the greatest figures of that conflict, both black and white, ever welcome no matter how bare the larder, how tiny the means. The larder *was* often bare, the family means incredibly small. How Mr. Garrison was able to support a wife and the five of his seven children who grew to maturity is hard to explain. Yet the hospitality of the home was unbounded and the children did their share of the household work with enthusiasm. Thus Fanny Garrison learned early the joy of working for others, of relieving and caring for her mother, in later years a complete invalid. For thirty years my grandmother bade her husband good-by in the morning without feeling certain that his enemies would let him return alive. My mother's vivacity, charm, and unusual beauty have been frequently recorded. In the latter she lived up to the family standard; according to the New York *Sun* her grandmother was a famous Nova Scotia beauty. In addition to all her household tasks, she made herself a competent teacher of the piano and thus contributed to her own support. Handicapped always by the smallness of her hands and the lack of adequate technical instruction in her youth, she was unusually musical in execution, interpretation and taste—in other words, a born musician. She gave to her children's musical instruction unending hours, however pressing her social and household duties might be.

At seventeen Fanny Garrison witnessed the coming of the Civil War. Under her father's roof she had seen John Brown of the Harper's Ferry curtain raiser to that great struggle—Brown being much disappointed that his host refused to countenance his efforts to free the slaves by force—and beheld in 1861 the realization of her father's demand that there should be no union with slaveholders. The great drama of the century was at hand. She remembered vividly the ideally handsome Colonel Robert Gould Shaw going off at the head of his black regiment, the Fifty-Fourth Massachusetts, to his death on the ramparts of Fort Wagner and to burial in an unmarked grave among his "niggers" where he and they fell. She saw her oldest brother, George, break amicably with his nonresistant father and go to the front as a lieutenant in the Fifty-Fifth Massachusetts, the companion Negro regiment to Colonel Shaw's. She never forgot the anxiety that followed her brother's departure, since the press of the South had announced that officers of Negro troops would not be taken prisoners but shot, and anyone who bore the name of Garrison must have been an especial target. With her other brothers she attended the profoundly thrilling Emancipation Meeting in Tremont Temple on January 1, 1863, to celebrate the unconditional emancipation of the slaves which the Abolitionist voices in the wilderness had demanded for three decades. It was a gathering electrified by the reading of the Emancipation Proclamation, a copy of which arrived just before its adjournment; her father heralded it in his *Liberator* the next day as a "great historic event, sublime in its magnitude, and eminently just and right alike to the oppressor and the oppressed."

Then war brought to her the young war correspondent, Henry Villard. They met at Dr. Dio Lewis's gymnasium where she, in the eminently respectable but none the less, for that day, extremely daring, bloomer costume, took part in what was the first gymnastic class for girls ever organized in Boston. Her younger brother had been thrilled to meet, at the home of Wendell Phillips, a war correspondent straight from the front and immediately invited him to the Dio Lewis performance. The meetings of my parents were few, but the future was settled for them both before he returned to the front, to the horrors that still awaited the Army of the Potomac. When on January 3, 1866, their marriage took place, there began the second and most romantic phase of Fanny Garrison's full, varied, and exceptionally interesting life. The first transition was startling and exciting. She, who in her twenty-one years had rarely left her simple paternal home, was whisked to Washington and plunged into the stirring first winter of peace by the side of her husband who, as Washington correspondent of the Chicago *Tribune*, was at the very heart of things. The capital was deep in the aftermath of Appomattox; uniforms had not yet left the streets; the tragedy of Lincoln still overhung the city; the curtain had risen on the tragedy of Reconstruction. For the impeachment of the President then in the White House her father was appealing to one audience after another. The young bride beheld at close range Salmon P. Chase, Gideon Welles, Charles Sumner, Schuyler Colfax, Thaddeus Stevens, Lyman Trumbull, John Sherman—the whole galaxy of men who were then endeavoring to remold the nation, men as to whose merits and demerits bitter controversies rage until this day—and found them glad to welcome the daughter of Garrison.

Amid the drama of Washington she met men at arms who had marched, camped, and faced hostile bullets with her husband. For one who had led so sheltered a life it was astounding how much at ease she was with them and how amazingly well educated for one whose formal education had been restricted to the public school. But the Winthrop School in Boston did for her what few of our many schools do for their pupils today—taught her a beautiful handwriting which never faltered while she lived, made her mistress of her own language and unusual in its expression. Nature had done the rest. It had given her a ready and quick mind; complete simplicity bordering on ingenuousness; the warmest of hearts, which often betrayed her and warped her judgments, and an unlimited capacity for sympathy with others; a winsomeness that never failed to attract, and a woman's skill to adjust herself to totally new scenes, to life with a man of foreign birth and a training so utterly at variance with hers. And he, in turn, opened up one world after another for her, took her overseas, and showed her that all men are kin and that the aspirations of all peoples are fundamentally the same.

Their stay in Washington was comparatively brief, being ended by my father's fruitless dash to the battlefields of the war between Austria and Prussia for the New York *Tribune*. They remained two years in Germany. Then followed alternate years of residence under Mr. Garrison's roof and sojourns abroad, years enjoyed with all possible zest despite the care of a household and three babies and, for a time, grave anxiety as to her husband's health. Within eight years of their marriage there began my father's rise from an impecunious journalist to one of the outstanding figures in the financial world, with corresponding wealth. That my mother remained entirely unchanged need not be stressed; her birth and training guaranteed that. Paradoxically, though always remaining quite unworldly, she became in the best sense a woman of the world. But wherever she went she carried with her the Garrisonian sympathy for the underdog, the Garrisonian sense of having some personal responsibility for injustice and wrong. She, too, knew that wealth obliges, and when the family reverses came she met them with a calm serenity and invariably sustained my father. In the darkest hours I never knew her courage to fail or

HENRY VILLARD

witnessed any doubt that the truth would prevail in the end. It was entirely natural for her to face criticism and financial loss if these were inseparable from the plain course of duty.

Always she was in her person a dainty aristocrat, dressing with exquisite taste and never with extravagance—an aristocrat in her fineness but entirely a democrat in her views and in her heart. Fear of the mighty and powerful she never had. She met all who came her way, whether laborer or crown prince, with a naturalness, a warmth, a disarming friendliness that had nothing to do with social conventions. Certain of the triumph of every cause to which she gave her devotion, she was incapable of compromise, without being either a bigot or narrowly puritanical. A tee-totaler always, she respected those who differed from her; when she asked the writer of these lines not to partake of alcoholic drinks, it was the easiest thing in the world to promise and to keep the promise, even in one's undergraduate days and when abroad. One could hardly refuse that mother anything! Though she was brought up in the straightest, and in certain respects the narrowest, of New England households, and for the greater part of her life regarded a sexual "sin" as the worst of all offenses, she was able, even in her eighties, to perceive and to understand the changes in standards and *mores* about her, to welcome them, and to believe that they meant a better, as well as a freer, association between men and women. To few is it given to have an open mind in the fullness of years and the readiness to accept modern ideas and novel policies. To modify any position she took for reasons of expediency—that was unthinkable; to shift her ground in order to gain a personal advantage, or to avoid unpleasantness, was as impossible for her as for her father, the strongest lines of whose countenance reappeared, with the years, in hers. But her certainty of the correctness of her positions, and her taking it as a matter of course that everyone she met agreed with her, quite often led her into difficulties and into injuring the feelings of others she would have been the last to wish to hurt.

When in 1900 my father died, and nearly thirty-five years of devoted happiness ended, there began the third epoch of my

mother's life. She had naturally been overshadowed by the powerful personality with whom she had shared those years. She reached
out now to build a life of her own. Other women of large wealth
have accepted widowhood as a commission to live idly and at ease,
to lay aside all cares, to roam as they pleased. For her it was a
summoning to devote her remaining years to the reforms in which
she was profoundly interested, notably woman suffrage and peace.
She found that she could speak in public and never quite got over
the surprise, being unaware how moving her voice could be, how
unfailing her charm and grace. Here I can do no better than to
repeat what I wrote when she left us in 1928:

Always the fact remains that hers was a lovely and inspiring presence.
. . . Men who had come to scoff at suffragettes went dumb when this
advocate arose who combined in herself every one of the lovely womanly
qualities. It is related of her that one rowdy legislative hearing became
quiet, respectful, and attentive the moment she began to speak. Here was
a great woman and a great lady; even the coarsest Tammany legislator
could see that and sense that hers was a testimony on behalf of her sex
not to be denied. Those white hairs above the still youthful face, those
flaming eyes, those earnest tones, that noble presence which was the
same and at ease in a sweltering children's clinic, or among the most
powerful of the earth, commanded immediate respect. And so did her
unfailing courage. A turbulent street procession moved her not at all;
she was of the few who dared to parade up Fifth Avenue at the outbreak of the war in protest against its folly and its crimes. Throughout
American participation in it she bore her testimony against war undaunted, to build up later the only kind of peace society she cared for—
one based on the inviolability of human life. It never occurred to her as
it did to some of her friends that she might be jeopardizing her social
position.[8]

She would not have cared a jot if she had. No thought of arrest or
prosecution could make her afraid in the days when there were
spies on every corner and a stupid government in Washington
eager to muzzle conscience and assassinate the character of whoever dissented. Finest of all was this indomitable spirit of hers.

[8] *The Nation*, New York, July 18, 1928.

Not even the greatest of human castastrophies, the World War, could cast it down or dim its radiant light.

These were the "divergent strains" which made me what I am. These were the parents who gave me every opportunity in life, every benefit that wealth could bestow, and forged for me the tools that I used in my effort to mold the public opinion of my time.

Chapter II. Our Life in New York

WHEN my parents moved to New York in the fall of 1876, because of my father's entering upon his railroad career and the unfavorable effect of the Boston climate upon his health, my conscious life began. The first winter we spent in the Westminster Hotel. In the fall of 1877 we moved into the Westmoreland, the first apartment house in the city with an elevator in it. Until a few years ago it stood on the corner of Seventeenth Street and Union Square, finally making place for the new, but always old, Tammany Hall. The Westmoreland was then in the center of the business and fashionable life of the city. Across the Square were Tiffany's, Brentano's, Gall and Lembke, the opticians, and other famous stores. Half a block above, on Broadway, there was the first Huyler's candy store (established in 1876), where ice-cream sodas were first introduced and the first commercial electric light plant was installed. There was not a shop on Fifth Avenue and years were to elapse before society was outraged by the news that a Fifth Avenue home was to be converted to business purposes. Washington Square was the most exclusive neighborhood and the "set" there ruled the city socially for several decades longer, combining wealth, good manners, family traditions, appreciation of music and art with the inevitably aristocratic and snobbish tendencies of any such group the world over. We had few friends there. Ours lived around us or as far uptown as the fifties. Seventeenth Street led east to Stuyvesant Square, St. George's Church, and the historic Friends' Meeting House, and to what was then also a fashionable section, Second Avenue, on which, near the corner of Fourteenth Street, stood the impressive residence of William M. Evarts, United States Senator and Secretary of State.

The New York of 1877 bore precious little resemblance to the metropolis of today. Its streets were filthy, and badly lighted, and so unsafe after nightfall that no well-dressed woman dared to go out alone. The police and the city government were hopelessly and brazenly corrupt. The purpose of the city's rulers was not to make a great city, or to render life easier and richer for its citizens, but to rob and exploit all of the weaker groups. There were gangs in plenty, contrary to the existing belief that gangsters are a product of prohibition and of the machine-gun and automobile age. A number of the gangs ruled supreme in their districts and were rarely bothered by the police. No wise man ventured into those districts after dark unless attended by others. It was a "wide open" city indeed; in the Tenderloin the brothels and crooked resorts of all kinds flourished openly, the police officials stationed there growing wealthy and admitting it, as when Inspector Williams told a legislative investigating committee that he had acquired hundreds of thousands of dollars by investing in "real estate in Japan." The city itself had no beauty save in such spots as Gramercy Park and Washington Square. Its architecture in all the new sections north of Madison Square was the hideous brown-stone dwelling. Every street was exactly like every other. No one then dared to violate convention by building what was known as an "English basement" residence and to discard the long steps up to the front door and the usual basement dining room.

There were many who contended that the indifference of New Yorkers to their corrupt politics and their dirty, ugly city was in part traceable to this total lack of architectural individuality and the complete domination of the conventional, as well as to lack of taste and of ethics. The docks and the water front were dreadfully run down, and the horrible slums through which ocean travelers drove to reach the inadequate hotels in cabs, whose drivers exacted five and ten dollars for short trips, made a most dismal and discouraging impression upon all foreigners. In the span of my life New York has been transformed into one of the most beautiful and impressive of cities, now very well governed as compared with the days of Tweed and Croker, and few people realize how degraded, dirty, and provincial Manhattan was; I was astounded when a Cabinet official asked me not long ago whether

New York had ever been badly governed! It seemed incredible that any New Yorker should be ignorant of the decades of civic struggle which have led up to the magnificent city of today. If there are still far too many slums and other evils, at least we have city governments, even under Tammany rule, which serve the poor infinitely better than was the case when we moved to New York. There would be a revolution if the city should retrace even one quarter of the way to the conditions that existed when the reform movement began and Edwin L. Godkin and *The Evening Post* began their ceaseless and invaluable attacks upon Tammany Hall and the corporation magnates who profited by it and supplied it with funds at election time.

At night Seventeenth Street was as quiet as a village thoroughfare save for a tiny one-horse, one-way street car, which ambled past the Westmoreland at decorous intervals, returning through Eighteenth Street. It often brought us our beloved New Jersey Garrison cousins from the Christopher Street Ferry and afforded us one of the nicest games we children played—recording the numbers of the cars until we had seen every one. To this day I can hear the horses' hooves pounding down the quiet street and the jangling of the bells. At night they gave me the assurance that all was well until they mingled with my dreams. Naturally our youthful friends came eagerly to ride up and down in that epoch-making elevator, but that new-fangled contraption cost the family dear. One day we children came in together and, finding the elevator upstairs, we boys stood by the front door. My sister, discovering that the elevator door was partly open, cried out, "It *is* here," and stepped in—only to plunge onto the cumbrous wheels at the bottom of the shaft. The injuries and the nerve shock she sustained laid the foundation for a life of semi-invalidism, too often nourished and not ended by the long array of doctors and surgeons called in at home and abroad.

None the less the Westmoreland years were happy ones, marked by the rapid improvement in the family finances. We grew from one apartment into two. We had a colored factotum, Hunter, who was butler, valet, and bodyguard for us youngsters and usually accompanied us when we left our playground in Union Square—then as conservative as it is radical today—for the long and adventurous trip by horsecar to school or to Central Park. Once we lost him while skating. Having but five cents between us, and I being the younger, my brother insisted on my riding home while he dared the long three-and-a-half mile walk through the early winter darkness, to be warmly praised for his unselfishness and his daring on his safe arrival home, while Hunter came in for a stiff scolding. Central Park had its thrills in those days. Once I saw a mass runaway in which seven carriages were involved, one coachman being pulled off his box and run over, while two women jumped from their victorias. It was worth going to the park just to see the exquisite carriages and horses of which I never wearied, the loss of which I regret to this day. Some of the turnouts were magnificent and the sleighs that appeared magically when there was enough snow were brilliant beyond easy description. The man I most envied drove a Russian troika with a splendid trotter flanked on each side by galloping mates; I felt that the whole outfit must have come direct from the Nevski-Prospekt in St. Petersburg. There was always a mad rush, when the snow was usable by sleigh owners, to be the first sleigh to reach McCombs Dam Bridge and McGowan's Tavern, for a magnum of champagne always awaited the first arrival of the winter. We never had a sleigh in the city but when the snow was very heavy the wheels came off our carriages and runners took their places.

We early acquired a coachman and horses, a Brewster landau, and a most solid, heavy, and comfortable victoria from the same firm, built to last. I veritably believe that it would be usable today if the motorcar had not appeared. For trips uptown we often used the old, high busses with straw on the floor in winter time and with the little hole in the roof near the driver. Through this one poked money and received change that was handed down in a neat, manila envelope with the amount printed on the outside. For schooling we boys went to the private school of James Herbert Morse, a Harvard graduate of fine taste and character, with pretensions to being a poet. I attended this school until I entered

Harvard. Its curriculum was conventionally barren. Mr. Morse was no modern school man and had no other thought than to teach the customary classical course. We had no laboratory, no chemistry, the merest smattering of physics, and the usual inadequate instruction in modern languages. It was considered a most daring innovation when we were given hot lunches under the supervision of Mrs. Morse, for the Morse family resided in the schoolhouse.

There were then only a few boarding schools and it had not yet become fashionable or necessary to send boys out of town. The tone of the Morse School was of the best and the friendships founded there have endured to this day. There were no stars among the graduates but they have represented the steadiest kind of solid, bourgeois citizens of the group that is so often described as the backbone of the Republic—conservative, of course, and generally Republican in politics, but men who have had my respect and affection throughout the years that have elapsed. Our annual reunions have meant more to me than those of my Harvard class. Perhaps my sole distinction in those school days was that I owned a pony and later a horse. Few believe me when I relate that I rode that beautiful little pony all the way up Fifth Avenue behind my mother's carriage and even occasionally found my way to and from Central Park alone. That is the fact, however, for my parents soon realized how trustworthy Dolly and I were together and how well she kept her dainty feet on the rough and slippery cobblestone pavements of pre-asphalt days.

We were sorry when we left the Westmoreland and moved into far more spacious and elaborate quarters uptown. Just before it was pulled down I wandered through those memory-hallowed rooms again—the one in which William Lloyd Garrison died in 1879, the poorly proportioned and low-ceilinged parlors that once had seemed so magnificent, the small bedrooms, the dark interior bathroom. As I passed for the last time through those Westmoreland rooms I suddenly remembered how, on one spring evening in 1879, my father had come to us children and told us we were to stay up far beyond bedtime to see something very wonderful.

FANNY GARRISON VILLARD AT THORWOOD

When it was dark he took us diagonally across the street to the Clarendon Hotel. There, sputtering and flickering away, and so bright as to be dazzling, were the first outdoor arc lights ever displayed in New York. I recalled, too, how we boys, immaculate in our velvet party suits, with our sister in a gay dress, white stockings, patent leather pumps, and her hair brushed back like that of Alice in Wonderland and well below her shoulders, left the Westmoreland with our parents to peek in at the great ball they gave at the Brunswick Hotel, or to go to receptions given by my father on board the, for that time, superb steamers he built for his Oregon and California Steamship Company which ran ships between San Francisco and Portland. Those receptions were considered genuine society events. We were tremendously thrilled by the ships and my father was proud that they were built in an American shipyard, that of John Roach at Chester. The old ships that he had found in service were horrible tubs, badly run, usually overcrowded, leaky, and quite unfit to keep the sea; my father never had a comfortable moment until they were retired.

One of the new vessels to which we children went to enjoy the consideration and freedom to roam given to the president's family was the *Oregonian*. A quarter of a century later I read one morning in Seattle that she had just arrived in port from Alaska. I rushed to my wife and gave her no rest until she went with me to see what I assured her was one of the loveliest steamers afloat. When we got on board she burst into laughter and I was utterly crestfallen, for I had completely forgotten the lapse of time and the progress of the shipbuilding art, and remembered the *Oregonian* as she had been in the pride and beauty of her youth when I was not even a dozen years old. We found her dirty, run down, worn out, more than ready for the watery grave soon to be hers. She was narrow, unbelievably small, incredibly antiquated, her staterooms tiny and primitive. As was the custom when she was built, her dining saloon was flanked on both sides by staterooms, so that those who reached the tables on those often terrible winter voyages along the California coast might have full benefit of the seasickness of the wretched people on the other side of the flimsy partitions. But when she left New York for the Pacific she was beautiful and a marvel of modernity.

As I look back on those Westmoreland days I remember that we children were never curious as to why our father should suddenly have risen as he did, why he should be building those fine ships and railroads, and founding electric light companies, and, when we traveled with him, as we did to California in the summer of 1877, why we should have occupied a private car, and how it was that we became possessed of such a magnificent country home. Those things seemed quite natural and befitting for Father. He was so big and impressive himself that it appeared the normal thing to have many people appeal to him, seeking his aid and advice and recognizing him as a distinguished leader. Not once, as I have indicated, did he ever suggest that wealth was an end in itself. He was far more interested in his great gifts to education and to philanthropies than in augmenting the family fortunes. He never urged that we should learn to make money; on the contrary he wished us to be professional men, and he never once spoke to us, not even when he knew that he was dying, of the size of his fortune or the amount that he would leave to us. If, as children, we feared his reproof and what seemed his great severity, none the less we knew how innately kind he was and how devoted to us even when he was at the height of his railroad career and one of the busiest men in America; we knew his bounty was "boundless as the sea, his love as deep," as is written on the beautiful monument by Karl Bitter at his grave in Sleepy Hollow, and our abiding faith in him was never shaken.

It was in December, 1879, that my father discovered and bought part of the hilltop at Dobbs Ferry, on the Hudson, which, as I write, is being developed for many homes by Joseph Patterson of the New York *Daily News,* and is named "Villard Hill." One of his advertisements calls it "an earthly paradise." So it seemed to us and I am sure to many of the thousands of visitors who came to Thorwood in the forty-eight years that it was our home—our real home no matter what city residence we occupied. I have met women in various countries and all over the United

States who knew that hill—and hated it—for the pupils of the Misses Masters' School "for young ladies" below us were compelled to walk up that hill, two by two, for exercise every Sunday morning after church service, a service in itself an ordeal. For the sermons preached for many a long year by Thornton Wilder's maternal grandfather, who had been a chaplain in the Confederate army, were usually about the pearly gates of heaven and anything but illuminating and inspiring. But if the Masters girls hated that climb, the neighborhood did not and on Saturdays and Sundays the place was visited by many, who rarely misbehaved and came to enjoy the glorious views. We looked forty miles to the north across the Tappan Zee to the Highlands around West Point; from a summerhouse in the rear we looked twenty-five miles down the river and saw the Statue of Liberty until the skyscrapers hid it; from the top of our water tower we saw many miles of the Sound and the ships on it. In a lifetime of travel at home and abroad I have never seen a situation to surpass it.

There were two houses on the hill; I believe they were the only habitations erected there after the wigwams of the Indians disappeared. They were built by two brothers Cochran, Scotchmen born, who were so devoted to one another that neither wanted anything better than the other possessed. So duplicate contracts were let for the two impressive, three-story, brick houses—they were alike to the very door knobs. The front lawns were made as much alike as the contours permitted and the stables were, I believe, practically identical—we tore both down. Father bought the house of the brother who died first; the second place, Dunedin, came to us only after Mr. Thomas Cochran's death. With his sister and two nieces he lived there for years after our arrival. Behind the two homes Father purchased the top of the hill, some eighty acres of superb woods, chiefly chestnuts, oaks, hickory and dogwood trees, with a few meadows. Through this park he built winding roads and paths, keeping the whole simple, natural, and dignified, giving us young people and our playfellows plenty of room to roam and ride and still be at home. To McKim, Mead and White, then at the outset of their architectural career, which

Father really inaugurated by three important orders, was entrusted the reconstruction and enlargement of Thorwood—Mr. McKim was my Uncle Wendell's brother-in-law and always like a member of the family. Indeed it was my father who induced McKim's Quaker parents to agree to his going to Paris to study at the Beaux Arts—they had considered it too wild and immoral a place.

Thorwood was the first large country house of the young firm and its six beautiful living rooms, some of superb proportions, did great credit to their skill and their artistry. To Stanford White we owed a small but beautifully paneled library with the most uncomfortable writing table and equally uncomfortable leather chairs ever inflicted by an architect upon his client. The white and gold music room designed by Charles McKim was a complete success. The fine California redwood hall, and the half-paneled dining room with its full-length windows and grand views, were not only most impressive but had the merit of never requiring any renovation or redecorating. For so large a mansion it had at first remarkably few bedrooms and bathrooms. It has always seemed to me the perfect country home of its type, one that fulfilled every material and esthetic need, and my life has been inseparably bound up with it. Not even the genius of those three architects could give to the semi-Georgian exterior any distinct style, but it was handsome in its dignity and simplicity.

At Dobbs Ferry we found ourselves in one of the narrowest of Scotch Presbyterian communities and, being churchless ourselves, shocked the neighborhood no end. For these godly Covenanters Sunday was a day of penance when the world was definitely renounced. The road to the Presbyterian Church was lined by the houses of Scotch families distinguished by all their sturdy qualities —Sinclairs, McCombs, Frasers, McClellands, Nivens, Williamsons, Wildes, and the home of Dr. Judson, our family physician, whose children have been our lifelong friends. The Cochrans were fine old people of a type not to be found anywhere today. When Sunday came every blind on their house was closed and not a ray of sunshine was permitted to enter. Usually they sat indoors; if they ventured out on the porch from which they looked straight down upon the river, they seemed to speak in muffled tones. Twice each Sabbath they went to church, swathed in deepest black, in their state landau, often with the curtains drawn as if on the way to a funeral, to return to the gloomy house for endless prayers, and, I believe, cold victuals—at least some of the community felt that it was sinful to ask a servant to prepare hot food on the Lord's Day save at breakfast. It was, I think, a great blow to this colony, and especially to Mr. Cochran, to find my mother what she was. They knew that her agitator father had left the church and violently assailed it for striking hands with the Devil to uphold slavery. They feared that she was godless, too, and were aghast when she actually refused to join any congregation in Dobbs Ferry. They shuddered when they heard our happy voices across the lawns on Sunday and saw us play tennis and croquet on the holy day. They knew that never a Sunday but our dining room held from a dozen to eighteen people, some of whom had usually come up from the city to revel—on Sunday—in nature's beauties.

According to all their theology and belief, my mother should have been a frivolous, worldly, hard-faced woman, seeking to hide the secret misery of her soul (because of its disloyalty to its Creator and its indifference to salvation) by potent drams, by paint and powder, by gay and daring costumes, and complete devotion to things carnal. Instead they found this new neighbor as disarming, as winning, as simple, and as lovely and trusting as a child. To their astonishment they discovered that she had the highest ideals, and principles as strict as theirs, nay, in one respect stricter, since wine never touched her lips and they had theirs—on weekdays. They saw that she used neither paint nor powder and obviously had never a secret sin to conceal; that she radiated happiness and communicated it to them and positively refused to be anxious about the future of her soul after death; that everything that concerned them became a concern of hers; that if they were ill never a day passed but she came to inquire and sit with them. Suddenly they realized that her visits opened up a whole new vista in their narrow lives. This lovely "sinner" must have given their theology a dreadful jolt, but of course she could never really shake their faith in their Sabbath and their Lord as something most solemn, most melancholy, most uncomfortable and dreary. I suppose they considered her a good woman gone wrong who somehow was not as wrong as she "had a right to be." When they found her husband as courtly and kind and considerate a neighbor as could be asked, I am sure that they attributed that to his wife, too. But as for her children! Well, I know what they thought of me for they soon found out my conscienceless depravity. I rode and drove my horses on Sunday for pleasure and gloried in it!

For that sin I was once reproved by one of the prettiest little Presbyterians at the Masters School. It was wicked of me to employ any person to work on Sunday, she said. When she married she would not have even a hot breakfast served on Sunday in her house. The groom who saddled my horse should not be asked to violate the Lord's injunction as to the day of rest. What if I saddled and fed him myself? Well, she replied, the beast himself was entitled to his day off. I explained that, on the contrary, it was not kindness to a horse to make him stand all day in his stall when he loved to be galloping along with me. But she would have none of that. It was too much for me; that, and the fact that, although Miss Masters had seen me grow up next door to her from a small boy into a virtuous subfreshman, she still insisted that if I called on any girl in her school there must be a chaperone in the room to hear every word uttered, put an end to my attentions to that lovely Sabbatarian. Many years later when I heard that she and her husband had smashed up and been divorced I was mean enough to wonder whether cold meals on Sunday had had something to do with it. Fortunately the Cochrans and Miss Lily Masters died before our modern decadence set in. Before we left Thorwood, with my own eyes I beheld the unbelievable—not less than a dozen Masters' girls sunning themselves, at the foot of our lawn on the hated Villard hill, in backless bathing suits.

Our music room was the center of our Thorwood activity. My

mother liked nothing better than to get up concerts; her annual entertainment for the Masters girls for the benefit of the Dobbs Ferry Hospital may have helped perhaps to give them a better opinion of the hill they were so often compelled to visit. She herself was constantly at her white and gold piano. I have always wished that I might have known her Boston teacher, Otto Dresel, for he inculcated in her a great love of the German classics and gave her a fine repertory. She was a rare accompanist and took lessons until near the end of her life, always bemoaning that her technical equipment made impossible her attempting the modern compositions, always overlooking the fact that her listeners forgave her lack of technical brilliancy in the solid musicianship she displayed. Those were wonderful hours we had together and when, after I abandoned my violin, I took to singing we had endless happiness with our interpretations.

Our Sunday midday chicken or roast beef dinners, winding up with the most gorgeous ice cream, were a real institution. No matter whether we had guests or not we had to dress formally for them. Often we wore cutaways, especially if there were ceremonious foreigners to be fed. Many Germans came and were duly overcome by the ravishing beauty of the place, for Germans have one specially good quality—they adore nature and love the outdoors, even more so it seems to me than the English. Numerous Englishmen came to us too. Indeed I learned much of international affairs through those contacts and the illuminating conversations we were so often privileged to hear. It was always a liberal group and never conservative or Big Business. Father was never liked by the leaders in Wall Stret. In the first place he was foreign-born and had never a sporting instinct; when he was through business he went home. He never attended their churches—often very important from the business point of view—or belonged to their pet clubs. They did not like his being a free trader and an independent Democrat, or "Mugwump," and they held him at least partly responsible for Godkin and *The Evening Post's* vagaries.

Of the American friends who came to us constantly none was

ever more welcome than Carl Schurz. His kindliness to young people, his devotion to my little brother Hilgard, his unfailing humor and gaiety of spirits endeared him to all of us. To hear him tell how he escaped summary execution by crawling through a sewer when captured with the revolutionary forces at Rastatt in Baden, and of his astonishingly daring rescue of Gottfried Kinkel from prison in Spandau, when there was a death sentence on his own head—why, there was no printed book to give one thrills like that. We fairly shivered when he told us how he stood outside the guard room in the Spandau prison with a pistol in his hand ready to kill himself if the guard should appear before Kinkel was freed; or related how he felt when, a major general and corps commander at Gettysburg, he lay for hours under Lee's cannonade among the tombstones on Cemetery Hill, wondering if he would not be killed and buried by the next shell. I believed Schurz then and believe him now when he said, very quietly and without boasting, that he never in his life had felt a qualm of fear in war—not even when first under fire. All his life I was devoted to this great man who held higher positions under the Republic than any other foreign-born citizen and I was proud indeed that during his last years after Father's death he called me his "adopted son" and never published an article or made a speech without showing it to me beforehand. His commission as major general, signed by Abraham Lincoln, is one of my most prized possessions. I owe him more for his aid and inspiration than I can well say.

After those tremendous Sunday dinners a drive was always in order and there I usually came in for I was willingly drafted to drive one team and show the points of historical interest between Thorwood and Tarrytown. When I was fifteen years old my father turned over the entire management of the stables to me, his only complaint being that I often stayed there so long as to make it quite noticeable where I had been when I turned up for meals. Our stable was something to be proud of, especially on Sundays, with its sanded floor in front of the dozen stalls and its plaited straw matting which the grooms loved to make. The stalls were decorated and the silver-mounted harnesses and shining carriages were always ready for inspection. As for the horses, gradually I was the only rider left in the family, but surely never did horses' coats shine more, especially after a faithful and devoted English coachman, Edward Hilley, took charge, to stay with us as long as he lived, to be buried from our house, and to be succeeded by his son-in-law.

Many were the amusing incidents that happened on those drives. I remember one German professor who gurgled with joy every time I showed him a colonial landmark. After he had seen the Washington Irving house, the André monument, the Headless Horseman bridge, and then the Revolutionary trench in Sleepy Hollow Cemetery he let out a whoop. "I haf always said," he declared, "that America had an historical underground." I had proved for him a long-held professorial thesis. Once my mother asked me to have my smartest rig, a natural wood Adirondack buckboard (still in my possession), and my light team of pretty bay horses in readiness as some old friends were coming from the West and I was to be particularly polite to the daughter. I promised, but that drive ended in disaster. Not a word could I get out of her save yes or no. Washington's Headquarters left her cold, so did a charming old Colonial cottage, and Cyrus Field's house. The Ardsley Club, one of the first country clubs, aroused not a flicker of interest. A half mile further on, in despair, I became reckless. "Do you wear corsets?" I asked, "because if you do this big house on the right may interest you. It belongs to Warner, the corset king."

The only response was a deep maidenly blush that I had never expected to see color the brow of one from the Far West. The rest of the ride passed in sullen silence. It was characteristic of that Mid-Victorian age that this guest went directly to my mother on our return to Thorwood and told her hostess that she had never been so insulted in her life, that never before had any man dared to ask her about her underwear. My peace-loving mother put on her fighting clothes and gave me one of the worst verbal drubbings I ever received. With what kind of females had I been associating, she inquired, that I could do a thing like that? She had thought that she had at least brought me up like a gentleman who knew how to behave in the presence of a lady, but plainly she had failed, and so on. She was actually grateful that that priggish, humorless prude had blabbed to her. Naturally for years I hated that girl with a deadly hatred. Years afterward she came to New York, married a fine fellow, and we became warm friends, and remained so until two dreadfully tragic bereavements broke her heart and, I believe, ended her life. Sometime before the second disaster we dined with her and her husband at the home of a mutual friend. Times *had* changed. It was the hour of the very shortest skirts ever seen; hers revealed what in my wanton boyhood were called underdrawers, well above bare knees. I laughed inwardly when I remembered that the brazen person in front ot me had been overcome with modesty and shame when, some thirty years previously, I had inquired if she wore another sacred and unmentionable undergarment.

Far more circumspect and praiseworthy than I was a certain young German who came up to a dance. I introduced him to one of the nicest girls of the neighborhood. He asked for the next dance and then, with infinite tact and most delicate consideration, gave her a kindly warning: "I marry," said he, "in October!" Our neighbor took the hint, and kept her ardent young heart in control, but her risibles gave her no end of trouble until, the dance ended, he took his irresistible charms to another. Even during our gravest trials the stream of visitors continued. They were all sorts and kinds, never assorted or chosen with any reference to position or power or congeniality. There were some strange mixtures! But never one person entered the front door whom my mother did not put at ease and welcome with warmth and friendliness. Best of all Thorwood was a family center to which came relatives from our large family circle scattered from Boston to San Francisco. Of these none was more welcome than my uncle, Francis Jackson Garrison, for many years with Houghton, Mifflin Company, and ever most kind, generous and affectionate. With him my ties became closer and closer as time passed; his counsel and aid were ever at my service. The letters which he and my mother wrote to each other every week from her marriage in 1866 until his death are in our archives.

The hardest entertaining we ever did was when, at the request of the heads of the New York Bar Association, my father turned over both our houses to the then Chief Justice of England, Lord Russell of Killowen, and the Solicitor General, Sir Frank Lockwood, who was, incidentally, one of the most gifted, witty, and charming Englishmen who ever lived. The Bar Association had invited them to speak at the annual meeting at Saratoga which opened on a Monday. As their ship arrived on Saturday morning the Association neither wished to transport them to some out-of-town resort for two days nor to have them spend a hot week end in the city, so my father stepped into the breach—Lord Russell had been Father's guest at the opening of the Northern Pacific. We knew that our simply-run home was hardly equal to the task and that we ourselves were not familiar enough with English country home customs to be sure that we could meet the situation but we plunged in and did our best. The guests arrived with several friends and relatives, with maids and valets, with trunks and bags enough, it seemed to us, to go around the world twice without stopping—the Russells alone had forty-five pieces. We gave two big dinners and a reception for them, doubling up ourselves and hiring extra servants galore. I had my hands full providing the transportation. As if we did not have trouble enough, soon after we adjourned to the living rooms from the state dinner, I was called out by the news that our engineer in peeking through the window to see the distinguished guests had slipped and fallen upon the iron spikes which helped to bar a cellar window. Sir Frank hurried out with me. We found that the engineer's lung, and almost his heart, had been pierced, and I recall with pleasure how the Solicitor General of Great Britain helped me minister to him until the doctor came. No nurse being available I had to apply ice to the wound most of the night.

It was at Thorwood that my younger brother, Hilgard, was born and died. He came to us when I was eleven years old, in time, as I shall relate, to play a role as an infant in arms in our most remarkable and dramatic experience. We all adored him and, while we are all prone to believe that those whom we lose at any early age are exceptionally gifted, after all these years I still feel sure that he had the most promise of any of us children. For this I have an outsider's testimony. I have referred to Carl Schurz's devotion to that little boy—he was only seven when he died from what was probably appendicitis, which medical men could not cure at that time. The beautiful address Carl Schurz made as he stood by the little boy's coffin in our flower-filled music room is printed in one of the volumes of the General's speeches and writings. He said that he spoke as a friend of this "dear little boy" for "he felt me to be his friend and called me so":

According to the ancient saying, those who are beloved of the gods die young. And this dear little boy certainly could be counted among those beloved. He was the late child of a most happy union. His birth was to his parents like the breaking of a fresh morning in the advanced day. Upon his cradle nature and fortune seemed to shower their choicest favors. That cradle stood in the lap of the purest and most beautiful family life. All that surrounded him was love and concord and goodness. He could hardly stand upon his little feet when he quickly grew into a distinct individuality. Of singularly delicate, almost feminine comeliness of shape, he soon developed in himself something like a real character, far away from common. His infant mind seemed to work in channels entirely his own. He had a habit of self-contemplation and self-criticism, looking at his own being and doings as those of a third person, which sometimes broke out in startling utterances. . . . And with all this his whole being bore the charm of an extraordinary—I might say a strange—loveliness. There was something in this boy that made older persons not only glad but proud to receive from him signs of friendship, and those who watched his ways, as almost everybody did who saw him frequently, would often wonderingly ask themselves what such a development would bring forth, being sure that it would be something very, very extraordinary.

Hilgard's death was for me one of those losses which time can never heal. We were ever the best of friends and playmates; the fact that he was so much younger, instead of separating us, brought us closer together and it hurts deeply to this day that modern science would have found no difficulty in preserving that sweet, winsome presence and all that promise, while the medical men of 1890 failed.

Hilgard's special joy was a darling black-and-tan terrier, as bright and clever a little animal as could be. They adored each other and Hilgard's nurse, Jane, cared for both of them with complete devotion. The dog was originally called Dot but I wickedly teased the little boy by calling him Tommy Dott, for I was steeped in Marryat's *Percival Keene* and *Mr. Midshipman Easy*. Finally the whole family adopted it and Tommy Dott he was to the end. When Hilgard died nobody needed to tell Tommy Dott that something dreadful had happened. He was in a state of absolute distress, running up and down stairs in every direction; once he slipped through the door and leaped upon the bed where his little master lay. I kept him with me at night and he cried hour after hour like a little child. He was shut up in the stable when we left for the cemetery and my first thought on our return was to go to him. The caretaker left in charge met me with a solemn face. Tommy Dott was dead. The little dog, who had never had a day's sickness, had fallen in a fit and died just about the time that we were at the grave in Sleepy Hollow. I have often read these stories of dogs not surviving their masters but this is the only case of which I personally know.

Dogs played a great part in our life at Thorwood for Father never wanted to be without one and I adored them. We had generation after generation of them—mastiffs, bull terriers, greyhounds, dachshunds, police dogs, I cannot recall them all, sometimes fifteen or twenty at a time. Two of them stand out, Brutus and Maida. The former, a superb, pedigreed, imported mastiff, suddenly appeared at Thorwood. We locked him up and advertised him at the post office and soon a groom came from Amzi L. Barber's place and took him home. Within four days he was back. We returned him and as soon as he was released he came back to us. That went on a couple of times more and then Mr. Barber sent him to us with a pleasant note to my father saying that as the dog plainly preferred my father to him, and was not to be won back to his early allegiance, he hoped my father would accept him. We needed no urging. Formidable as that beautiful dog was and terrifying as was his bark, we all loved him. But his heart went out to only one—my father—for he was a one-man dog. They were a wonderfully matched pair as they walked around the place, both superb specimens of their type. Every night Brutus lay at my father's feet until bedtime came. Never once did he misbehave and he belied his name for he was faithful and loyal to the end. The remarkable thing about his coming to us was that after he got there he never wandered from Thorwood and that, in finding the way to us, he covered nearly two miles and passed a number of large places on the way without, so far as we could ascertain, stopping anywhere else. We had no female attraction for him in our kennels and he left a number of his kind at Mr. Barber's. Why should he have headed straight for us and have adopted my father as his master? I can find no answer to this.

My pet among many dogs was the dachshund called Maida. I brought her back from Harvard and she was a universal favorite. She became the progenitor of a long line of dachshunds among whom a fat Fafner was a good miniature of Wagner's dragon save that he was meek and mild. My mother allowed me to have Maida in the house during the day but a stableman called for her and Brutus at ten o'clock to put them in the stable for the night. The family sat evenings in a small reception room, for its coziness and, in the fall, for its open fire, eschewing the great parlors. Each had his chair and my father soon covered Brutus, at his feet, with the foreign dailies he read and discarded. Maida learned to tell time perfectly. Apparently sound asleep, about twenty minutes of ten first one eye would open and then the other. Soon, if she thought we were all absorbed in our reading, she would sneak out without a sound, to hide under a parlor sofa. When the stableman came there would be a hunt and we would have to drag her out, completely crestfallen at her capture.

One night I was at a dance and got home about two o'clock, let myself in, put out the light, and went up the stairs, past the motto in stained glass on the landing which read, "Peace Be Unto This House." There at the top stood Maida wiggling all over with joy. If ever a dog laughed Maida did then. "You see," she said as plainly as if she had spoken, "I put one over on them this time." She had sneaked up the stairs to my room and so could not be found. A good watchdog, she had never barked nor made a sound when she heard me enter, knowing full well who it was, and came out to meet me. Naturally I let her stay. My mother was so amused she relented and thereafter whenever I was at home Maida slept in my room and never once disturbed me. She was not only well-behaved, she was extremely modest. Whenever I got down to nudity in undressing she invariably turned her eyes away! I tried it out many times. I have never seen a dog who could express her feelings so clearly at all times. You could read them in her eyes as in a human's.

As to the friends who worked for us, what they thought of my parents as employers can be guessed by the fact that of the six permanent men workers, who were with us when my mother died, one had been with us forty-eight years, three twenty-five or more, one fifteen and another ten. The old superintendent, Michael Hayes, Father literally bought with Thorwood. When the place was sold he had been over fifty years with us and could no longer remember how long he, as a boy, had served Mr. Cochran. The domestics were devoted to their tender-hearted mistress as they should have been. Every generation of employers complains of the dreadful deterioration of the "help," but looking back a half century I can list one man and one woman after another who were fidelity itself. Once someone telephoned to Father's office that we needed a groom at once. The German assistant secretary had never filled an order like that. He strolled over to Castle Garden and as he got there he saw a likely looking young Irishman with bowlegs coming out with his baggage. Guessing from his legs that he was a horseman, he went up to him and said: "Are you familiar with horses?" "I am," was the reply. "Are you looking for a job?" "That is what I came to America for." Within an hour William Stephens was on a train bound for Dobbs Ferry and as groom and chauffeur he remained with us until he stood by my mother's grave a quarter of a century later. These were real friends; they would have brooked no condescension and they never showed a trace of servility. They were fine Americans whether born abroad or here. Certainly no estate ever was more faithfully served or made fewer demands on its owners. Whether we were in Europe or New York City there never was a time when we did not feel certain that that lovely home was as well and as honestly cared for as if we were there.

So the years rolled on. It seemed to me that Thorwood and its one hundred beautiful acres grew lovelier every year, the views finer, the sunsets—to see which my mother led us all, especially our guests, every evening to the summerhouse above the river— more glorious. My father hoped an impossible hope for the America of today—that Thorwood would be like an old English manor and stay in the family for generations. It was a farm when we first went to it, for we had cows and chickens and ducks, to say nothing of a priceless donkey sent to us by a Colorado admirer of my father's, and the annual haying was a serious business. When the end came it was a highly taxed piece of suburban property, quite beyond our means to maintain. I am glad that when Joseph Patterson purchased it, to build upon it the many homes that my mother hoped might rise there in all that beauty, he tore down both Thorwood and Dunedin and every other building. It was fitting. The home in which we had had such happiness, in which my parents and Hilgard died, ought never to have passed into other hands and other uses. The chapter was full and rounded; the new one rightly started upon a blank page.

THORWOOD

THE AUTHOR, IN CART, WITH HIS ELDER BROTHER AND SISTER, AT
THORWOOD

Chapter III. The Golden Spike

OUR greatest family experience came in 1883. May had brought us the unexpected but joyously welcomed brother, of whose coming my elder brother Harold and I had no suspicion until Father walked into our joint room early one morning and told us what had happened. That event put horses and dogs and everything else into the background and daily enriched our lives during all of the little boy's brief span of life. When August arrived he became a real problem for my mother because the completion of the Northern Pacific in that month was to be celebrated on a grand scale at the beginning of September. There was no Walker-Gordon milk in those days; to wean the baby and leave him behind was something neither parent could contemplate and my father would rather have postponed the ceremonies than to have gone without his wife. As it turned out the baby, in Jane's excellent care, stood the trip perfectly. In Chicago, on the return trip, my mother terrified us youngsters by fainting in the street, the natural result of the exhaustion of weeks of hard travel, never-ending excitement and public ceremonies, and, toward the end, very bad news.

Fortunately she needed only a few days of rest to be herself again. She was physically so strong and well, her spirit was so indomitable and her temperament so sunny and cheerful, that when anything went wrong with her it seemed to us as if the bottom had dropped out of everything. From her we were always sure to receive an overflowing sympathy and comfort, and even aid in mitigating paternal strictness—sometimes to Father's dismay. But any weakness she may have shown us was offset by her own rigid, often Puritan, standards. No one ever saw her in careless attire or a negligee; never did she fail to appear on the moment for breakfast. She was punctuality itself until advancing years made her anticipate the time for trains and engagements. Her ability to keep herself always well in hand, the total absence of moods and humors and "nerves," not only made her the mainstay of the family but made possible those reserves of strength which carried her through such a strain as the driving of the Golden Spike, and other experiences that were to come.

The first and last spike of the Northern Pacific Railroad rests in my safe. It is of iron; it is rusty; it shows the mark of two sledge hammers, for it punctuated the beginning and the end of a momentous industrial and social enterprise. The press of America, when it told of the completion of the first railway to span the Northwest, described this object as the "Golden Spike" and at least one editor rebuked the completor of that great and hazardous undertaking for his senseless and ostentatious extravagance in wasting so much of the stockholders' money on a mere symbol. Although I was only eleven years old when we crossed the continent on one of the first trains ever to run from St. Paul to Portland, Oregon, the events of that expedition are entirely clear and distinct in my mind, where far more recent events have begun to fade. That is hardly surprising. Any boy who saw his father the center of a tremendous celebration in one city and State after another, who beheld him ranked in public honor with the then President of the United States and acclaimed almost as much as the distinguished ex-President and conqueror of the Confederacy, General Grant, could not fail to have those events indelibly impressed upon the recording film of his brain.

Never was there a more spontaneous and wholehearted celebration. The hamlets, towns, and cities which that railroad served were convinced that no greater service could be rendered to them, and indeed to the outer world, than the completion of that line. In speech after speech the declaration was made that the opening of the Northern Pacific meant the lowering of the cost of living and the cheapening of bread in England and all the nations of Europe.[1] A great empire was now accessible. No longer would the

[1] The New York *Times* wrote (September 9, 1883) that "a wilderness is now open to civilization, and one which is adequate to support in comfort the surplus population of all Europe . . . which will within a very few years work economic and social changes [in Europe] of which what has already happened in Great Britain affords but a faint far-off hint."

grain of the North Pacific slopes have to be taken around Cape Horn to Liverpool in sailing ships, a matter of months. No longer would the railroad journey to that slope be interrupted by days in coaches and wagons. This portion of the West was conquered at last; this iron span signified the end of hostilities between pioneers and Indians. Endless stretches of uninhabited land, which could not possibly be occupied fully for generations, it was thought, were now open to settlers. The largest farms the world had ever seen were to be had for the asking or for trifling sums. There was no caviling or doubting throughout the Northwest. The men who had achieved this miracle were hailed as the greatest benefactors that part of the United States had known since Lewis and Clark had found the overland route.

Multitudes knew of their own experience what this achievement signified. They were aware, as the modern critic cannot be, what it meant to force that road to completion through the wilderness, through the Bad Lands, over the Rocky Mountains, through dense forests, and how many hundreds of its creators lay in unmarked graves, among them many of the army of 15,000 Chinese who made the building of this railroad possible. Those cheering crowds that greeted us at the opening knew how the surveying parties had gone into that primeval country at the risk of their lives, how the construction gangs had had to be guarded by portions of the little regular army from warring Indians driven to despair by the greed of the white men and by the endless perfidy and betrayals of the government in Washington, whose only interest in treaties with the tribes was how soon they could be made "scraps of paper." As my father stood on the platform of the pavilion erected to seat a thousand persons for the Last Spike ceremonies at Gold Creek, fifty-five miles west of Helena, the heroic tracklayers were foremost in his mind. There, at the apex of his career, in the most eloquent passage of his address of welcome, he said that the achievements of the actual constructors of the railroad "form a great sum of human patience and perseverance, energy and bravery, hardship and privation." It was, he declared, "a mighty struggle of mechanical and manual force against the direst obstacles of primitive nature."

Facing his guests who had come from England and Germany, from all over the United States, he added: "You have the testimony of your own eyes that this highway had to be carved out of a very wilderness where we found nothing to help us—no labor, no food, no habitations, no material, no means of transportation." He could have reinforced these statements by report after report. Thus Henry Thielsen, supervising engineer of the Western department of the railroad, wrote on February 17, 1882: "Snow lies five feet deep on the work, but the men—8,000 of them—march out bravely to their tasks, the snow up to their armpits." Of a contractor Mr. Thielsen reported: "His ox teams break a road through the woods and use it till dark, but by the next morning the wind has drifted enough snow to completely obliterate the tracks and a new road has to be made"—all this with a temperature often sixteen and twenty degrees below zero. The Chinese, be it noted, stuck to this grim job when white men failed. The Rocky Mountains had to be scaled, for the Mullen tunnel through the main spur could not be finished in time. It is not surprising that my father felt it to be his most important duty to recognize "by this public acknowledgment, as much as possible, the heavy debt of gratitude" that he who had carried the line to completion felt for the achievements of the actual physical builders of the railroad.

But the men in the wilderness were not the only ones to perform herculean labor. The raising of the money for the enterprise, which had already been sixteen years building when Henry Villard brought his enthusiasm and energy to the task, was in itself a tremendous undertaking. For it seemed hopeless to connect the two ends. How could bankers and the public be expected to put up money for an enterprise that after completion would still perhaps for a generation be running through uncultivated plains and mountain fastnesses without the possibility of adequate support? Where others had failed, or had proceeded only with maddening slowness, how could a man who had been only five years or less in railroading hope to succeed? But thanks to my father's German and English connections the money was found and the road hurried to completion—hurried because of the fear that Congress might revoke the land grant, which was the subsidy granted by Congress to the builders of the road.

It is the fashion now to criticize that policy of giving to the company alternate sections of land along the route—I have seen denunciations of my father because of this "squandering" of our national resources, although he did not join the Northern Pacific until sixteen years *after* the award of the land. The truth is that the first Pacific railroads were launched or pushed forward during the Civil War, when the government lacked money for anything except the war and believed that there was so much land in its inexhaustible empire that this was the cheapest and easiest way to aid in the construction of these iron highways. It was not due to corruption or infidelity to the people. The man who signed his name to the act incorporating the Northern Pacific and awarding it the land grant was no less a person than Abraham Lincoln, who will hardly be accused of having been the tool of selfish business interests and rapacious capitalists. As we look back now from the vantage point of 1939 it is easy to see that another policy would have been wiser but the country which was fighting for its life in the 1860's felt differently. Cash subsidies or government construction and ownership we know now would have been far better. In 1883, however, it was not clear that even with the aid of those alternate sections of land the railroad could possibly succeed. As my father made that address bankruptcy was near at hand.

The large company invited by Henry Villard to witness the Last Spike exercises comprised nearly five hundred persons. The number caused a good deal of unfavorable comment but the management, judged especially by the publicity standards of 1939, would have been lax if it had not adequately celebrated the completion of what was then the longest railroad in the world and let everyone know that it was open for business. Undoubtedly it was an advertising and publicity scheme as charged by some newspapers; the journalists of three nations in attendance were invited in the hope that they would describe what they saw. The publicity actually obtained could not have been purchased by a half million dollars of advertising. The expedition was, however, far more than a publicity venture. My father intended it to be not only a recognition of the actual manual builders and those who had preceded him in the management but a public acknowledgment of the part played by English and German investors in the building of the road. Without their aid, as stated, it could never have been finished when it was. It seemed only proper, therefore, that representatives of both countries should be present to see and record what had been done with their money, and the character of the empire opened up by the Northern Pacific.

Some of the press recognized this. Thus the influential Utica *Observer* felt that "never was money better invested," although it warned its readers against yielding to the lure of Dakota lands without the most careful inquiry into them. The Portland *Oregonian* asserted that "no railroad company ever made a better investment than the Northern Pacific in carrying this excursion through. Great as is the cost of it, the outlay will come back ten times over, both to the company and to the country. Indeed, the results will be of immeasurable value." If a defense of it were really needed it would be furnished by the spontaneity and enthusiasm of the reception all along the route. Wherever the trains halted the people turned out to express their gratitude that this section of the country was now really tied to the rest by an iron link, and they were especially pleased that men from across the seas had come to behold.

Towns and cities fought for the privilege of entertaining the visitors and there were bitter feuds when the excursionists failed to stop or stopped only for a short time.[2] It is impossible to believe that this was all pumped up by clever press agents or that the settlers along the line would have fallen for a mere stock-selling venture as some newspapers declared it to be. Indeed, it is

[2] The St. Paul *Pioneer-Press* reported on September 5: "The progress of Mr. Villard and his guests seems to be one of triumph and ovation. . . . All along the road, so far as reports have come, there is nothing but rejoicing. But few men in the history of the country have ever been the recipients of such ovations as greet Mr. Villard and will continue to greet him as he moves to the westward."

a tragic fact that my father paid a heavy price, and the Northern Pacific a far greater one, for some of those foreign guests. Accustomed to the dense populations of England and the Continent some of them were appalled at the vast desert stretches, the Bad Lands of Dakota Territory, the apparently interminable forests, the tremendous distances—sometimes seventy-five miles—between stations and the few visible habitations. They believed the railroad would never pay its way and cabled back to sell their securities, thus expediting the impending crash of the Villard railroad and steamship companies.

The entire Villard family left New York in my father's private car attached to a special train filled by the German guests, including my German aunt and her husband, Major General Von Xylander of the Bavarian army, the British and American sections following a day later. Among the Germans were Professor Hermann von Holst, the distinguished commentator on the American Constitution and historian of the United States, later professor at the University of Chicago; Georg Siemens, a director of the even then extremely powerful Deutsche Bank; Herr Von Schauss, the head of an important South German bank; Baron Georg von Bunsen, a member of the Reichstag distinguished for his opposition to Bismarck; Professor Rudolf Gneist, a great historian and also a member of the Reichstag; Doctor Paul Lindau, journalist and novelist, and a group of journalists and officials of various municipalities, besides distinguished representatives of Bremen, Hamburg, Stettin, and Frankfurt am Main. In the English group were James Bryce, then a member of Parliament and already collecting material for his *American Commonwealth,* and at least nine other members of Parliament in addition to two earls, with a couple of lords thrown in for good measure.

There were two future Chief Justices of England among the judges present, and the then Chief Justice met us for a day en route. The Earl of Onslow came in for a great deal of unfavorable publicity because it leaked out that he had, through a misunderstanding, demanded a private car for himself and his Countess. The diplomatic corps in Washington was well represented. In recognition of the Scandinavian settlers of the Northwest there were officials of the Danish, Swedish, and Norwegian Legations, together with Count Lippe-Weissenfeld, the Austrian Chargé d'Affaires, Baron Von Eisendecher, the German Minister, and the Honorable Lionel Sackville-West, the British Minister, who later achieved a permanent place in American annals by committing a political indiscretion the publication of which resulted in President Cleveland's sending him back to England in disgrace.[8] The German Minister, Von Eisendecher, who died only a few years ago, was without doubt the most charming, sensible, and able minister Germany ever sent to this country and, so far as I know, was the only German ever to be both an admiral in the navy and a minister in the diplomatic service and, incidentally, commander of the Kaiser's famous sailing yacht, the *Meteor*.

The Washington government was represented by John Davis, then Assistant Secretary of State, the Secretary of the Interior, H. M. Teller, and the Attorney General, Benjamin H. Brewster, besides whom there were governors, senators, territorial delegates, consuls, and numerous other federal officials. The roster of journalists included Edwin L. Godkin, Carl Schurz, Joseph Pulitzer, Harvey W. Scott of the Portland *Oregonian*, Joseph Medill of the Chicago *Tribune*, E. P. Mitchell of the New York *Sun*, Henry L. Nelson of the Boston *Herald*, W. N. Haldeman of the Louisville *Courier-Journal*, C. W. Knapp of the St. Louis *Republican*, and A. K. McClure of the Philadelphia *Times*, together with numerous correspondents and reporters. There was a galaxy of soldiers: Grant, Sheridan, Terry, Slocum, H. H. Sibley, Frank Wheaton, Nelson Miles, Cuvier Grover, John Newton, and still others who had been actively identified with the protection of the frontier. As it appears today it was a striking cross section of the political, governmental, military, and social life of the United States of 1883. The then President, Chester A. Arthur, met the expedition in Minneapolis and took part in the celebration there for a day on his return journey from a vacation in Yellowstone Park.

[8] See V. Sackville-West, *Pepita*, Doubleday, Doran, 1937, pp. 178-83.

F. Jay Haynes

THE LAST SPIKE CEREMONIES. HENRY VILLARD, STANDING WITH
HAT ON, AT SECOND COLUMN, MAKING THE OPENING ADDRESS

In Chicago we were royally entertained and much written up in the press, the English guests being continually interviewed as to what was going to happen in Ireland! The rival cities of St. Paul and Minneapolis outdid themselves and the parade in the latter city remains in my memory as the most remarkable civic and industrial display I have ever witnessed. The enthusiasm for the four guests of honor, President Arthur, Grant, Sheridan, and Villard, was unbounded, with Grant, as everywhere, the chief hero. Besides what seems now a tiny military display—twenty-one companies of regulars and militia—there were 820 wagons and floats, depicting the history of Minnesota and the life of the pioneer, and thousands of workers from the flour and lumber mills as well as from the trades and industries of Minneapolis. There were Indians in plenty, half-breeds proud of their divided ancestry, covered wagons galore, "Red River carts," immigrant trains complete and also a railroad construction one. The parade took hours to pass and President Arthur was happy to escape for a time and rest in the West Hotel in front of which the stand was erected. At St. Paul that afternoon there was a smaller display. It was a thrilling day for me and my brother, but we soon began to expect a thrill every day. We were allowed to sit up until ten o'clock and hear our father speak at the great banquet given in a hotel at Lake Minnetonka. As for shaking hands with lords and earls, the trepidation which came over us when this first happened is vivid still.

I soon got over that, however, and one afternoon I even called all by myself upon a lord who wore a bandage on his head instead of a coronet. It was Lord Carrington, later Earl Carrington and Governor General of New South Wales, who was the first to be injured on the trip. The car in which he was quartered jumped the track when running onto the ferryboat that was to take it across the Snake River; hence his injury. A much worse accident was to come. Running down the Pacific slope of the Rocky Mountains the train of which our car was a part broke in two. When the rear portion caught the front half it nearly demolished the old private car furnished by the Baltimore and Ohio Railroad— all the big railroads of the country had contributed private cars—

splitting it in two for half of its length. By the door sat the British Minister. He was saved as by a miracle. The split stopped right at the table at which the Danish Minister, and the daughter of Sackville-West and the famous dancer Pepita, were playing cards; I picked some out of the wreck the next morning and cherished them for a long time. To me it was a grand adventure but Father's feelings when he stepped off our car in the dark and came across some of the wreckage can well be imagined. Not for one moment was he unaware of the responsibility put upon him by those four special trains running over a brand-new line which had never before been tested in any way.

Another unforgettable boy's-eye view was that at Gray Cliff in Montana where 3,000 Crow Indians were encamped alongside of the railroad for the express purpose of letting the guests see a genuine Indian encampment. Deerslayer, the last of the Mohicans, Uncas, all of Cooper's heroes rose up before me as the train slowed down and we all scrambled off to enter the camp of the yelling and grunting Indians who crowded around us begging for anything they could get and eager to sell anything they had, even the little they had on, for good tourist money. But often you got something you hated to keep because of its odor. Such filth, such squalor, such smells, such degradation! The noble red man in the state to which he had then been reduced by the Great White Fathers in Washington was not a romantic object or one to reflect credit upon our country. Still the novelty of it all enthralled. It was truly a feather in one's cap to be able to go back to school and boast of acquaintance with such chiefs as Medicine Crow and his father, Bull That Goes Hunting, Plenty Coups, and especially Chief Two Belly, with which euphonious gentleman Carl Schurz pow-wowed at length over the Crow war when he was Secretary of the Interior. One could hold one's head in a tepee for at least a couple of minutes, long enough to gaze with amusement upon the little papooses all tied up in readiness to be slung upon their mother's backs and to shudder at what passed for food. Then there were horse races. Here the Indians were beaten at their own game by two young English officers, both captains in crack British regiments, riding bareback like their rivals. One officer became Colonel Halford, owner of a magnificent palace in London and for decades the favorite aide-de-camp of Edward the Seventh; many years later the other, then Earl Grey, Governor General of Canada, called upon the writer and upon his mother in New York City, to see, he said, "what that little American boy has grown up to be."

As for the towns, Mandan, Jamestown, Bismarck, one after the other they turned out for us. The decorations were remarkably well done for they did not confine themselves to flags and bunting but used wheat and corn and magnificent fruit and vegetables to decorate their triumphal arches. In Bismarck, Sitting Bull, who had been but such a short time before in the field against our troops, Herr Von Eisendecher, Carl Schurz, and my father laid the cornerstone of the State capitol, destined to stand until it burned down with priceless archives in 1931. Then came Helena, the capital of Montana, proud in its belief that it had a great future before it, only to find that Butte, on a parallel branch line, was the predestined success in the race between the two towns, for Helena has grown but little either in numbers or in influence. One could not be sure in those days when one named a settlement or town just what its future would be. For instance, where the branch of the Northern Pacific that ran through Helena and the one from Butte met my father had named a hamlet after his father-in-law. The first time I saw it in later years it comprised about twelve houses and I hate to think what my temperance grandfather would have thought had he heard that at least six of them were saloons and dives.

It was at Gold Creek, 1,025 miles from St. Paul and 706 from Portland, that the official last spike was driven. Actually the railroad was finished on August 22, 1883; the chief engineer's triumphant dispatch is a treasured family possession. Besides the pavilion there were a bandstand and large platforms, and up to them drew, one after the other, the four great trains from the East with their decorated and festooned locomotives and the one from the Pacific coast. In front of the grandstand there was another roadbed with only the sleepers laid, in readiness for the final scene. The accident to our special had caused a serious delay, serious because the program was long, the list of speakers extremely formidable, and at least one of them, William M. Evarts, ex-Secretary of State, the orator of the day, certain to take a lot of time. The grandstand was well filled; around it swirled a motley crowd, cowboys, tracklayers, railroad men, settlers who had driven many miles, for there was not a house in sight, soldiers from General Miles's Fifth Infantry who fired the salute, women well-attired and wearing the huge bustles of the day in sharp contrast with frontier women in ill-fitting, homemade garments and, wandering about, a most picturesque group of seven Crow Indian chiefs, headed by Iron Bull.

After my father's introductory remarks, from which I have already quoted,[4] there spoke the former president of the Northern Pacific, Frederick Billings, Mr. Evarts, Sir James Hannan, representing the English guests; the German Minister, Doctor Rudolf Gneist; no less than five state and territorial governors, and, in response to the demand of the crowd, General Grant, the taciturn, himself, with his inevitable cigar. He declared that it was proper that he be given especial consideration on that day for, when Jefferson Davis was Secretary of War, he, Grant, then a lieutenant and acting quartermaster and commissary at an army post on the Columbia River, had issued the supplies for the first expedition to survey the route of the railroad, headed by General Isaac I. Stevens, Governor of Washington Territory, who later gave his life for the Union at Chantilly. General Grant said that he knew that Mr. Billings and others had put a lot of their money into the Northern Pacific but he himself had put in some of Uncle Sam's and that was a greater feat which entitled him to especial honor. The afternoon wore rapidly on; the sinking sun warned everybody that there was no time to lose. Once or twice the program was interrupted by music from the band of the Fifth

---

[4] "President Villard read a very excellent speech, sound in sense and good in tone and taste. . . ." Lord Chief Justice Charles Russell, *Diary of a Visit to the United States*, New York, 1910, p. 83.

Infantry, whose bandmaster had composed an especial railroad march, *The Iron Horse,* in honor of Henry Villard. It was to be punctuated by whistles from a locomotive which was backed down to the platform to play with the band. Unfortunately my father had not been tipped off. When the locomotive's whistle almost blew us out of the grandstand he hastily sent an aide with peremptory orders to the engineer to stop interrupting the music! The bandmaster's heart was broken.

It was Iron Bull who made the last speech, and pathetic and moving it was when translated from the sign language in which it was delivered. Concluding, he said: "There is a meaning in my part of the ceremony and I understand it. We have reached the end of our rule and a new one has come. The end of our lives, too, is near at hand. . . . Of our once powerful nation there are now but a few left—just a handful—and we, too, will soon be gone. After the Indian has given way to civilization the whites will come." As he finished he handed to my father the same iron spike that is now in my custody, perhaps as a token of resignation and the submission of his people to a cruel and inexorable fate.

Then came the dramatic moment of the day. At a given signal picked men from the construction gangs from West and East laid the missing rails in a final cheering and yelling race, the East winning. The rails for the Eastern gang were drawn to them on a flat car pulled by a black horse who bore a sign reading: "My name is Nig. I have drawn the rails 750 miles." [5] As soon as the rails were laid down Henry Villard and his guests quitted the grandstand and proceeded to the exact point where the rails had met. But here we got into trouble; no one had thought to rope off the space. Guests and spectators crowded to the spot until the crush became alarming and prevented photographing of what actually occurred, which was very unfortunate because of the legend that has since arisen as to what took place. I have read the testimony of several "eyewitnesses" who swore that it really was a golden

[5] Nig joined the Villard family on our return from the celebration by the gift of his owner and spent his last years with every care and equine comfort in our Dobbs Ferry stable.

spike that was used, and there is at least one painting which por-
trays my father and General Grant driving the spike in comfort
in a nice, large, open space.

My mother, carrying her infant, my elder brother, my sister,
and I fought our way to the last rail. I saw my father hand the
spike to H. C. Davis, an official of the Manitoba Railroad, who
had driven it down on the first Northern Pacific rail in 1870. After
that the crush was so great that I was shoved aside and saw little.
But what happened is incontestably this: My father struck the
next blow after Mr. Davis. He was followed in turn by Frederick
Billings, Mayor Carter Harrison of Chicago, William M. Evarts,
Carl Schurz, General Grant, and my mother. The tiny hand of the
baby was also placed on the hammer, and Iron Bull, a superb
figure in full ceremonial regalia, with immovable features, had his
turn. The artillery fired the salute. The assembled engines demonstrated the power of their whistles; the crowd cheered and cheered
again—and the ceremony was over. Today there stands on the spot
only a simple wooden sign to inform the traveling public that the
last spike was driven there on September 8, 1883.

Even after the Last Spike ceremonies there was no let-down
in the interest and excitement of the trip. The receptions were just
as spontaneous and warm,[6] the scenery more romantic and impressive as we approached the Pacific, reached Lake Pend d'Oreille,
Spokane, Walla Walla, Wallulah, and then went down the ma-
jestic Columbia River to Portland. The beauty of the situation of
that terminus of the Northern Pacific, with its three glorious snow
mountains, profoundly impressed the visitors who were quick to
sense an Eastern influence which has always distinguished Portland from Tacoma and Seattle and is one reason why it is more
conservative. Portland seemed a far older community and then, as
today, it was one of the loveliest of American cities, a really ideal

[6] "The popular demonstrations on the way were amazing. We saw literally,
during our journey, more than 2,000 miles of decorations and flags; and the
merchant millionaires of the city, the lonely squatter on the prairie, the Chinese
woodcutter in the forest all had 'welcome' written over their doors, as well as
on their faces and in their hearts."—W. S. Furay, editor of the Columbus, Ohio,
Sunday Herald, in its issue of October 7, 1883.

place to live, barring its rainy season. Here, too, we were welcomed with great parades, banquets, speech making, an evening at the Chinese theatre, and everywhere demonstrations of regard for my father, to warm our hearts even in the black days ahead, for Portland never lost faith in him.

Seattle and Tacoma provided the usual enthusiastic demonstration. In Seattle the formal ceremony, in the exquisite setting of the old campus of the University of Washington looking out over the waters of Puget Sound, was distinguished by an address by Carl Schurz and a most moving and touching speech of welcome by a young woman, a Miss Powell, the daughter of one of the professors—a novel happening, indeed, in the eyes of the foreign visitors. The university had reason to be grateful to my father for he personally carried it for a couple of years when the legislature refused to appropriate the small budget of this struggling school; curiously enough, the university has long since forgotten this whereas the University of Oregon always remembers with every evidence of gratitude my father's similarly generous gifts to what has now become a great university at Eugene. Finally we came to Vancouver across the waters, to be welcomed there under another flag with every courtesy, though without the familiar enthusiasm. It was journey's end for us. I have few memories of the trip home save a growing awareness that something was going very wrong and that Father began to look more and more worn.

It was then that we children learned how unstable public favor is and never forgot the lesson. I have not exaggerated in portraying the pinnacle to which my father had risen. His financial fall took him correspondingly far in the opposite direction. The Villard stocks had dropped from twenty to twenty-five points during our absence on the Last Spike expedition. Judged by the collapse of 1929 and present day fluctuations, that hardly seems enough to send a whole system crashing. But the hammering of the stocks continued and then appeared the signs of the depression of 1884 which affected gravely not only the United States but a considerable portion of the world. Still Henry Villard fought on, his sanguine temperament leading him to put in all his available resources to bolster up his stocks. He bought largely and urged his friends to do likewise, assuring them of his sincere belief that the bear raids would soon be weathered. But the fates were against him. In addition, he lost heavily at this moment in the collapse of the West Shore Railroad in which he had invested to oblige friends.

The earnings of the Northern Pacific which were expected to shoot up when the road was completed failed to do so and even showed losses because construction materials were no longer being hauled. The cost of the final links turned out to be much greater than the chief engineer had estimated and the flotation of a $20,000,000 second mortgage only partly relieved the situation and further depressed the stock. The fact that the mortgage could be floated was a pleasant dividend on the excursion expenditures, for the bulk of the bonds was sold by the Deutsche Bank and other German bankers whose representatives on the trip had not been stampeded into selling out by the pioneer conditions they had beheld. Meanwhile the Oregon and Transcontinental Company, the proprietary company created by Father to aid in the financing of the Northern Pacific, got into trouble because of its huge advances to the railroad; two of the directors, becoming frightened, used their official knowledge for enormous short sales of its stock. My father's own means were soon exhausted and he himself by the end of November was approaching a complete nervous collapse from the terrible strain. Without my mother's never-weakening support he could not have weathered it. On December 17 the end came. A committee of friends offered to advance him the money he needed to avoid personal bankruptcy and to save the Oregon and Transcontinental, provided that he pledge every single thing he owned—and provided also that he resign his presidency of both the Oregon and Transcontinental and the Oregon Railway and Navigation Companies. That meant likewise his resignation as president of the Northern Pacific. He retained only the headship of the Oregon and California Railroad Company at the request of his English backers.

So, at not yet fifty, the king was deposed and there were ex-

tremely few so poor to do him justice let alone honor. The newspapers turned upon him ruthlessly. Those individuals who had
fawned upon him when all was going well, and had fought to
pay a 40 per cent premium for participation in his Blind Pool,
forgot all that he had done for them and joined in the hue and
cry. Not until it became known that he had almost wholly sacrificed his means was there a turn in the tide. A well-known clergyman of Boston, the Reverend Cyrus A. Bartol of a Unitarian
Church, helped unexpectedly by preaching a sermon of praise for
the man who was ready to donate all he had to save his companies
—not a usual Wall Street happening. But failure is always a crime
if you have lost other people's money besides your own. It was
not until four years later that, against his own better judgment,
he yielded to the demand of the directors of the companies that
he resume his controlling position in the two Oregon companies
and the Northern Pacific. Many of the very men who had turned
against him in 1883 demanded in 1887 that he put aside his own
wishes and rescue the companies.

Of all this tragedy in 1883 we children were well aware without, of course, understanding its details. What made it worse was
that in order to save hotel bills we had moved into our new house
at 451 Madison Avenue, with the courtyard in front of it, which
my father had had built from McKim, Mead and White's plans,
as a wing of the Florentine block between 50th and 51st Streets.
There were six houses in the block (two have since been combined) but, because of this courtyard, even to this day many
passers-by think that there is only one huge house. Ours was not
even wholly furnished when we moved in just before the crash.
Soon ugly crowds gathered before it and, believing it to be the
greatest and most luxurious palace ever created by a single individual in New York, showed their disapproval. "The railroad is
wrecked but look what the president has built himself." It was not
possible to tell them that it was a six-family structure. Our residence there was always a nightmare and when we moved out it
was for good. Fortunately for my father it was purchased within
a year or so by Mr. and Mrs. Whitelaw Reid. The money helped

to put him on his feet and relieved him of a tremendous tax burden. He easily got over his disappointment in losing it and was always able to take satisfaction in his creation of that block. But the front courtyard plan, which he adopted in the hope that it would be widely followed in the city to give more light and air for homes, was never imitated; the cost of land was too great. Today the block is only one third occupied but there, just behind St. Patrick's Cathedral, it stands—a monument to the skill and artistry of McKim, Mead and White and still one of the finest American edifices.

Deeply as I sympathized with my father in the dreadful disappointment of his breakdown of 1883, and the loss of his commanding railroad position, I have long been convinced that it was a blessing for him and his family—though it was quite well enough disguised at the time! While it was never possible that great wealth could have made my socially-minded parents, with their compelling sense of community obligation and public spirit as demonstrated by their ownership of *The Evening Post*, as unsocial and as hostile to progress and to a fairer distribution of property as are most of our present aristocracy of wealth, it is well that they and their children were never exposed to any greater test. Had my father had a different fate in 1883 there is no telling where his financial genius would not have led him, with the aid of his powerful following in England and Germany. There is evidence that he would have been a great railroad administrator as well as organizer and financier; the men who served under him in his companies were devoted to him and praised his fairness and readiness to reward deserving men.[7] The disaster of 1883 seemed almost unbearable to him but for all of us, I am convinced, it proved that "sweet are the uses of adversity."

[7] Only a few years ago, more than thirty years after my father's death, a fellow passenger in a Pullman car turned out to be a locomotive engineer on the Northern Pacific. I told him that my father had also been employed by that railroad. When he heard who my father was he jumped up and asked if he might shake the hand of the son "of our fairest and squarest president who did more for the men than any other, under whom I began my service with the road."

Chapter IV. Berlin in 1884-86

THE winter of 1883-84 had so nearly wrecked my father nervously that an entire change of scene and complete rest for him were plainly called for—if a man with such an active and creative mind could ever rest. He decided to reside for a time in Berlin and there we spent two most profitable years. He selected Berlin instead of Munich primarily because his brother-in-law and sister were living there, General Von Xylander being the military representative of Bavaria in the Bundesrat. Berlin also lured him because Germany was in the tremendous industrial and political upsurge that followed the Franco-Prussian War, then only thirteen years in the past, the establishment of the empire, and the final elimination of all hindrances to complete freedom of trade within its confines. The speed of its development rivaled that of the United States. Father was soon in contact with the heads of the German General Electric Company and also with the great Deutsche Bank with which he had already had close relations. He found the German financiers much more ready to put money into electric developments than were the American; they have always been quicker to take up scientific advances and apply them to industry. Father also welcomed the opportunity to renew his friendship with Friedrich Kapp, who had spent so many years in the United States before returning to Berlin and had been an outstanding leader of the German-American group and a devoted republican.[1] Unfortunately within two months after our arrival in Berlin Friedrich Kapp died and, in a few months more, General Von Xylander was compelled for physical reasons to retire from active service and returned with my aunt to Munich.

My military uncle was anything but a militarist. Indeed he and

---

[1] Thirty-six years later the son of this republican headed the Kapp Putsch which came near to overthrowing the German Republic.

his brother Emil, who rose to still higher rank as an able cavalry commander, reminded me of the Civil War generals who came to our home in New York, all of them hating war and being opposed to a large army and navy.[2] Both were veterans of the Franco-Prussian War in which my uncle was attached to the personal staff of the Crown Prince, later the tragic Kaiser Friedrich. They wanted no more war and when I asked them what they thought about our being so unarmed they replied that they considered the United States the most fortunate of nations since it needed no army and navy and, in their opinion (like that of all the other foreign officers of rank I have since met), it was beyond the possibility of attack and invasion. Both of them died before the World War; my uncle would have fitted into it not at all. A tremendously powerful militarist Germany did not interest him in the least. Indeed, he was much frightened when the son of his old commander came to the throne so suddenly for, like all those close to the Crown Prince, he disliked the future Kaiser Wilhelm. He was certain that this impetuous man would speedily embroil Germany with its neighbors. However, twenty-six years of peace actually lay ahead.

When not on military duty my Uncle Robert was the typical Bavarian of that day, easygoing, soft-spoken, with delightful manners, and nothing of the heel-clicking Prussian about him. He was all for maintaining the exceptional status of Bavaria in the Reich, a sort of State's rights feeling, like our American tradition. We children loved to see him in his stunning full dress Bavarian blue uniform, his cocked hat and feathers. My aunt was much more of a martinet. She abused her husband constantly and nagged him no end, especially as to his personal appearance. As a matter of fact she adored him; her abuse, which he took so good-naturedly, never fighting back, was mere camouflage. Let anything happen to him and she was devotion itself, and she was a deeply

[2] Notably Sherman. When I once asked him if he would advise my going to West Point he replied: "Under no circumstances. It is not a career for anyone," and it was not at that time of small frontier posts and complete stagnation in promotion.

sad and lonely woman after his death—they never had children. She had a beautiful figure, carried herself perfectly, was always tightly laced and well-gowned and her wealth of white hair was always carefully coiffured. She was genuinely a *grande dame*, belonged in court life, and regretted bitterly her husband's retirement from their high official position in Berlin. She could never wholly understand us Americans, or our points of view, but was always fond of us, and in her last years I was as close to her as possible for one who lived overseas and appeared only at intervals. My aunt often horrified my mother because she gossiped and— worst of all—smoked cigarettes! Their joint devotion to my father held them together, however, the one so worldly, the other so completely unworldly. As a matter of fact my aunt was far more strait-laced than her sharp tongue and bold speech—for those days—made her out to be. I was astounded once to hear her sharp denunciation of a bachelor friend whom she had run into with his mistress at Monte Carlo; my mother could not have been more censorious.

Morals in Germany were as lax then as in later years. My aunt must have known that in the fashionable regiments every officer kept his woman. She certainly could have had no illusions as to habits and customs in court circles. This was all fostered by the absurd conventions of the day and the utterly unnatural relations of the sexes. The young people were so kept apart, and the girls so chaperoned, that of course the young men sought companionship among women of the stage and other "outcasts." The latter were often stimulating friends and loyal lovers (as well as frequently blackmailing leeches) but they were sought because they dared to have the same moral, or immoral, code as the men who supported them. Even adolescent boys were rarely allowed to be alone with girls; skating was extremely popular because then you could talk with one of the opposite sex without a chaperone within earshot.

A lieutenant of the Prussian Railroad Regiment (there was only one then, I believe), who had been at the opening of the Northern Pacific, gave my sister her first lesson in Berlin as to how carefully a young woman should behave toward young men. His card was brought in one day when our parents were out. Having known him at home she did what any American girl would have done—went into the parlor to greet him and tell of her parents' absence. The lieutenant's embarrassment was as obvious as inexplicable and within two minutes he had fled from the house. As soon as possible he called again, asked to see my father alone, apologized, and explained his strange conduct by saying that he knew that Miss Villard did not understand German customs but that he had had to leave at once or he would have compromised her with our servants! I returned to America convinced that we were far ahead of the Germans when it came to normal and sensible relations among young people. But I have since learned that there is little or no difference in the sex morals of the several nations.

We occupied an apartment in a new house on what was then the Kurfürstendamm but is now the Budapesterstrasse, a continuation of it having received the former name and becoming the famous night-life avenue. In 1884 the city extended only a little beyond the Zoological Garden. The hypocritical Kaiser had not yet built the hideous church on this street in memory of his parents. From our back windows we could hear the animals roaring at their mealtimes. To reach the Grunewald people walked past sandy building lots or cultivated fields. There were one-horse street cars on the single-track line to Charlottenburg and, only a couple of doors away at the head of the street, was an excellent restaurant whose proprietor, having lived in New York, occasionally imported a barrel of Blue Point oysters by which we naturally profited. Beyond the restaurant was the Lützow Canal, along which we loved to walk and watch the great canal boats being poled along by men and women, with a mast and sail lying on deck to be erected when lakes and rivers were reached. As Americans we were shocked to see women doing hard manual labor like this and wondered how a couple of people could keep such a huge boat going.

To our home came many new and old friends, often distinguished people. Among the first to appear were the members of

the Last Spike excursion, who presented to my father a magnificent album containing their photographs and a suitable, beautifully painted and illuminated dedication—the English guests
gave him a great, gold loving cup. Among those my parents saw
much of were Von Helmholtz, the distinguished physicist, and
Virchow, the medical pioneer, who was one of the greatest scien-
tists the world has known, being an Egyptologist, archaeologist,
anthropologist, ethnologist, a marvelous physician and surgeon, a
leader in public health, and a prolific author. In 1848-49 this great
man was a revolutionist; in 1856 the author of the epoch-making
Cellular Pathology; and, in addition to all this, for forty-two
years he served Berlin as city councilor, was for sixteen years a
member of the Prussian Chamber, and for thirteen of the Reichstag—a universal genius who worked nineteen hours out of every
twenty-four! Others were Gneist and Mommsen, the historians;
Von Hoffmann, the chemist; Von Bunsen the statesman, and
numerous journalists and liberal editors—there were such then
despite Bismarck—and one of the finest of them was Doctor Theodor Barth, who founded and edited the Berlin *Nation* after becoming acquainted with ours in the United States. To his weekly
my father frequently contributed. Werner von Siemens, the foremost German electrical pioneer and head of the General Electric
Company, and almost the only captain of industry to visit us, was
still another welcome guest. Indeed, for our elders it was a most
stimulating intellectual life and for us a constant education in liberalism and the liberal world of affairs.

Mommsen on one occasion deeply incensed my loyal American
mother at her dinner table. First he told her, the woman suffra-
gist, that woman's place was in the home and kitchen, that she
should not aspire to anything else, and that if any German women
should attempt it the German men would check them, for they
did not propose to have intellectual wives; they preferred them
simple, domestic, and beautiful. To which my mother, who had
been struck by the absence of beauty and the lack of chic and
charm among the German women, answered with rare anger that
Mommsen's countrywomen would have to work hard to achieve

that third quality. Next Mommsen severely criticized the United States. When my mother replied that at least he must admit we were a very young country and had had tremendous obstacles to overcome, he answered: "I knew you would say that. Americans always do. It is no excuse at all. You Americans had the opportunity to build a new country and a new social order and of profiting by all our mistakes, and now you are making all these mistakes yourselves"—a biting truth which was never more to the point than in the post bellum period thirty years later. Mommsen was the father of no less than fifteen children. My mother wrote of him at that time: "He is a tall, thin, wiry man with absolutely piercing eyes and he is well armed with sarcasm and willing to use it any moment." Ludwig Bamberger, the author and parliamentarian, was perhaps more understanding of the difficulties of the American democracy. My father enjoyed greatly his constant intercourse with him and the other opponents of Bismarck. Mommsen, Virchow, Von Bunsen, Barth had all encountered the Chancellor's might.

They had a hard row to hoe against their great and unscrupulous adversary, and so did the Socialists who were then regarded much as Communists are in the United States today. The wily Bismarck stole some of their political clothes and instituted the great social security reforms which put Germany far ahead of the rest of the world, for which the United States has had to wait until the Presidency of Franklin Roosevelt. In August, 1884, Bismarck had yielded against his better judgment to a German demand for colonies—chiefly for purposes of "side," for there was then no allegation that Germany needed territory for surplus population or lacked adequate raw materials. He seized the Cameroons which the English had already looked over and refused to annex,[3] and one of my clearest Berlin recollections is of seeing a parade of the crew of the first German cruiser to return from the new colony. With them marched a group of natives—captives at the chariot wheels—and the people who witnessed the spectacle ap-

[3] Cf. William Osgood Aydelotte, *Bismarck and British Colonial Policy*, University of Pennsylvania, 1937.

plauded loudly. The taking of that territory, however, was not a happy venture. The German administration of the Cameroons, although better than that of their West African colony, was none too good. I am one of those, like General Smuts, who believe that the Germans should never be allowed to govern native races.

During these Berlin years my parents met the Crown Princess several times in connection with her effort to build up the first high school for girls. She had heard of my father's gifts to his birthplace, Speyer, in the Palatinate, and to Kaiserslautern, and sought his help. It was hard for Americans to understand why this English princess was so unpopular, but it was plain that she was far too liberal and too advanced for that day in Germany. Indeed, it has been well said that she was destined for unpopularity because she was too German in England and too English in Germany. Naturally the Mommsens were bitterly opposed to her efforts to make thinking humans out of German women. In addition, she had the tactlessness which so often marks English people when domiciled abroad. Her inability to get on with her elder son is now historically revealed—to his complete discredit. Even with her daughters things were not easy; at one bazaar my mother heard the Princess Victoria defy a maternal order to remove her gloves with as flat an "I won't" as any commoner might have snapped out. When my mother met the Princess Wilhelm, the Princess said something to her that she could not understand. For a minute or two she was in utter confusion, then, forgetting etiquette, my mother burst out: "Oh, you are speaking *English*," and pretty poor English it was. Royalty was easily seen because the members of the royal family frequently went to the great balls which are still to some degree notable features of Berlin life, or were up to the time that Hitler came in. They also skated democratically on the pond in the Thiergarten unguarded and mingling freely with the public.

The Crown Prince seemed to us all the physical embodiment of what a king ought to be; I can recall none other of those rulers that I have seen who was so truly regal in stature and appearance, and so genial and kindly in his manner. There is no doubt that if

he had lived to rule Germany for even ten years the whole story
of modern Europe would have been a different one. My father
was also sent for by the old Kaiserin Augusta and was painfully
impressed by her enameled face and other evidences of great age.
In later years he was approached with the inquiry as to whether
he would accept decorations in recognition of his gifts to the Palatinate, of the considerable help he gave to the German government's exhibit at the Chicago World's Fair in 1893, and for his
bringing to this country a number of young German students and
technicians to carry on their studying. An ingrained republican, he
declined all such suggestions.[4]

Musically Berlin was then at high water mark. The operas were
excellent, the Joachim-DeAhna Quartet the acme in chamber
music, while the Philharmonic Orchestra, of course, set a far
higher standard than that of any American organization of that
time—it was the period just before the founding of the Boston
Symphony. My mother saw quite a little of Joachim and never
attended one of his many concerts without entering in her diary:
"Joachim played superbly." He was kind enough to give my
sister what is now called an audition, to speak well of her talent
as a violinist, and to recommend a good teacher for her. She and
my brother Harold, with his cello, and I with my violin worked
hard all the time we were in Berlin. Soon my mother was playing
Beethoven trios with her elder children, for it was impossible not
to be stimulated by the deep love of music and the high artistry
of the performances of those days. This was also a period when
the German stage had reached great heights.

In Berlin the ignorance of everything American, and especially of the size of our country, was colossal. Once in school I
was asked by a teacher how long it took to cross our continent.

---

[4] My father never showed better judgment than when President Cleveland,
after his re-election in 1892, asked him if he would like to become Minister
to Berlin. My father thanked the President but told him that he considered himself ineligible because he had contributed to the President's election funds, because he was a Wall Street man, and because he had never learned to bow down
before kings—the blood of 1848 was still in his veins. It was some time before
he told us of this.

I answered: "About five days." The teacher turned to the class
and said: "Boys, boys, don't believe him. He is lying to you."
When, much outraged, I replied that I had actually made the
journey, and over my father's railroad, and therefore knew, it did
not help me. None of them believed that any country save Russia
could be so large, and when I added that Texas was as big or
bigger than France I was set down as a hopeless Munchausen.
There was a tremendous enthusiasm among all German boys for
everything relating to our Indians. Every boy and girl read
Cooper's novels. These made the children believe that contem-
porary America was absolutely wild when one went beyond the
confines of New York and Philadelphia.

My father was once called upon by Count Von der Goltz, one
of the great and successful commanders of the war with France.
The Count's son had had to resign from the most exclusive cavalry regiment, the Garde du Corps, because of too much wine, too
many women, and too much gambling, and had been sent as a
remittance man to the United States. The Count read to my father
two letters from his son begging for immediate additional pecun-
iary aid because of the extraordinary bad luck he had had. He
had been robbed of all he had by cowboys in Central Park and
soon thereafter, when he had been so imprudent as to visit Niagara,
had been stripped of all his possessions by marauding Indians. His
father remarked that he knew America was very wild and unset-
tled outside of the East but wondered whether there was not a
little exaggeration in those stories. Father told him the truth and
on his return to New York looked up the young Count, found him
in Ludlow Street jail for debt, bailed him out, and sent him to
Montana where he brought prosperity to a dry goods store when
the women found that they could be waited on by a real count.
Subsequently he moved to Milwaukee, married a hard-working
stenographer, and, so far as we knew, lived happily ever after.

Of all the various phases of my education I count those two and
one-quarter years in Berlin the most valuable, and ever since have
been a strong advocate of sending young Americans abroad whenever possible. This is not only because I learned another language

but because those years knocked out of me the American bumptiousness and spread eaglism which characterized most Americans at that time, both young and old. That stay in Europe made me an internationalist, and I came to love the German people, to realize that all peoples are not very different and that there are other points of view than one's own. Our summers spent in Switzerland, on the Rigi, and in the Engadine confirmed this. What I learned in Berlin has stood me in good stead all my life, helped to fit me to write on Germany as soon as I joined the staff of *The Evening Post,* and aided me in understanding, if not in approving, the feelings with which the German people entered the World War.[5] Not then, of course, nor in later visits, did I fathom the German character. Indeed, there have been times since the coming of Hitler that I have had to ask myself if I have ever understood the German psychology, or ever could. In later years I have recalled how at school in Germany the deceit practiced by German statesmen towards Napoleon after their subjugation was held up to us as honorable and praiseworthy in high degree. This should have prepared me, but did not, for the secret violations of the Treaty of Versailles, violations carried on from the very signing of the Treaty. I have been reluctantly compelled to believe that only a few Germans were opposed to this deliberate dishonesty.

When I finally was qualified to enter the Kaiserin Augusta Gymnasium in Charlottenburg in March, 1886, our stay was drawing to a close. I was, however, long enough in the "Untertertia" class to get a good insight into German scholastic methods of that time. I found that the progress of the class was determined by that of the slowest mind in it but I have to admit that what I learned there I really knew and have never lost. Naturally the contrast with Mr. Morse's small and relatively easygoing and superficial school was great. The German boys permitted things to be done to them that independent American youngsters would never have stood for. There was some corporal punishment though I never heard of any regular whippings. Some of the teachers pulled

[5] As set forth in my *Germany Embattled,* New York, 1915.

or pinched ears and slapped faces or twisted arms. Several of them were overbearing and arrogant. I early made up my mind that I would walk out of the school if any teacher laid hands upon me, but as a foreigner I was never molested. I did not do very well in my studies, partly because I knew that we were sailing for home in the fall before the examinations leading up to promotion to the next class and partly because I lived alone for six weeks in our apartment after our brief summer vacation, being cared for by the butler, with no one there to supervise my home work.

The entire class and all the teachers and the rector of the gymnasium were astounded when they learned this. It came out through my refusal to take home my weekly reports for parental signature. They could not believe that I, in my fifteenth year, had traveled alone from Switzerland to Berlin, or rather from Heidelberg to Berlin, for an old friend had traveled with me to that university city. While there I witnessed the beautiful and historically most impressive parade that marked the five hundredth anniversary of the founding of the university. Traveling alone to Berlin seemed perfectly natural to me as an American boy. Once there, the butler got me my breakfast and made me my two sandwiches for my lunch, and for dinner I went to the neighboring restaurant. Saturdays and Sundays, with or without friends, I went off on my bicycle. It was one of those extremely dangerous affairs with a high wheel in front and a little one behind and I was always glad when I toppled over on a sandy road and not on a pavement. "Oswald's velocipede" my mother called it, and there were still so few that anyone who rode on such a machine attracted much attention. Sometimes I accompanied old friends on picnic trips to the beautiful near by lakes and suburbs. Our family doctor, who had also witnessed the driving of the Last Spike, kept an eye on me and I was never lonely. But the school authorities refused to credit my story and sent the school janitor, when I was safe in my class, to interview the butler and verify the facts. Whereupon my parents' stock would have sunk considerably on account of their strange and heartless conduct in turning a fourteen-year-older adrift in so great a city had their conduct not been laid to the notorious eccentricity of Americans.

This incident, and the refusal to believe my statement about the size of the United States, illustrated well the difference between German and American children at that time. No German boy would have been trusted as I was. We in our family, and all our friends, had been brought up at home to be independent and were always trusted unless we proved ourselves unworthy. The German attitude was just the opposite; teachers and parents never thought of granting independence or responsibility and some of our teachers certainly went on the theory that a child's first instinct was to deceive. They placed upon the boys the burden of proving that they told the truth and so a number of them naturally fell into the role assigned to them and lied and cheated and cribbed. Why not, if that was what was expected of them? None the less there were some nice, clean, and upright lads in the class, with one of whom, also a writer, I have kept in touch ever since. I learned later that the gymnasium was not considered one of the best. The "Ordinarius" of our class, which is perhaps best translated by "Dean," was a quiet, gentlemanly man who won everybody's respect. Dietrich Hahn, our instructor in history, was by all odds the most interesting and the best teacher. Soon after he resigned, went into politics, and was elected to the Reichstag. There he had a meteoric rise by reason of marked oratorical ability and because he became a most subservient adulator of Bismarck and representative of the Prussian Junker. Finally he disappeared, almost as suddenly as he had risen.

In the German schools at that time there was no sign of militarism or even marching. When the pupils went out with their teachers it was for all day hikes which were correlated usually to their instruction in botany and natural history. Not until the middle of the World War did Germany begin to drill her schoolboys. Until then her military men had believed that drilling boys before they obtained their full growth was hurtful and not helpful—an opinion shared by some of the best instructors in physical training in this country. Few of the boys in my class sought the military career. Of course I as one who had practically never seen troops was deeply impressed by the military displays. Almost every day in the spring and summer regiments marched through the Kurfürstendamm between five and six in the morning with their magnificent bands and superb regimental singing, and it was impossible not to rush to the windows to see them. The parades and drills on the Tempelhofer Feld, now the greatest civic aviation field possessed by any city, were amazingly impressive displays which quite naturally gave the Germans the feeling that there could be no other army to compare with theirs.

At that time there was no love for the enforced three-year service and many parents made genuine sacrifices to put their children through the gymnasiums in order to have them pass the graduation examinations which reduced this period and enabled them to serve as one-year volunteers. These recruits were slightly favored since the officers were drawn from this group except when they came in from the cadet schools. Even then there were plenty of true stories of the brutalities in the barracks and on the drill grounds. The noncommissioned officers had far too much power and the other officers were too remote from their men and trusted the sergeants too much—a condition which is reported to have been largely remedied in the army of Hitler. In the eighties the officers were not yet as overbearing as in later years but what I picked up in my school days, together with my steady reading of German dailies, made me a sharp antagonist of the whole German military system; I had been writing critical editorials denouncing it for sixteen years when the World War came.

Eager as I was to get back to the United States it was a real wrench to leave Berlin, and I have ever since felt myself completely at home when residing there. Among my most cherished memories of our Berlin years are those of my brother Hilgard; he developed from a little baby into a lovely little boy, always sunny and happy, always the joy of the whole family. His nurse stood her exile from home as best she could but was never able to pick up more than a few words of German. On October 1, 1886, we left for London and after nearly two weeks in England we sailed on the North German Lloyd steamer *Saale*, "a great ship" we called it, but it gave us a terrible passage, with storms all the way over. It seemed a relief, indeed, on the tenth day to set foot in New York again. But, after the cleanliness and order of Berlin, my mother entered in her diary: "The filth of New York is appalling."

The home we occupied on our return to New York comprised the three lower floors of the Louis C. Tiffany house which stood at the corner of Seventy-second Street and Madison Avenue until 1937. Our apartment contained a two-storied dining room done in Mr. Tiffany's best taste and a very large drawing room. To it came on one occasion nearly three hundred guests to witness and to hear something very remarkable—Lilli Lehmann singing into Edison's improved phonograph and then having her magnificent voice come thinly and scratchingly back to her from the wax cylinder upon which it was recorded. This was considered the last word in scientific marvels. Edison himself was there. We were far from the first movie and the radio yet this curious squeaking instrument, with its fragile and easily broken records, was actually a long step on the road to the permanent preservation of the human voice and personality for the use of future generations, the end of which we have not yet reached. The blocks directly opposite us, on the south across Seventy-second Street, were part of the old James Lenox farm and, though I can find few not of the older generation to believe it, there were still a farmer, still a stable and some cows on the land in 1887. For some years thereafter we watched the farmer do his chores in the mornings. We saw the farm buried under great drifts of snow in the blizzard of 1888, during which we rescued a man who was leaning up against the farm fence dazed and exhausted, got him into our house, and gave him food and drink as if we were all dwellers on a Dakota prairie.

I did not attempt to go to school on that day for the horse-cars stopped early and I was subject then, and for several years thereafter, to serious bronchial attacks. On the second day it was considered a feat that I was able to walk all the way down to Forty-ninth Street to Mr. Morse's school (which I had reluctantly re-entered) and home again. Commuters were marooned in the city for two or three days and the drifts were frequently far over one's head. The metropolis has never seen anything approaching this storm since; indeed, whatever the weather bureau may say, I for one am convinced that New York's climate has changed. The good nature with which the city took its complete paralysis by that storm was typically American. Snowbank after snowbank was decorated with amusing signs and everybody forgot financial losses and grave personal inconvenience in the excitement of being part of a tremendous natural phenomenon which, fortunately, cost only a few lives. No more than nine or ten men reached the office of *The Evening Post* on that blizzard day but that skeleton crew actually got the paper out. I do not suppose that more than fifty copies were sold but the record of never having failed to appear in eighty-seven years was kept unbroken, and thereafter the staff always insisted that the newspaper would appear automatically even though no one came to the office to get it out.

We slipped easily into our old New York way of life save that my elder brother had entered Harvard. My father drifted quickly back into the railroad world although he had planned not to become active again for some time and always to remain an independent business man allied to no company and responsible for nobody's investments except those of the Deutsche Bank and a large Frankfurt banking house as whose representative he had returned from Berlin. Within ten months two of the companies he created, the Oregon Railway and Navigation Company and the Oregon Transcontinental, got into serious financial difficulties and would have collapsed had not my father's European backers cabled him five million dollars within thirty-six hours of his laying the case before them, to the serious derangement of the international exchange market. At first he declared that he would not again become a director of these companies and of the Northern Pacific; unfortunately, as has already been said, he yielded to the tremendous pressure brought to bear upon him and to the argument that loyalty demanded that he come to the rescue of the endangered companies. Later he declined the presidency of the Northern Pacific but took the chairmanship of the board, another step that he repented deeply in later years.

With my Harvard entrance examinations behind me in June of 1889, with my brother and a school friend I spent six most valuable weeks in Yellowstone National Park and the Jackson's Hole country at the foot of the Tetons. This region, now so familiar to hundreds of thousands of automobile tourists, was then one of the wildest portions of the West. We found only two or three ranches in Jackson's Hole. There was any amount of game, deer, moose, antelope in particular. We killed only what we needed for food. Few of my experiences have been more rewarding. I widened my understanding of frontier life, saw a small portion of our army at work, for Yellowstone Park was then in the custody of the First Cavalry, and came to know as wonderful and as beautiful a portion of our country as can be found. Those days and evenings in the saddle, the lonely camps, the open air meals, eaten with the seasoning of a glorious fatigue, the untouched beauty of nature, the sense of almost being a pioneer, remain in memory to this day.

Here in Jackson's Hole was America primeval, America in the making. Here were men who lived snowed in for eight months with no sign of other human life; I found the works of Robert Ingersoll and Thomas Paine the only books in one lonely cabin. Here were health and strength, liberty and freedom from all conventions, with never a fence nor the sign of a road, and the sight of deer took on new significance because there, on four legs, was the food we must have. Here were unfished streams and the loveliest emerald lakes, and trees that sought the heavens, and, a marvelous back drop to all, the great Tetons themselves with their perpetual snow and their then unconquered heights. I think it must have been only because my home opportunities were so rare and so all-promising that I did not yield wholly to the lure of that West and return as Theodore Roosevelt and Owen Wister did again and again; it certainly awoke in me my pioneer inheritance.

Much strengthened and invigorated I entered Harvard and had the great benefit of sharing rooms with my scholarly brother during my Freshman year—a privilege gratefully appreciated.

Chapter V. Harvard Days

THE Harvard of my undergraduate days was a Harvard entirely satisfied with itself. It had reason to be. Its leadership of the collegiate world was never clearer. President Eliot was the outstanding figure in American education. Its scholars were known everywhere and there was nowhere else in America a body to challenge their superiority. Royce, James, Childs, Charles Eliot Norton, Alexander Agassiz, George M. Lane and Greenough in Latin; George L. Kittredge, LeBaron R. Briggs, Adams S. Hill, and Barrett Wendell in English; Goodwin in Greek; Channing, Hart, and Emmerton in history; Taussig and Dunbar in economics; Shaler and Whitney in geology; George H. Palmer in religion and philosophy; Putnam in archaeology; Pickering in astronomy; Santayana, then nearing the end of his brief but brilliant teaching years; Boucher and DeSumichrast in French—these, the really extraordinary law faculty, and still others were great teachers and usually rare personalities. If I aver that we have not their equals today I must not be accused of looking at the past through the rosy spectacles with which the old always seek to regard the days of their youth. They were the flowering of an age. Their disappearance marked the end of an era.

There are, of course, striking personalities and great teachers at Harvard today, notably in the sciences. Yet President Conant's own utterances and his rigid search for outstanding *men* bear out the fact that there is not yet a group of scholars to measure up to that which gave Harvard its remarkable tone and standing in 1889. We were at the tail end of the great period of New England. The literary traditions in Massachusetts were yet compelling. Moreover, the leading men I have mentioned had, most of them, their roots in Civil War days. Shaler had commanded a battery of artillery in action in his native Kentucky at twenty-one. Hill had been a Civil War journalist in close association with my father and Horace White. Those who were too young to serve, or were born in the war period, were, like Albert Bushnell Hart, none the less deeply affected by it and the post bellum political strife. Channing once begged me to write a life of Jefferson Davis to combat the new school of Civil War history which seeks to make black white and white black and to wipe out all the fundamental ethical differences between the North and the South of slave days in one sappy, sentimental portrayal of an innocent, kindly, and vilified ante bellum South which never existed. Consciously or unconsciously, many of these Harvard scholars had been molded by their background of the period of union and disunion and affected by that outpouring of unselfish devotion to the Union in 1861-65 which Harvard especially typified in New England.

These great teachers and savants had, moreover, a polish, a courtliness, almost an old-worldliness, that cannot be replaced today. They were the product of the time of leisure and of good manners, when people wrote long letters to each other in their own handwriting to record their feelings and beliefs, to exchange experiences, and to match comments on happenings all over the world. There was intellectual intercourse, not only among the faculty but between it and the Boston Brahmins. The faculty, although growing rapidly, was small enough for every member to know every other. It was still a debating body and, under the wise guidance of President Eliot, was a notable scholastic senate in which the elders forged out educational policy and were free to challenge and even to reject presidential proposals, in which young men could establish their claim to intellectual parity with their seniors.[1] It was not until President Lowell's regime that, because of his own personal characteristics and the great growth of the faculty, this meeting of free minds in debate gradually came to an end.

In an America undergoing the astounding economic and political transformations of the years from 1865 to 1898, the Harvard

---

[1] The most outspoken, at times savage, and successful critic of Mr. Eliot was Professor Kittredge.

community held fast to ideals, to traditions, to ways of life which were remarkably apart from the great surge toward riches, toward monopoly and special privilege of every kind, toward gross materialism, which characterized the national life. Its scholars kept alive and watered richly a green oasis in which men were mentally absolutely free, could cherish the graces of life, and could even think as a group. No important national or international issues were there to distract or to divide, nothing until the Spanish War to arouse even a tithe of the fierce passions born of the World War and the subsequent political and economic developments. Naturally the undergraduate body reflected the economic currents of the day and many of its members were slow to understand and appreciate what Harvard offered to them. Some of my classmates were of the new order. The wealth that sent them to college was newly acquired. Just as the Civil War had meant a final break with the type of undergraduate which Harvard had received after the days when all its students were destined to be pedagogues or preachers, so our group heralded the time when going to college was to be both conventional and good form—something for rich young fashionables to do before going on with lives of ease. There were a number of such in my class, boys whose parents had only social aspirations for them.

They thronged, for example, the classes in fine arts of Charles Eliot Norton and in geology of Nathaniel Shaler, because they were "snaps," easy to pass with the aid of a coach such as the famous "Widow" Nolan (a man, if you please). They sneered at Norton's priceless and caustic comments on men and affairs in our public life and were apt to sleep through some of Professor Shaler's wide-ranging discourses. Professor Norton deliberately included in his lectures discussions of the events of the day, of every phase of manners and morals and social happenings, called politicians by their right names, and found so little to praise as to meet the usual fate of the high-minded, idealistic, and consistent commentator upon public affairs. Yet if there ever was a patriot it was Charles Eliot Norton; he always upheld the theory that the university teacher was profoundly concerned with public affairs and had the duty of going on record when in his judgment the country deviated from its principles and fundamental tenets. When the Spanish War and our lurch into imperialism came on, he spoke out at once and, like the rest of the anti-imperialists, became extremely unpopular but rendered yeoman service in criticizing the Administration and making it conscious that it was being watched and tested every moment. He instituted a gathering at the little village in Massachusetts, Ashfield, where he had his summer home, to which free spirits came to discuss the ominous new trend toward conquest and imperialism and to reassert the old American ideals.

In our time Harvard College was still so small (our class numbered less than four hundred on graduation) that the professors, not then being pursued by the specter of research and of having to print a book every two or three years, were able to know and influence their students outside of their classrooms and to invite some of them to their homes. Perhaps the tutorial system, and the opportunity within the new Harvard "houses" for the undergraduates to come into contact with the masters and other faculty residents, may now have filled the void which existed for many years after the older social association of teachers and pupils came to an end because of the greatly increased numbers and enlarged demands upon the professors. As to that I cannot say, but I must truthfully record, as have so many others before me, that what I remember most clearly today about my life at Harvard is my contacts with some of the notable men I have named. Many books I then read are now forgotten; there is not a trace within me of some of the courses that I took, but the individualities that influenced me most have never been dimmed. Their example and their reasoned beliefs remain with me and to them I most gratefully record my lasting indebtedness. Undoubtedly my two postgraduate years played a greater part here, as will appear later, than my undergraduate period. Still if I had left Harvard permanently when my class was graduated in 1893 I should none the less look back to my teachers with a gratitude and an admiration which I do not seem to detect for its instructors in the generation to which my sons belong.

President Eliot himself was an institution. He stood as straight as Bunker Hill Monument and was obviously as unshakable on his foundations. One looked at him and felt instinctively that our institutions were safe and justified when they produced one such as he. Undergraduates found him austere and unapproachable. They were awed by him and his rectitude; he seemed to them an unyielding Colonial Puritan come to life. They were wrong. True, one could never conceive of catching him off his guard, or in a dressing gown, or even relaxed as men justifiably are after a hard day; one felt that never was there a man who had himself so completely in hand. Yet he was by no means unapproachable or too puritanical. He had a charming smile and I always found his voice most agreeable. Naturally he varied it little in speaking; he knew nothing of the orator's arts and would not have used them if he had. His choice of English was superb and some of the finest inscriptions in the language came from his pen. His speeches were clear and direct, perfectly framed, with never a repetition—ready for the printer as a stenographer took them down. In other words, he was a great thinking machine with a completely balanced mind —and his heart was not cold or indifferent, not at all, but a heart controlled and never permitted to run away with him.

His faculty often quarreled with him but their admiration for him was complete. Even when his tact failed him—as it often did, sometimes cruelly, in his relations with them—they still upheld him. They all felt when that presence appeared this *was* the leader. Never, I believe, did any college head so completely honor and perfectly typify in himself the institution over which he presided. If he had been no educational innovator at all he would still have ranked as a great man, a great gentleman, and a great American. Indeed, many of his friends, and I, too, mourned that he did not accept Theodore Roosevelt's offer to send him to the Court of St. James's. No one else could have raised the overseas prestige of the United States as he and there never would have been the slightest possibility of his yielding to the insidious flattery of London and becoming faithless to America. He never, never would have gone hat in hand to the Foreign Office to ask for his orders.

That he was a conservative goes without saying and he could dislike heartily and lastingly. He never forgave Wendell Phillips. Not because Phillips had sided with the slaves and taken up with agitators. He might have been forgiven for that in view of Emancipation but unpardonable was that golden orator's later career. He had headed a labor ticket in Massachusetts as candidate for Governor and had declared that Lincoln had freed only a portion of the American slaves. Mr. Eliot is on record as denouncing Phillips, one of the greatest and quite the most unselfish of Harvard's graduates, as an untrustworthy and reckless demagogue. Yet he did not toady to wealth as so many college presidents have done and still do and he recognized relatively few—though too many—of the magnates of the business world with honorary degrees. Although he dared to violate the historic Harvard tradition in not bestowing the LL.D. on one Governor of Massachusetts, Benjamin F. Butler, he was ready to honor William McKinley with it in the face of innumerable protests but that, fortunately, never took place. Mr. Eliot's reform instincts confined themselves largely to education and such undertakings as civic or civil service reform. He was never in touch with the masses and their aspirations.

With President Eliot I got on capitally. When I became Harvard correspondent for *The Evening Post* he gave me his confidence and the occasional interviews that I asked for. One of these had to do with one of his blind sides, the lack of a uniform architectural plan for Harvard's development. It was under his regime that some of the worst buildings were put into the "Yard," and though Charles Eliot Norton and others kept urging a return to Colonial architecture and a unified plan, these had to wait upon the coming in of President Lowell. Nor could President Eliot see any need for the application to Harvard of the modified English college plan, as to which I was also directed to interview him. The university was turning out splendid men everywhere, leaders in their communities; there was, he thought, surely no need for a radical change. Curiously enough he was even quite content that during the greater part of his administration there were no bathrooms in the dormitories. The era of bathing by the hundreds under the showers in the old gymnasium had not yet ended when my class entered college.

Ninety-three has not been an overly distinguished group though ranking well with those in college with it. Few men within it have achieved nation-wide distinction. William Vaughn Moody was our greatest talent and he died prematurely. One great judge we have contributed to the nation, Learned Hand of the United States Circuit Court of Appeals, whose breadth of vision, liberalism, and freedom from archaic legal traditions long ago marked him as one who should have been upon the Supreme Court bench of the United States and doubtless would have been had not Justices Stone, Cardozo and Hughes blocked the way by also being New Yorkers. Judge Hand is, and for years has been, intellectually the foremost member of the class. Within our ranks have been some other outstanding lawyers, notably Robert Gray Dodge, the leader of the Boston Bar. We are proud of several excellent doctors, of whom Freeman Allen was a distinguished anesthetist, Charles R. Bardeen was long the dean of the Medical School of the University of Wisconsin, and William H. Robey is to this day one of the foremost physicians of Boston. We have had one college president, Murray Bartlett, and several distinguished professors. We have been represented in Congress by some worthy, hard-working, conservative Congressmen, have furnished an inconspicuous governor or two and an ambassador to France in Jesse I. Straus, who won everybody's respect and the warm regard of many. We were good friends but he once told a director of *The Nation* that I was the only black sheep in '93, which is after all eminence in its way! A most unusually attractive personality was that of James A. Wilder of Honolulu. Musician, capital actor, unexcelled *raconteur*, Chief Sea Scout of the United States, and portrait painter of no little merit, his friends were legion. Indeed he was an institution in himself.

There were and are some able journalists in our class: Frederick

Roy Martin, for a time General Manager of the Associated Press; William O. Taylor, for so many years, with his father and elder brother, a manager and owner of the Boston *Globe;* and Frederick Sibley, who was one of the few war correspondents at the front in the World War to make a name for himself with the public and the troops with whom he served—General Clarence R. Edwards' Yankee Division. Of the other members of the class, Frederick Converse has been a noteworthy composer and prominent in the Boston Conservatory of Music. Patrick T. Campbell was long the able superintendent of schools in Boston, while Frederick Winsor is the head of a fine Harvard preparatory school, Middlesex, which he himself created. Our first scholar, David S. Muzzey, has been a professor of history at Columbia, a leader of the Ethical Culture Society, and the writer of conventional and, in spots, superficial histories. Thomas A. Jaggar is an international authority on volcanoes and has, therefore, resided in Hawaii, the best natural laboratory in the world for him. As a whole I cannot say, as I should dearly like to, that '93 has been a class to which the university might refer with especial pride. But at least we have upheld the Harvard tradition of contributing greatly to the steadfast bourgeoisie and the satisfactory maintenance of the *status quo.*

As to my own undergraduate life there is absolutely nothing to be said; I enjoyed it to the brim. I lived alone after my brother's graduation which made it easier for me to give a good deal of time to studying the violin under one of the greatest musicians of our musical history, Franz Kneisel; I have counted it a great honor that I was at this time the only amateur pupil he would take. From him I learned much more than the fundamentals of violin playing. I found depths in him that I had not suspected in musicians and a sound judgment on affairs that astonished me. In later years Kreisler, Paderewski, Zimbalist, Gabrilowitsch, Schumann-Heink, and many other friends have made me realize how completely the musician has evolved from the old mid-Victorian ideal of a long-haired, temperamental, impossible person, wrapped up only in his or her music and without another thought in the world beyond musical expression. There are others besides Paderewski who could have shone in world affairs. That prince of men, Kreisler, would have proved his genius in any role to which fate might have assigned him. Gabrilowitsch might easily have played a great civic part and I have found to my delight that many of this group were not only citizens of the world but, like Zimbalist in particular, had their minds attuned to new ideas and to proposals for a nobler world. With Kneisel my friendship lasted until his early death; it was my joy to follow his concerts for many years and once, when his purpose faltered, to help to continue his glorious quartet for a short period.

I never attained high rank at Harvard. I had worked hard in my Freshman year and hoped for good marks but in the middle of the final examinations came that dreadful blow, the death of my brother. I lost several of these tests and had to take them in the fall, with poor results, for I spent most of the summer in a health resort in the Black Forest trying to get over the shock and to cure my continuing tendency to severe bronchial attacks. When I found that my low marks barred any hope of my obtaining a high stand, and that I could not take additional courses and substitute them for those in which I had received low grades, I lost nearly all interest in marks and must have graduated well down in the class, which has always made it seem extraordinarily unreal to me that I should be wearing a Phi Beta Kappa key voted to me in after years. Those were happy college years! Life was easy and without a care. I had a sufficiently large allowance to profit by theatres and concerts as much as I pleased and I was profoundly interested in politics and the world of political affairs. There were few, indeed, in the class who shared these interests— only two or three, one of them being a son of Senator Brice of Ohio. Practically nobody in the class was interested in world events; the eager, well-trained, thoughtful, even brilliant groups of undergraduates in the universities with which I have discussed foreign affairs of late years were unknown until after the World War.

The itch to write made itself felt strongly. I contributed several articles and stories to the *Harvard Advocate* and *Monthly*, but

never tried for the *Crimson* or any other undergraduate publication, probably because I was too close to *The Evening Post,* whose
Harvard correspondent I became in 1891. This was excellent training, for *The Evening Post* did not care much for undergraduate
news but wanted serious discussions of Harvard trends, studies
of university events, and personalities. I was told to send letters
"which will interest the alumni and those who are looking for
places for the education of their sons." I preserved for many years
a letter from the managing editor telling me that he had been
directed to extend to me Mr. Godkin's praise for one of my articles.
It was a great encouragement for I knew how rarely he patted
anyone's back. He also once rebuked me for criticizing some members of the faculty and had the passage struck out because he held
that "no undergraduate should criticize his professors anonymously."

The very first class—compulsory English—that I attended on
entering Harvard was presided over by William Lyon Phelps, so
long of Yale, and it was the first class ever taught by him who
has since become one of the most successful of American lecturers
and the most prolific and easily pleased book reviewer the country
has ever possessed. He was then, as now, a fluent speaker, able to
make a charming impression upon his listeners, and I was naturally
pleased when my first theme was read by him, with approval, to
the class. Later in the year he startled and moved us by reading
out a filthy theme handed in by one of our classmates. It was not
then considered bad taste for a college teacher to read a moral
lesson. Phelps did so without cant or false sentiment, so earnestly,
and so sincerely, and so wisely that I am certain that every one
of the rather irresponsible youths who heard him genuinely
profited.

I was one of those who sought admission in our senior year to
Professor Adams S. Hill's English V, the most advanced course
in English composition open to graduates and undergraduates and
strictly limited in the number of students. Professor Hill made
all who appeared to enroll write down why they desired to take
that course. I was stupid enough to say that I needed it in order

to get an honor in English and was also drawn to it by the fact that Professor Hill had been a war-time associate of my father. The statements were handed in; Professor Hill read out a few in what remained of the hour. Mine was one he pounced upon and if ever a hapless undergraduate was flayed it was I. Both reasons were pronounced unworthy with a sarcasm that reduced me to a pulp. I felt certain that I had spoiled my chances. But Professor Hill forgave me, I entered the class, enjoyed it thoroughly, profited enormously by it, and at the end got my honor. Never was there a more biting tongue than was possessed by this gifted author of the then standard textbooks in rhetoric. He had also the deadly power of silence. After a theme was read aloud by the author he would often allow two or three minutes to elapse while the class shiveringly anticipated the coming verbal execution of the criminal who had just performed. Once the low-lived classmate I have referred to read another not merely risqué but vulgarly low theme. Professor Hill sat silent for nearly five minutes, then gave us no moral lecture but so demolished the offender in two sentences that the class almost felt a glimmering of sympathy for him. Nothing could have been more perfect than those few words.

Once our task was to write a child's story and we were each warned it would not be accepted unless it had been read to a child before being turned in. When the class assembled Professor Hill asked a heavily-mustached graduate student to read his. It was very bad. There ensued the long and ominous pause. "Did you try that on a child?" asked Professor Hill. "I did. I read it to my eight-year-old son," was the reply—to the class's astonishment. "Well, what did your son say?" "He said," answered the father, "that it was rotten." Like a flash came the rapier-like reply: "Well, *he was right.*" The class roared with joy. I got off easily with my tale of a deserter from a Western army post and was much elated when *Harper's Young People* paid me fifteen dollars for it.

Barrett Wendell was another of the outstanding English teachers. His affected English accent and speech at first prejudiced students against him. He often seemed to be straining after startling effects and his loose tongue did him great injustice, as when he once told a class that he had two brothers of whom one was a fool and the other an ass. He adored everything European and once cried out as if in pain when he saw me removing a Swiss hotel sticker from a bag. "Don't do that," he said, "they remind me of the happiest days of my life." He was an ultra Back Bay conservative and confided to me his belief that Henry Cabot Lodge was the greatest man in our public life. *The Nation* and *The Evening Post* he constantly jeered at and he always had a sharp fling at them or a jest when I hove in sight. Underneath his poses he had a kind and sympathetic heart, saddened, I thought, by his consciousness that he had not achieved what he should have.[2] He exerted a fine influence upon the young instructors in the department and they were extremely fond of him. I was as astonished as I was deeply touched when, having heard, in 1896, that I was not going on in the History Department, he came to me and offered me an instructorship in English, for I thought he valued me far below par. When I said that I knew I was not competent for the position he replied: "Leave that to me. I know you are." We did not meet often in later years but when we did his greeting and the cordiality of his hand clasp warmed my heart.

The fifteen months that followed my graduation in June, 1893, were full of travel and sight-seeing. First came the glorious World's Fair at Chicago. I have seen several since but nothing to compare with its classical architecture so consistently and so beautifully carried out. I know it is the fashion in some quarters now to sneer at it as lacking in originality and in American character and for other reasons. In my judgment it is still to be regarded as one of the great milestones in our national life. Its beneficial effect upon our architectural development can never be measured; as an educational institution it was a tremendous success. Its beauty, especially at night, was beyond adequate description. The lighting

---

[2] He wrote me on March 7, 1915, of his "despondent wonder whether one's life has been futile." I was bowled over when he wrote me in 1915 in praise of my *Germany Embattled* for its "beauty of style," "sweep of its sentences" and "flow of the paragraphs."

effects which would appear conventional, probably inadequate today, seemed wonderful; indeed, we saw here for the first time the use of electricity on a great scale. Although this remarkable enterprise apparently used up for a time almost all of Chicago's limited reservoir of civic pride and achievement, nevertheless it is something for the city to be proud of for all time. Its situation was perfect, its lagoons and beautiful landscaping entrancing. The foreign buildings—my father had much to do, unofficially, with the German—were very well done and characteristic. Every line of civic and social endeavor was stimulated by that exhibition and in many respects it marked the coming of age of the United States.

We sailed for Gibraltar on November 4; the *Fulda* rolled and pitched for nine long days during which we wedged ourselves into our bunks and got precious little sleep. Spain proved as fascinating as expected; the beauty of Ronda moved me to an article for *The Evening Post*. But the physical beauty of Spain, its glorious architecture of the past, its exquisite museums and galleries, were offset for me by the wretchedness of the people, the unending beggars, many of them horribly crippled and malformed, the constant evidences of moral degradation, and the ubiquitous priests. Those priests and beggars have always presented themselves whenever I have thought of Spain. They convinced me, boy that I was, that there was no hope for Spain until the stranglehold of the Church, the great landlords, and grandees, and capitalists, was broken. We had to wait a lifetime to see the coming of the social revolution of which the people may now be robbed by the criminal connivance of the French and British governments and the intervention of two foreign despots.

After a month in Madrid, Seville, and other cities, we departed from Malaga for Northern Africa. Our ship spent one day at Melilla. Since hostilities had been going on between the Moors and the Spaniards, and the latter were actually penned up in the city, we were surprised when we were permitted to spend one entire day in the town and the military encampment. As a matter of fact, hostilities had been temporarily suspended pending negotiations for peace. Melilla seen at sunrise from the harbor presented a wonderfully picturesque appearance, being built upon a great rock jutting out into the sea. The roadstead was full of heavily-laden freighters and transports and a half dozen old-fashioned warships. There were not even sentries at the landing place. The general effect of the town was absolutely depressing. It was overcrowded and filthy; there was no evidence of the simplest sanitary precautions. The forts were old and badly built; one new fort had collapsed owing to the rain. There were 30,000 troops encamped or rather deep in mud. They were undersized, underage, and were given food which would have driven Anglo-Saxon soldiers to mutiny, but the men were well-handled when a division drilled on the plain in the afternoon.

What I saw prepared me when war came in 1898 for the ease with which Shafter's army defeated the Spaniards and for the Spanish failure to make headway against the Cubans. The article that I wrote about my observations in Melilla became my first contribution to *The Nation*, January 11, 1894, the beginning of a series that has now lasted forty-five years. Many years later, soon after the World War, there was another great, and for the Spaniards, disastrous and bloody campaign against the Moors. During it I met at Munich an aunt of the King of Spain. The Princess said to me: "I wish I could understand this war. We were so happy not to be drawn into the World War by which we legitimately prospered enormously, and now we are spending all that we gained and more in Africa and are losing thousands upon thousands of our fine young boys. My nephew tells me that our national honor demands that we do this. I wish I could understand that kind of honor. It seems to me a dreadful disaster."

Throughout the winter we wandered through Northern Africa, reveling in Constantine, Biskra, Tunis, and Algiers, and going thence to Sicily and by an English steamer to Alexandria. Two months in Egypt were enormously remunerative. My first magazine article was the result of my study of the Egyptian army. In the course of that stay I met Major Reginald Wingate, later Sir Reginald and the distinguished successor of Lord Kitchener, still living in London. I was astounded to find on the walls of the

Cairo War Department huge maps all marked, "Drawn in the year of American Independence, 1876," or some such year. The explanation was that these maps were the creations of former Confederate officers who entered the service of the Khedive, some of them because they refused to take the oath of allegiance.[3] The Chief of Staff had been General Charles P. Stone, that tragic figure of the Army of the Potomac who, after the Battle of Ball's Bluff, was relieved of his command and confined for six months in forts in New York harbor as a common criminal. He was never able to ascertain the charge (supposedly treason) made against him nor to obtain justice; even appeals to Lincoln brought no relief. Finally he was restored to his rank and given command of another brigade but his promising career was ruined so he sought balm in Egypt. The English officers in Cairo spoke in the highest terms of the work done by these American officers, especially of their staff and its topographical labors.

Major Wingate was most extraordinarily kind to so young an American as myself and when, after our return from a perfect trip up the Nile, I was confined to my bed with rheumatic fever he brought to my bedside Father Ohrwalder, the Austrian priest who had been for eleven years a captive of the Mahdi and had just escaped. Ohrwalder showed me the marks on his wrists of the chains that he had worn during most of those years; his story of the whole situation in the Sudan was thrilling to a degree, for at that time the Mahdi was at the height of his power and tourists rarely went beyond the first cataract. Kitchener had still to fight the Battle of Omdurman. Major Wingate was giving a large portion of his time to efforts to rescue the remaining prisoners, in the same way that he had freed Ohrwalder, by sending fast camels and trustworthy natives to Omdurman. After many failures he finally succeeded in bringing out Slatin Pasha, one of the most romantic figures of modern times.

From Egypt we traveled to Greece and Turkey and through the Balkans to Vienna but those were not happy months because

---

[3] Cf. W. W. Loring, Major General in the Confederate Service, *A Confederate Soldier in Egypt*, Dodd, Mead, New York, 1894.

my mother came down with a light attack of typhoid when we
arrived in the Austrian capital and my father had his most trying
business difficulties to confront at long range. It was part of my
duty to decode long cablegrams from New York and our situation
can be imagined when, at Budapest, as we were leaving the railroad station at two o'clock in the morning, my father's handbag
with his most private papers, his passport, and his code was stolen
from under our eyes. We had placed it on the small seat in front
of us in the fiacre; it was gone in sixty seconds and no amount
of searching or offering of a reward recovered it. Fortunately the
passport was totally unnecessary. I had never seen one before and
my father never showed his but once during that long journey—
a far happier situation than that of today.

As the weeks passed, despite the attractions of Vienna, including
an extraordinary Corpus Christi parade, with the most magnificent
display of horses, uniforms, and royal equipment that I have ever
seen, and the Emperor Franz Josef walking in the center of it,
I got very stale and began to feel that I was going downhill because of lack of regular work. Suddenly out of a clear sky came
one of the most welcome letters I have ever received. It was a
note from Professor Albert Bushnell Hart of Harvard asking
me if I would accept an appointment as his assistant in United
States history in charge of the written work of his large course,
History XIII. My parents and my sister were as pleased as I and
I lost no time in accepting. I spent several weeks following this
at a water cure institution on the shore of Lake Constance in order
to put myself into the best possible trim for the winter ahead,
rowing a great deal and learning to enjoy the cold water of the
lake.

It was well that I did this. For I had only been three months
at my task in Cambridge when I came down with a critical attack
of appendicitis. My Cambridge physician failed to diagnose it correctly and let me lie in my room for three days without nurse or
care until I demanded that he take me to the Massachusetts General Hospital for, in addition to the intense pain, I felt my strength
rapidly ebbing. I literally saved my own life. Arrived at the

hospital a young interne took one look at me and rushed to the telephone to summon Doctor H. H. A. Beach. He asked me if there was any reason why he should delay operating. I said no, that my family were all in Europe. My devoted Boston uncles came; I wrote a hasty letter to be sent to my mother if I died, Doctor Beach having told me very earnestly, in answer to my question, that if I had any letters to write I had better write them. Within two hours of my arrival I was on the operating table. They found that the abscess had burst and, the surgery of that day being what it was, abandoned the operation, took me back to my room, and told the nurse to give me whatever I wanted as I would certainly die before morning. I came out of the ether suddenly; the special day nurse was giving her instructions to the special night nurse. I caught the words: "The operation was unsuccessful." When I asked what she had said the nurse replied: "Oh, they didn't get the appendix but were successful in every other way."

On the following Saturday, five days later, Doctor Beach came to me and after examining me said: "I've a piece of good news for you, young man." "Yes?" I asked. "Yes. You are going to live." I was conscious through those days of violent nausea how near the end was, for I felt after the retching that if my heart beat one single stroke faster I could not live. My clerical friends will be interested to know that I, a nonchurchgoer, asked the nurse to read the Bible to me. She wanted to know what passages. I had no ideas on the subject but I can testify that whatever it was that she read soothed me by the beauty of the language.

Christmas was only a couple of days off when the doctor awarded me life. I decided to celebrate the fact and through my musical aunt, Mrs. Frank Garrison, engaged one of the best church quartets and a violinist of the Boston Symphony Orchestra to play on Christmas Day in the ward. But Doctor Beach would not let me have much music and so the musicians played in a number of the other wards. Happily there was a woman visitor in the hospital who witnessed this and was so struck with the pleasure it gave that she donated a considerable sum for Christmas music thereafter. The handsome check that my father sent to Doctor Beach was used by him as the first contribution to a new laboratory and the impulse it gave enabled him to raise the rest of the amount needed. Therefore I had the satisfaction of knowing that my illness produced some lasting advantages for that splendid old hospital with its beautiful Bulfinch building. However, I myself did not get off easily. It was seven and a half weeks before I could leave the hospital—a time busily employed in making love to two charming nurses—and then I had to go to Augusta, Georgia, to recuperate. Before I left Doctor Beach volunteered the statement that he regularly took wine, and whiskey as he needed it, but that he wished to tell me that if I had had any alcohol in my body I should never have survived.

I did not return to my work at Harvard until after the Easter vacation, a sad blow indeed. Though I was never really competent, I enjoyed my teaching, and carried on my studies for a master's degree as best I could. But whatever vanity I might have had about my appointment was effectively removed at the end of my second year when, in a burst of confidence, Professor Hart confided to me that he had selected me because of my social standing, the fact that I wore nice clothes, and was a member of a couple of good clubs. He was tired, he said, of having to pick "greasy grinds," as the men who did nothing but study were termed, because they so often lacked the appearance and the ability necessary to win the regard and respect of their students. It was a dreadful blow to my pride and it is certainly the only time, so far as I am aware, that I owed anything to my tailor.

Another blow came at the end of that teaching period. At the outset Professor Hart had asked me if I would also supervise the work of a small class of seven students that he had at Radcliffe. He explained that there would be no pay—Harvard paid me the munificent salary of $200 a year—and that I should only have to give one or two hours a week to the work. Of course my inherited interest in higher education for women made me accept with alacrity. I found, however, that I had let myself in for something serious. I think that with two exceptions all the Radcliffe students were older than myself and they knew a great deal more, some of them, than their instructor. I managed to carry on my Harvard work by reading ahead plus monumental bluffing. But those unfair Radcliffe women insisted on being at least a couple of jumps ahead of me, which was no way to treat a superior male however young. One of them was so extremely pretty that most of the young instructors were more than ready to have her in their classes; it never got beyond that for she soon proved as uninteresting as she was lovely.

At the end of my second year I met Miss Coes, the secretary of the college, and asked her how Radcliffe was getting on. "Very badly," she said, "financially very badly." I replied jokingly that I knew that must be the case since I had never been paid for my valuable services. She at once said that could not be. I explained that the arrangement was that I should not be paid and that I had only been joking. She indignantly replied that Radcliffe did not accept charity from its instructors and that she would call the attention of the treasurer to the situation at once. I protested in vain. Two weeks later I received a letter from the treasurer of Radcliffe enclosing a check and a voucher. The voucher read: "For two years' service as assistant in United States history, payment in full, $20." With this painful estimate of the value of my teaching before me I endorsed the check to the treasurer's order and returned it with a polite note saying that it was so very far in excess of what I felt to be my deserts that I begged to donate it to the college to be used for the purchase of books dealing with United States history. I thought I had come back rather neatly. I was wrong; being a woman's college, Radcliffe had the last word. The following winter when I was in Philadelphia I received the annual report of the college. It opened with a sentence which read that Radcliffe had received during the past year two gifts, one of $100,000 from Mrs. Agassiz and one of $20 from Oswald Garrison Villard! There was no come back to that.

I lectured infrequently to the Harvard class. The first time I nearly lost control of it. There was a determined move to break me up by shuffling of feet, uncalled for applause, and laughter at nothing. Finally, in desperation, I said to the class that I knew

I was green at this sort of thing but that I asked their co-operation and appealed to their sense of fair play; that I needed their help to succeed and must have it. I then began anew. Again came the shuffling of feet and I felt that I was lost. Fortunately for me I had many personal friends of undergraduate days in the course and they rallied to me and hissed down the troublemakers. I finished in control and had no further difficulty. Many of the men before me were as old or older than I and they knew it. That lecture was doubly important. It was on John Brown of Harper's Ferry and it led in time to my biography of him, *John Brown; Fifty Years After;* I believe it to be the only first-class job I have ever done.

Chapter VI. From History to Journalism

MY second graduate year at Harvard was a preposterously busy one. In addition to my work in History XIII at Harvard and Radcliffe I was collecting material for a thesis on Henry Knox, the first Secretary of War, making a careful study of fifty volumes of his papers in a Boston library, trying to carry four courses for my master's degree, giving a weekly talk on current events in a Boston girls' school, keeping up the Harvard correspondence for *The Evening Post,* and serving in Battery A, First Massachusetts Coast Artillery. I also drilled with a Harvard student company and obtained the grade of A in the military science course, for I was slow to come to my pacifist position and could not at that time accept my grandfather's views. I joined the militia in the belief that it was a necessary police force. Like almost everyone else I was totally in the dark as to the merits of the Pullman strike of 1894 which led me to enlist. I approved of President Cleveland's intervention in that strike and for many years considered Governor Altgeld a very dangerous person. It was not until our conquest of Cuba and the Philippines, with its needless waste of life and, in the archipelago, shocking cruelties, that I arrived at my antiwar position. I liked soldiering in peace time so much that it was a clear case of reason triumphing over sentiment and inborn liking.

Naturally all this work was more than I could do well; by the grace of my professors I was allowed to count my teaching as a half course and my research was accepted in lieu of my thesis. As a result I duly received my degree from President Eliot before whom I appeared at Commencement as the elected representative of the graduates receiving similar degrees. During this college year I took my meals at the Colonial Club, then the nearest approach to a faculty club, with a membership of town and gown.

There I ate at a table whose varying attendance included Professors Hill, Royce, James, Wendell, Farlow, Richards the chemist, later the Nobel Prize winner and father-in-law of President Conant, George A. Bartlett, Archibald Cary Coolidge, and numerous others. It was my role to be as inconspicuous as possible for I was the only youngster in the group. That did not prevent endless teasing by my elders, Hill, Wendell, and Farlow leading, with James now and then putting in a thrust with quiet smile and grave, searching eyes. There was never a sting to what he said; but he often took the opinions of the twenty-three-year-old neophyte before him and demolished them completely. Farlow, who was professor of cryptogamic botany, a little bent man with an impish sarcasm, I also met often at the home of mutual friends and we saw much of one another at the club as we were among the most regular "mealers." He enjoyed razzing me no end; still we were most sympathetic friends despite the difference in years. In George A. Bartlett, for so many years the Regent of the college, I had not only a warm friend but a defender always ready to come to my rescue when he could. He had a charming, honest face, often lit up with humor, and a kindly smile but as Regent he was often very stern. He was as modest, as kind and unselfish as anyone could be.

It was he who stood by me when I was all but choking to death because of a throat abscess when visiting at Northeast Harbor in the early summer of 1896. I was a ghastly sight fighting for breath with a terribly swollen tongue but he sat up all night with me and took charge of me as if I were his son until my parents arrived and he could confirm the good news that the abscess had burst in the nick of time, just when surgeons were leaving Bar Harbor to undertake a very dangerous operation. Professor Bartlett was also a Civil War veteran with a deep hatred of war and all that made for it but he regularly participated in a *Kriegspiel* and enjoyed it to the brim. He enlisted in the First Maine Cavalry when only eighteen and in their first serious engagement was wounded and fell under his horse where he lay until the Confederates pulled him out and sent him to the horrors of their prisons. About these experiences he would never talk. I kept in close and grateful friendship with him until he died. Archie Coolidge came only rarely; I had already known him for some years and, like all who knew him, valued highly his sterling qualities, his quiet ability, his freedom from any selfish ambition, and the range of his knowledge which was not widely recognized until the World War and the Peace Conference led to his playing important parts. Richards was also modest and quiet, never seeking to lead in the conversation but speaking clearly and to the point whenever moved to do so.

I am sure that during that winter I paid for all of Mr. Godkin's sins, and my own deficiencies as well, by the verbal castigations I had to undergo. I had not sense enough to make daily notes of the brilliant conversations I heard or this might be a really valuable record. Those Colonial Club hours were quite the most useful and stimulating of my six Cambridge years. For all their readiness to make me a butt of their jokes and sarcasms my elders were all so kind, so generous, and forbearing, that I recall those contacts with profoundest gratitude. I knew how fortunate I was to be able to sit, metaphorically, at the feet of so unsurpassed a group of American scholars. Given my especial bent toward politics, what impressed me most was their great concern with public affairs, the care with which they followed every happening in our foreign policy, and the daily events in Washington. They were deeply stirred by President Cleveland's Venezuelan message and some of them joined a group of Harvard teachers and undergraduates who immediately signed a public protest declaring that "the intense war spirit now manifested in our treatment of foreign affairs seems to us a menace to the welfare of our country and to her high stand among civilized nations"—which sounds as if it had been written much, much later. Curiously enough those men in public life who at that time were most in favor of Cleveland's twisting the British lion's tail were the very men who twenty years later were abusing President Wilson for delaying in putting us into the war to save England!

Of the Colonial Club group Royce and James were naturally

the most impressive. When they spoke everyone listened; I recall particularly James's seriousness and earnestness and the impression he gave of a controlling desire within him to get to the bottom of things, really to arrive at the facts. He was a great admirer of my Uncle Wendell, the editor of *The Nation*, and of *The Nation* itself, and was long one of its most valued contributors. Cambridge was full of the stories of Royce and his remarkable twins, one of whom was said to have hastened the death of James Russell Lowell by playing a hose upon the poet as he was passing on a wintry day, but that story has been denied. Royce's appearance was very striking but not prepossessing; his face told a story of character, calm resolution, and deep, constructive thought. He had a kind voice and, if I remember correctly, he was not an eager conversationalist; none of them sparkled quite as much as did Professor Hill.

Naturally they discussed Harvard and Harvard conditions unendingly but had any outsiders attacked it they would have defended Harvard from the drop of the hat. They made me think of great English oaks such as one sees standing mighty and alone in those exquisite meadows leading right down to the Thames, oaks completely and roundly developed as nature would like to make every tree. These men were exemplifications of the intellectual *genus homo* developed to the uttermost, yet they were extraordinarily modest and unassuming and never as inclined to be lords of all they surveyed as some of the German savants I have met. Nor was there anything of the ceremonious politeness of any corresponding German group. These Harvard scholars were informal and friendly; not above having at times sharp and caustic exchanges of opinion; [1] withal they were friends and peers and workers for a common cause.

As for Albert Bushnell Hart, I have never been able to repay my indebtedness to him and never shall. I do not think he has

---

[1] For one example, James wrote of Santayana, April 2, 1900: "I now understand Santayana, the man. I never understood him before. But what a perfection of rottenness in a philosophy!" William James, *Letters of William James*, Boston, 1920, Vol. II, p. 122.

ever realized what his choice of a well-dressed assistant did for me. It was a turning point; it bolstered up my morale; it won me his friendship and, I believe, his regard. At least he has often given what seem to me proofs of that. In a way he was different from many of the other professors, largely because of his Middle Western background. He was and is rightly proud of his Ohio birth and ancestry and that he came from that great battleground of the Abolition struggle. No more devoted son of Harvard ever taught within its walls. His was a methodical mind and he had worked out for History XIII a series of differently colored sets of folders of four pages each on which the students were supposed to write certain of their themes and studies. He was most fertile in his selection of subjects and in this way obtained a good deal of material of value. He himself was a storehouse of information as to our nation's past and he gave out this knowledge with virility, a deep understanding, and a passionate devotion to our country. There were much more graceful and more moving lecturers and it was sometimes the fashion to criticize his peculiar methods. The answer was that we had no less than 400 students in History XIII each fall and if any student left the course without a thorough understanding of that period of our national life which led to disunion it was his own fault.

Professor Hart's controlled exterior has belied the fires within him. Occasionally they have broken out, as during the Bull Moose campaign of his classmate, Theodore Roosevelt, when he and another Harvard teacher scandalized Cambridge and Boston by standing on their chairs in the Bull Moose convention, waving their arms, and yelling like undergraduates at a football game. When the war came on he who had spent much time in Germany, where he had won his Ph.D., became an ardent advocate of preparedness and finally of our going to war; had he been younger he would certainly have been at the front. For years we could see eye to eye on hardly anything; I am happy that our friendship survived that period and has remained unbroken and warm. One tie that has bound us together has been our great interest in the Negro and our similar views of Abolition and its leaders. At eighty-four he is still active on the Board of Trustees of Howard University, the great college for colored students which has received such an impulse from the Roosevelt Administration. I did not need to be assured of the satisfaction with which he voted to confer its LL.D. upon his former assistant—of the good clothes. He and I were also woman suffragists and he heartily approved my first public address. I always thought it especially fitting that my "maiden" speech was for woman suffrage. My father approved, too, happening to be in Boston at the time; his presence, while gratifying me, added to my fear that I should not do him credit.

It was hard to give up such priceless associations as those at Harvard, such a wonderfully stimulating atmosphere in which to live and work. Had I been older I might not have relinquished them but the spirit of adventure was strong within me. When the hour came in which I had to decide whether to make teaching there my life's work or to go into journalism, my father wished me to stay at Harvard. With his usual prophetic insight into the future he declared that I would work for years for a public which did not want as fine a daily as *The Evening Post* and that I should some day lose it in return for a life's pains. I told him that at Harvard one was too safe, too sheltered, too at ease. "It is," I assured him, "like sitting in a club window and watching the world go by on the pavement outside." I laughingly reminded him that, after all, he was responsible for my having journalism in my blood. It was the easier for him to assent because he knew that I would be at home or near by. I have never regretted the decision in spite of all my defeats and failures. When the time came to say good-by, Professor Hill's last words to me were: "Despite your total abstinence I wish you a hearty Godspeed. Tell your mother I am sorry to see you have inherited her virtues."

It was not until the late fall that, after a hasty trip to Europe with my father, I was able to join the staff of the Philadelphia *Press*. It seemed to me unwise to go directly to *The Evening Post* for I had the feeling that I should not be treated on my merits in its office and so might not be able to ascertain promptly whether

I had or had not in me the makings of a journalist. I felt that some of the men I knew on the editorial staff, like Horace White, would be too kind and too lenient in their judgments and that those that I did not know might feel that they could not treat me like an ordinary employee and would assume that I had turned up to represent the ownership rather than to carve out my own career. So, having met Talcott Williams of the Philadelphia *Press*, I applied to him for a reporter's job and obtained one. I thought my motives decent and considerate of others, yet some years later Arthur Brisbane wrote in the Hearst papers that I had gone to the Philadelphia *Press* because I considered myself too superior and too aristocratic to be willing to serve with the employees of the family newspaper! It was a valuable lesson indeed as to how easily proper motives may be twisted into the reverse.

From a number of points of view my choice of the Philadelphia *Press* was a good one. At least I learned from my six months' service with it exactly what a newspaper office ought not to be; therefore when I came into authority on *The Evening Post* I always endeavored to make it the exact antithesis of the *Press*. In Philadelphia we were housed in a shockingly broken-down structure, a perfect firetrap. The plaster was falling from the walls of the small rooms, there was no whole chair and only battered desks, nothing which remotely resembled the city room of a modern newspaper. It was a bedlam, with men singing, whistling, talking, and yelling for copy boys, and therefore a most admirable schooling in concentration. That is one of the great advantages of being a journalist. Your literary man who writes at home can indulge himself as much as he pleases in moods and await the most favorable circumstances. The journalist learns to write under any and all conditions, whether he is ill or well, nervous and tired to a degree, or otherwise. My father had once said that he had some hopes of me save for the fact that I could never learn to concentrate, but he could not have said that after I had been a few weeks with the *Press*, and ever since I have been able to write at all times, afloat or ashore, in railroad trains, even in trolley cars, subject to innumerable interruptions, and always able to pick up the thread again without delay. Few of us in the *Press* office used typewriters; we wrote in long hand and how well we wrote was a matter of complete indifference as long as we presented the gist of the story in the first paragraph and kept it to the length ordered by the city or managing editor, of whom everyone was in awe with the exception of the two or three star writers.

We reported at noon and worked twelve hours; at least once a week I was on the late shift and sat round the office for emergencies or hastened out into the night until as late as two or three o'clock. I usually slept until ten or eleven, had breakfast, and, after not more than an hour to myself, wandered down to the office. We got our other meals when and where we could; they were often sandwiches eaten on the back platforms of trolley cars. Our pay was ridiculous; mine was $10 a week at the beginning. After I had been there four months I demanded an increase and was actually raised to $12.50 for six long and arduous days. That is at the rate of $2.08 a day. Of course the business manager knew that I was not living on my pay but there were a number of poor devils on the staff who didn't get very much more and some had wives to support. Many years later, in 1921, at a dinner of graduates of the Philadelphia *Press*, then long gone to the graveyard of newspapers, at which dinner Governor Brumbaugh of Pennsylvania and others recalled their association with the *Press*, I told this story. When I spoke of my having wrung my increase of salary out of Mr. Townsend, the business manager, if the large company before me had rehearsed for weeks there could not have been a greater unanimity and quickness in the roar, "You lie, nobody *ever* got any increase of salary out of Townsend," that came back to me and almost prevented my going on.

In view of the remarkable loyalty to the *Press* of all who worked for it, I am sorry to have to say that it was a good deal of a journalistic harlot, but that it was. It was absolutely subservient to its advertisers; it was a partisan Republican organ; it had a tremendously long list of sacred cows and a corresponding black list. The managing editor, being a Catholic, saw to it that no stories detrimental to Catholics appeared in the newspaper, as I shall illustrate later. No reporter could tell how his story would appear. Many were written that were one-sided or misleading; some of them were out of whole cloth, such as atrocity stories about the Spanish in Cuba, for the noble crusade to free Cuba from Spanish tyranny was being carried on in full blast by the least worthy and most ignoble of the journalistic profession. I cannot acquit Talcott Williams, afterwards for so many years the head of the Pulitzer School of Journalism and expounder of journalistic ethics to his students, of knowledge of what was going on in his shop if only because on one occasion he apologized for and condoned the printing of certain advertising, the character of which was unmistakable. He was, of course, an employee. The editor of the paper was Charles Emory Smith, who had been in 1890 Minister to Russia and in 1898 became Postmaster General by appointment of William McKinley. The newspaper itself belonged to the Wells family which was represented in the office and fought a long but losing fight to keep the paper alive.

Grateful as I was to Williams for my opportunity on the *Press*, he irritated me greatly. Whenever an abuse was cited to him, or a wrong described, he invariably minimized it or he drew from his extraordinary storehouse of history instances to prove that similar or worse things had happened under John Adams, or Andrew Jackson, and especially under James Buchanan or Abraham Lincoln. This was something more than merely a desire to see everything in as cheerful a light as possible. It is one of my failings, I know, but I have never been able to work happily with men or women who were incapable of hot indignation at something or other—whether small or big, whether it stirred me personally or not, if only it was *something*. To minimize every evil is to my mind to condone it and in time to destroy one's influence.

I came into the office of the *Press* one night all excitement, with a great beat, for I had seen, with horror, what was the closest approximation to a lynching mob that I have ever run across. The man who caused the trouble was an ex-priest, Slattery by name, whose wife was a former nun; they were making a living by touring the country and "revealing the secrets" of convents and monasteries and were frequently assailed. In this case they succeeded in getting into a closed carriage after their lecture but had hardly taken their seats when a bullet crashed through the window of the carriage. They drove off and I, returning from an assignment, found myself gathered up by that horrible, bloodthirsty mob. I trailed Slattery to a hotel, got an interview, satisfied myself that no other reporter was around, and rushed to the office to write the dramatic scene that I had witnessed. My announcement that I had a beat was at first welcomed but all enthusiasm died out when I reported the happening to the city editor and the managing editor. I was told not to "overwrite it." I said I would give it what it was worth and went to my desk. Three times the genial and kindly city editor, Benjamin Gordon, who liked me as I liked him, came in and cautioned me; and it was then that the reporters tipped me off to the fact that King, the managing editor, was a Catholic and would not permit anything anti-Catholic to be featured. I continued to cover sheet after sheet.

Finally King himself walked in and said: "Oh, about that story of yours: don't make it sensational, just write it in a corner grocery style." That was too much for me. I blazed at him that I had not been brought up in a corner grocery, that I was writing all the facts, and that he could do with them what he pleased. The reporters around me almost fell off their chairs; no such insubordination had ever been heard before. The only reason that I could indulge in it, of course, was my economic independence. The memory of the way those good fellows with whom I worked were compelled to do what they knew was wrong lest they lose their jobs is one of the reasons why I so heartily favored the creation of the Newspaper Guild, why I hope that it will make newspaper employees as a group so strong that they can refuse to take assignments they know to be unworthy or to misrepresent the facts when ordered to do so. Needless to say that when my great beat appeared the next morning I had to search the *Press* twice before I could find it. It was about eight lines long, carefully buried between advertising on the least important news page.

Mondays were my days off and I was graciously allowed to leave the office at quarter to twelve on Sunday nights in order to catch the midnight train to New York so that I could breakfast with my parents the next morning. I returned on an early train Tuesday morning and on one occasion came out of the Pennsylvania Station to find the place in a state of great excitement. Across the square Wanamaker's store was on fire! I immediately called the city editor and was assigned to get hold of John Wanamaker as soon as possible and seek an interview with him as to the damage done. First, however, I was to enter the store myself and see just what the damage was. The firemen would not let me in for all my police card. I found an unguarded freight elevator at the sidewalk and darted through it into the store. The damage was not serious and some of the sales force were still on duty, despite the burning of a tower on the corner of the building and considerable damage by water, but as a good deal of this was in the china and crockery department it could have been worse. When I reached the sanctimonious John Wanamaker, he of the Bible classes, he assured me that the loss was very great indeed, that he didn't think he would ever be able to estimate how great it was, and then dictated a statement for the *Press*. I also met his son who, not knowing what his father had said, gave me an opinion that coincided with my own. The next day there was a grand fire sale which netted a handsome sum, indeed, for Honest John. In the evening one of the reporters brought in a fine pair of lined gloves and told us what a bargain he had picked up. Another reporter looked at them and sniffed. Said he: "Why, I bought a pair just like that at Wanamaker's a couple of weeks ago and didn't pay as much."

The star reporter was Ralph D. Paine, to whom we all looked up with envy. He had been a crack Yale oarsman and was a whopping big fellow who could hold his own in any tight place that he might get into. He was the one reporter who did not have to worry about the attitude of his superiors; he was sure of his job and drew a large salary. He could use his time largely as he saw fit and came and went as he pleased. His Sunday stories were great features for he had a lively, engaging style and put things picturesquely. He was soon assigned to the Cuban situation and joined one of the voyages of a famous filibustering captain who regularly ran guns and men through the Spanish blockade. But here Ralph Paine's flair for romance sometimes took control; atrocity stories read well. Another reporter handed in a number of similar ones, and, in his case, the staff believed that when this man was supposed to be in Key West or Tampa collecting his material he was conjuring it up out of his imagination or in consultation with Cuban cigar makers in Philadelphia.

When the war came we who had worked with him all thought that Ralph Paine's great hour had struck and that he would come out of it as large a figure as Richard Harding Davis. This did not prove to be the case; indeed, he never realized the expectations of his friends. In later years he retired to a country home and wrote some books of adventure and sea tales. After his too early death some of his friends and classmates established a Ralph D. Paine Prize to be awarded to a member of the senior class at Yale for the best prose style; thus I had a double reason for being pleased when my younger son and namesake was one of the two recipients of this prize in 1938. Paine's charm remains with me as it has with the men who were his college intimates. He was a warm-hearted and loyal friend and a grand companion.

Within a couple of months after I joined the staff I was getting some interesting assignments. One of these cases was a murder committed in the Norristown Insane Asylum to which criminal insane were sent. The place was not originally intended for that purpose and the bulk of its patients was of a harmless variety. Naturally the attendants resented the coming of these dangerous men with whom they were not prepared to cope and all sorts of abuses developed. Every now and then a criminal would die mysteriously—at the hands of his attendants it was generally believed. In this particular case an attendant was arrested, charged with the killing, and jailed in the police station in the Philadelphia City Hall. With the consent of the *Press* I got myself locked up for some hours in the night with this man in the hope of getting something startling out of him; instead, he convinced me that he was innocent. Fortunately he was able to prove it and also to convince the jury that he had been "framed" by the inner clique of attendants whom he had not joined, being a new man and trying to do his work honestly. Still it was touch and go for him. The victim had been horribly injured internally yet there were no outward signs of bruises. It was claimed that he had been "kneed" and it was explained to me that jumping on a man with one's knees does not leave exterior marks.

My interest in this case led to my being assigned permanently to an investigation of the prisons and asylums then being carried on by Judge James Gay Gordon, who happened to be one of the honest and fearless judges not subject to political pressure. It was he who interested himself in the case of this innocent guard and then, using his magisterial right, he added Norristown to his investigation of what was going on in the asylums. He had already been at work on the prisons. For the rest of the winter I reported his doings when they had news angles and we became good friends. It was in connection with this inquiry that I got into the Eastern Penitentiary. I have never forgotten the horror of it and the condition of the prisoners in antiquated cells without anything resembling adequate sanitary conditions, while the cells themselves were so unwholesome as to invite illness. In some cases water stood deep on the floor. The crusade carried on by Judge Gordon had some excellent results and led to the building of an asylum for the criminal insane. I was interested to read a few years ago that there was another exposé going on of the terrible conditions in Eastern Penitentiary. A civilized community would have destroyed it decades before I saw it.

Once I reported a visit to the Matteawan Asylum on the Hudson. Judge Gordon filled a private car with people of influence and politicians in order that they might see how New York was handling its insane of this type and took me along. We were immensely impressed by what we beheld, the fearlessness which the attendants displayed, and their willingness to allow us to roam as we pleased. In one room we found Oliver Curtis Perry, a man of excellent education, who had been adopted by worthy people but had suddenly turned into a most dangerous criminal. Riding on the roof of the express car of a fast train on the New York Central after it left a station he tied one end of a rope to the ventilator and lowered himself to a side door upon which he knocked while swinging with the motion of the train. The express messenger threw open the door and pulled him in, for which Perry rewarded him by killing him and robbing the safe. Some months before we saw him he had broken an electric light bulb in his cell and had sought to blind himself with one of the pieces. When I asked him why he had done it he replied in these words: "I thought that if I blinded myself and so proved that I could no longer do injury to anyone the Governor would let me out. I had rather gaze upon the world with clouded vision than look upon four blank walls with perfect sight."

In the women's ward I noticed a sweet-faced, white-haired woman sitting in a rocker and embroidering diligently. She might have posed for the typical American mother. It seemed so amazing that she should be there that I asked the nearest attendant who she was. "Why, she," he said, "is the Veiled Murderess." When I had to admit that I had never heard of the lady he explained that she was a famous poisoner who had been guilty of removing from this world some sixteen or eighteen people and was distinguished by wearing a heavy veil at her trial. No one who beheld that benign countenance would ever have feared any action that she might have taken. Looks were entirely misleading here, which was not the case with Perry; but Perry's smooth tongue on one occasion had corrupted one of his guards and he had made a miraculous escape from Matteawan over the roof and down a conductor pipe.

Naturally, keeping the hours that I had to, I met few Philadelphians except as I encountered them in the course of my reporting but a number of acquaintances begun then ripened into lasting friendships. The first important political speech I reported was one by James M. Beck. In the last year of his life I had a delightful evening with him at his home in Washington, in which he showed a most amazing knowledge of the details of the Battle of the Marne and expressed views as to the situation in Europe which astonished me when coming from one so closely associated with the conservative policies of the Republican party. No figure stands out more clearly in my memory of my Philadelphia days than that of Mary Channing Wister, soon to become the wife of her cousin, Owen Wister. Still in her twenties, she was laboring valiantly through a women's civic association to redeem the city of her residence. Her grace and charm as a presiding officer, her modesty and ability, her winning presence and lovely brown eyes impressed all who knew her, among them my father who met her when she was the chairman of a welcoming committee in Philadelphia for the annual meeting of the Civil Service Reform Association. My father was much disappointed when he heard the news that she was engaged to Owen Wister for he had hoped, it appeared, that I might fall in love with her and she with me. If I had laid siege to her heart I could certainly never have hoped to come off successfully in any rivalry with Owen Wister—he was for one thing a man of the world and twelve years older than I. I did steal some few evenings between assignments, notably on Sunday (when I sometimes turned in as many as four sermons), which stolen time I spent at the Wister home, singing my favorite German *lieder* to Mary Wister's most musical accompaniment. She died sixteen years later on the birth of her sixth child. I doubt if anybody could have been more beloved by his or her friends than she was.

By all odds one of the most interesting of my assignments was to report the march of the battalion of the Sixth United States Cavalry then stationed at Fort Myer, Virginia, from New York to Philadelphia to take part in the unveiling of the Grant monument. I joined it in camp on the Palisades after my brother's wedding on April 29, 1897. The next morning a soldier was assigned to see that my mount was saddled and the stirrups adjusted. He insisted that I get on the horse while he was still tied to the picket rope. Against my protest and better judgment I did so. The horse at once reared, slipped on the straw under him, and fell on my left ankle. Soon after we marched, the horse plunging and rearing when the band struck up. I had never ridden on a McClellan saddle before, I was very soft, and my ankle pained me and puffed up steadily, so that by the time we went into camp at Elizabeth that afternoon I was ready to fall off my horse. None the less I enjoyed every minute. For once I was with horses enough to satisfy me. The officers were a fine group of men. The colonel, Samuel S. Sumner, who, when a lieutenant on the staff of his distinguished father, General Edwin V. Sumner of the Army of the Potomac, had on occasion shared his tent with my father, welcomed me warmly. He was prominent in the Cuban campaign and died a major general on the retired list only a couple of years ago.

Colonel Sumner was an excellent regimental commander, controlling his officers quietly and justly, and this squadron was one to be proud of. Among his officers were several who rose to high rank—Charles Dudley Rhodes, Robert L. Howze, and Walter C. Short, an ideal cavalryman and horseman; George T. Summerlin is Chief of the Division of Protocol in the State Department. My particular friend was Lieutenant Edwards C. Brooks, later on General Wood's staff in Cuba, and I kept up my friendship with some of these officers for many years. Those camps of the regiment en route to Philadelphia stand out to this day. At Princeton we had an ideal setting and the next morning we paraded before the university and then left for Trenton. None of us suspected what the next sixteen months would bring to that regiment. In September of the following year I found it in camp—at Montauk Point—a regiment of feeble, yellow, fever-stricken ghosts as a result of that brief Cuban campaign. The men of the old Sixth still say: "Once a Sixth Cavalryman always a Sixth Cavalryman." I hate to think how I should have been tempted if someone had offered me a lieutenant's commission in it when that march was over.

My connection with the Philadelphia *Press* ceased soon after that experience. I was sent for by my father and Horace White of *The Evening Post* to consult with them as to a situation which had arisen in that office because of the sudden leaving of a number of the staff. I had intended to stay on in Philadelphia until I had completed a year there and then to go to the Washington office of *The Evening Post*, to serve under its veteran correspondent, Francis Leupp. Instead I yielded to my father's and Mr. White's request that I join *The Evening Post* at once, and I began work with it on May 24, 1897. Later I rejoiced that I returned to our home when I did for my father had only three and one-half years of life before him and the happiness of our communion in those years remains a possession beyond price.

Chapter VII. *The Evening Post* Gets a Recruit

WHEN I arrived at the office of *The Evening Post* to begin my long connection with it, and reported to Horace White, I found him and some other editors in a blue funk because of the desertions from the staff to that of the *Commercial Advertiser*. That was characteristic of Mr. White; whenever his emotions were deeply stirred his pen was paralyzed and his judgment failed. Never was there a kinder or more benevolent person but his fighting days, during which he had helped to supply John Brown with Sharps rifles in Kansas when assistant secretary of the Kansas Emigrant Society, had long since vanished. He could then see ruin ahead and the only remedy he and others had to suggest was that I become city editor and shoulder the whole situation. I was, of course, pleased that these experienced journalists should think me when but twenty-four years old fitted for that job but this was one of the very few times in my life when I displayed excellent judgment. I pointed out to Mr. White that I was utterly ignorant of New York from the news point of view and that if I took over the city desk I should not know how to give a single assignment to the reporters who had not already regular beats such as police headquarters and the City Hall and that I could not successfully direct the men when I myself had not served in the ranks in New York City. So I declined the offer with thanks.

After studying the situation for several days, and talking with the veteran managing editor, William A. Linn, a most able journalist who was not frightened like the rest, I asked that a position be created for me as editor of the Saturday feature supplement which was badly in need of invigoration, from which point of vantage I could familiarize myself with the entire problem, both in the editorial and counting rooms. The assistant city editor was made acting city editor, new reporters were taken on, and my friend Edward P. Call, of the Philadelphia *Press*, appointed business manager. I decided to train a reporter, Henry Beach Needham, son of Judge Charles W. Needham, so long a distinguished legal adviser of the Interstate Commerce Commission, as real estate editor and was rewarded by my choice; he was later succeeded by Burton J. Hendrick who subsequently made a name for himself by his service with *McClure's Magazine* and the *World's Work* and by his *Life and Letters of Walter H. Page*, for which he received the first of three Pulitzer Prizes. I did my best to assure all concerned that the owners had complete faith in the future of the newspaper and had no intention of quitting because a rival had robbed us of some of our best men. Here my Philadelphia *Press* experience stood me in good stead. There we were accustomed to a changing staff and knew that there were plenty of good journalists to be had for every job.

Nearly a dozen men had left *The Evening Post* and others gradually followed. The chief losses were H. J. Wright, who had a great reputation as city editor; J. S. Seymour, the business manager, and several of his assistants; an unusually able real estate editor; Norman Hapgood, then a star reporter, and, later on, Lincoln Steffens, who did not find me wholly appreciative of his work as city editor, for which desk job he was never intended by nature. Under Mr. Seymour *The Evening Post* had made its best financial showing; a remark attributed to him that they would "have the shutters on *The Evening Post* building in six months' time" was chiefly responsible for the office alarm. My youth and inexperience made me refuse to share that fright; I could not believe that the daily which had such editors, such standards, and such a following could be made to lose its place overnight. Yet I could see how the talented younger men had chafed under the rigid conservatism of the editorial management with which they had little or no personal contact and some had welcomed the chance to join a newspaper which was to be light, amusing, full of "human nature" stories, and unhampered by tradition. Here it may be said that while the *Globe*, into which the *Commercial Advertiser* turned, drew to its staff some other able men such as

Bruce Bliven, now of the *New Republic*, and Robert L. Duffus, now of the New York *Times*, it lacked our prestige, editorial strength, and freedom, and passed from the New York newspaper stage well before the eclipse of *The Evening Post*.

The editorial writers and staff editors I found in the latter's offices at 210 Broadway were, with a couple of exceptions, a group of rare men, able and fearless and absolutely devoted to the highest journalistic ideals and content with small salaries because of their complete editorial freedom and the absence of all ownership dictation. They were a remarkably congenial group and there was an almost total lack of that office intrigue which has been and is the bane of so many newspaper offices. At the head and front stood Edwin L. Godkin, who remains in my opinion the greatest editorial writer the American press has ever produced. No other leader writer in this country could match him in irony and sarcasm, in power of phraseology, in clarity and logic, in his masterly style, in his ability to dissect a proposition and to destroy it merely by restating it. Few other journalists have had such a prophetic vision. None surpassed him in the extent of his knowledge of affairs in America or abroad—all driven home by his absolute devotion to principle from which he never swerved. "Never write," he said to me, "without conveying information or expressing an opinion with reasons."

He was a democrat of democrats in his political beliefs—with certain limitations due to his time and early training. For example, he could never favor the political emancipation of women although demanding every possible educational opportunity for them, and he never had a real understanding of the significance and need of a labor movement to phases of which he was strongly opposed. But he never compromised on any issue of human liberty or republican institutions. Above all he was as devoted an American as ever lived although constantly accused of being an Anglomaniac and of taking Cobden Club gold; of course he encountered the familiar demand of those who could not meet his arguments to "go back where he came from." Having seen one war, the Crimean, at first hand as correspondent of the London *Daily*

News, and the aftermath of several, he was an absolute devotee of peace, once even writing in his ardor that eventually the place of the soldier in the social scale would be next to that of the hangman. He feared no one and nothing and knew how to honor his complete intellectual liberty, for he once told me that he had never met another man who, he felt, would have had the generosity and unselfishness to do what my father had done—subordinate himself and the family interest in *The Evening Post* and allow absolute liberty of conscience and expression to its editors without a financial care or responsibility.

Godkin shunned the limelight, made no speeches or public appearances, but enjoyed to the brim the friendship of an intellectual and social elite in this country and in England, moving in New York in the Washington Square set. As an editor he unquestionably suffered from not getting into contact with other elements in New York life. The other journalists in the city knew him not at all. In fact all the editors of *The Evening Post* of that time were open to the charge of insularity which the journalists of the rest of the country forcefully laid against their brethren of Manhattan Island. Godkin was really shy when he ventured outside his milieu and it was that shyness, as well as a certain reserve, which kept him entirely remote from the staff except for the editorial writers, the managing editor, and the critics. An occasional letter of praise reached the outer offices but he often failed to recognize and greet men who had served *The Evening Post* for years. He had no interest in the personal lives and office problems of most of the men he worked with; once he declined an invitation to dine with heads of departments to discuss office matters, writing that he saw enough of them at the office. To the reporters he was only an awesome name. The business office admired but dreaded him; his biting editorial comment was the chief obstacle to its success, for he would as soon ridicule the owner of a big department store as a Tammany politician. It is impossible to deny that there was some snobbishness in him, probably a residue of his life in Ireland and England, for he always looked down upon people who were in small trades.

From the beginning of his career with *The Evening Post* it was the fashion to decry him as a perfectionist, or a bilious critic, or an habitual faultfinder who could see no good in anything and was always destructive and never constructive. Those who criticized him thus could not themselves show one one-hundredth part of his record of constant constructive suggestions for the improvement of our government and national life. James Bryce told the truth when he said that among those who really understood Mr. Godkin it was not "for his intellectual gifts that Mr. Godkin was most admired but for the moral qualities that directed the exercise of these gifts." And an anonymous writer in *The Atlantic Monthly* for January, 1897, in discussing Mr. Godkin's book entitled *Problems of Modern Democracy*, wrote thus: "If the question is asked, to what single influence is the fact chiefly due that there is visible today a definite ideal of good government which beckons the country steadily forward, and a coherent body of independent thought which supports us in the hope that we may attain it, the answer must be, to that of the author of these essays."

Godkin's *Evening Post* is often spoken of now as a pretty conservative, semiliberal journal and the wonder is expressed that I, who was trained in that school, should have become "so radical." The fact is that we were always much more liberal, even radical, than most people gave us credit for being; we were even denounced by some as dangerous radicals, which many will find it hard to believe when they read that Godkin supported Grover Cleveland in the Debs strike and generally upheld his bond policies. We *were* radical on peace and war and on the Negro question; radical in our insistence that the United States stay at home and not go to war abroad or impose its imperialistic will upon the Latin-American republics, often with great slaughter. We were radical in our demand for free trade and our complete opposition to the whole protective system as the source of innumerable evils in our social, political, and industrial life, and later were radically for woman suffrage.

When we fought for free trade we fought for labor; when we fought for the purification of our political life, notably our civic life, we fought primarily for the workingman. There was hardly a forward-looking cause planned for the benefit of the masses which Godkin did not espouse. The reason for Wall Street's dislike of us was not merely our exposure of its abysmal ignorance in matters of finance, especially national finance, but because Godkin never ceased to point out that Tammany Hall was merely a front for the big business men without whose constant support, financial and otherwise, the Hall could not have lived. The biggest men in Wall Street were usually the biggest cowards, not to designate them otherwise. They preferred to pay blackmail rather than to fight the Hall, although there has never been a period in my lifetime when they could not have purged the city, destroyed Tammany Hall, and ended the injustices in our courts and the exploitation of the poor people of the city by Tammany. They did not clean up the Hall because they profited by misgovernment. If they contributed to the Citizens' Union or some reform committee, it was to salve their consciences. Godkin's attacks upon them were the more remarkable because he met many of them socially, notably the good and virtuous Republican leaders who supported the Republican organization though they knew, as well as Godkin, that it was not a whit better morally than Tammany. His social contacts never influenced his civic indignation.

Indubitably Godkin suffered from the limitations of the liberal political philosophy of Cobden and Bright; he did not live long enough to see the staunchest English Cobdenite recognize that the policy of *laissez faire* was ended by the tremendous developments of modern industrialism, capitalism, and nationalism. He would never have ceased opposing Socialism—one of his indictments of protection was that it was the mother of trusts and Socialism—but he clearly realized the inevitability of the extension of the control of government into the fields of private enterprise, such as in the establishment of the Interstate Commerce Commission. We sought to be open-minded and to welcome evolution but there were certain principles which we could never surrender or compromise and these were precisely the ones bound to make for the welfare of the great majority of our citizens. By other journalists, who stooped low to win large circulations, *The Evening Post* was derided and called a class paper because our appeal was primarily to the well-to-do and the intellectual. That its audience was extremely limited is true, but that its objectives were the betterment of the well-to-do and the privileged—that is the most absolute falsehood. It served the whole people far more faithfully, for all its limitations, than many a paper which professed its devotion to the plain people and to the workers as such.

The great power of Godkin's *Evening Post* lay in its profound effect upon the press of the country and its public men. Perhaps the finest compliment paid to Mr. Godkin was Governor David B. Hill's remark during the Maynard campaign in which the reformers, with Godkin leading, waged a successful, although at first hopeless, fight against Hill's efforts to elect a totally unfit man to high judicial office. Said Hill: "I don't care anything about the handful of mugwumps who read it [*The Evening Post*] in New York. The trouble with the damned sheet is that every editor in New York State reads it." So did most men in public life. To Grover Cleveland it was a Bible which he never failed to read— until Mr. Godkin denounced him for his utterly inexplicable Venezuelan boundary attack upon Great Britain. Then he turned upon it and got a laugh out of an audience by saying that he always read *The Evening Post* editorial page for the little jokes which appeared in the lower right-hand corner under the headline "Waifs." That was unworthy of him for if ever a man was indebted to an editor it was Grover Cleveland to Mr. Godkin. Never should the President's tongue have lent itself to a sneer at, or a criticism of, Mr. Godkin, because what he owed to *The Evening Post* for day by day political education and guidance was literally immeasurable. And this was true of many another public man. Often they were not aware of it, nor were all the editors who profited by Godkin's leadership and wisdom. But the latter's steady pounding away at wrongs and upholding ideals inevitably affected the readers, however they might dissent from some of the positions taken.

Finally, credit must be given to Mr. Godkin as well as to the owners for the clean pages and high news standards of *The Evening Post*. Like the *Christian Science Monitor*, we showed for years that a high-grade daily could live without featuring crime, or sensations, or resorting to comics, or to society gossip, or violating the proper privacy of the individual. We were never ashamed of any story that appeared in our pages and the dispatches were edited with a care which at that time was unusual. As long as Mr. Godkin was connected with this newspaper he insisted on rigid standards of accuracy in reporting and, despite the vehemence of his editorial attacks, we had far fewer libel suits than any daily in the city; we lost only two, both due to reporters' errors. Of course this editorial policy limited circulation and profits, and so did the three-cent price. I often wonder if a major mistake was not advancing the price to five cents at the outbreak of the World War. But this I know: if I had the job to do over again I would uphold the same standards, plus the illustrations and cartoons we eventually printed.

When I entered the office to begin my work Godkin received me with genuine kindness, although much disturbed by a report that my appearance meant that I was to supplant him and that I would radically alter *The Evening Post*—a bit of malicious gossip whose author I was not long in discovering. I am deeply indebted to him for the inspiration and training, notably in his magnificent fight against the war with Spain, that I received at his hands during the three years that remained of his active service. So far from being gloomy, grim, and sour, I found that he had a mordant sense of humor and that his editorial conferences were punctuated by roars of laughter—nothing caused him greater amusement than the charge that he opened the editorial conference every morning by singing with his staff "God Save the Queen." He insisted on the highest standards of literary style and it is my mature judgment that not even the editorial page of the *Sun*, our only real rival, exceeded that of Godkin's in excellence and its amazing uniformity.

The vigor of the writers was largely due to the fact that throughout the Villard ownership each editor wrote what he really believed—unless he was insincere, and we had only two such in thirty-seven years. If a man did not agree with the policy in a given case he did not write upon that subject. The first momentous morning that I was asked to write a short editorial paragraph it took me two hours. I wrote it, rewrote it a second and even a third time. It was not so very long before I, too, could do my column of a thousand words within an hour or so despite interruptions. The happiness of those editorial mornings, the generous kindliness of the older men, the sincere and earnest and enlightening discussions in the editorial council, the comradeship, and the pride in our joint production made me value highly my new associations.

The speed with which the editorial page was produced—between ten and twelve o'clock—amazed other journalists. Joseph Pulitzer once asked me, when he was taking me around Frenchman's Bay in his motor launch, how it was that we often had long and extremely well-informed editorials on events news of which sometimes did not come out until half past ten or eleven o'clock. I explained that we had a large and competent staff of writers, all of whom were specialists in certain fields and all of whom were accustomed to turn out a column editorial of a thousand words or more in an hour and a half. Very few news bulletins reached us without our having someone capable of dealing with them, especially in the foreign field, as to which American editors, even down to the World War, were almost completely ignorant outside of the Eastern seaboard and one or two large cities of the Pacific Coast and the interior. Mr. Pulitzer did not conceal his admiration and asked me: "Do you really get down to the office every morning at nine o'clock?" I said that I did and the others did, too, or soon thereafter. He said: "I wish that I could get the gentlemen of my staff to be as good journalists. They cannot even stay late enough at the office to write on news that appears on the front page."

Horace White, the second in command, who took charge in Mr. Godkin's absences, was of an entirely different type. Extraordinarily unworldly, gentle, and well-disposed toward everyone, he had a completely American background and always won the respect and affectionate admiration of all who came into contact with him. He, too, wrote with great clarity of style, without, of course, Godkin's sarcasm, vigor, and drive, but his lucid arguments were frequently more convincing to the reader. He had a great reputation as a writer on economics, currency, finance and international monetary affairs, and contributed largely to *The Evening Post's* great prestige in the financial field. His friendships with the financiers of the day were many for they respected him highly for his knowledge and his rugged intellectual honesty, and knew that he could not be "reached." From the standpoint of 1939, Mr. White ranks as a great economic conservative; had he lived to see the days of the New Deal financing he would probably have cried out loud and promptly demised.

It is true that he was blind to much that was going on about him in our economic life, partly because of his inborn naïveté and guilelessness. He could not see the significance of Thomas W. Lawson's *Frenzied Finance* revelations; nor was he able to view in proper perspective the fight that Theodore Roosevelt and William J. Bryan and others were making against the growing domination of American life by Wall Street influences, the rise of monopolies, and what has so long been dubbed Big Business. Against Bryan's silver heresy Mr. White fought magnificently although he hated with all his heart about everything that McKinley stood for. Indeed, I believe that if he had been able to foresee what did happen under McKinley he would reluctantly have accepted Bryan. He was not afraid of forlorn hopes or standing with a small minority, as he showed when he became a Greeley Republican and, again in 1898, in opposing Theodore Roosevelt's election as governor.

He, too, was wedded to principle and could rarely see anything good in expediency. He had been much more of a working journalist in his early life than Godkin but when I joined the staff he was well along in years and the title of "Uncle Horace," bestowed upon him by the staff, indicated both the affection in which he was held and the absence of vigor in his leadership. He took far more interest in the business management of *The Evening Post* than his great colleague but was soon eager to turn over the presidency of the company to me. Responsibility he more and more avoided and important decisions likewise. But he could still lash out strongly when his feelings were stirred. When, as I have said, he was too deeply moved he quite went to pieces. This resulted in a dangerous situation on the day of the shooting of President McKinley. As soon as the flash came announcing the crime we realized that our position would not be an easy one; that we would be charged with having led up to the assassination by the severity of our attacks upon that "great and good man" and our government. We could not know then that the responsibility for Czolgosz's act would soon be laid at Hearst's door. Everything would depend, for us, upon the tone and the wording of our next day's leader.

Mr. McKinley was shot at midday on a Friday and as usual we had to prepare the long articles for Saturday's issue that afternoon because of our early Saturday appearance. Mr. White's great shock and distress were manifest at the hastily called editorial conference, but he undertook to write the McKinley leader. The afternoon passed; finally he turned in an article and left for home. The other editors read what he had written and were horrified by it; its publication would have been a disaster and exposed us to ridicule, if not contempt. They came to me and said that it must under no circumstances appear. I agreed with them. They then declared that I must write the leader. That bowled me over. I still had little or no confidence in my writing ability and said frankly that I doubted my power to rise to the emergency. They insisted that I could; that Mr. White would accept my overriding of his article but no one else's. That clinched it and I went to work with the aid and advice of my elders and produced an adequate leader—it took me until late at night. The next day Mr. White accepted my interference with a magnanimity that endeared him to us more than ever.

Similarly, when my father died in the previous year, Mr. White was wholly unable to write more than a dozen lines—all devoted to his illness. I was, of course, not there to aid and the newspaper which Henry Villard re-created, and made financially possible, passed over his services without an editorial appreciation though with a long and accurate obituary. Mr. White was a minority stockholder in *The Evening Post* and the investment meant a great deal to him, but he never once considered the risk he ran of losing it all and never complained if there were no dividends. I was fortunate, indeed, to be able to work under Mr. Godkin and Mr. White when I was so young. It is true that it gave me what I know now to have been an inferiority complex which made me always doubt my own abilities and judgments. But again I have no regret and only gratitude for having lived among and worked with giants.

Among the many fine men who made *The Evening Post* what it was I recall with especial gratitude Edward P. Clark—the wheel horse editorial writer and our authority on State politics the country over. His style was never easy and flowing but he brought to his task a fidelity, an independence, a fearlessness, and a skill in political interpretation beyond praise, and limitless industry as well. He had a little cubbyhole of an office and, as soon as the editorial page was out of the way, he plunged into the exchanges from all over the country so that at times he almost disappeared behind the discarded papers piled on the floor. He knew well the politics of every State. No one welcomed me more cordially or aided me more; he could not have been kinder or more helpful. A graduate of the *Springfield Republican,* he embodied the finest New England characteristics and died in *The Evening Post's* service, devoted to the end.

A different type was Joseph Bucklin Bishop, who set himself deliberately to run down my editorial work in the hope of getting me out of the office. A painstaking imitator of Mr. Godkin's style, he prided himself that his work was often mistaken for his chief's. He was an expert on the local political situation and knew well the reformers who in those days sought to rescue the city from Tammany's clutches. He stood their blunders, jealousies, amateur-ishness, and vagaries as long as he could but one day burst forth with entirely justifiable wrath and said to a couple of them: "If you expect me to continue to back you up, then, so help me God, you must keep away from me. If you talk to me any more at this office or at the club, I'll go over to Tammany." That has been, I fancy, the experience of many an editor. To keep one's balance and rise above the din and confusion and conflict of personalities some detachment is often necessary. It reminded me of Lydia Maria Child's famous remark in Abolition days as she surveyed some of the antislavery brethren at one of their conventions: "The good Lord uses tools I wouldn't touch with a forty-foot pole."

When I told Mr. White of Mr. Bishop's constant picking upon my writing and saying it was hopeless, he rose in his wrath and declared: "Why, you write better today than Bishop ever did." When because of his plain disloyalty we eased Bishop out, he, too, went to the *Commercial Advertiser*. With us he had been one of the bitterest critics of Theodore Roosevelt, writing some of the editorials to which the latter objected most. On leaving, Bishop underwent a sea change and became one of T.R.'s greatest upholders, with the result that he landed a fine job as secretary of the Panama Canal Commission. He witnessed the building of that great work and became its adequate historian besides editing well T.R.'s letters to his children. I never met any other man who had so low an opinion of women as human beings.

Another outstanding figure in the office was my uncle, Wendell Phillips Garrison. Cofounder, with Godkin, of *The Nation*, when it was amalgamated with *The Evening Post* he filled the dual role of editor of *The Nation* and literary editor of the daily, the same reviews appearing in both papers until I was compelled to inject more literary material into *The Evening Post*. Mr. Garrison was one of the greatest American editors—using that noun in its original, narrow sense of one who corrects and revises manuscripts and editorials. His knowledge was encyclopedic; his proofreading unsurpassed. No other editor could have worked harder over his proofs and striven more meticulously for absolute accuracy. He had assembled the greatest group of reviewers and writers who ever contributed to a scholarly American publication. Yet he relied upon none of them but verified, so far as was humanly possible, every statement of fact that they made. Six o'clock in the morning usually found him at his desk at his home in West Orange, New Jersey, reading proof or writing letters before breakfast. Forty-one years of absolute devotion he gave to *The Nation* until, because of his failing health, I was compelled to urge his retirement which took place on June 28, 1906. I never had a more trying duty to perform. He survived only a few months. When he died no less than twelve hundred letters of regret and sympathy reached his family. His correspondence—all in his own hand, for he never would have a secretary—covered the world. That he, Godkin, and *The Nation* profoundly influenced the entire intellectual development of the United States is beyond question; the bound volumes of his period are prime source material for any historian who writes of the years from 1865 to 1906.

Well described as "learned and humble, peaceable and quite unafraid, a soul freed and possessed in quiet," Mr. Garrison's modesty and self-effacement made it impossible to obtain for him the recognition of his services that he deserved but never sought. Harvard, his college, gave him an A.M. when upon politicians and men of far less scholarship and intellectual eminence it bestowed LL.D's. Towards the end his great work was recognized publicly by an appreciative group of friends and contributors. They looked up to him not only with admiration, but with profoundest respect, especially for his complete intellectual independence and integrity. He seldom wrote himself but he had an excellent political as well as literary judgment—he never could abide Woodrow Wilson and considered him to rank very low as an historian—and sometimes *The Nation* struck out for itself. Spartan in his control of his life, Puritan in his rigidity and his high standards, he lived largely for his weekly and his family. To me he was a tolerant and kindly critic and the tie of affection between us grew steadily closer and warmer. When I heard that he had accepted my article on the Spaniards at Melilla, and for republication in *The Evening Post*, I felt elated for I knew that our kinship would make him more severe in his criticism than if I had been a stranger. His detached judgments towards those whom he loved were sometimes too stoical. But I can recall no event that marred the happiness of our association.[1]

To speak of Hammond Lamont here is to take him out of turn for I did not woo him away from Brown College until 1900. But as he belongs to the giants of *The Evening Post* this is the fitting place to bring him in. A brother of Thomas W. Lamont, he was of a different fiber and larger caliber. Graduated from Harvard in 1886, he was a reporter on the Seattle *Post-Intelligencer* when he interviewed President Eliot and made so few notes as to worry the head of Harvard not a little. The next day the interview as printed proved to be the best with him that Mr. Eliot had ever seen. It was not only beautifully written but absolutely correct and marked by an understanding so keen and far-reaching that Mr. Eliot sent for Lamont at once and offered him an instructorship in English. Lamont did not stay long at Harvard before being called to a professorship at Brown, where he took high rank at once. When I heard of him I was in search of a managing editor. I was told to see President Eliot first and that the battle would be won if I could get his aid. I left at once for Cambridge.

President Eliot heard me, declared that he would help me, and said: "Go right down to Providence but don't tell him you've talked with me." I found that Lamont's eyes lighted up when I told him my mission. He was a natural-born journalist and if you are that, and have tasted newspaper life, you are never again immune. He did not commit himself but said he would write. I left for New York. A half hour later he was on the road to Cambridge! What Mr. Eliot said to him brought me his assent. Never did I make a better choice. Everybody in the office admired and loved him. He took hold in 1900 as if he had been one of us all his life, was the ideal managing editor, and became a most valuable contributor to the editorial page for he wrote clear and superb English, had great breadth of vision, and excellent judgment despite the intensity of his feelings.

[1] See Wendell Phillips Garrison, *Letters and Memorials*, Cambridge, 1908.

He, too, could burn with indignation and often did so, but although he hit hard there was no malice in it. For Wall Street he had the bitterest aversion but this was before his brother became prominent; he did not live to see his brother in the Morgan firm. A great sense of humor smoothed Hammond Lamont's too brief road through life. Of course he was generous, unselfish, and never a self-seeker, and was possessed of such a sense of justice that he would have made a great judge even if he had never read a page of law. When it became my sad task to ask my uncle to retire, the latter begged me to let *The Nation* die. There was no one he could think of fit to carry it on who would respect it and its traditions. I said, "Oh, yes, there is." He guessed one man. To his relief I said, "No." Then I said, "It's Hammond Lamont." I can think of no finer tribute to Lamont than the look which came over Mr. Garrison's face. "To him," he replied, "I will turn over *The Nation* with joy. He has character, ability, understanding, literary taste, and is a man of highest principle."

There were only three years after Lamont's transfer to *The Nation*, before this friendship and joyous association came to an end. In May, 1909, Lamont decided to go to Roosevelt Hospital for a minor operation on his jaw. It seemed inconsequential but, on the afternoon of May 5, he came into my office and without warning said some things to me that nearly robbed me of my composure. I jumped up, took his hand, and, out of the depths of my heart, gave him back for himself what he had said to me. Then I said, "Why do you speak so? You are running no risk. The doctors say it is of no importance." He looked at me steadily and then he said: "I'm not so sure, I'm not so sure. You can never tell. I hope for the best, but I couldn't go if there is any risk and not tell you just how I really felt about you." The next afternoon Rollo Ogden came into my room. "Do you realize it's four o'clock and we have not heard from the hospital? We were to be told right away." I jumped up in alarm. The telephone brought no satisfaction. I rushed for the elevated. When I reached the hospital Hammond Lamont was with the *Stelligeri*. He had known. That pure and magnificent spirit had sensed the end at hand and a life was finished whose great powers were but beginning to unfold. The doctors could not stop the flow of blood from an artery they were compelled to cut.

Many men have passed through my life and vanished into the Beyond. Only two or three others live as closely to me today; for them the wellspring of abiding affection rises within me now and then and, for a moment, pours over its rim. Lamont's loss was incalculable to me and to *The Evening Post*. I know, as I know that the world exists, that had Hammond Lamont lived and gone on with us the whole story of *The Evening Post* would have been different; that in the hardest of the years to come, when the whole world went mad, I could have leaned upon him. Nothing could have swept him from his moorings or tarnished the pure gold of which he was made.

Is it any wonder that when there were men like these upon the staff we who were of *The Evening Post* believed that there was no other American newspaper to compare with ours?

Chapter VIII. Rough Seas and Hard Going

FATE obviously intended that *The Evening Post* under my management should not encounter calm and peaceful seas. True, the internal disturbances which caused my joining the staff when I did were soon ended and confidence restored. Within six months, however, the threat of war with Spain, which we were bound to oppose, was intensified by the blowing up of the *Maine* and then by the hostilities brought about by President McKinley's dishonest handling of the situation. We were naturally in favor of the Cuban demand for self-government, sympathized with the rebels, and severely criticized the Spanish offer of autonomy made in the fall of 1897, feeling certain that it "could prove only a mockery and a source of fresh disaster to the Cubans." On the other hand, we were under no illusions as to the insurgents, knew that most of the newspaper stories about them were fakes, and were quite prepared for the proof, furnished when we got into the war, that they were in no position to aid United States forces.

We stood with McKinley in his message to Congress of December, 1897, when he declared that forcible annexation was not to be thought of; that by our code of morality it would be criminal aggression; and we stuck to the position when William McKinley abandoned it and seized the Philippines. But the influence of *The Evening Post* in the days leading up to the war was slight when compared with the orgy of lying and sensationalism indulged in by the yellow journalists of the day, with Hearst and Pulitzer setting the pace. I believe that those months of unbridled sensationalism and the throwing off of any pretense of journalistic responsibility to the public left permanent marks upon almost the entire American press—certainly in the matter of typography. Despite this lurid furor McKinley could have prevented war had he been sincere in his desire to do so. Yet to this day the myth appears in many histories and memoirs that the good and benign McKinley fought to keep us out of war until an overwhelming popular and congressional demand drove him into it.

Nothing could be further from the truth, which is that Spain had surrendered on nearly every point and had offered to submit to arbitration those on which she had not yielded *before* the President asked Congress, on April 11, 1898, what he should do in regard to the situation which he had previously characterized as intolerable. As the historian James Ford Rhodes puts it: "McKinley feared a rupture in his own party, and on account of that fear had not the nerve and power to resist the pressure for war. We may be assured that if Mark Hanna had been President there would have been no war with Spain." [1] The actual facts did not come out until three years later, June, 1901, when we of *The Evening Post* discovered, among documents relating to the war published in routine fashion by the State Department,[2] the complete messages from General Stewart L. Woodford, our Minister to Spain, announcing the Spanish surrender. One of these messages, the crucial one of April 5, 1898, had been suppressed by President McKinley. In it General Woodford announced the Queen Regent's readiness to suspend hostilities in Cuba immediately and unconditionally for a period of six months. "I believe," General Woodford cabled, "that this means peace, which the sober judgment of our people will approve long before next November, and which must be approved at the bar of final history." In reply McKinley merely cabled that he "highly appreciated the Queen's desire for peace" but that he could not "assume to influence the action of the American Congress," but if an armistice were offered he would "communicate that fact to Congress." How did he do it in his war message? As Walter Millis puts it: "The fact that Spain had surrendered was imparted in two brief paragraphs, inserted at the end of nine closely-printed pages written on the

[1] James Ford Rhodes, *History of the McKinley and Roosevelt Administrations*, New York, 1922, p. 64.

[2] See *The Nation*, July 4, 1901, p. 4; Feb. 20, 1902: "Our Preventable War with Spain."

assumption that she had not." [3] It was so slurred over that even we editors, who were so opposed to our going to war, failed to grasp the significance of those paragraphs.

The President merely stated that he had received official information that the Queen Regent of Spain had directed General Blanco in Cuba "in order to prepare and facilitate peace to proclaim a suspension of hostilities, the duration and details of which have not yet been communicated to me." This in the face of General Woodford's cablegram stating that the Queen would agree to an armistice until *October 5!* In addition, Mr. McKinley said that he was sure that "this fact . . . will . . . have your just and careful attention in the solemn deliberations upon which you are about to enter." This he could only have written with his tongue in his cheek, for few Congressmen and Senators in the face of the yellow press, and the demand for revenge for the loss of the *Maine* and 260 lives, were in a condition to deliberate solemnly over anything. Yet if Congress had been squarely told that all reason for hostilities had been removed, that fighting in Cuba would cease immediately, and that the dying *reconcentrados* could then be saved, it could not have declared war. Actually our going to war insured months and months of additional suffering for the victims of Spanish misgovernment, military incapacity, and brutality; our relief ships with food and medical supplies, instead of going in April, were sent in the early fall; hostilities with Spain did not cease until August 12.

Several years later I met General Woodford and heard from his lips the whole story. "When I sent that last cable to McKinley," said he, "I thought I should wake up the next morning to find myself acclaimed all over the United States for having achieved the greatest diplomatic victory in our history—the surrender of the proud Castilian nation. I heard only that the President would lay the matter before Congress—without a word of personal congratulation. The next thing I knew he went before Congress, failed to tell it all that I had accomplished, and prac-

[3] Walter Millis, *The Martial Spirit*, New York, 1931, p. 138.

tically asked for the declaration of hostilities." It was in this wise that we went into our totally unnecessary, indeed, criminally needless, war with Spain. The blood of every American who died in that war and in the subsequent Philippine hostilities rests squarely upon the head of William McKinley. In view of the continuing misrepresentations of his acts, is it any wonder that others besides Henry Ford declare that "history is bunk"?

What followed in the Philippines was worse. Until Manila was captured we were all for the Filipinos; our officials encouraged and aided Aguinaldo and gave him every reason to believe that we were interested only in establishing a Filipino republic and turning over the country to its inhabitants. After the battle of Manila we ignored, abused, and exasperated Aguinaldo in every way. Finally hostilities began when American sentries fired upon four Filipinos who did not stop when challenged and Filipino troops returned the fire. The war that followed lasted for more than three years, costing us $170,000,000, and many thousands of lives of Americans and Filipinos. We made that war because McKinley, having put his ear to the ground on a Western speaking trip, returned convinced that the American people desired to become an Asiatic power. Thereupon he committed himself to a "benevolent assimilation" that required 70,000 American troops, the loss of many fine American men, and the ravaging of Luzon, and also to a brutal refusal to treat with the Filipinos until they were entirely vanquished.

When we began the war with Spain, Professor William Graham Sumner of Yale warned his countrymen that the immediate results would be that we would be doing before long the very things that we had reprobated in the Spanish conduct in Cuba and that the spirit of cruelty and oppression we had set out to exorcise by military force would in turn enter into our own souls. He was ridiculed where he was not written down as crazy. Yet we had not been long at war in the Philippines before we had instituted the very reconcentration camp system which had aroused our indignation when utilized by the Spaniards in Cuba. We not only burned villages and crops, as is inevitable in all wars, but actually took over from Spain the "water-cure" torture in order to get information. This is one of the most diabolical means of inducing confessions ever devised by the sadism of man—the insertion of a hose or bamboo into a man's mouth and pumping him full of water until his organs are ready to burst; dirty water was actually recommended by one American officer as much more effective than the pure kind! Subsequently more than eighty officers and men of the American army were tried for the commission of this crime or for other abuses or murders of unarmed Filipino prisoners.

One of these officers, Lieutenant Preston Brown, a Yale graduate who later became a major general, was found guilty of killing "an unarmed, unresisting Filipino, name unknown, a prisoner in his charge," and was sentenced by a court-martial of his fellow-officers to dismissal and five years' imprisonment. Theodore Roosevelt mitigated this sentence to the loss of only thirty numbers on the promotion list! Captain Cornelius M. Brownell was declared guilty of the cold-blooded murder of a Catholic priest, Father Augustine, when seeking to obtain information by torture so terrible that the priest died.[4] On April 14, 1902, I lunched with President Theodore Roosevelt at the White House and laid before him some of the facts which had come to my knowledge about these Philippine happenings. The very next day he issued an order calling on the military for a most rigorous investigation. Some of the phrases in that order had a remarkably familiar sound, as I had used them in my talk with him.

We of The Evening Post threw ourselves into the breach on behalf of the Filipinos with the same passion for justice with which we championed the cause of the Boers against England. We insisted that the American principles of liberty and freedom should be applied to the archipelago and demanded that hostilities be stopped. We and the many other editors of like minds were promptly and viciously attacked as "little Americans," as traitors giving aid and comfort to the enemy, and it was officially reported from the islands that articles from the dissenting minority news-

[4] See The Nation for March 5 and 12, 1903.

papers were stiffening the resistance of the Filipinos to our troops. After the war I learned from Lyman J. Gage, who during those war years was Secretary of the Treasury, that the Cabinet had devoted the greater part of one session to discussing a proposal that the editors of *The Evening Post* and *The Nation*, the Springfield, Mass., *Republican*, and the Boston *Herald* should be prosecuted for treason. Fortunately for the government, as well as for ourselves, the views of Mr. Gage and some others prevailed.

It is true that under the McKinley administration no direct censorship of the press similar to that of the World War was undertaken and the great American tradition of allowing dissent in war time was upheld. But official suppression of facts and of military and naval reports went on through the whole struggle and the censorship in the Philippines was as rigid as it could possibly be made. We had there in General Wheaton and General Otis as tyrannical militarists as were ever produced in Germany. They did not hesitate to criticize Jacob Gould Schurman, of the first Philippine Commission, because he failed to portray the Filipinos as savages, and it was characteristic that General Wheaton denounced the circulation among the Filipinos of the Declaration of Independence as treasonable and seditious! Unlike Admiral Dewey, Major General Henry W. Lawton (our only general killed in battle since the Civil War), and others, these officers showed that they had but the slightest veneer of American democracy and that they had in them the makings of the perfect satrap and the ruthless dictator.

I cannot deny that we hit extremely hard in our fight; that we spared McKinley, and particularly his senatorial upholders, not at all, Godkin leading until disabled by his apoplectic stroke on February 4, 1900. Then, the most passionate, and perhaps for us the most dangerous, articles came from the pen of Rollo Ogden, later our chief editorial writer, at that time a complete pacifist and opponent of war. We had magnificent support from the Anti-Imperialists headed by Carl Schurz, Moorfield Storey, ex-Governor Boutwell, Senator George F. Hoar, and Charles Eliot Norton—Massachusetts did itself proud. Yet a large part of the country which was vocal and politically influential was blinded by the thought that we were to become like England, a world empire, with the sun never setting on our flag. This spread-eagle-ism was reprobated by some notable Republicans in addition to those mentioned, such as Senator Thomas B. Reed and ex-President Benjamin Harrison. Grover Cleveland spoke out well also against the prevailing jingoism of which the following is from the pen of Senator Albert J. Beveridge of Indiana:

We will establish trading posts throughout the world as distributing points for American products. We will cover the ocean with our merchant marine. We will build a navy to the measure of our greatness. Great colonies governing themselves, flying our flag and trading with us, will grow about our posts of trade. Our institutions will follow our flag on the wings of our commerce. And American laws will plant themselves on shores hitherto bloody and benighted, but by those agencies of God henceforth to be made beautiful and bright.[5]

It is but just to add that Senator Beveridge lived to repent this folly. Theodore Roosevelt was not much behind him in fustian.[6] For example, on October 1, 1898, he said that the war had not been a great one but: "Nevertheless it was a war which has decided much for our destiny and which has been of incalculable benefit to the country; a war because of which every American citizen can hold his head high, for now the nation stands as the peer of any of the Great Powers of the world, and we who fought in it hope we have proved that we are not unworthy of the men who so valiantly wore both the blue and the gray in the years from 1861 to 1865"—as if the great United States were not already the peer of any other country! However, the prize for cold-blooded frankness as to our underlying motives must go to the San Francisco *Argonaut* which felt that "the talk about benevolent assimilation is insufferable cant," and then said:

[5] Claude G. Bowers, *Beveridge and the Progressive Era*, Boston, 1932, p. 69.

[6] Two years earlier Roosevelt had written (*Bachelor of Arts*, March, 1896): "At present the only hope of a colony that wishes to attain full moral and mental growth is to become an independent State. . . . There is no chance for any tropical colony owned by a Northern race."

We do not want the Filipinos. We want the Philippines. The islands are enormously rich, but, unfortunately they are *infested by Filipinos*. There are many millions of them there, and *it is to be feared that their extinction will be slow*. . . . The development of the islands cannot be successfully done while the Filipinos are there. Therefore the more of them killed the better.[7]

William J. Bryan promptly espoused the anti-imperialist cause but he was too unpopular with the country's real, business rulers to win on this issue. The voters could not take his criticisms of the imperialist policy too seriously when he had urged the ratification of the peace treaty. Had he defeated it, as his power within his party made it possible for him to do, our whole history would have been different. More than that, he laid himself open to ridicule when he donned a colonel's uniform and, entirely inexperienced and incompetent as he was, announced his readiness to lead his Nebraska regiment into battle, the real commander being, of course, the experienced lieutenant colonel. Bryan did some fine work then, yet the editors of *The Evening Post* could never believe that he was a trustworthy champion of the cause of the people or a sound and consistent statesman. The worship of the gold standard was complete in our office and sound-money theories held to be all-important. Hence *The Evening Post* in the Presidential campaign of 1900 sat squarely upon the fence while continuing to fight hard for the anti-imperialist cause.

The far-reaching results of the abandonment of our old American ideals in 1898 and 1899 are obvious. The annexation of Hawaii,[8] made possible by the Spanish War and our taking over the Philippines, have constituted the chief excuse for our tremendous naval expansion and are the reasons for our ever present danger of war with Japan, although military and naval men admit frankly that the Philippines cannot be successfully defended or reconquered if Japan should seize them. Today, in spite of what-

[7] Quoted in *The Nation*, June 12, 1902.

[8] *The Evening Post* and *The Nation* bitterly opposed this, attributed it to a conspiracy of the large landowners and asked: "What is Hawaii?" Our answer was: "Sixty millionaires."

ever politicians and military and naval men may have in mind, the American people wish to get out of all overseas commitments. The dream of American world empire has long since ended. The surviving anti-imperialists have every reason to look back with satisfaction upon the stand they took and their vindication by the passage of years. Unfortunately only a few of them are left.

That *The Evening Post's* course from 1898 to 1902 did not add to its circulation need not be stressed. Far more detrimental from the business office's point of view, however, was our being boycotted in 1899 by all the department stores that had advertised with us, with the sole exception of John Wanamaker whose business rivals accused him of "scabbing." The cause of this boycott was merely Mr. Godkin's violent attacks upon the law which permits the returning American traveler to bring in free of duty only $100 worth of goods purchased abroad. This law had been dictated in Washington by the New York Merchants and Manufacturers Board of Trade. The battle for its repeal that Mr. Godkin lost illustrated both his best and his worst qualities. He fought brilliantly, with complete courage, refusing to be intimidated by any advertisers whatsoever, and in this he was loyally upheld by the owners of *The Evening Post*. A more flagrant and determined effort by advertisers to control the opinions of a journal is not on record.

On the other hand, Godkin's methods of conducting the fight were most unfortunate; here the snobbishness to which I have referred came into play. He stressed the fact that the Board of Trade was "officered by two tailors, one tailor-trimmings dealer, one shirt maker, one auctioneer, one shoe dealer, one dealer in dressmakers' supplies, and one furrier"—"one impudent furrier" Mr. Godkin always called him. He was correct in maintaining that this group of local merchants should not have been allowed to put this regulation over on the entire American people but his sneers aroused the Board and our advertisers to such fury that some of the latter were never ready to forgive *The Evening Post* or make terms with it again. When a settlement was finally reached many of the stores returned to our columns but it is a conservative estimate that that fight cost *The Evening Post* by and large more than a million dollars, so serious a loss as to render it impossible for me to make a financial success of the paper on any considerable scale. For when I took it over it had no working capital whatsoever. Still I weathered the boycott, the serious depression of 1907, and the shock of war in 1914.

Never was there a more remarkable demonstration of good will and support than was given to us by our readers in our struggle against the boycott. Day after day we printed letters from outstanding men and women of the community. They tried to help financially, too, but we were under no illusions for we knew that interest would wane in time, as it did, and that the financial help proffered could only be a fraction of what we were losing. Still we were cheerful about it; there were fortunately only a few minority stockholders and most of these I gradually bought out. The rest were accustomed to long periods of going without dividends—*pro bono publico*. Our circulation never went beyond 33,000 during my leadership; indeed, most of the time it was in the twenties, yet advertisers did profit by using our columns, and openly acknowledged it, for we possessed a quality of readership unsurpassed by any other daily and also the highest purchasing power in proportion to numbers. That was the explanation of our keeping alive—that, and our editorial ability and independence.

My father's death in November, 1900, was an irreparable blow to me and *The Evening Post*—to say nothing about the severance of the happiest of relationships between a father and son. The loss of his counsel and of my ability to profit by his long journalistic and business experience weakened my faith in myself. My father's attitude towards *The Evening Post* was unique. When he purchased it and *The Nation* in 1881 and combined them, he gave his majority stockholding to my mother and then trusteed it, giving complete power of control to three trustees, David A. Wells, the great tariff reformer, Benjamin H. Bristow, Secretary of the Treasury under Grant, and Horace White, in order that no one should say that *The Evening Post* was dominated by a Wall Street man and also to assure to the editors their complete independence. He never sought to influence the newspaper's editorial policy but was, of course, often consulted by the editors. So far as the business management was concerned he was never approached except when the newspaper was in trouble or loans were needed as they often were in summer since we lived from hand-to-mouth. Editors and publisher turned at once to him in an emergency like the boycott. The independence of *The Evening Post* is best illustrated by the fact that on more than one occasion criticisms of my father's railroad policy appeared in my mother's newspaper without protest from him beyond a friendly one. That was what Mr. Godkin meant when he said that he never knew of any other man who would have borne himself as my father did in connection with *The Evening Post.*

During these first decades of the new century we never let up in our attacks upon the Morgan type of business methods and Morgan himself whose mismanagement of the Shipping Trust, the New Haven Railroad, and other companies should have retired him from Wall Street. As for the politicians, is it any wonder that they writhed when Mr. Godkin wrote, as he did on the election of Thomas C. Platt to the United States Senate, that the boss was "probably the most despised [man] in the community"; "who has neither character nor intelligence fit for legislative purposes"? The New York Legislature, Mr. Godkin declared, had chosen a man "popularly believed to be the most of his time engaged in bribery and corruption," adding the belief that Boss Platt had no knowledge of our government and laws "except as much as may be necessary for the purchase of officials"! [9] These were extremely dangerous and daring words for they charged him with the commission of many crimes under the law. When it came out that money had been given to Platt by a life insurance company for political purposes we called it a "criminal misuse of corporate funds" which naturally endeared us to the insurance magnates. Yet Platt never dared to sue. Our record on Platt alone should have convinced everybody that *The Evening Post* was

[9] *The Nation,* Jan. 21, 1897, p. 42.

free from capitalistic control, for Platt was the darling of the Wall Street gods who could "see him" at any time and regularly bought from him what they wanted.

With Theodore Roosevelt our relations were always difficult. We supported him warmly when he was Civil Service Commissioner, and, with few exceptions, when he was Police Commissioner, and in those days, like all politicians when we praised them, he thought highly of *The Evening Post*—for the moment. But the editors were under no illusion as to Roosevelt and insisted up to the time that he became President that he had a boyish and unstable mentality. Horace White had been well aware of the Roosevelt propensity for not telling the truth when it served their purposes because he had had an experience along that line with Theodore Roosevelt in 1884. Coming out of the Republican convention in Chicago, Mr. White, who was reporting it for *The Evening Post*, met in the telegraph office Theodore Roosevelt and Henry Cabot Lodge. He found them as entirely outraged by the nomination of James G. Blaine as he was himself. Both told him that they had decided to bolt the ticket. When Mr. White asked Roosevelt if he might telegraph what the latter had said, he replied, "By all means." Before Mr. White could reach New York, however, the press received a telegram from Theodore Roosevelt, who was then on his way to his Western ranch, to the effect that Mr. White's published statement that he proposed to bolt Blaine was erroneous. Said he: "I shall not bolt the convention by any means. I have no personal objections to Blaine. I think you will find there will be no fatal disaffection. I believe Blaine will be elected. I have been called a reformer but I am a Republican." [10] On talking it over further, Roosevelt and Lodge had decided that they, as young and rising politicians, could not afford to break with the party machine. This incident is the key to Theodore

[10] Dispatch from St. Paul, Minnesota, in Boston *Herald*, June 10, 1884. Speaking in Brooklyn on October 18, 1884, Roosevelt said: "I know that Mr. Blaine, if elected, must represent the honesty and must obey the will of the mass of honest and upright Republicans who have nominated him and who will elect him."

Roosevelt's entire political career; the reformer in him always surrendered to the politician and to his ambition when it came to a
tight place and he never hesitated to twist the truth.

I learned this personally as one of the Independents who offered
a nomination for the governorship of New York to Theodore
Roosevelt on his return from Cuba with his regiment in 1898.
While I was not of those who actually obtained the Colonel's
promise to take the nomination if it were offered to him, and not
subsequently to withdraw if he took it, I was in the closest contact
with John Jay Chapman, R. Fulton Cutting, Paul Fuller, James
W. Pryor, Richard Welling, Abner Haight, Isaac H. Klein,
Everett V. Abbott, Boudinot Keith, Preble Tucker, and Meyer D.
Rothschild, who actually carried on the negotiations with Roosevelt. The Colonel eagerly accepted the proffered nomination with
its conditions; as to this the facts are indisputable and have recently
been set forth again in the letters of John Jay Chapman.[11] The
Independents did not object to Roosevelt's running both on their
and the regular Republican ticket. They simply did not wish to
launch the boom and then be told that "T.R." would not, by order
of Platt, remain on their ticket. Yet this is precisely what happened. The brave Rough Rider, who always posed as being anti-
machine, yielded to the boss the minute pressure was exerted.

There were two long interviews with the Colonel at Montauk
where Mr. Rothschild also obtained, on the day of the Union's
convention, his consent to nomination by the Citizens' Union.
Then, when he began to play false, there was one of two hours at
the City Club on September 23, 1898, and one of an hour the next
day with Chapman and Paul Fuller, the latter a distinguished
New York attorney. The only defense Roosevelt gave was that
he "didn't understand." As Chapman wrote in 1919 in reviewing
the event after twenty-one years, "Roosevelt never afterward told
the truth about the situation. He persuaded himself that he hadn't
understood my original proposition—whereas he had understood

[11] M. A. DeWolfe Howe, *John Jay Chapman and His Letters*, Boston, 1937, pp. 138-46.

it; only events had caused him to change his mind as to the expediency of it." At one time during the encounters Roosevelt was shown a letter of his to Mr. Tucker enclosing and approving an address which recorded his pledge. All he could say in the face of that overwhelming evidence was that he, the experienced politician and officeholder, had really not read the address he approved but had only "glanced at it!" As Chapman wrote at the time, "a mere collocation of the correspondence without a word of comment would damn him."

The climax came on September 24, at an extraordinarily dramatic meeting at the Reform Club presided over by R. Fulton Cutting, one of the most cultivated, most distinguished in appearance, and aristocratic of the reformers, of courtly bearing and manners. Chapman, who, by accident, was absent but saw Roosevelt the next day, recorded the event thus: "They say that last night— he [Roosevelt] could hardly walk when he left, and that Fulton Cutting (if you know Fulton Cutting you'll see how remarkable this is) dismissed him like a French noble dismissing a lackey. . . . [Said Cutting:] 'Mr. Roosevelt, I don't think we need discuss the matter further.' " I can confirm this because I talked with the members of the group the next day. They added to Chapman's picture the fact that, after that remark of Cutting, Roosevelt rose to go and turned to shake hands but not a man in the room moved toward him or bade him good night. I may add that not one of them ever had any faith in the moral integrity of Roosevelt thereafter though doubtless later some agreed with Chapman's 1919 opinion that Roosevelt "became the most vital, most interesting, and most important figure of his generation." Roosevelt in later years referred characteristically to the group as like "the lunatic fringe" to every reform movement; "another knot of extremists who at first ardently insisted I must be 'forced' on Platt and as soon as Platt supported me themselves opposed me because he supported me." He wrote this in his *Autobiography;* [12] it was as

[12] Theodore Roosevelt, *Theodore Roosevelt—An Autobiography*, New York, 1913, p. 296.

false a statement of the case as any Machiavelli could have devised.

The Independents at once determined to defeat Roosevelt and nearly succeeded in doing so. On a third ticket we nominated Theodore Bacon of Rochester—a highly respectable, but not an inspiring, figure or an impressive orator. Carl Schurz and other prominent men came out for Bacon and to my great satisfaction *The Evening Post* supported the ticket, Godkin and White being unable to stomach the Roosevelt performance and seeing very clearly what was going to happen—that if Roosevelt was elected he would hurt the machine and Platt not at all. With all his Rough Rider prestige, his posing as a hero in his uniform, and the war excitement, he won the election by only 17,786 votes. A change of 9,000 would have stopped his progress toward the Presidency— a narrow squeak indeed.

My association with Jack Chapman then and later was most stimulating. He was nearer to genius, I think, than any writer I have known. This I feel in part accounted for his periods of depression which at times led to his retirement for shorter or longer periods. He was charming to fascination, had a wonderful sense of humor, was as brilliant in conversation as in his writing, and could see further through the shams of our social and political life than anyone I knew. His courage was without limit and I deemed it an honor to be allowed to contribute once or twice to his *Political Nursery*, as fearless and mordant a political publication as one could ask. He had wealth, social position, a beautiful wife, and fine children and, had his nature and his nervous system permitted, would have been a great leader. Something of the reformer within him he inherited from his antislavery grandmother, Maria Weston Chapman, and he had her witty tongue as well. He understood clearly the true function of the reformer, which is one reason why his biography of William Lloyd Garrison is so remarkable. Once he wrote: "As soon as the reformers give up trying to be statesmen, and perceive that their function is purely educational, and that they are mere antislavery agitators and *persons of no account whatever*, they will succeed better." [13] How my grandfather would have applauded that! It is the complete truth for all reformers. From his courage I gained courage. Through his eyes I learned to see much that I had not seen or understood. Partly because of his inspiration I gave a great deal of time to civic affairs. As long as we worked together I profited by the electrical dynamo that was his mind, that shed sparks every second. The World War, in which he lost his gifted poet son, Victor, separated us, but years later we came together again. His head and his heavy beard were Jovian; Michelangelo would have immortalized such a one. Against the startling honesty of this man, Theodore Roosevelt seemed in 1898 small indeed and his election of Chapman to his famous Ananias Club merely a laughable gesture.[14]

[13] John Jay Chapman, *Causes and Consequences*, New York, 1901, p. 33. The italics are mine.

[14] A sample of Chapman's fearless writing even as to Harvard is the following: "Pierpont Morgan is the actual apex as well as the type, of the commercial perversions of the era. The political corruptions, etc., the power behind all . . . Now then, at the dedication of the New Medical School, Eliot goes about in a cab with Pierpont, hangs laurels and wreaths on his nose, and gives him the papal kiss. Now what I want to know is this—what has Eliot got to say to the young man entering business or politics who is about to be corrupted by Morgan and his class? How eloquently can Eliot present the case for honesty? Can he say anything that will reverberate through the chambers of that young man's brain more loudly than that kiss? If Eliot is a great man, I want a small man." Letter to William James, February 13, 1907. M. A. DeWolfe Howe, *John Jay Chapman and His Letters*, Boston, 1937, p. 226.

Chapter IX. Roosevelt, Wood—and a Rascal

ON February 12, 1900, Theodore Roosevelt declared: "Under no circumstances would I accept the nomination for the Vice-Presidency . . . it seems to me clear that at the present time my duty is here in the State, whose people chose me to be Governor. Great problems have been faced and are being solved in this State at this time, and if the people desire, I hope that the work thus begun I may help to carry to a successful conclusion." He added amusingly enough, in view of what happened later, that he was "happy to state that Senator Platt cordially acquiesces in my views of the matter." Platt did so only because he knew what Roosevelt's weakness was: "Ambition, combined with the dread of breaking with his party machine was the magic ring, Platt discovered, upon which he had only to rub in order to bring the rough-riding jinn obediently to heel, saying: 'Here am I!'"[1] When the Republican convention met in Philadelphia on June 18, 1900 (I reported it for *The Evening Post*), he again deprecated talk of his nomination as Vice-President, reiterated that the field of his best usefulness was in New York State, and said: "I very earnestly ask that every friend of mine in the convention respect my wish and my judgment in the matter." But Platt issued the orders and the convention obeyed. The Governor yielded, of course, accepted the Vice-Presidency with alacrity, spent the next four months campaigning for the national ticket and forgot the reform program at Albany. He had had considerable success as Governor—enough to prove that it could have been much greater. But because of politics he showed hesitation and vacillation instead of uncompromising thoroughness in the cause of reform and he was more than most governors ignorant of the actual business of the State.

[1] *The Nation*, January 3, 1901.

Often I have felt that the only adequate way to treat of Theodore Roosevelt would be to list a large number of adjectives and let the reader choose those that he felt fitted this complex and many-sided personality. The choice would be large. Here are some: loyal and disloyal; intellectually honest and dishonest; truthful and lying; brave and (politically) cowardly; sincere and insincere; ingenuous and disingenuous; scrupulous and unscrupulous; unyielding and compromising; brilliant and commonplace; modest and altogether immodest; dignified and undignified; boyish and mature; an actor, a poseur, a passionately sincere advocate, amazingly deft and quick; highly beloved and deeply hated. All of these have been applied to him, and fitted at one time or another. But one thing is certain: few people could resist his buoyancy of spirit, his extraordinary vitality, the force of his ego, and his cheery good nature. I know that I could not any more than I can escape the, to me, even greater charm of Franklin Roosevelt.

I have already written elsewhere that Theodore Roosevelt did more to corrupt the press than anyone else. By that I meant that he warped and twisted, consciously or unconsciously, by his fascinating personality the judgments of the best of the reporters and correspondents and many of the editors. For example, Francis E. Leupp, for so many years *The Evening Post's* altogether admirable Washington correspondent, never lost the judicial attitude he sought to maintain until he succumbed to the charms of Theodore Roosevelt. He finally yielded to the President's blandishments, resigned, and accepted a federal office from him. Once "T.R." appeared before a group of correspondents and waved two "stories" at them. "Here," he said, "is a story and here is the denial which you will print the next day"—the press men accepted both. They adored him for himself, because he created so much news, because he was so stimulating, so vital, and so athletic. Moreover, he took a deep interest in them, their lives, their interests, and their hobbies. He would talk birds with one until two A.M., horses with another, boats with a third, and one was especially welcome because his grandfather rode in the Charge of the Light Brigade. In spite of all those friendships he no more escaped the intense and hostile gossip which centers upon the White House than any other President. If ever a man led an exemplary family life it was Theodore Roosevelt. To charge him with intemperance was almost as outrageous as the New York *Tribune's* declaring that President Cleveland in a drunken rage had driven his wife out of the White House with only a nightgown to protect her from the storm. The only possible excuse for believing that Theodore Roosevelt was ever over stimulated would have been a misunderstanding by strangers of his sometimes excited volubility, his grimaces, his occasional falsetto. He was as "clean as a hound's tooth" in his habits, as he urged everybody else to be.

One luncheon at the White House with him I shall not forget. I had been asked in to discuss army matters with him and the Secretary of War, Elihu Root—it was on April 14, 1902. There were present at the table three of the children, Mrs. Roosevelt, Colonel Albert L. Mills, later General, a foreign Minister, Mr. Root, and myself. We were discussing important national affairs when suddenly Theodore, Jr. jumped up and disappeared into what was then a near by conservatory. He returned bearing a vicious-looking yellow, red, and blue macaw. The minute he hove in sight the President burst out with: "Take it away, take it away." In calm defiance of the Presidential order, Teddy, Jr. came nearer and nearer with the menacing bird. Meanwhile Alice Roosevelt had set up a chant: "Father's afraid, father's afraid, father's afraid, father's afraid." That was more than the President could stand. The boy in him came to the surface, he leaped from his chair, went over and took the bird, rather gingerly, and, showing his teeth, turned upon his offspring and said: "Now who's afraid, now who's afraid, now who's afraid?" He then handed the macaw back to Teddy who bore it off without a word, took his seat at the table, and we renewed the discussion of the fate of nations. I looked at Secretary Root and the Minister during this episode but they never moved a muscle of their faces. I came to the conclusion that that was a familiar sort of happening.

We of *The Evening Post* were never in doubt as to what Roosevelt really thought of us. Thus he wrote as early as June 13,

1893, to Captain Mahan: "I greatly enjoyed the clipping from the *Tribune*. What a real donkey *The Evening Post* is. And what fearful mental degeneracy results from reading it or *The Nation* as a steady thing." To him Godkin was "not a good patriot." We were all of us liars, falsifiers, the truth was not in us. Personally I remained on pretty good terms with Roosevelt. There were times when he thought very well of me; one of my magazine articles, for example, was of "inestimable value" to the army, and made him and Elihu Root feel "humble and ashamed." What he truly felt about me was revealed by a delightful happening at a White House luncheon. One of the guests told the President that when Edison dispatched to Berlin in charge of his first assistant the latest model of his phonograph, the Kaiser sent for the assistant and the machine. Three times the man came, on the first two visits, at the Kaiser's request, taking the instrument completely to pieces and putting it together again. The third time the Kaiser did that himself. When Roosevelt heard this he demurred, especially when it was truthfully added that Edison had said that he knew nothing about the Kaiser but he did not believe there were five or six men anywhere who had the mentality to put that machine together again after having seen it demonstrated only twice, and that he believed the Kaiser to be a most extraordinary man. A friend of mine at the table assured the President that the story was true as he had had it from Oswald Villard, and that Oswald Villard got it from Thomas Edison himself. Whereupon Roosevelt burst out in his highest falsetto: "I *wish* that somebody would take Oswald Villard to pieces and forget how to put him together again!" No single anecdote concerning me has ever given me such pleasure as this. It recalls the fact that I had the distinguished privilege of taking the great German scientist, Von Helmholtz, out to Thomas A. Edison's laboratory, introducing these two great men to each other and then for a couple of hours acting as interpreter for them. It was then that Edison told this story of the Kaiser's extraordinary achievement.

At that time I was supposed to resemble Theodore Roosevelt and there were sometimes amusing happenings in consequence.

Because of the presence at Montauk of the remnant of Shafter's army I decided in September, 1898, to take my vacation on horseback and to visit the troops, and I did so, riding 375 miles in eighteen days with my saddlebags behind me—by no means an easy trip because of the absence of adequate inns. I began my journey from Dobbs Ferry and when I reached New York and rode down Fifth Avenue I was saluted and waved to by one policeman after another. That afternoon when I rode onto a Long Island ferry I was followed by a motley crowd of commuters and idlers who surrounded me and then stood and stared. Finally a fireman climbed out of the engine room, walked up to me, and said: "Excuse me, sor, be you Colonel Roosevelt?" When I said "no" the crowd promptly disappeared. Hotels were few and far between and my horse was leg weary and tired out when about half-past ten that evening I got into a dirty and suspicious-looking inn— only after insisting that I could go no further. The next morning the surly proprietor assured me that he would not have let me in had he not thought that I was the Rough Rider. Soon after leaving him I skirted Camp Black where a new volunteer regiment was training and ran into the Officer of the Day. He wanted to turn out the guard for me and told me the Colonel would take it as a personal hurt if I failed to call on him. He was bitterly disappointed when I explained that I had important business at Montauk and rode on. At Montauk I found Colonel Roosevelt making a stump speech in front of his tent to a mixed crowd of soldiers and visitors. I thought the Rough Riders just as undisciplined as their brief existence would lead one to expect. The Fort Myer battalion of the Sixth Cavalry bore no resemblance to the smart, trim organization I had known. The men still on duty seemed hardly strong enough to mount guard and the few officers left were, as I have said, like ghosts, hardly recognizable.

The first colonel of the Rough Riders, Leonard Wood, was Governor General of Cuba when I met him in Havana in March, 1900. *The Evening Post* had had a good deal to do with his becoming the head of Cuba because it had warmly praised his work in cleaning up Santiago immediately after the surrender. I thought the General as attractive and winning as he had been represented and I was the recipient of marked attention from him. The Cuban Cabinet, for example, was asked to meet me at dinner and he gave me so much of his time that I became suspicious; I was too young a journalist to merit such favors. I soon found myself repelled both by his methods and his cynical frankness. He asked me if I had seen the Rough Riders at Montauk. I answered that I had. "What did you think of them?" I replied that I had seen a number of raw militia regiments but never a regiment so undisciplined and unmilitary as the Rough Riders. "That," he said, "began with the day Colonel Roosevelt took over my regiment." He was savage about Roosevelt's book, *The Rough Riders*, and showed that he was thoroughly antagonistic to the Governor of New York. He stated: "I have received letters from Maine to California asking me to denounce *The Rough Riders* because of its misrepresentations." He then asked how Roosevelt was doing as Governor, plainly with the hope that he would hear unfavorable things, and wound up by declaring that he considered him "a medical case." When Roosevelt became President, however, the breach was promptly healed and they became more devoted allies than ever.

The last time that I was with General Wood at the palace I found out what it was that he wanted of me. There had appeared in the *North American Review* for February, 1900, an article from the pen of Major James E. Runcie, violently attacking the administration of the Governor General of Cuba, Major General John R. Brooke. General Brooke's removal and his replacement by General Wood were generally attributed to this article but actually they took place well before its publication. After its appearance the Secretary of War, Elihu Root, had ordered General Wood to dismiss Major Runcie from the several offices and places on commissions which he held, for indiscipline in attacking in print his superior officer. General Wood complained to me that this had deprived him of his most valuable lieutenant and besought me to write an editorial on my return to New York deprecating the action of the War Department and asking for the restoration of Major Runcie on the ground that the editor of the *North American Review*, Colonel George Harvey, had agreed to publish Runcie's article anonymously and had then appended Runcie's name. I did this immediately upon my return and received a great shock the next day when there came a letter from Colonel Harvey demanding an immediate retraction else he would sue for libel and ask heavy damages.

I was badly frightened, more so than at any other time in my journalistic career, for I was just beginning my editorial writing and this was the first time that I had made trouble for the paper. My feelings were not improved by the fact that the elder men were as much upset as I. So I went around to Franklin Square to Colonel Harvey's office, explained the situation, and threw myself upon his mercy. When I told him who my informant was he said: "That does not surprise me. I have come across that man's trail before." He then told me that the Runcie manuscript was interlined and corrected in the handwriting of General Wood, and I so reported to our editorial council. The next day we duly apologized to the *North American Review*. Three years later we printed in a letter from a Havana correspondent the charge that the manuscript had been both instigated and interlined by General Wood. This time Colonel Harvey denied his statement to me, and *The Evening Post* and *The Nation* promptly made a most complete apology to General Wood.[2] For this contretemps we were roundly scored by the press. I still believe the statement to have been true. Major Runcie, whose friendship I highly valued and enjoyed, admitted to me, as to others, that General Wood asked him to write the article, and I am very certain that he never would have misinformed General Wood as to any promise of Colonel Harvey to publish the article anonymously. Others beside myself heard that Wood had edited the article. Major Runcie would not, however, come to our defense because he was under a deep personal obligation to General Wood. When a lieutenant of artillery at the Presidio at San Francisco, Runcie had received a grave injury in

[2] *The Nation*, May 7 and May 14, 1903.

"CIVILIZING" THE MOROS. JUST AFTER THE ATTACK BY GENERAL WOOD'S TROOPS ON MOUNT DAJO. NOTE THE DEAD WOMAN AND HER BABE. THE NEGATIVE OF THIS PICTURE WAS "ACCIDENTALLY" DESTROYED BY A HIGH AMERICAN OFFICER.

a mounted artillery drill, which injury brought about his retirement from active service. The surgeon who took care of him with rare devotion and the greatest skill was Leonard Wood and Runcie always felt that he owed his life to him. That did not prevent his letting intimates know his disappointment in the General as the head of Cuba.

Whatever else may be said about General Wood it cannot be denied that more and graver charges were made against him than against any general officer the army has known since the Civil War. When his nomination for the rank of major general of regulars was being considered it took nine hundred pages, printed as *Executive Document C, Confidential, 58th Congress, Second Session,* to record the charges of disloyalty to and conspiracy against his superior commander, abuses of authority, favoritism, improper acceptance of a valuable gift, broken faith, duplicity, and untruthfulness and the evidence on the other side. Had he not been confirmed by the Senate as major general he would have been dropped out of the army and that fact influenced in his favor the committee majority, who were Republicans. For a long time I and others believed that Wood was responsible for the removal of General Henry W. Lawton, his old commander in Arizona, as head of Santiago, which resulted in Wood's succeeding him. This information came to me from high officers at Santiago at the time but Hermann Hagedorn, the general's biographer, has convinced me that I was misinformed. Naturally I regret that I did the General any injustice.

In no other case has it been as difficult to get at the whole truth and as easy to go wrong, for at every point in Wood's career there were charges and countercharges until I finally believed that only a high civilian court could establish all the facts. Thus there is great conflict of testimony as to Wood's whereabouts during the Battle of Santiago. An officer of high standing, who was also with the Fourth Cavalry under Lawton in Arizona when Wood received his medal of honor, declared that Wood never heard a hostile shot fired in that Arizona fighting. For this Lieutenant Colonel H. C. Benson was rebuked but never ordered before a court as he should have been in order to establish the truth. One thing is undeniable. General and Mrs. Wood received valuable gifts from the backers of the Havana jai alai betting game which General Wood licensed, something that he should never have done. Secretary Root investigated the gift and acquitted the General of misconduct. But I am old-fashioned enough to believe that it was a grossly improper thing for an American general to accept a silver service worth more than $5,000, and his wife pearls valued at more than $3,000, from such a source.

Two Secretaries of War, Garrison and Baker, told me that General Wood was so guilty of insubordination that they could have court-martialed him but that they did not wish to make a martyr of him. General Wood would not have denied the insubordination and would have declared that he deliberately transgressed in order to rouse the army and the country to the need of preparedness. Curiously enough, his zeal for the public service always went hand in hand with his zeal for his own advancement.[3] Ahead of our troops he and a number of other generals were sent to France to witness and be instructed in the new warfare. General Wood made trouble immediately and talked indiscreetly and this was one of the reasons why General Pershing would not permit him to go to France again—it was Pershing's decision and nobody else's.[4] When Wood was Chief of Staff, "the atmosphere of the War Department was one of spite, jealousy, and intrigue." [5]

Of all the men whom I have known and studied Leonard Wood seems to me to have been the most blindly ambitious. Were he living today he would be the ideal fascist leader and would have no more compunction in "purging" any rivals than he showed when he was deliberately buying people off in Cuba to end their

---

[3] General Adna Chaffee, after being Wood's Chief of Staff in Cuba, wrote: "General Wood needs about him very steady and cautious men—men who are not his tools—sycophants; but he does not want such material. It is necessary to serve him as he wishes, that his assistants think as he does and believe in his infallibility." General William H. Carter, *Life of Lieutenant General Chaffee*, Chicago, 1917, p. 172.

[4] Frederick Palmer, *Newton D. Baker*, New York, 1931, pp. 232-42.

[5] George Creel, *The War, The World and Wilson*, New York, 1920, p. 89.

opposition to him. Naturally the moneyed interests supported him enthusiastically when he sought the Presidential nomination and they poured out money in such quantities that again the General was the center of a scandal; some of his agents were guilty of corruption. He lacked vision and background, read little, knew nothing about economics and modern trends, and would have taken the Big Business viewpoint as to labor and strikes. He was always a man to be reckoned with and had a host of devoted and loyal friends who would believe no evil of him. His ability was unquestioned and he was an excellent commander of troops; there is no doubt that the division that he trained was the best that arrived in France.

No one admired General Wood more than Edgar C. Bellairs. It was I who opened a journalistic career to this remarkable rascal. In January, 1898, he brought me a letter of introduction from Fabian Franklin, then an editor of the Baltimore *American* and later one of my own editorial staff on *The Evening Post*. Accepting Mr. Franklin's recommendation I gave Bellairs permission to write for our Saturday paper—he was in dire need. He had evidently come from a good family and I have always believed that he was a noncommissioned officer, if not a commissioned one, in the routed army of Valentine Baker Pasha in Egypt, for whom he had the most unbounded regard, beyond that for any other man until he met Leonard Wood. Then he transferred that adoration. "I would lie down and let General Wood walk upon me," he once said to me. He wrote badly but I licked his articles about Baker's army into shape and then printed a series by him on the chain gangs in Florida, with which he said he had served as an overseer. They created a sensation and called forth violent protests but no one could deny that he knew what he was writing about. When the war with Spain came, Bellairs asked and received an appointment from me as one of our correspondents with the army because of his military experience.

We sent him to Florida and received some interesting articles. One that we displayed prominently told of his having made his way on a fisherman's boat to Cuba, where he had most interesting experiences until he was stricken with fever, after which he worked his way back to the United States. Some days after the article appeared—it was accompanied by a very considerable expense bill including the cost of one mule eaten when other food gave out— Rollo Ogden was rereading it and noticed that Bellairs gave the latitude and longitude of his furthermost point in Cuba. Mr. Ogden looked them up and found that they placed Bellairs in the middle of the Atlantic! We made discreet inquiries and found that there was no doubt that Bellairs had never left the United States and so we paid him off and dismissed him without further action. He then went to the Associated Press and, on the strength of his having been connected with *The Evening Post,* was immediately employed by Melville Stone. Probably I should have denounced him to Stone but it never occurred to me to do so. Stone sent Bellairs to Santiago where he reported favorably upon General Wood's achievements and when the General was transferred to Havana Bellairs accompanied him, almost as a member of his family. When I was in Havana it seemed to me that Bellairs was acting as *maître d'hôtel* of the palace; I know that he supervised dinner parties. Soon Melville Stone got rumors about Bellairs' record and finally a letter from Florida vaguely urging him to probe into Bellairs' past. He was about to do so when, as he wrote, "the General [Wood] appeared on the scene and vouched for the man's character in unmistakable terms. He assured us that Bellairs was the victim of malice and was wholly trustworthy."

After a while the Associated Press sent Bellairs to the Philippines where he again began his hero worship, this time of General Chaffee. At the time of the Boxer Rebellion, in accordance with that general's request, Bellairs was assigned to the American expedition into China which General Chaffee commanded. After this he returned with our little army to Manila. Finally Mr. Stone found out the truth and in June, 1902, recalled him. On July 2 of that year the Army and Navy Club of Manila gave a farewell dinner to Bellairs, the program of which lies before me. He was then "Captain Edgar Gerald Bellairs" and the fifty foremost

Americans in the islands were present, including General Chaffee, the Chief Quartermaster, the Chief Commissary, the Chief of Artillery, the Chief Ordnance officer, Martin Egan, later connected with J. P. Morgan & Co., General Jesse M. Lee, and W. Morgan Shuster, then Collector of Customs. It was a glorious send-off and Bellairs must have gone aboard ship with feelings of exaltation. He brought back with him the manuscript of a book, which soon appeared, denouncing Governor General Taft of the Philippines for his inefficiency, weakness, and toadying to the Filipinos and demanding the substitution for him of the greatest of all administrators, Leonard Wood. Bellairs had intended to dedicate this volume to me out of gratitude but something quite unexpected intervened.

I was then acting as managing editor of *The Evening Post* in a little cubbyhole on the composing room floor of the old *Evening Post* Building which still stands, empty and desolate, at the corner of Broadway and Fulton Street. When the office boy brought in Bellairs' card I told him to let the visitor come in and reached into my desk for a memorandum which I had prepared for this event. When Bellairs entered he held out his hand with a warm, "My *dear* Villard!" "Just one moment," said I. "Before we shake hands let's clear up one point. Am I shaking hands with Ernest Gerald Bellairs, or Ernest Alaine Cheriton, or E. Ellaine, or E. A. Cameron, or Charles Ballentine?" Nothing more melodramatic ever happened on the stage. He threw up his hands, said, "*Oh, my God*, have you heard that awful lie?", walked over to the armchair by my desk and collapsed into it as if stricken. "Give me time," he cried, "give me time and I'll prove my innocence." "You can do that now," I answered. "Why not roll up the sleeve of your coat and show me that you have no anchor tattooed on your right arm?" He made no move to do so but sat as if stupefied.

The record in my hand I had taken from a book called *Famous Criminals,* by Inspector Byrnes. Bellairs' real name was Charles Ballentine. He was the son of a clergyman in Norfolk County, England, and according to Byrnes he had "visited every country on the face of the globe and the number of his victims runs into the thousands. The most successful part he plays is that of a society confidence man. The best families in England, France, and Canada have been taken in by his suavity. . . ." On June 10, 1891, after being arrested in New York, he was delivered to the State Agent of Florida and taken to Tampa where he was wanted for forgery and was sentenced, on December 23, 1891, to seven years on the chain gang. He had grown no mustache or beard, and he had actually had the nerve to return to Florida as the correspondent of *The Evening Post*.

Our interview was quickly concluded—by his act as soon as he could pull himself together. He left assuring me that he would return and disprove the charges. He never did. On November 23, 1902, he wrote to me: "I cannot leave America, probably forever, without a line of farewell to you and a repetition of the thanks due you for your kindness at a time when I sorely needed it. . . . I trust when I write you from another part of the world I may be in a position to prove to you that 'the devil is not as black as he has been painted.'" I made no publication about him for some time. Then one day the New York *Sun,* which was opening up a tremendous fire upon General Wood, came out with a short editorial about Edgar G. Bellairs and wound up by asking: "Who is this man, Edgar G. Bellairs?", with the evident intention of answering this in full with Bellairs' record the next day. They were mad as hornets when I spoiled their game by telling them in *The Evening Post* of that afternoon all about Bellairs and his connection with Leonard Wood.

I must not forget to add that it was Melville Stone who tipped me off when I met him on the street one day and expostulated with him at the way in which Bellairs was booming General Chaffee and attacking Mr. Taft. Years later I saw Bellairs pass through the lobby of the House of Commons. For years after his exposure in the United States he actually acted as a special correspondent for the London *Times,* under what name I do not know. I do not think that I should have published one word about him if the *Sun* had not opened up, for there was a chance that, although he had repaid my kindness by cheating me and *The Evening Post*, he was trying to go straight. A beautiful jade piece which was part of the loot of Peking is still in my possession. Bellairs sent it to me from Manila and I have never been able to discover the proper owner.

Chapter X. A Centennial and a Conference with Consequences

The Evening Post's centennial was celebrated on November 16, 1901, at a luncheon tendered to the officers and editors in the library of the Equitable Building. Abram S. Hewitt, probably the foremost citizen of New York at that time, presided and we listened to eulogistic addresses by Carl Schurz, St. Clair McKelway, Andrew Carnegie, James C. Carter, Archbishop Corrigan, Joseph C. Hendrix, President J. G. Schurman of Cornell and President Francis L. Patton of Princeton. Three editors responded, Mr. White, Mr. Garrison, and I, mine being an easy task since all the praise applied to the older men and none to me. Unfortunately the two men who most deserved recognition were not there—Henry Villard and Edwin L. Godkin, the latter then living crippled in England. In the evening there was a dinner for our entire force of 180 employees from all departments. The centennial issue reviewing the history of the paper I had personally supervised.

The celebration served a double purpose, to recognize the work of the veterans of the staff and to recall *The Evening Post's* outstanding record. True, that had not always been unblemished; the scandal of the trial for corruption of Isaac Henderson, part owner and publisher and New York Navy Agent under Lincoln, lingered long, and in the last years of the Bryant-Godwin regime there were quite unsavory business connections with Tammany Hall. Still it had been on the whole a great and high-minded institution, dignified, clean, and able in its pages which had always been conducted by outstanding men. Undoubtedly Alexander Hamilton was privy to its birth by which his political fortunes immediately profited but the bold assertion of the present owner upon the editorial page that the newspaper was founded by Ham-

ilton lacks any historical authority so far as I could ever discover.
That William Coleman, the first editor, was Hamilton's devoted
henchman, and that Hamilton wrote editorials for it, is beyond
question. It is also more than significant that on the second page
of the first subscribers' book—in 1801 one signed one's name in
the register in order to become a subscriber—was the signature of
Aaron Burr. Hamilton may even have been at the residence of
Archibald Gracie on the Battery at the meeting of his supporters at
which it was decided to launch the venture,[1] but as to this there
is no record to guide us. When Hamilton himself had not the
moral courage to refuse to fight Aaron Burr and his amazingly
brilliant career was ended, the editors and printers of *The Evening Post* walked beside or behind his coffin and the funeral was
described and the order of the procession illustrated in their paper
between deep black lines. If Hamilton was not the proprietor of
The Evening Post or its editor he was surely its demigod.

And what a roll of editors there was to recall: William Coleman,
William Leggett, William Cullen Bryant (from 1826 to 1878—
52 years), Parke Godwin, John Bigelow, Carl Schurz, Edwin L.
Godkin, Horace White. Surely no other daily ever had a more
distinguished group. It was Leggett who committed *The Evening
Post* as early as 1835 to the antislavery cause and William Cullen
Bryant properly celebrated this coeditor of his in these lines:

> The words of fire that from his pen
> Were flung upon the fervid page
> Still move, still shake the hearts of men,
> Amid a cold and coward age.

These were words that applied as well to Godkin.

On the retirement of Horace White, Rollo Ogden became the
chief editorial writer, with complete power over the editorial page
—he freely edited my articles at all times. I never once overruled
him. In the heat of righteous indignation Mr. Ogden rose at in-

---

[1] The second Archibald Gracie, New Yorker born and bred, was a Confederate brigadier general; the third went down with the *Titanic* with the
calm courage to be expected of one of his talent and lineage.

tervals to the height of Godkin himself and I personally believe
that in those years he even surpassed in vigor, breadth, and frequently eloquence, the work of Frank Cobb on the *World*. Originally a clergyman by profession, he startled his congregation in
the leading Presbyterian Church in Cleveland by announcing from
the pulpit one day that he could no longer believe what he had
taught and that therefore he must resign, which he did and became a missionary in Mexico. This was a highly creditable incident
in his life which he strove always to conceal; his was a contradictory nature. It was the World War which swept him from his
old bearings, which dimmed his moral perceptions, and swung
him away from that brilliant course he had pursued during all
those years of our Philippine invasion, and the power of his pen
finally disappeared behind the mask of the editorial page of the
New York *Times*, whose owner, he once told me, he would under
no circumstances ever serve. But to Rollo Ogden, when he was the
moral reformer, *The Evening Post* owed a very great deal. No
editor ever did a better job of unearthing and properly character-
izing a politician's skulduggery than did Mr. Ogden when he
handled the Roosevelt-created Panama revolution which resulted
in our taking over the Canal. Year in year out he revealed the
trickery and falsity of our Panama aggression. Of this act of gross
international immorality Mr. Roosevelt boasted later to the students of the University of California, saying frankly: "I took the
Canal."

Never was there a more terrific denunciation of a man than
Mr. Ogden's "Unthinkable Hearst" published on March 1, 1904,
as to which Henry Watterson wrote me six days later: "My belief is that you have killed the Hearst boom." Sent to every editor,
every educator, every clergyman, every public man in the South,
that editorial *did* have a tremendous effect and unquestionably
marked the beginning of the end of the Hearst boom for the Presidency. The following excerpt is worth preserving here if only as
evidence of Ogden at his most powerful:

It is not simply that we revolt at Hearst's huge vulgarity; at his front
of bronze; at his shrieking unfitness mentally, for the office which he

sets out to buy. All this goes without saying. There never has been a case of a man of such slender intellectual equipment, absolutely without experience in office, impudently flaunting his wealth before the eyes of the people and saying, "Make me President." This is folly. This is to degrade public life, but there is something darker and more fearful behind. It is well known that this man has a record which would make it impossible for him to live through a Presidential campaign—such gutters would be dragged, such sewers laid open. . . . It is not a question of politics, but of character. An agitator we can endure; an honest radical we can respect; a fanatic we can tolerate; but a low voluptuary trying to sting his jaded senses to a fresh thrill by turning from private to public corruption is a new horror in American politics. To set the heel of contempt upon it must be the impulse of all honest men.

This was one of the many editorials for which I was made the whipping boy, for the Hearst press opened up on me and accused me of every possible crime and of being in my looks one of those monstrosities "usually to be found upon the shelves of an anatomical museum." That sort of thing I was slowly inured to; it was not easy at first but it was part of my job and seemed a small price to pay for the tremendous privilege of engineering the course of so great a journal.

Of the other veterans of *The Evening Post* who were with us at the time of the centennial, and for years afterwards, I recall with particular affection our two critics, J. Ranken Towse, who dealt with the drama, and Henry T. Finck, who for many years held forth in the field of music. They were at opposite poles in their attitude toward their work. Mr. Towse prided himself on the fact that he had never once met an actor or an actress, a policy he pursued in order that no one should ever say of him that he had been influenced by a friendship. I broke his heart one day by luring him into my office and introducing him to the lovely Julia Marlowe. He nearly wept at having the record of a lifetime spoiled and I was deeply cast down that a mischievous prank had hurt him so much, for we all loved him and admired him. If ever there was a Spartan it was he. He was an old 'varsity oar from Cambridge and had come direct to the United States after graduation but, although he lived into his eighties, he never became an

American citizen and remained an Englishman to the core. As he joined *The Evening Post* as a reporter soon after his arrival he practically spent the whole of his life in its service and no one else during his long connection with it ever set up higher ideals and lived up to them more determinedly. As the years passed, however, he found it harder and harder to say a good word for an actor of the current day and lived more and more in memories of Booth and Macready and the other great lights of past generations.

If Mr. Towse was always the reserved and controlled Englishman, Henry T. Finck was all emotion and distinguished by a charming boyishness which he never outgrew. When I first entered the office I shared a cubbyhole with him and we were called "the twins" and were very congenial. Far from shunning musicians, Finck loved being with them and especially adored the beautiful women among them. He saw no impropriety whatsoever in falling in love with them and raving about them in his writings. Correspondingly he was filled with fury against all who took the contrary view. They were all in a sinister conspiracy. Indeed, the musical world was then largely composed of feuds. Finck thought that anybody by the name of Damrosch was Public Enemy No. 1. But the full force of his invective was directed toward those who sneered and scoffed at Wagner when Wagner's operas were first produced in New York. He likened them to the critics who had found fault with Beethoven and the other great masters in their day and correspondingly rejoiced as, with the passage of years, Wagnerian operas became the most popular and were admitted to be the products of the greatest genius of modern music. Curiously enough, Henry Finck was just as violently antagonistic to the introduction of the music of Brahms as those whom he assailed were prejudiced against Wagner. With all his unusual sense of humor, he could not see that the cases were exactly parallel. Gradually he was compelled to admit that a particular quartet, or concerto, or symphony of Brahms was really good. But when he made a damaging admission like this he always covered his tracks and declared that all the rest of Brahms was trash.

Both of these critics had, of course, absolute freedom of expression and they jealously guarded this right—or would have had there been occasion to do so. Once Finck, who could be extremely absent-minded, thought he had a clear case. He picked up one of our early editions and found to his amazement that his review of a concert given the night before had been entirely altered. He rushed to the managing editor exploding with wrath and, holding the paper in his hand, read the statements as they appeared and told him what he had actually written. Together they started for the composing room and demanded to know of the superintendent who had altered Finck's copy. The old superintendent, a magnificent specimen by the name of Morris Van Vliet, took the paper away from Finck, looked at it, laughed, and showed him that it was the *Commercial Advertiser* and not *The Evening Post* that he held in his hand. There was great similarity of type at that time. A more crestfallen man than Finck never returned to his office. The staff laughed so immoderately that the next edition almost failed to appear.

Once Hammond Lamont and I played a trick on Rollo Ogden. We deliberately altered a savage editorial that he had written on Theodore Roosevelt, making it much worse, quite indecently libelous when not wholly wild. This was set up in a bogus editorial page with all the other editorials. Lamont, who was a capital actor, took the fake page into Ogden's office, laid it before him, and said that he wished it understood that he considered this the most scandalous and indecent editorial that he had ever read. His voice trembled with the utmost indignation as he added that if that editorial went out on the street he would resign and leave the office that day. Ogden took one look at it and headed for the composing room as had Finck. He, too, was boiling with indignation so that he did not notice that practically the entire staff of the paper was assembled there. Rushing up to Van Vliet he demanded to know what this interference with his copy meant. "It means," said Van Vliet, "that we are very happy to have you with us and wish to congratulate you on your fiftieth birthday." Whereupon the staff applauded and cheered the utterly bewildered Ogden. There *was* a genuine camaraderie in *The Evening Post* in all those years; it *was* in many respects like one great family bound together by devotion to a common end—the production of the best and freest paper we could create.

The financial editor, Alexander D. Noyes, was another who had complete control of his department. His is naturally a conservative point of view and his mind has a strong historical bent which leads him—he still writes for *The Times*—often to overdo his comparisons with past events which he always has at his finger tips in most amazing detail. He and I did not see eye to eye on many things; it was therefore a satisfaction to have him testify that I never interfered with his financial leader which he wrote as he pleased. He has lived to see public financing of a kind the mere suggestion of which would have turned his hair snow-white thirty years ago. If his writing usually led into beaten paths, it was a source of great strength to us to have in his position a man known for his absolute incorruptibility, respected for his financial knowledge, and feared because of his readiness to scourge the lords of Wall Street when he felt that they deserved it. I believe he is still of those who think that capitalism can be saved, just as he was formerly among the sincere and misguided who were certain that the world could be made safe by our entering the World War and that Prussian militarism could be wiped out by fastening militarism on us and all the world.

We never had to worry about Arthur F. J. Crandall's handling of the telegraph news; besides being an extremely efficient editor, he was a gentleman and also, by training and bent, an artist. His sense of news values was perfect, his taste in headlines of the best. When the World War came he rose to that emergency in a way to make us proud. The flood of war dispatches was handled with intelligence and discrimination and when their sources were dubious that was indicated. I cannot say that we escaped all the baneful effects of the false British propaganda, for that was manifestly impossible,[2] but we tried our best to keep the scales even and

---

[2] I, for example, was profoundly influenced by Lord Bryce's signing the report on German atrocities in Belgium, which, I am reliably informed, he lived to regret.

I think that we succeeded as well as any. I look back upon the hours which I spent editing dispatches under Mr. Crandall in my first years on *The Evening Post* with gratitude and rejoice in his friendship to this hour.

It is impossible to recall here all the long list of men who were part of the great training school which was our *Evening Post*. I may be allowed, however, to add to the names already cited those of Simeon Strunsky, Harold Phelps Stokes, Reginald Cleveland, Franklin Clarkin, Harold J. Learoyd, Charles A. Selden, H. I. Brock, Harold Littledale, Ralph Graves, Walter B. Hayward, and Charles McD. Puckette, all fine journalists and loyal and devoted workers who later went to the New York *Times*. Among the other editorial writers of distinction were Frank J. Mather, Jr., later of Princeton University, Royal J. Davis, Fabian Franklin, beloved of all who worked with him, Allan Nevins, and Philip L. Allen who died in the great promise of his late twenties. Garet Garrett and Frank H. Simonds later made names for themselves in other fields; Simonds' service at Albany and elsewhere for us—he cordially disliked and distrusted Charles E. Hughes—gave us no inkling of the great influence he was later to exert as a military commentator during the World War and a writer on international subjects thereafter. Paul Elmer More was an editor of *The Nation*; Stuart P. Sherman helped out during vacations. Robert J. MacAlarney, one of our best city editors, later took the charm of his personality to the Pulitzer School of Journalism; A. E. Thomas turned to the stage with success as a playwright; George Henry Payne is a militant member of the Federal Communications Commission; Lawrence Perry has continued his great success as a sports writer and author; Arthur D. Howden Smith became the first biographer of Colonel House; Frederick W. Gehle went to the Chase National Bank where he is a vice-president; Charles P. Sawyer, who spent practically his whole life with *The Evening Post*, completed his service in the dramatic department and Amy Loveman has long been an editor of the *Saturday Review of Literature*. William J. Boies of the financial department, Norman Duncan, Leonard J. DeBekker, R. L. Barnum, Herbert

Reed, Walter Randall, Horace Green, Foster Ware, Josiah D. Whitney, Elizabeth King, Marian Storm, Clara Savage, George B. Fife, Chester Parrish, and Henry J. Case all added to our strength, while in the business department Edward P. Call, William J. Pattison, and Emil M. Scholz fought faithfully and bravely in the hopeless fight to make a financial success of our enterprise.

In the year after *The Evening Post's* centennial there occurred the most important—and most educational—event in my life. My interest in Negro education led to my being invited in April, 1902, to join the first of the southern educational trips which were made possible by the generosity of Robert C. Ogden, the merchant philanthropist. These journeys were made by special train to the annual "Conference on Education in the South"; the company was large and influential, with numerous journalists included to assure publicity. Stops were made at a number of institutions, Hampton Institute being the first to be visited en route to the conference city. For many years the head of the Wanamaker store in New York, an earnest, straightforward speaker, of a sincerely religious nature, Mr. Ogden was the ideal leader for a movement which, thanks largely to Rockefeller generosity, out of small beginnings brought about an extraordinary educational revival in the South, with most notable results. Out of it had already come the General Education and Southern Education Boards which have dispensed millions for schools and colleges for both races and deeply influenced educational policy in that section. It was a situation calling for the utmost skill and tact and these Mr. Ogden, William H. Baldwin, Jr., the able and lovable president of the Long Island Railway and head of Tuskegee's trustees, Edgar Gardner Murphy, Albert Shaw, George Foster Peabody, Wallace C. Buttrick, and others who took the lead, all displayed.

To one of my temper and training it often seemed as if they compromised too much and held their tongues too carefully in check in the face of grievous inequalities and injustices. There was certainly a tendency to lean over backward because the Southern prejudices were still deeply ingrained, feelings were easily hurt,

FOUR "EVENING POST" EDITORS

Top Row: EDWIN L. GODKIN (FROM AN ENGRAVING BY G. KRUELL), HORACE WHITE

Lower Row: WENDELL P. GARRISON, HAMMOND LAMONT

and memories of the Civil War and Reconstruction were still keen thirty-seven years after Appomattox. This may be illustrated by a story long joyously told by Mrs. C. W. Ide of Brooklyn, a sister of Mr. Ogden. At Athens, Georgia, on this 1902 trip, being a guest of two charming spinsters, she sat with them at one of the first meetings of the conference. They had heard something almost unbelievable—that by some lapse a grandson of that horrible William Lloyd Garrison had been permitted to join the party. Out of that curiosity which makes one desire occasionally to see a freak, they asked Mrs. Ide to point out the man so cursed in his ancestry. I happened to be sitting on the platform. When they looked at me their astonishment was not to be controlled. "Why," said they in unison, "he is *nice* looking!"

In the face of widespread feelings like these, the whole enterprise was dangerous. Northerners bearing gifts were to be as mistrusted as Greeks in the same role and listeners had to be convinced that this was not all a covert scheme to put wrong ideas in Negroes' heads, make them less efficient servants, and possibly even establish race equality; had the adjectives Bolshevik or Communist been in use then we should have heard them, too. The speakers naturally went out of their way to emphasize the glories of the South and Lee and Stonewall Jackson were always worked as hard in those early conferences as they once were in the Shenandoah or on the Potomac.

Mr. Ogden was both generous and daring in asking me for I was young, radical, none too tactful, and ready to believe that truths which shocked were sometimes called for. At Richmond, in the historic old Governor's Mansion, I was first called on to speak on this trip and I could not refrain from dwelling on the changed conditions which made it possible for me to speak where my grandfather would so cheerfully and happily have been hanged. It may have been historically worth dwelling upon but I cannot say that that brief talk was a great success! I was asked to speak again but in competition with such men as those I have mentioned and Walter H. Page, St. Clair McKelway of the *Brooklyn Eagle*, Hamilton Wright Mabie, the Reverend Francis G. Peabody,

John Graham Brooks, Bishop McVickar, Percy Stickney Grant, Edwin A. Alderman, then president of Tulane University, later long head of the University of Virginia and always one of our most eloquent and gifted orators, and Talcott Williams, I was the veriest flop. It was all a most remarkable trip. The conference itself, and its successors, were truly what Charles W. Eliot termed them in an inscription for a large bronze tablet, the work of Karl Bitter, which was presented to Mr. Ogden by his guests: "Excursions into ennobling experiences." Sometimes, however, feelings did rise high among the participants in the excursions. On a station platform I once heard Andrew Carnegie who had been debating the Philippine wickedness with one of its apologists, the Reverend Lyman Abbott, editor of the *Outlook*, say calmly and deliberately to that divine: "You lie and you know you lie. The truth is not in you!" Some of us promptly terminated that debate.

As we neared Athens, on April 24, 1902, the heat was intense; we had been living on the train and the lack of bathing facilities made the high temperature the less bearable. The train stopped at a junction several miles out and was boarded with true Southern friendliness by a welcoming group of young and old. George Foster Peabody suddenly appeared in the observation car and said to William Jay Schieffelin, A. E. Thomas, and myself: "There are some very pretty girls in this welcoming party and you young men must come and make yourselves agreeable." The one to whom I was assigned, Julia B. Sandford, of Covington, Kentucky, who happened to be visiting in Athens, fully lived up to the description given. We found seats on the rear platform and I got in wrong at once. The train passed a shimmering pool. "My," I panted, "I wish I were in that!" "Really," said she, "to get away from me?" However, I made amends. Miss Sandford, with her hostess, Miss May Hodgson, was asked by Mr. Ogden to go on with us to New York and in November we became engaged at Plattsburg Barracks, at the quarters of Captain and Mrs. John L. Hines of the Twenty-Third Infantry, the former one of our most efficient, and one of the six most distinguished, generals of our war with Germany. At a reunion dinner of the "Ogden party" in November, I was suddenly called upon without warning to explain what I "had found in the South" and how it was that I had surrendered on sight to the daughter of a Confederate captain and whether my education was now complete. We were married in Athens in February, 1903, and after thirty-six years the surrender is still complete and my education is still being taken in hand.

Among many other enduring benefits this alliance aided me in my work for colored and white education in the South by giving me a far better understanding of the Southern point of view and background than I could otherwise have had. It intensified my interest in the innumerable special problems of that part of our country which even in August, 1938, President Roosevelt called our most backward section economically; which today in its continuing injustice to and repression of its colored workers, its denial to them of all self-government, its taxing them without representation, and its open violation of the Constitution of the United States, has created a situation which is still fraught with tremendous danger to the republic.

As a direct result of that trip to Athens I felt that I must identify myself with one of the Southern educational enterprises, and so I became president of the Board of Directors of the Manassas Industrial School in 1903. This was a small, struggling imitation of Hampton, erected near the battlefield of Bull Run—our plows used to turn up relics of both the armies that had encamped on our fields. The founder was a remarkable colored woman, Jennie Dean, who had been born a slave and had had very little education indeed. Her honest countenance and moving appeals for her people loosened many a purse string. For twenty-two years I directed the destinies of that little school without any success whatever beyond the raising of considerable sums of money and the modernizing of the physical plant. Here I must gratefully acknowledge most generous help from Andrew Carnegie who first came to our aid with a check for $1,000 without solicitation because of an article of mine. I flattered myself that it was my moving picture of the school's needs which had brought this check. Not at all; he told me that he sent it because the name Jennie Dean reminded him so of Scott's heroine of the Midlothian, Jeanie Deans! Later Mr. Carnegie gave us a library building but with a warning that no library should ever go beyond 100,000 books. When I asked him what one did when one passed the 100,000 mark, he said, "Give away the oldest." In the depression of 1907 I tremblingly asked him for a renewal of his $1,000. He said: "In these times? Absolutely not. I'll not give you $1,000, I'll give you $2,000." And his check for that sum was annually forthcoming until he died. My work at Manassas was one of my outstanding failures but it gave me so clear an insight into the underlying problems, the weaknesses, and shortcomings of the colored people that I have felt more than compensated for my time and trouble. At least I know why it is that they have been so retarded in achieving the economic or political power in our national life which a solid front of twelve millions of Americans could exercise. I believe that I got more education out of my connection with Manassas than any pupil who sat upon its benches. Finally I resigned because the colored people of the neighboring counties would not do their share in financing the enterprise.

With *The Evening Post's* absolute devotion to the gold standard and its hostility to Theodore Roosevelt, which was as intense in June, 1904, as it could possibly be, it is not surprising that the editors were thrilled by Alton B. Parker's telegraphic declination of the Democratic nomination unless the platform contained an out-and-out gold plank. Rejoicing in the final elimination of Hearst, and forgetting that one telegram does not necessarily make a good candidate, Mr. Ogden headed his paean of praise "A Man at Last" and defied the adulators of Theodore Roosevelt to show a single instance in which their idol had taken a stand approximating the moral courage displayed by Judge Parker. Never before had a plain citizen "declined a Presidential nomination already made unless his convictions and his honor were cleared. . . ." It was, Mr. Ogden wrote, a "calmly heroic act," so "bold in conception, so triumphant in execution" that it drove the last nail into the coffin of free silver and established the gold standard "better than an act of Congress." In his enthusiasm Mr. Ogden forgot that a year previously, when Judge Parker had discussed the Fourteenth Amendment before the Bar Association of Georgia and never once mentioned the grave political issues involved, he had also written:[3] "If wholly to avoid the burning questions of the day is to show yourself a fit man for the Presidency, then Judge Parker's address should have sensibly advanced his candidacy."

Still it was difficult not to enthuse for one who had been so excellent a chief judge and had now deliberately preferred to lose the nomination and perhaps the Presidency rather than to run under a false flag. I was in Europe at the time of the conventions but returned in time to hear Judge Parker's dignified, judicially written speech of acceptance at his home at Esopus. That address was particularly satisfactory to us for its really admirable demonstration of the un-American character of the tawdry militarism (tiny, indeed, beside that of the Democrats in 1939) in which the Republicans had been indulging. His Philippine views were also entirely in accord with ours and his tariff pronouncement sane, realistic, and patently honest. That speech enthused me, too, but I got a chill one day when calling upon the Judge to find him in close consultation with Thomas F. Ryan and August Belmont, whose influence upon the campaign became greater and greater as it waxed. Mr. Belmont alone put up more than $250,000 for the Parker campaign fund. There can be no doubt that if Parker had been elected the Wall Street crowd would have had nothing whatever to fear from him. At that we infinitely preferred him to Theodore Roosevelt for whose brilliant and audacious campaigning, however, the solemn Judge's straightforwardness and dignity were no match.

Curiously enough, as the campaign waxed Theodore Roosevelt, the bold and the brave, became panic-stricken because of a fear that he was really in danger of defeat when there was no danger

[3] *The Nation*, July 16, 1903.

of that whatsoever. Defeat he could not face and so, yielding to his terror, he stooped to the most pitiful if not contemptible act of his career—he sold himself for campaign funds to the very Big Business men whom he had so long been calling, with truth, "the malefactors of great wealth." He sent for them, made terms with them, and the campaign coffers of the Republican Party were correspondingly enriched by a quarter of a million dollars. Among those involved in this purchase and sale was Daniel S. Lamont, a former private secretary of President Cleveland and then the president of the Northern Pacific Railroad. At the eleventh hour of the campaign he told the whole story to Judge Parker whose election he, as a Democrat, favored, but swore the Judge to secrecy as to names and details. The Judge made general charges that President Roosevelt and the Chairman of the Republican National Committee, George B. Cortelyou, had used their official positions to induce large corporations and Big Business men to contribute funds. Roosevelt did the only possible thing. He flatly denied, on November 4, the truth of the insinuation that Mr. Cortelyou had made use of knowledge gained in office to obtain contributions from corporations. He similarly denied that anyone "in my behalf and by my authority" had made any pledge or promise. He said that "it is a wicked falsehood" that "there has been any understanding as to future immunity or benefits in recognition of any contributions from any source." Judge Parker, being unable to respond by giving names, amounts, and the place where the surrender occurred, was at a complete disadvantage. Most of the public considered Parker's attack a last-hour campaign roorback and it undoubtedly injured Parker. When the election returns were in, Theodore Roosevelt wrote to his son: "I am stunned by the overwhelming victory we have won. I have the greatest popular majority and the greatest electoral majority ever given to a candidate for President." [4]

But the matter of Judge Parker's charges did not end there. Not even a year later George W. Perkins, of the New York Life

[4] J. B. Bishop, *Roosevelt and His Time*, New York, 1920, Vol. I, p. 335.

Insurance Company, testified that that corporation gave nearly fifty thousand dollars to promote the election of Mr. Roosevelt. More than that, it was done in a devious manner. Mr. Perkins gave his personal check for the amount and not until a month after the election was the New York Life check drawn. Naturally Judge Parker took the opportunity to point out how this revelation upheld his contentions. He did not pretend that his party was of superior virtue in the matter of accepting funds from corporations but only reiterated what he had charged the year previous—that the *big corporations'* checks went to the Republicans. More than a year later Edward H. Harriman made the public charge that Roosevelt had requested him to raise $250,000 for the Presidential campaign. Again Mr. Roosevelt made a sweeping denial, saying: "I never requested Mr. Harriman to raise a dollar for the Presidential campaign of 1904. On the contrary, our communications as regards the campaign related exclusively to the fight being made against Mr. Higgins for Governor of New York. . . . He was concerned only in getting me to tell Mr. Cortelyou to aid Mr. Higgins so far as he could, which I gladly did." There the matter rested until Roosevelt was running for the Presidency on the Bull Moose ticket in 1912.[5] There was a period during that campaign when many people really feared Roosevelt's re-election. During this time I was called on the telephone by a man who said: "You do not know me but you may have heard of my banking house, Thomas L. Manson & Company. I am Mr. Manson. I have a matter of the utmost importance bearing on the campaign that I wish to discuss with you because I believe that you are the one editor who will handle the matter. I am afraid that for certain reasons I must ask you to come to my office to talk with me. I hope you will forgive this and come." Naturally I went at once.

As soon as we were alone Mr. Manson, who turned out to be

---

[5] On the night of his triumphal sweep in 1904 Roosevelt had issued the statement reading: "The wise custom which limits the President to two terms regards the substance and not the form, and under no circumstances will I be a candidate or accept another nomination."

a very high grade man, told me the following story: "I asked you to come," he said, "because I am afraid that Roosevelt is going to be elected and I think that that is the worst thing that could happen to the country. I hold him to be thoroughly dishonest and proof of that is what I am going to tell you now. I was one of the most intimate friends of the late Hamilton McK. Twombly, a director of the Jersey Central Railroad.[6] From him I learned not once, but on several occasions, the true story of what took place between Theodore Roosevelt and prominent Wall Street men in the campaign of 1904. I think it should be published now and that if it is published it will defeat Roosevelt. I cannot, however, figure in the matter myself because of personal reasons and so I have asked you to come in the hope that after I have told you the facts you will be able to print them in *The Evening Post*." He then revealed that Roosevelt had sent word to Twombly, Harriman, Frick, Lamont, and others that he wished to see them at the White House and that it would be well worth their while to come to see him. The group assembled at Twombly's magnificent home at Morristown, had dinner there, and were driven in automobiles to a private car which was sidetracked at the further end of the Pennsylvania terminal in Jersey City. No one was allowed to know who was in the party or what the purpose was except those who composed the group. The midnight train to Washington picked up the car and dropped it early the next morning some distance from the Washington station.

There the travelers were routed out and driven in automobiles to the White House which they reached at seven o'clock. They were taken in by the entrance opposite to the Treasury Department and were immediately ushered into the President's presence. They found him in a complete funk. He told them that unless a large sum of money was raised Parker would carry the election. He must have at least a quarter of a million, and at once. He then promised this group, whom he had so bitterly attacked, whose business methods he had usually so correctly criticized, that if they

[6] He was also an officer or director of no less than forty-nine other corporations.

gave him that money they would have nothing further to fear from him during his second term as President. He declared that it would be much worse for them if they allowed Parker to be elected if only because of Parker's stand on the tariff. They took his word, accepted his surrender, and gave him the money he desired. It was not possible to doubt Mr. Manson's sincerity or the depths of his indignation that a man capable of such an act might really be again elected President. I pointed out to him, however, the gravity of the charges. I could not publish the story as he told it to me without being certain of a violent attack if not a libel suit. He then suggested that I get into touch with Henry C. Frick and find out the truth from him. As soon thereafter as possible I made an appointment with Mr. Frick who was at his home at Pride's Crossing, Massachusetts.

As soon as Mr. Frick heard the object of my coming he related the whole story with the utmost frankness. I did not have to tell him what Mr. Manson had said to me, and his narrative corroborated the former's at every point. He gave a graphic description of that early morning call at the White House and then said with astounding bluntness: "He got down on his knees to us. We bought the son of a bitch and then he did not stay bought." [7] When I asked him whether he did not think the story should be published he declared that it should be, but of course added that he would have to consult his lawyer before I could quote him. My heart sank at that. I could not conceive of any lawyer who might be employed by Henry C. Frick encouraging him to invite the vituperation and denunciation which he would face if he stood for this story. My forecast was right; in a few days I received word that Mr. Frick regretted his lawyer's decision but that he must stand by it. On August 28, 1912, I published an emasculated story in *The Evening Post*; it had no effect whatever, not any more than a broadside of a page I compiled for *The Evening Post* con-

[7] Mr. Frick doubtless had in mind, among other things, a violent attack by Roosevelt on August 20, 1907, at Provincetown, Massachusetts, upon the rich "malefactors" who, he said, had "combined to bring about financial stress" in order to "discredit the policy of the Government"—i.e., himself.

trasting Theodore Roosevelt's promises and preachments with his actual practices.

As I rose to leave Mr. Frick he asked me if I would not like to see his pictures. I accepted with alacrity for I had never seen that wonderful collection which is now one of the great assets of the City of New York. While looking at them I asked him if those that I beheld there were the same that he had in New York and found that they were. "Do you *really* venture to bring them up here every spring and take them back every fall?" I asked him. "Yes, indeed," said he. "I have a steel car specially made for their transportation. They come out on the night train to Boston and then the car is shunted across Boston and brought up here." "Still," I replied, "aren't you afraid that something might happen to them even then?" "Oh, no," said he, "they are insured." This recalls my once hearing Charles M. Schwab say, in reply to a man's praise of the exquisite Titian in his New York city home, that it had cost him $150,000 and was lovely but that if he again had such a sum "to blow in I would put it in a blast furnace. I get so much more pleasure out of that."

Chapter XI. Hughes, Taft, and a New Crusade

I HAVE often been accused of yielding to misguided enthusiasm for public men and believing that in this one or in that one a political savior was at hand, and I must plead guilty to the charge—until Woodrow Wilson and Ramsay MacDonald cured me of that habit. Probably I did stress too much getting a "good man" into high office rather than changing fundamental conditions. That was partly because McKinley proved how easy it was for a foolish, weak, or unfaithful man in the White House to alter all by himself the whole policy of the country. Moreover, it takes many years to alter fundamental economic conditions or the governmental structure, so one always hopes for a short cut. At any rate, during the years Charles E. Hughes was en route to the Capitol at Albany, and during his residence there, I was enthusiastically for him and once set forth my belief that he realized my ideal of a public servant "more nearly than anyone else whom I have seen in office. I do not mean that he agrees with me on policies, but that he is in every respect that which Roosevelt pretends to be, a true reformer and a real public servant. . . . That he feels that he owes his allegiance solely to the people every official act bears witness. Thomas Mott Osborne agrees with me that he is the best Democrat we have in the State today." [1]

Like the *World*, and other independent newspapers, we had been pounding the insurance companies whose heads owned them and treated them as their private property to be milked as they saw fit without the slightest regard for the rights of the policyholders. We had long charged the companies with playing politics and paying out what should have been trust funds to the campaign treasurers of the two parties. Yet no one was prepared for the

[1] To Francis J. Garrison, January 28, 1908.

revelations which came when President Alexander of the Equitable Life, and his vice-president, James Hazen Hyde, fell out. Then it was discovered that Mr. Hyde, still a very young man, had had his salary increased, with the aid of Chauncey Depew, from $30,000 to $100,000, had added $27,000 more as salaries paid him by subsidiaries of the Equitable, for which he gave no return, and had attempted to use the company's funds for defraying the expenses of elaborate social occasions of his own. When the Equitable Life stock was suddenly purchased by a Thomas F. Ryan syndicate and Paul Morton put in as president, we promptly protested that it was grossly improper that a man whose questionable railway career was at that moment under investigation by government law officers should be given such a responsibility.

During this preliminary scandal the other big companies protested their own virtue. When the official inquiry began, Mr. Hughes, keen, fearless, and unapproachable, tore the masks from them all and what came out deeply stirred the public by its rottenness. Naturally this brought Mr. Hughes straight to the front and led to his immediately being considered for the highest office in the State, without inquiring whether he was actually fitted for the administering of the affairs of the great commonwealth; a prosecutor's talents are not necessarily those of a great executive. But Governor Hughes proved from the beginning that he did have the necessary qualities and carried to Albany his readiness to give every ounce of strength to the office that he had assumed. We, in our shop, were particularly delighted with the campaign which he made against William R. Hearst in 1906 after the Democratic Party had been so foolish as to allow itself to be bribed or talked into nominating that editor for Governor. Mr. Hughes won that election by the force and drive that he put into the campaign.

With lucidity and precision he put the case in his telegram of acceptance when he declared that his task was: "To defend the honor of the State, to represent the common sense of the people in the cause of decent government." Never were party platforms as rapidly discarded. It was just a question of Hearst or Hughes. Decent Democrats everywhere bolted Hearst; not a reputable

Democratic newspaper in the Democratic city of New York supported him. He who had been violently and usefully attacking Boss Murphy, Grady, and the Sullivans of Tammany rushed into their arms—Murphy he had been calling the greatest criminal of the age, a thief, and the hireling of the corporations; to send this man to Sing Sing, he had again and again declared, was his greatest aim. Hearst, we said, "will go through the State carried on the back of Murphy, infamy joined to freebooting." Yet, despite the clarity of the issue, despite the utter disparity in decency and character of the two candidates, Hughes won by only 55,000. It had been thought that his majority would be at least 200,000.

The explanation of this was not a low moral tone on the part of the electorate. It was the era of muckraking and of a tremendous popular upsurge against the mismanagement of the great corporations, of the insurance companies, of the Standard Oil Company as exposed by government investigators, and of the New York Central as illustrated by its rebates to the Sugar Trust. It was an era of indignation against the anthracite monopoly and the Ice Trust, against the stock jobbing and stock watering and exploitation of the public by the utility corporations in practically every city in the State of New York. The people wanted redress, knew that the time was ripe for it, and turned to Hearst because his newspapers had been so outspoken in their attacks upon the great evildoers; doubtless they brushed aside Hearst's surrender to Tammany as necessary in order to obtain office. To many of them Mr. Hughes seemed merely a corporation attorney who had done one good job in clearing up the insurance companies. We, and the other liberal newspapers, warned Mr. Hughes in the hour of his triumph that if he did not do his utmost to check abuses and redress grievances, and if the rotten Republican machine prevented his obtaining reform, then Hearst or someone else would certainly succeed him. We admitted that corporations had rights to be respected but we said: "Our common carriers cannot be allowed to use their immensely valuable franchises from the public as instruments of discrimination; our traction and lighting companies are not licensed to loot our cities; our antimonopoly law must not be violated with impunity."

Mr. Hughes showed at once that he needed no warning but he found it extremely difficult to obtain from the boss-ridden Legislature what he wanted. Still, by January, 1908, the beginning of his second year, we were able to say that the attention of the whole country was fixed upon the Governor of New York to a degree unequaled since the days of Tilden and Cleveland. He was already being much talked about for the Presidential nomination and his second message to the legislature was carefully scanned to see if there were not some views in it for general consumption. It was a quiet, straightforward, unemotional, and businesslike utterance which dealt only with State affairs. There was not the slightest appeal to the country as a whole or indication that he was then taking the talk of the nomination seriously. On January 26 I called upon him and asked him if he would care to discuss with me the question of the Presidency and a coming speech. He said: "It will do me good to talk to you." And he gave me a great deal of time.

Because of the light it throws upon his development at that period, part of our talk is worth printing here. He confessed frankly that he had not had time to think his way through the many national problems for he had been wrapped up in his professional career until he had been sent to Albany where he had been driven, night and day, "until I am often at the end of my strength." He declared that if the nomination were offered he would accept it because he thought that no man in good health had the right to decline such an honor. "But," he added, "if I should have to take the nomination, it would be with the profoundest misgiving of my ability to do it justice and with full cognizance of the fact that three-quarters of our Presidents have been such insignificant characters as not to be worth writing about in the book of history." He talked freely about his relations to President Roosevelt, stating that the latter did not consider him a practical man but that the kind of practical politics which he was urged to play was repugnant to his moral sense and also seemed to him the worst kind of politics. "In fact," he said, "I find the practical politician is one who cannot see beyond his nose or is wholly wrapped up in his own petty jealousies and his disgust over this grievance or that grievance. When I am free from office I shall want to write or speak on the duty of a statesman in a democracy and the first thing I shall say will be that it is not a statesman's duty to blurt out the first idea that comes into his mind." This was a direct slap at Roosevelt.

Mr. Hughes agreed with me that it is a misfortune that our people, once they place a man in office, accept everything from him as wise and good merely because he says it. He spoke of himself as being "a tariff reform protectionist" but as being entirely ignorant of the tariff schedules of that day. On my return to my office I noted: "He is naturally a States' rights man but he feels that it is impossible to lay down a definite line beyond which there shall never be federal legislation because no one can tell what industrial conditions may be confronted fifty years hence. Above all, the man's transparent sincerity and honesty and his great earnestness give the listener the absolute conviction that no amount of pressure could make him swerve an iota from the course that he has laid down for himself. Indeed, this year at Albany makes this absolutely clear. The Governor stated that he would on no account accept a re-election to the governorship as he could not afford it. He will also not accept the Vice-Presidency on any terms." I added that if anyone should get the impression that Mr. Hughes had been, and still was, a narrow man, it would not be altogether wrong. He *was* narrow, obstinate, and opinionated.

As the time for the gubernatorial nomination came around, Mr. Hughes did accept it again, the Presidential nomination having gone to William H. Taft by order of Theodore Roosevelt. Mr. Hughes felt that he must carry on the battle against the evil forces in Albany and in sticking to the task he rendered a genuine public service at heavy cost to himself, because he never liked the job, because he hated life in Albany, and it was steadily impoverishing him. Up to that time he had never compromised with a politician, made his appointments for office from merit solely, and had exposed himself to the bitterest attacks from the machine politicians of both parties. He had given battle to the bosses of his own party and he—the corporation lawyer—was determined to make still more complete the divorce between the public service corporation and the politician and he wanted direct primary nominations and a reform of the election laws written on the statute books before he gave up public office. At the time, the common verdict was that he was "the best Governor since Grover Cleveland." The Republican politicians were thoroughly opposed to his renomination but Roosevelt, Taft, and Hitchcock forced the State bosses to swing into line for the Governor. This time his plurality was larger than in 1906—being 69,462.

When William H. Taft accepted the Republican nomination at the hands of Theodore Roosevelt, he invited the disaster which overtook him. No man should put himself under such an obligation to another, especially when that other is one of Theodore Roosevelt's temperament; if he does, grave trouble is certain. Mr. Roosevelt did the handsome and wise thing in leaving the country soon after Mr. Taft's nomination. While he was away, however, his thick and thin adherents, who would not believe that any successor could be worthy of Theodore Roosevelt, began making trouble by writing him reports of Mr. Taft's delinquencies. Before the Colonel emerged from Europe, where he was lecturing to crowned heads—and actually told Lord Cromer to his face, after a few days in Egypt, wherein that veteran English administrator had failed—I was called upon by one of Taft's closest associates to get my opinion of what would happen on Roosevelt's return. I made a correct forecast and told him that I believed Theodore would return in a hostile spirit. My questioner was not convinced and insisted that I was letting long-standing prejudices influence my judgment.

Mr. Taft's administration was no greater success because he was never by nature intended for this office. He was a charming gentleman, one of the finest who ever entered the White House. He was kindly, well-meaning, absolutely honest, and entirely guiltless of any purpose to turn the United States over to the reactionaries. He was merely true to his training and ultraconservatism. His

great vice was that he was extremely lazy and a great procrasti-
nator—William J. Bryan called him "The Great Postponer"—and
these traits led him into one pitfall after another. Take the cases
of his mistaken decision as to the merits of the Ballinger-Pinchot
controversy and his famous Winona speech on the tariff. I happen
to know the facts as to both. The papers in the Ballinger-Pinchot
case, when they were ready for the President's final decision, came
to a sizeable pile, one which called for hours of labor adequately
to digest, even although one had had Mr. Taft's experience as a
judge and a high administrator. He put off reading those papers
until the last day. He was at his summer White House in Beverly.
It was a beautiful day and the President could not resist the
temptation when the Yale golf team appeared and challenged
him, to go out and play with them. He yielded and had a wonderful time, ate a huge dinner, and napped off after it. Finally,
awakened by his secretary, he set himself to the task and tried,
between that time and a couple of hours after midnight, to master
the controversy which did so much to wreck his administration
politically and to stamp it as reactionary. For in this last-minute
study of the case he reached the wrong decision.

The next day he started for the West and at Winona met with
disaster—later he admitted that he had written the Winona speech
"between stations"; again he was tricked by his procrastination.
In that speech he stood with the stand patters when his own party
was surging with a new spirit, when George W. Norris, William
E. Borah, and Robert LaFollette were already voicing the real
desires of the Republicans of the Middle West. These men naturally offered no quarter to the President who signed the Payne-
Aldrich Tariff Bill. That represented a repudiation of Republican
pledges but this did not prevent Mr. Taft's signing it and prais-
ing it as a great achievement. Naturally Mr. Taft opposed the
initiative, the referendum, the recall, and the direct primary. A
number of valuable laws were passed in Mr. Taft's Presidency
but for these he personally never received due credit; they were
offset by his opposition to the insurgency in his own party, by his
dismissal of Gifford Pinchot from the office of Chief Forester for

insubordination, and by his restoration to private entry of one and one-half million acres of public lands in Montana and Wyoming. To the faults already cited must be added that he had too great readiness to entrust heavy responsibilities to men around him whom he had not always selected wisely.

When Mr. Taft's term ended in 1912, our journalistic judgment upon him was:

He fell upon a time of huge discontent and ferment. His party split beneath his eyes. He was made the object of venomous calumny and treacherous betrayal. A veritable scandal machine was set operating early in his administration with the deliberate purpose of discrediting him and breaking him down. Finally came the supreme disloyalty: first the hidden and insidious attack, then the open and vengeful assault, by Theodore Roosevelt. What man could have stood up before all this? [2]

On the other side of the ledger was Mr. Taft's total lack of the higher political imagination, of "quick sympathy and popular quality which would have enabled him to take arms against his sea of troubles. . . . Political disaster after political disaster he failed to recognize in its beginnings." We might also have added that his personal ties with the men of influence in Wall Street were much too close; they had been his warm friends and he continued the relationships.

The great glory of Mr. Taft's administration was his refusal to be stampeded into war with Mexico although the temptation to go in, and thus direct attention away from the dreadfully unhappy domestic situation, must have been great. That was a real and vital contribution to the cause of peace which should not be forgotten in any judgment of Mr. Taft. Similarly, no one should overlook his consistent friendliness to the Filipinos and his unusual understanding of their point of view, together with his freedom from color- and race-prejudice, notably when he was Governor General in the Philippines. He never failed to insist that America should live up to its pledges to the people of the archipelago. These

[2] *The Nation*, March 6, 1913, p. 222.

things make it all the sadder that the higher attributes of national leadership were denied to so clean, kindly, and honorable a man in a time which demanded a great and farsighted statesman.

I look back upon my own relations with Mr. Taft with the greatest satisfaction.[3] For a time his private secretary in the White House was Charles Dyer Norton, one of the most attractive and brilliant young men of his day, who had married at Thorwood my cousin, Katherine Garrison, to whom I have always been bound in ties of especial affection. This gave me a particular interest in the Taft administration, so far as that was possible for one of my radically different political philosophy. On one occasion, at a great dinner of the New York Peace Society on February 26, 1909, my wife and I had the privilege of being at a small round table chockablock with President Taft, Elihu Root, Joseph H. Choate, and Andrew Carnegie. On the way out—I had to leave early—I met William Jennings Bryan coming in to speak, perspiring violently—sweating would be the truer word; he had already made one long speech somewhere else. We had a pleasant chat in the hall. Strangely enough, he and I were the only ones of that whole group who thought that when you believed war was the sum of all evils and that no good whatever could come of it, you should be true to that belief not only in times of peace but when war came. Five years later the war was upon us and all those public men at the tables of the New York Peace Society that night in 1909 were for our joining in.

The centennial of the birth of Abraham Lincoln took place the month before Mr. Taft became President. On that anniversary there met in New York a national conference to discuss the plight of the Negro, which conference was instigated by Mary White Ovington, William English Walling, Henry Moskowitz, and myself. Walling was a Southerner, a Socialist of a flamingly liberal spirit, married to a fine Russian-American, Anna Strunsky, who

[3] It is true, however, that he was, near the end of his Presidency, bitterly incensed by criticisms in *The Evening Post*, Indianapolis *News*, and Boston *Herald*, and put into a message to Congress a passage denouncing us as intellectually dishonest and tools of the criminal rich! He finally omitted it.

had suffered imprisonment when quite a young girl for taking part in the revolutionary movement in Russia against the Czar. Walling had become convinced, despite his upbringing, that the Southern treatment of the Negro was as blind and as stupid and as inimical to the interests of the white people as it was un-American, contrary to the spirit of our democratic institutions, and often wickedly cruel and immoral. Like the rest of us he had become gravely alarmed by the spread of lynching and race rioting to the North. In the summer of 1908 the North had been shocked—while a large part of the South exulted—because of the grievous race riots in Springfield, Illinois, the home of Abraham Lincoln. There a mob, including, the press said, many of the town's "best citizens," took possession of Springfield for two days, killing and wounding scores of Negroes and driving thousands from the city. This was too much for Walling. He declared in *The Independent*: [4] "Either the spirit of the Abolitionists, of Lincoln, and of Lovejoy must be revived and we must come to treat the Negro on a plane of absolute political and social equality, or Vardaman and Tillman will soon have transferred the race war to the North."

Mary White Ovington had already been fired with a desire to aid the Negro; she was at that moment living in a Negro tenement on a Negro street in New York and had been for four years studying the terrible conditions under which Negroes were then living there—they are little improved today. To the Negroes she has given the greater part of her life with an unselfishness, a patience, a sweetness of spirit, and a kindliness hard to describe adequately. Henry Moskowitz was later prominent in the administration of Mayor Mitchel. With the broad knowledge which he possessed he joined Mr. Walling and Mary White Ovington in a preliminary conference at which Lincoln's birthday was chosen for the beginning of the campaign and they arrived at the decision that their next step should be to enlist my aid—no greater compliment has ever been paid to me. Naturally I received them with enthusiasm, aided them in securing the co-operation of able and representative men and women, and drafted for them the call for

[4] *The Independent*, September 3, 1908.

the Lincoln's birthday conference and helped in giving it wide publicity. In that call I declared that the centennial celebration would fail to justify itself if it made "no recognition of the colored men and women for whom the great Emancipator labored to assure freedom." I felt that to honor Lincoln adequately we should inquire how far the country had lived up to the obligations of the Emancipation Proclamation and how far it had gone in assuring to each citizen, irrespective of color, the equality of opportunity and equality before the law, which underlie our American institutions and are guaranteed by the Constitution.

The call continued thus:

If Mr. Lincoln could revisit this country in the flesh, he would be disheartened and discouraged. He would learn that on January 1, 1909, Georgia had rounded out a new confederacy by disfranchising the Negro, after the manner of all the other Southern States. . . . He would learn that the Supreme Court . . . has laid down the principle that if an individual state chooses, it may "make it a crime for white and colored persons to frequent the same market place at the same time, or appear in an assemblage of citizens convened to consider questions of a public or political nature in which all citizens, without regard to race, are equally interested. . . ." [5]

Silence under these conditions means tacit approval. . . . "A house divided against itself cannot stand"; this government cannot exist half slave and half free any better today than it could in 1861, hence we call upon all the believers in democracy to join in a national conference for the discussion of present evils, the voicing of protests and the renewal of the struggle for civil and political liberty.[6]

The call was signed by Jane Addams, Samuel Bowles of the Springfield, Mass., *Republican,* Harriot Stanton Blatch, John Dewey, William Lloyd Garrison, Jr., William Dean Howells, the Rev. Dr. Charles H. Parkhurst, Anna Garlin Spencer, Charles Edward Russell, Hamilton Holt, Lincoln Steffens, President

[5] The words of Justice John M. Harlan in his dissent from the decision of the Supreme Court in the Berea College case.

[6] See Mary White Ovington, *How The National Association for the Advancement of Colored People Was Founded,* pamphlet, New York.

Charles F. Thwing, of Western Reserve University, Horace White, Lillian D. Wald, President Mary E. Woolley of Mount Holyoke, Professor Charles E. Zueblin, and a distinguished group of colored men, among them Doctor W. E. B. DuBois, the Reverend Francis J. Grimke of Washington, Bishop Alexander Walters, the Reverend Doctor J. Milton Waldron, and W. L. Bulkley. The date set for the conference was May 30 and more than one thousand persons were invited. Of the large number who came, many engaged in religious, social, and educational work "for the first time met the Negro who demands, not a pittance, but his full rights in the commonwealth. They received a stimulating shock and one which they enjoyed. They did not want to leave the meeting." The latter went on for several days.

The result was the birth of the National Association for the Advancement of Colored People with its platform of the abolition of all caste distinctions based simply on race and color, and the recognition of the principle of human brotherhood. From the first it has always stood unequivocally and uncompromisingly and militantly for the absolute right of the Negro to every privilege guaranteed to the white man by the Constitution of the United States. Its founding marked a milestone in the development of the colored people in the United States and was one of the movements which I helped to originate as to which I have no regrets, in which I can take unqualified satisfaction. It has had at times more than 100,000 members and it has achieved extraordinary results, not only in increasing race solidarity but in developing leadership and in stiffening the backbone of white politicians and spurring the white friends of the race to renewed efforts. That was my conception from the beginning—that it should be aggressive, that it should be the watchdog of Negro liberties, and that it should allow no wrong to take place without its protesting and bringing all the pressure to bear that it possibly could.

Under the leadership of Doctor W. E. B. DuBois, so many years the editor of our monthly publication *The Crisis*, of the lamented James Weldon Johnson, of Walter White, Professor Joel E. Spingarn, Mary White Ovington, Arthur Spingarn, Mr. Walling, John E. Milholland, Henry Moskowitz, and a number of others, the work has gone steadily on. The victories won in the Supreme Court on behalf of the Negro alone would have justified the founding of the Association and all the labor and money put into it. That the federal antilynching bill has come so near passing has been solely due to the Association and latterly to the leadership of the present secretary, Walter White. I feel strongly that tremendous progress has been made since that historic Lincoln Centennial call was sent out. I am especially happy to add that most of my encouragement comes out of the South; the growth of the anti-Negro prejudice in the North is the discouraging factor. The number of emancipated and fearless Southerners who dare to stand up for the rights of the colored people has tremendously increased. When I reached Athens, Georgia, in 1903 for my wedding, I was waited upon by a delegation of colored people who begged my aid. Their spokesman was the superintendent of the Negro schools. The committee told me then that their greatest danger came from the undergraduates of the University of Georgia and that no Negro girl child of twelve was safe at night upon the streets of Athens. More than thirty years later on another visit to Athens I was again asked to see some colored people among whom, curiously enough, was the then superintendent of Negro schools. When I asked my visitors about the undergraduates I was told that their relations with the white young people of the university and the town were of the friendliest and best.

I have dwelt upon this most encouraging change of opinion in the South elsewhere.[7] There is a notable improvement in the matter of the sex relations between the white men and the colored women. There is still a tremendous amount of miscegenation; there are still thousands of illegitimate mulatto children born to black women and this condition will continue as long as laws exist preventing intermarriage and placing the Negro woman at the mercy of the white man; public opinion in most communities will

[7] O. G. Villard, "The Crumbling Color Line," *Harper's*, July, 1929.

not permit her to sue the father of her child for its support. Nevertheless, things are happening all over the South that would have been absolutely impossible in 1909. For example, I have photographs of a group of young white and colored people traveling North together from Virginia to attend a religious conference, the members of the party sharing Pullmans and having their meals together in the dining car. There are militant young white Southerners of excellent families who do not hesitate to enter Negro homes in order to know, in the most honorable and friendly spirit, the residents therein. In December, 1938, there happened in Birmingham, Alabama, something almost unbelievable. The Southern Conference for Human Welfare met there 1,200 strong, whites and blacks in fullest fraternity. When police marched in and compelled the races to sit by themselves the angry Conference promptly resolved that Congress pass at once the Federal anti-lynching bill and a Federal uniform suffrage law which *would give votes to the blacks!* So far has the South advanced since the Athens Conference of 1903. To the Interracial Conference movement we also owe great progress. Until the Atlanta riots it had never occurred to anybody in the South that it would be a wise and statesmanlike move to form joint committees of Negroes and whites in the large communities to discuss amicably and fairly the problems arising out of the juxtaposition of the two races—problems that were by no means one-sided but were often due to the absence of efficient, just, and modern administration of towns and villages. There is still a long road to go but no just man can deny the astounding progress already made.

This can be illustrated in the North also. On April 27, 1908, a year before the founding of the N.A.A.C.P., a group of us met at dinner in a restaurant on Fulton Street, solely to discuss the economic relationship of the races in New York City. Of course there were whites and blacks of both sexes present. How would it have been possible to treat this subject with colored people absent and the rest of us unable to obtain their point of view? Unfortunately the secretary had sent notices to the press—at that early stage in the brief existence of the Cosmopolitan Club publicity was

not desirable or needed. A drunken reporter from a Hearst newspaper, so drunk as hardly to be able to stand, came up to me as
to others and asked in his befuddled condition what it all meant.
The story which the Hearst papers printed the next day was one
of the falsest and foulest that I have ever read in any newspaper.
It declared that coal-black colored men were leering at white
women and forcing their attentions upon them; there was much
worse than that and the whole meeting was portrayed as a movement for social equality instead of for civic betterment. This story
was copied all over the United States and those of us whose names
appeared in it were overwhelmed with the most violent abuse,
much of it foul and obscene. For six weeks Mary White Ovington,
in herself the personification of lovely and spiritual womanhood,
was compelled to have her mail opened by male relatives.

As for the editorial writers, why, they were in clover and, as
is the habit of the fraternity, few indeed stopped to inquire into
the facts. One of the most amusing editorials appeared in the
New York *Times*, in which the Southern prejudices of Adolph S.
Ochs came to the surface—it is a fact that some of the most rabid
anti-Negro Southerners that I have met during my life have been
Jews. In this editorial the *Times* said:

This particular banquet, we think, provoking as it must the public disgust and indignation, will serve to call the attention of the community
to certain forces of evil that have been rather actively at work of late,
and will, if we mistake not, tend in a marked degree to check and destroy them through the odious exhibition now made of what they really
mean. . . . In the North we may be said to have no Negro question,
but there is a Negro question in the South, and it would be well-nigh
impossible to do the Negroes of the South a greater injury than was
done by these flabby-minded persons who assembled in New York City
on Monday to talk about and to exemplify the social "equality" of the
races.

It then went on to charge that the whole dinner was a deliberate
attempt on the part of Socialists to spread their doctrine—"the
real Socialists, the persons who are seeking by pen and speech and

by all the arts of agitation and mob leadership, by revolution if necessary, to destroy society, and with it the home and religion"! The attitude of the Southern press toward the Northern "nigger-lovers" we were represented to be need not be described. Here, too, time has wrought its changes. It is a commonplace now to see colored men and women at public dinners in all the leading hotels in New York City. At a recent dinner in the Mayflower Hotel in that great citadel of anti-Negro prejudice, Washington, D. C., I rejoiced to see colored among the whites—this in the capital in which, until a few years ago, it was impossible for colored people to sit among white people at the concerts given by the great artists of their own race, like Roland Hayes. Even the white friends of Southern education belonging to the groups behind the General Education Board, the Phelps Stokes Fund, and similar organizations, no longer are afraid of having it known that they dine with colored people. At a dinner given by one of these groups to a great British colonial administrator I noted with satisfaction that forty per cent of those present were colored. Of course the *Times* did not attack that dinner; for one thing there were rich and influential business men there.

My work for the colored people was by no means my only non-professional activity during these years. On January 1, 1907, there appeared the first issue of *Yachting*, a creation of mine which bids fair to be as permanent as any specialized publication can be. Robert M. McBride, the book publisher, had charge with me of the launching of this craft, and the first editor was Lawrence Perry. He was succeeded by my schoolmate and lifelong friend, Herbert L. Stone, who has been its clever and popular skipper ever since. I parted from it at a time when I was too absorbed in other matters to be able to give it personal attention and I rejoice that its present success, and the tremendous development of the sport, even during the depression, give every indication that my belief in the need of a high-class yachting publication was thoroughly warranted.[8] *Yachting* was the outgrowth, too, of three sum-

---

[8] In 1918 I became the owner for a number of years of *The Nautical Gazette*, but here my judgment went entirely wrong. The trade was averse to any inde-

mers of ownership of a 35-foot sloop, the *Hilgarda*, which gave me great happiness and added to my thrilling memories one of being rescued by a coast guard lifeboat when we were dismasted in a heavy blow and high seas off Sandy Hook.

At all times I eagerly shared my mother's enthusiasm and labors for the woman suffrage cause and joined with Mr. Ogden in committing *The Evening Post* to it. On our side of the water campaigning for votes for women was wholly without risk and tame enough—not nearly so thrilling as the battle to keep this country at peace. Only two experiences stand out: I was one of the eighty-four men who marched in the first joint suffrage parade in 1911. As luck would have it we formed right under the windows of the University Club and I could discern in them the faces of scoffing friends, who were doubtless much outraged at this latest proof of the insanity of that crank Villard. From the club to Union Square we were booed, hissed, and ridiculed without a moment's cessation. The crowd generally assumed that we were not there of our own free will and reflections upon the masculinity of our wives and our low estate in our own homes were common. "Did she make you come?" "And who's doing the cooking while you're out?" were among the milder queries. At Union Square, Anna Shaw, one of the greatest and most effective of the leaders, a lovely person if there ever was one, my mother, and I, spoke from our automobile, Miss Shaw scintillating as usual, for her sense of humor never deserted her and she knew just how to handle crowds. Writing the next day I said: "I have felt perfectly elated ever since. I feel like beginning work now for next year's parade and I am determined to have at least 500 men in line at that time, and instead of 3,000 women there ought to be 20,000. I do not know when I have enjoyed a day more and wish I could do it over again tomorrow."

There were two humorous incidents during that parade. When Mrs. Frederick Nathan, tall and superb in bearing and, as always,

pendent publication opposed to ship subsidies and a government-underwritten merchant marine, which, as it is operated today, is chiefly a means of further increasing the federal deficits.

beautifully gowned, hove in sight, one man looked at her and said:
"That one'll be President!" As we men were forming in line
Norah Stanton Blatch observed that we had no banner. "That
won't do," said she and rushed off. In a minute she came back in
triumph bearing a tightly furled banner. When we opened it out
we hastily returned it to her with thanks. It read: "Men have the
votes. Why not we?" Once in Washington there were no men in
the line-up and the crowd was rough and menacing, actually laying hands upon some of the marchers. My wife and others kept
near my mother and so did I, for her white hairs and serene and
lovely countenance did not prevent her from being the target of
coarse and vulgar abuse. There were times when it looked as if
the parade would be broken up but it went through to the end
albeit in considerable confusion. When suffrage finally came there
wasn't a ripple. The male and female Tories who had opposed
this reform, as they did every other, were busy killing Huns—
that is, if words counted for that end.

Chapter XII. The Case of Jotham P. Allds

THE greatest "beat" and sensation of my *Evening Post* career happened in January, 1910, as a result of a bit of healthy moral indignation on the part of Senator Josiah T. Newcomb who had formerly been a telegraph editor of *The Evening Post*, and then had been elected State Senator from an uptown New York district. At the beginning of the legislative session the corrupt Republican organization in Albany, then headed by Speaker Nixon, elected Jotham P. Allds to be the temporary president and Republican majority leader of the Senate. Seven pro-Hughes Senators bolted their party and voted against Allds, among them Frederick M. Davenport of Clinton, J. Mayhew Wainwright of Westchester, Harvey D. Hinman of Binghamton, George B. Agnew of New York City, and, curiously enough, Benn Conger of Norwich, who had never been known as a reformer or independent but had been supporting Governor Hughes. These Senators met in a room at the Ten Eyck Hotel in Albany on January 4 and there Senator Conger told his associates that he himself knew of bribes having been paid to Allds to hold in committee a bill amending the highway law, which amendment took away from the town boards the right to award contracts for bridges. It was one of the many blackmailing "strike" bills presented to the Legislature from time to time, a number of which would emerge from committee toward the end of the session and then, just as mysteriously, be referred back to the committee to remain there for another twelve months. Had this particular bill passed it would have ruined several small bridge-building companies in which Conger was interested. There was no sound reason for it.

Unfortunately for Benn Conger and Jotham Allds, the former made one great mistake. He failed to add to his story the usual: "Now, boys, you know that this is all in confidence, just between

you and me," with the result that the others left the room
without feeling under obligation of secrecy while Conger never
dreamed that any one of them would peach and so violate the
usual code of honor among the Albany legislators. Newcomb was
the most sensitive and also the most inexperienced of the group
in the Legislature. Conger's revelation stirred him deeply so that
he could not sleep comfortably and could not get it out of his
mind. He could not endure sitting in his senatorial seat with Allds
presiding. He began to wonder whether some civic organization
could not be induced to take up the matter and on the 6th of
January wandered into *The Evening Post* office and asked Rollo
Ogden and myself whether the City Club, of which I was a vice-
president, or the Corrupt Practices Association, or some other
society would be interested in taking the matter up.

I told him that the City Club could not do so under its charter
and that the other association dealt only with election matters.
Then I said that I did not see any reason why we of *The Evening
Post* should not publish the story and that I would be willing to
do so provided that the other senators, aside from Conger, would
agree to stand for the story so that we should have backing for
its publication. Newcomb's gratitude equaled his surprise. It had
not occurred to him that any newspaper would dare to touch so
dangerous a matter. He told me that he was certain that the
bolters would stand by me if I should print the facts. He added
that Senator Wainwright had told Senator Allds himself about
Conger's charge and that the others were talking freely about the
revelation. We then spent some time discussing the best method
of getting the facts out. It seemed to me that we should act with
all possible speed lest the gossip in Albany embolden some other
newspaper to print an emasculated story. I left New York that
same night by the midnight train for Utica.

On arriving there I went straight to the Clinton home of Senator, later Congressman, Frederick M. Davenport, having telephoned him before leaving that I must see him on an important
matter. He confirmed all but a few details of Senator Newcomb's
story and explained that when Conger was speaking he was draft-

ing a resolution to be signed by the seven insurgents and therefore was not listening as intently as the others, particularly as Senator Conger had informed him beforehand of the facts Conger revealed to the group. Mr. Davenport also declared that he was not under any obligation of confidence and that he would, of course, stand by us if we brought out the truth; as it was a group matter, however, he did not wish to act until he could communicate with Senator Harvey D. Hinman. He then strongly advised my going forthwith to Albany and laying the matter before Governor Hughes as the Chief Executive of the State. I returned to Albany by the next train, reaching the Governor's Mansion at a quarter of five.

For two hours we discussed the Conger charges at great length. Mr. Hughes was naturally most eager for the publication of the Conger story, stating that the showing up of Allds and the crookedness of the Legislature would be a godsent aid to him in the fight he was waging on the machine. He told me of a recent call from Senator Allds during which the Senator assured the Governor of his desire to do whatever was right, to have a short session, and to co-operate with him in any way to bring about the legislation which Mr. Hughes desired and that the machine had refused to give him the previous winter. He also asked the Governor to get together with him and a number of prominent party men and settle the whole question at one sitting as to what the Legislature should do. This the Governor declined in emphatic terms, saying that he was always accessible if they came in a group and asked for a conference; that he had been there for the previous three years and that they could have come to him singly or in a body at any time, instead of which they had done everything possible to defeat the measures he advocated. His language to Senator Allds was pretty emphatic.

As for the next step, the Governor advised me to go at once to Binghamton to see Senator Hinman, as his support would carry me "a great distance." I reached Binghamton early the next morning and received a cordial welcome from Senator Hinman and a promise of hearty co-operation. But he declined to take the lead himself, since he had been a candidate for president pro tem of the Senate in opposition to Allds and people might therefore say that his action was due to spite. "If necessary," he said, "I will travel a thousand miles to come into court and testify to the correctness of Senator Newcomb's statement." He told me that the Governor had called him up to notify him of my coming and that he had assured the Governor that, if *The Evening Post* would publish the story, it would be the best thing that could happen for the Republican party and the State. I had intended to return to New York but he induced me to proceed at once to Groton, the home of Senator Conger, and see the latter myself.

It was quarter to seven in the evening when I arrived at that little town. The setting was as perfect for a melodrama as one could possibly ask. It was snowing and cold enough to make the lighted homes seem inviting indeed and quite suggestive of Christmas cards. It was entirely in keeping that I should find the Senator not in his home but at a prayer meeting. I went straight to the church and stood for a cold half hour looking up at the lighted, stained-glass windows, listening to the organ and the singing within. There was really nothing lacking to make it seem like an old-fashioned detective story, with a young reporter ready to tear the mask from the face of the hypocritical pillar of the church.

Though I had never seen Senator Conger, I picked him out of the congregation as it emerged and followed him to his house. He had never heard of me and was reluctant to admit me when I said that I was a representative of *The Evening Post* until I told him that I had come by direction of Senator Hinman. Then I read to him a statement that I had prepared and told him that Newcomb's story had been in every essential detail verified by both Senator Hinman and Senator Davenport. Despite the fact that he had just left his church, where he had probably heard something about not bearing false witness, he denied the truth of Newcomb's report of the meeting at the Ten Eyck, refused to say that he had paid any money to Senator Allds, and admitted only the payment of money to the Republican Campaign Committee. I warned him then that Senator Allds had informed Senator Davenport that he planned to make a statement about the whole thing and urged him to take the offensive before Allds did. We parted with the request from him that I come to his office at nine o'clock the next morning.

I was at his office in the building of the Standard Typewriter Company on the minute. He kept me waiting for nearly an hour, then he dictated to me a weak and colorless statement putting the whole matter up to the campaign committee and mentioning no names. Bitterly disappointed I left, telegraphing Senator Hinman as I did so to meet me when the train passed through Binghamton. His failure to appear—because of the slowness of the dispatch—still further discouraged me. Just as I entered my apartment in New York that evening the telephone was ringing. It was Senator Hinman who informed me that after I had left Groton Senator Conger had had a long telephone conversation with him in which he had warned Conger that he must tell not half-truths but the whole truth about Allds. Then he asked: "Where are you now, at your office?" I replied: "At my home." He said: "When you get to your office tomorrow morning you will find a telegram from Senator Conger telling you that he will stiffen up that statement." Sure enough, Conger's dispatch was lying on top of my mail when I reached my office the next morning. I at once called him on the telephone to confirm his promise of a stiffer statement.

Two days later, Wednesday evening, I met the Senator at the Ten Eyck Hotel and this time he told the whole truth. He had seen the money passed to Allds in thousand-dollar bills. When I asked whether he had corroborative evidence he told me that he could get a clerk, who had helped him to place the money in the envelopes and had delivered it, to testify. The bridge constructors would also testify to his having gone to them and urged them to put up money. He explained that the first year that the bill was introduced he was able to hold it in committee by his own political influence. The next year he and his brother paid Allds, Jean Burnett, and Nixon, three of the Republican leaders. The next year they again paid these rascals. The fourth year, after the introduction of the bill, the demand of Allds and others for still larger sums had become so insistent that he was compelled to raise a fund

of $7,500 among the different bridge companies but, at the last
moment, a Rochester and an Albany company had refused to pay
their promised share and withdrawn, believing that the Conger
brothers would make up the deficiency. "There is," he said, "supposed to be honor among thieves but there was none in this case.'
He and his brother declined to step in, the combination went to
pieces, no money was paid, and subsequently the bill was passed
by the Assembly. I urged him to make a clean breast of the whole
thing in the interest of common decency and of the welfare of the
State and he promised that he would do so on the following
Monday.

On Saturday morning a card was brought into my office. It was
that of my friend, Herman Ridder, the proprietor of the *New
Yorker Staats Zeitung*. To my surprise he brought in with him a
huge man, wearing a heavy overcoat with a fur collar. With every
evidence of embarrassment Mr. Ridder pushed the man up to my
desk, saying: "This is my friend, Senator Allds. I know you will
do the right thing by him. I'll leave you two together to settle
the matter between you." Then, without another word, he turned
and fled. My feelings can be imagined, especially when I noted
the Senator's bulk! He took off his coat, sat down, and we went
to it. He declared that he had framed the amendment to the highway law only because it cut down the opportunities for graft in
the town boards, asserted that Senator Conger was a man of bad
character whose agents and companies were under indictment in
several states, and that he had no fear whatsoever of the outcome
of any investigation, as any Senate inquiry "would prove my innocence in two minutes." Waxing very earnest he said: "Mr. Villard,
I have a mother ninety years old and she *knows* that I couldn't do
a wrong thing." When I suggested that if he and she were so
certain of his innocence the prompt publication of this charge with
his evidence to confute it would be the best possible way of putting an end to a story which all Albany was beginning to talk
about, he replied that, even if one proved one's innocence, some of
the scandal always stuck.

I informed him that *The Evening Post* had no ax to grind in

the matter, was not in search of a sensation, was without malice
and without desire to injure him or anyone, but believed that it
had a public duty to perform. I could only promise him that his
refutation and denial would appear side by side with the charges.
I reminded him that I was no child or ignoramus in these matters
and that he knew and I knew that he had been for years connected
with one of the most corrupt and rascally political organizations
that had ever disgraced an American state. I challenged him to
deny, if his own hands were clean, that others near him had
bought and sold legislation and that the career of the bill in question was highly suspicious since it had taken precisely the same
course the other corrupt "strike" bills always took. I asked him
why, if this was a good bill and worthy of passage, it had been for
four years before the Legislature before being passed and put on
the statute books. I referred to the bill, which appeared annually,
to compel ferry companies to provide toilets on their boats, which
always came out of committee only to go back again at the end
of the session, and asked him to deny that the annual dropping
of this bill was paid for by the companies. He did not reply.

He was next reminded that his political associations put upon
his shoulders the onus of proof of the untruthfulness of such
charges as were brought against him. Again with great earnestness
he assured me that conditions at Albany were now pure and would
continue to be, that there was no "third house," and had not been
since Governor Higgins's administration and that it would be unfortunate from the point of view of what was to be accomplished
at Albany to have the charges brought out. If they were, there
could be no question as to the outcome in view of his "fifteen years
of unblemished service." He was certain, after having talked with
me and seen my fairness and desire to do what was right, that
there would be no publication at all after I had read his denial
and the facts as to Conger's character which he would lay before
me. I warned him to be under no misapprehension about that;
that even if his denial might seem to him and his friends conclusive, it would still be our duty to bring out the charges and
countercharges in order to ventilate a system which was intoler-

able and to air a scandal that could only be disposed of by publicity. He finally left my office swearing that he knew that I would
do the right thing by him and not print a single word.

The following Monday evening I was at Albany with our Albany correspondent, Walter T. Arndt, and our attorney, William
M. Wherry, Jr., a brilliant young lawyer who distinguished himself throughout this case by his skill and the fertility of resource
he displayed. Senator Conger put me off again and again, and it
was not until five minutes past ten o'clock in the evening that I
finally entered his room. It was as critical a moment for me as I
have ever had in my journalistic career for, just before entering
the room in which the Senator and I were locked, I had released
by telephone large advertisements for the morning newspapers
announcing the greatest "beat" in our history. I took this risk
because Mr. Wherry had, a few minutes before, approved the
publication of a statement wheedled out of Senator Conger by
Senator Newcomb, outlining the former's accusation of bribery
against Senator Allds. At the last minute Conger had welshed
again and it took Newcomb a long time to get him to agree to
this relatively mild statement. But Mr. Wherry warned me that
we could not go ahead with its publication unless I obtained Conger's signature to the document. When I sat down with him I had
burned my bridges behind me.

Disaster faced me immediately—Conger refused to sign! Said
he: "You are asking me to go to my political death, and moreover you will blow out of political life several good fellows. Why
should I commit suicide?" Thus he replied again and again to my
insistence that he sign his political death warrant. It was as difficult a question to answer as could well be framed. Again and again
we swung around the hopeless circle, he always asking: "Why do
you ask me to destroy myself?" Over and over I marshaled my
arguments: Senator Allds was calling him a liar and a scoundrel;
I reminded Conger repeatedly that I had shown him great consideration, that I had treated him in the straightest and frankest
manner; that I could have published the story in an indirect form
that he would not have liked at all; that I had refrained from

doing so for a week out of consideration for him. I pointed out
anew that it was too late for him to retreat, as the story was all
over Albany, and that he had much better have it come from him
as a repentant bribe-giver than to have it appear as a clear-cut
indictment of both himself and Allds.

Again he refused and it then became just a question whose will
would dominate, his or mine. His lawyer had told him to sign
nothing; he was bound to take that advice. With each refusal I
became more desperate. It was then even too late to recall the
placards for the newsdealers' stands. I could see thousands buying
The Evening Post the next day in response to those sensational
advertisements, only to find nothing in it but the most humiliating
apology ever made by a daily; there would hardly have been time
to recast the articles already in type. Then a thought came to me.
The statement from Conger that Newcomb had tossed upon the
bed in my room was in his handwriting and not that of Conger.
I asked the Senator for the manuscript of that statement. He refused for the very reason that made me desire it—that it was in
his handwriting.

I took another tack, saying: "I am a trustee in this matter; the
publication of the story will probably involve *The Evening Post*
in long-continued litigation into which I cannot enter in justice to
the stockholders without a signed statement from you"—I might
have added that a large verdict against us might have put us out
of business. Conger was unmoved. I reminded him that he and I
might both drop dead before the suit came to trial in which case
The Evening Post might be without warrant in law for the publication. I told him of the sudden and unexpected death of Hammond Lamont in the previous year, as an example of the sort of
thing that might happen, and said that I *must* have his signature.
He refused. Then I took a more compelling and rougher tone,
threatening him with the full hostility of our paper if he let us
down, and saying that we should have to describe him as a man
who had made criminal charges against an associate and then had
refused to substantiate them. It was the right course. He began to
weaken and finally said that he would sign if I would give my

word of honor that the statement would not be printed with his
signature either in type or facsimile and that I would put it in my
safe to be used only in the event of a lawsuit. I then began copy-
ing the statement in pencil, with none too steady a hand, as the
manuscript before me testifies. This time he would not state spe-
cifically that he had himself given money to Allds. All he would
say was:

I have personal knowledge that when Republican leader of the
Assembly he, Allds, received money for aiding the defeat of legislation
before that body. . . .

Question: Who were the others besides Allds?

Answer: Some are dead; others are out of public affairs and I will
not name them.

Question: How do you come to have personal knowledge of the
transaction?

Answer: My company was one of the victims of the holdup. I shall
be ready to state the facts, the exact truth, before a regularly constituted
committee of the Senate.

With this in my hand, signed "B. Conger," I left the room almost
exhausted—my coat was wet through; if I had not sweated blood,
I had done the best I could! I rejoined Mr. Wherry and Mr.
Arndt, whose anxiety at my failure to reappear had equaled my
own. Mr. Wherry grabbed the statement and after some moments'
cogitation decided that it would do. Soon thereafter Mr. Arndt
got Senator Allds out of bed at the Fort Orange Club to tell him
of the impending publication, to read him Conger's statement, and
to assure him again that *The Evening Post* would print any reply
that he wished to make in the column next to Conger's charges.
Allds became very indignant, declared that we had not played fair
with him but said that we would have the statement next day and
it duly arrived in time by telephone.

As I stood at the forms in the composing room with the managing editor the next day putting the finishing touches to the story,
having just received Senator Allds's denial, there was placed in
my hands a letter from Martin W. Littleton, Allds's lawyer, noti-

fying me that the charges we were about to publish were utterly
false and both criminally and civilly libelous, and that I and *The
Evening Post* would be held absolutely responsible. I admit that
for a moment I had a sinking of the heart. Everybody in the
group about me was watching my face. But there was only one
thing to do—"let her go in, please." The page was rolled into the
near by "foundry," *The Evening Post* appeared with its largest
headlines, and the results were astounding. As a newspaper "beat"
it was all that we could ask. We were never sued nor arrested.
The revelation stunned political circles and the newspaper world,
and it was so far-reaching that no other newspaper could fail to
take notice of it. It completely wrecked the session of the Legislature, for the Senate did practically nothing but try Allds, while
the Assembly marked time. So little legislation was passed that
year that no "strike" bill had a chance; I must have saved some
people large sums of money—certainly the Albany income of many
of the legislators was the smallest in years.

For two months the Senate tried this man who had assured me
that he could prove his innocence in two minutes. It was largely
a battle of wits between Martin W. Littleton on behalf of Allds
and James W. Osborne whom the Senate retained as prosecutor,
with Osborne winning as he should have. His letter of gratitude
to *The Evening Post* for our loan to him of the services of Mr.
Wherry lies before me. He rightly praised our counsel as "extremely competent in the handling of men," as "full of suggestions," with the imagination to look ahead and foresee our opponents' next moves. Mr. Wherry's work was indeed invaluable, his
judgment unfailing, his resourcefulness unlimited. The final vote
stood 40 to 9 for conviction. The victory presaged to Mr. Osborne,
and many others, "the beginning of a new era in politics." It put
Mr. Hughes in complete command of the situation at Albany.
Hughes and Conger, and *The Evening Post*, had struck the machine a deadly blow. The following November the election of a
Democrat, John A. Dix, as Governor to succeed Hughes, was
largely due to the Allds scandal. It was some time before the

"black horsemen" began to ride again; indeed, there are those who believe that the Legislature has never been as crooked since.

Among other interesting facts brought out by the cross-examination of Allds was that he was receiving a retainer of $100 a month from the New York Central Railroad. He had admitted banking large sums of cash at the close of every legislative session. We had some anxious moments during the trial, partly because of the determination of the Republican machine to uphold Allds at any cost. Thus, Timothy Woodruff, the former lieutenant governor and Republican boss of Brooklyn, told Lloyd C. Griscom, then county chairman in New York City, that "my five senators will vote in favor of Allds no matter what the testimony," which led Griscom then and there to say to himself: "That insures your going out of the leadership, Mr. Woodruff." Conger resigned during the proceedings, realizing that the "gang" would show him no mercy after Allds was convicted, and so proved the correctness of his statement to me that he was committing political suicide. Allds hung on until just before the Senate voted, on March 30, to convict him. In a desperate and cowardly attempt to avert his fate, he then technically saved himself from expulsion by resigning, but he was as ruined as he was guilty; that was beyond dispute. On his resignation he announced that he would immediately bring suits against Conger and *The Evening Post* for $100,000 apiece. They were never brought. Threats of his that he would shoot me reached me frequently for a time and convinced me of my safety at his hands, for men who threaten publicly do not act. He died years afterward in obscurity in his home town of Norwich, after having been for that brief time when under fire the acting lieutenant-governor of the State. There was even some doubt as to whether his clairvoyant ninety-year-old mother really was his actual mother or a foster mother, but his devotion to her was beyond question.

When it was all over I wrote as modest an editorial as I could with some regard for our own part in the victory. I could not fail, however, to dwell upon the fact that *The Evening Post* was entitled to credit for having obtained the conviction of the first

legislator ever impeached, tried, and found guilty of taking money
in the State of New York, something of an achievement in view
of the many who had been, and were, notoriously corrupt. My
surprise and chagrin were great, indeed, when I received within
twenty-four hours a letter from a reader who declared that my
editorial was in error. A Senator Jasper Ward had been impeached,
tried, and convicted in 1826 and—what seemed almost incredible—
because of revelations as to him published by the New York *Evening Post!* What is even more astounding, Senator Ward also resigned to escape expulsion. A search of our files proved this to be
correct, and so we had to confess editorially our ignorance of our
own past. I had not made history; history had but repeated itself.

A few days after the vote I had a talk of three-quarters of an
hour with Governor Hughes, who thought the revolution in the
character of the Legislature nothing less than marvelous. I noted
then that "he looked worn and his hair is turning gray; he complained greatly of the terrific strain he is under and the overwork.
He was quite complimentary about the work of *The Evening Post*
and told me that the investigation into the Adirondack land
frauds, which he started after our publication as to the graft going
on there, has more than justified our article and is producing some
very startling facts." At this time President Taft, Chairman Gris-
com, and Governor Hughes were determined to drive Senator
Depew and Timothy Woodruff out of public life as soon as possible—Depew when his term ended.

Probably no man in American life did more to debase the politics of his State than Chauncey Depew during his long service as
political manager of the New York Central Railroad. He was
deeply besmirched by the investigation of the Equitable Life Insurance Company when it appeared that he received a salary of
$20,000 a year for doing nothing but exercising his political in-
fluence for the company and that he had obtained a loan of
$250,000 from the Equitable for a Depew land company, of
which he was part owner, on property which the State Insurance
Department appraised at only $150,000. To make good, after suit
was brought by the Attorney General of New York against Depew

and his associates, they settled for $293,850.82.[1] To explain his part
ownership of this land Depew told two totally conflicting stories.
Is it any wonder that Mr. Hughes and Mr. Taft wished to rescue
the Empire State from the disgrace of being represented by Platt
and Depew? Yet when Depew died, after having presented a
statue of himself to his native town of Peekskill and delivered the
address at its unveiling, press and public men united in paeans of
praise for him and his noble career. Thomas W. Lamont actually
stated:[2] "Sorrow at the death of Mr. Depew will be as universal
as it is real. For three generations he has had a place all his own
in the esteem and affection of his countrymen. They have been
helped by his optimism and humor, encouraged by his example as
a citizen, inspired by his *fine and straightforward political life*.
Mr. Depew was an institution and he will become a tradition."
Myron C. Taylor of the United States Steel Corporation was not
to be outdone by Lamont. Said he: "Senator Depew was a great
American beloved by everyone throughout his long and useful
life. He was an outstanding example of the highest standards and
an inspiration to the professional and business life of the country.
He was a fine type of the courteous Christian gentleman." Whenever I hear men attributing all our ills to immigration into the
United States, notably of the "scum of Southeastern Europe," I
always smile and recall that Allds, Nixon, Burnet, Boies Penrose,
Matthew Quay, Platt, Depew, and numerous others, who were
beyond question the most dangerous or the most corrupt men in
our public life, bore the best of Anglo-Saxon names and boasted
that they were of old American ancestry—and all exemplary
Christians.

The fight for good government in Albany did not long profit
by the ruining of Allds and the exposing of the high-placed Republican archpriests. By a single disheartening error of judgment,
Governor Hughes himself undid much of what he had accomplished and put a stop to further progress. President Taft visited
him early in April in Albany and begged him to run again in the

---

[1] *The Nation*, September 7, 1905.
[2] New York *Times*, April 6, 1928.

coming fall election. The Governor refused; he had had three and one-half years of the most arduous service and was receiving only $10,000 a year, which meant that he was rapidly exhausting his savings. On April 26, less than a month after the Allds vote, all of us who had fought for and with the Governor were appalled to read that Mr. Taft, accepting Mr. Hughes's "no" as to the governorship, had then appointed him to the Supreme Court to succeed the late Justice David J. Brewer. Nothing could have been worse for the cause than that announcement. Hughes had abandoned the fight just when victory was certain. From that moment the machine politicians in both camps snapped their fingers at him; in their parlance he was "a dead one." He was not going to run again, why should they listen any longer to the cracking of his whip? As Burton J. Hendrick subsequently wrote in *McClure's Magazine:* [3] "the Governor's action was immensely popular in certain quarters. The Albany gang made no attempt to conceal its delight. With Hughes now safely out of the way they proceeded to ride roughshod over his proposed reforms of the nomination system." I went to Albany to remonstrate with Hughes. He was perturbed but he had accepted and there was nothing left to be done. "But why, Governor," said I, "could you not have let this be a secret between you and President Taft? The Supreme Court will not meet until December, neither will Congress, and you cannot take your seat until the Senate confirms your appointment." The Governor could only reply that having given his acceptance to Mr. Taft it would not have been right to withhold the fact, a process of reasoning I still cannot understand. So the bosses beat the Governor. "The conqueror of the giants had gone down before the Lilliputians." [4]

[3] *McClure's Magazine,* September, 1910, p. 511.
[4] *Ibid.*, p. 512.

Chapter XIII. Woodrow Wilson to the Fore

WHEN I told my father one summer day in 1895 that I was going over to Philadelphia to listen to some lectures in American history he was incredulous. "I never before heard of your wishing to get any more education than you had to acquire," said he. "What's the reason for this?" "Two," I replied. "I am stagnating here at home with nothing to keep me occupied and there's a professor whose books interest me who is going to lecture in this university extension course." "Who is he?" Father asked. "His name," I replied, "is Woodrow Wilson and he's beginning to have quite a reputation." After assuring himself that my temperature was normal, Father gave his consent and I journeyed to Philadelphia —Philadelphia in July and, as it happened, at its very hottest. There and then began my acquaintance with the future President of the United States. We were not long in locking horns. When he lectured on the Abolitionists I begged leave to dissent from his views. It is needless to say who held the upper hand in the debate; I am sure the other students enjoyed it.

While I occasionally met Mr. Wilson after joining *The Evening Post*, or heard from him, I began to know him only when my wife and I embarked on the steamer leaving Bermuda on March 5, 1910, and found ourselves seated next to him and the captain. The latter was a typical small-steamer master mariner, whose yarns were not always too elegant or his views too erudite. It was delightful to see how quickly Mr. Wilson covered any *gaucherie* by an amusing anecdote introduced with a "that reminds me." Often he helped us over the embarrassment of a pointless story by taking it as the peg on which to hang some remarks leading in the direction the captain had meant to take. Mr. Wilson was at his best in those days. He was approachable, mellow, altogether attractive, delightfully witty, with a story for every five minutes. As he knew no one else on board save a Princeton alumnus, I had him considerably to myself. We went all over his admirable fight against the Princeton clubs in order to democratize undergraduate life, a conflict in which *The Nation* and *The Evening Post* supported him. After that, as we were walking up and down the deck I broached the subject of his entering political life and seeking the governorship of New Jersey. He declared that, while he had not definitely decided, his mind was headed in that direction. As a matter of fact he vacillated until the last moment. On July 9, 1910, he stated to the Newark *Evening News:* "The mention of my name in connection with the governorship, senatorship, or Presidency, is a matter which I have never [*sic*] and do not now attach any importance whatever. Make it just as forcibly plain as you can, so that it may perhaps put an end to all these stories, most of them absurd, which have made me appear as being a candidate for office." Three days later, July 12, Wilson formally declared his readiness to run.

On the steamer I told him that we would back him to the limit if he became a candidate—and we did so. We treated the governorship campaign in New Jersey as fully as we would a similar one in New York. Throughout his governorship we exercised considerable influence because ours was the only newspaper which he read—a circumstance that appalled his New Jersey backers when they found that they had a candidate on their hands who was not sufficiently interested in his State or its politics to read a New Jersey newspaper,[1] and had often not voted. A newspaper man found him wandering around in Trenton after his inauguration and to him Wilson confessed his utter ignorance of what to do and said: "I do not even know how to choose a secretary." Fortunately for the Governor two men came to his aid who had originally opposed him for the nomination and gave him the education that he needed; their pupil was in the kindergarten stage. Both were absolutely destitute of self-seeking, interested only in Wilson's success in order that the cause of good government might profit.

[1] James Kerney, *The Political Education of Woodrow Wilson*, New York, 1926, p. 82. Statement of Wilson to Kerney.

They were Joseph P. Tumulty, who relinquished other ambitions to become his secretary, and James Kerney, the owner and editor of the Trenton *Evening Times.*

Mr. Wilson had asked me to recommend a suitable secretary and I had suggested Charles A. Selden of *The Evening Post,* who had been covering the Wilson campaign for us. On June 2, 1911, the Governor wrote me telling me of his decision: "But the plot thickens about me here; the Smith forces are trying to coil me about with plans of their own which it will take more knowledge of past transactions here than I now have to checkmate and defeat. I am therefore going to ask one of the ablest young Democratic politicians of the State if he will not act as my secretary in order that I may have a guide at my elbow in matters of which I know almost nothing. If he declines the field will be open again." Tumulty promptly accepted and gave ten years of his life with absolute devotion to "the Governor" as he always called him even throughout the White House years, until Mr. Wilson severed the friendship between them. Kerney, one of the most kindhearted of advisers, the most loyal of supporters, and, as I can personally testify, one of the most delightful and truest of friends, rendered inestimable service and never received or sought any reward. When I think of Wilson the Governor, I always see Tumulty and Kerney also, not forgetting Thomas Pence and Martin P. Devlin and others who helped to make Governor Wilson's administration a success.

I shall not outline his governorship because that has been done definitively by James Kerney in his *The Political Education of Woodrow Wilson,* by all odds the best and most reliable book written about Mr. Wilson's political career. It is accurate, detached, restrained, not glossing over Wilson's faults and weaknesses but treating him with unfailing kindliness—despite the author's awareness that Wilson's Presidency became a disaster for the United States because of our entering the World War. The way Mr. Wilson went about the job of governing New Jersey made the greatest appeal to me and my editorial associates. After all the noisome and crooked governing by compromise and sordid bargaining behind closed doors, with which we were familiar, it was exhilarating to have another State executive administering public affairs in the broad light of day as had Governor Hughes. Wilson actually had his desk in an open office where all might see him, where he was accessible to every citizen who walked in, and after his first year he went to some county seats to account for his stewardship and to answer any questions which might be put to him by any citizen. On August 13, 1912, my notes say: "I found him in the State House democratically wandering about and talking to the people in the outer office who were waiting to see him. There are no fuss and feathers where he is."

Up to the time that he was a candidate for the governorship Wilson was what any fair-minded man would have called a conservative if not a reactionary. He even thought that our system of elections could not work unless candidates were picked by a few. "They are the political bosses and managers whom the people obey and affect to despise. It is unjust to despise them." He was "a fierce partisan of the open shop" and largely opposed to the organization of labor. Wilson was even absolutely hostile to the regulation of public utility and other corporations by the States' or the Federal governments, saying that federal regulation was based on a theory "compounded of confused thinking and impossible principles of law." [2] The panic in November, 1907, he steadily charged to the "aggressive attitude of legislation toward the railroads." Yet when he became governor he sponsored the strictest regulatory legislation ever passed in New Jersey—the so-called Seven Sisters Laws. There is no doubt in my mind that when he was selected by George Harvey and others connected with Big Business they thought they were choosing a man who would in most matters be the antithesis of Theodore Roosevelt and represent their point of view. But Mr. Wilson had made up his mind, as he said to me, that what people wanted was " a modified Rooseveltism."

Somehow or other the many who felt as I did on these questions

[2] Kerney, *op. cit.*, p. 33.

were still drawn to Wilson if only by the belief that the entrance into politics of a man of his type, even if he were conservative, would do much to purify the rotten politics of New Jersey. In this we were not mistaken but none of us dreamed that he would swing completely over to the other extreme and that within two years he would be campaigning for the Presidency on a platform which may be summed up by his repeated statement that "the masters of the Government of the United States are the combined capitalists and manufacturers of the United States"; that "the Government of the United States at present is a foster child of the special interests. It is not allowed to have a will of its own. It is told at every move: 'Don't do that; you will interfere with our prosperity.' And when we ask, 'Where is our prosperity lodged?' a certain group of gentlemen say, 'With us.' " [3] This from the man who, up to that time, had held the extreme Big Business view that there could be no prosperity as long as the government interfered in any way with the corporations!

I should have paid much more attention to the significance of these sudden changes on the part of the Governor as soon as he entered public life. If I had I would have been prepared for much that happened. When it appeared that he had become a really liberal leader I told him that *The Nation* and *The Evening Post* would support him for the Presidency enthusiastically. Then and there I gave him the positive assurance that I wanted nothing from him, was not a candidate for any office, and believed that newspaper reformers to be effective must refrain from receiving favors from any administration. He expressed his gratitude, and, as it happened, Jim Kerney and I were about the only men who worked hard for Wilson's elevation to the Presidency who did not ask or receive some office. I was the second influential newspaper man to put myself behind the Wilson boom. [4] The first was George

[3] Woodrow Wilson, *The New Freedom*, New York, 1921, pp. 57-59.

[4] "Spurred on by the New York *Evening Post*, then under the direction of Oswald Garrison Villard, the intellectuals were flocking to Wilson. Next to Harvey, Villard had perhaps given the greatest nation-wide impetus to the boom."—Kerney, *op. cit.*, p. 131.

Harvey who had been urging him steadily until the time came when it seemed to Wilson's advisers that the Harvey advocacy of Wilson's election to the Presidency was injuring his chances to appear as a radical leader since Harvey was closely allied not only with J. P. Morgan & Company but with Senator James Smith, Jr., the most influential Democrat in the State of New Jersey, whose coming over to Wilson, through George Harvey's influence, insured Wilson's nomination for the governorship. When Wilson, in response to a question of George Harvey as to whether the latter's support was hurting him, bluntly replied that it was, Harvey took Woodrow Wilson's name down from the masthead of *Harper's Weekly* where he had been long carrying it as his candidate for the Presidency. This, and his break with Henry Watterson, was the beginning of that long series of broken friendships which illustrated one of the worst sides of Wilson's nature.

No sooner had Wilson been safely nominated than he turned upon Smith and James R. Nugent, the Chairman of the Democratic State Committee. The latter had not favored Wilson's candidacy but was always ready to obey the slightest wish of "the old man," as he called Senator Smith. As Kerney put it: "Like Roosevelt, Wilson was a bit abrupt and rough in canceling what seemed like obligations to his benefactors—a habit of the more or less idealized politicians, who usually convince themselves that their own human conceptions are infallible." After Wilson's election, on December 9, 1910, he made a public statement attacking Senator Smith and saying: "I know that the people of New Jersey do not desire Mr. James Smith, Jr. to be sent again to the Senate. If he should be, he will not go as their representative." At that time New Jersey had a primary law intended to afford an opportunity to the voters of the State to express their preferences for those whom they wished to have chosen as United States Senators. There was very little interest in this expression of opinion and, in the election in which Mr. Wilson won the governorship, only 48,000 Democrats took the trouble to vote for James E. Martine, who was more or less of a joke in New Jersey and was little fitted for the office of senator aside from being a lovable personality.

With the election over everybody was puzzled as to what stand to take, except Smith and his cohorts. The Senator had said in Wilson's presence that he would not stand for re-election but later declared that his health had improved and that he would be a candidate to succeed himself. On the other hand, it took a good deal of persuading to get Mr. Wilson to stand by Martine. One of those who convinced him was William W. St. John, one of the two men who had induced Martine to run. Mr. St. John also converted us to the belief that whether the choice of the primary was wise or unwise it was the democratic course to uphold it, and I allowed him to write a series of articles for *The Evening Post* supporting Martine—articles which were carefully read by the Governor-elect. When he took his position Mr. Wilson said: "For me that vote is conclusive. I think it should be for every member of the Legislature." From then on Wilson repeatedly attacked Smith, even declaring that he was planning to make use of Republican votes to bring about his choice. When the ballot was taken in the Legislature, on January 24, Smith was overwhelmingly defeated and Martine elected to an inglorious career at Washington, marked, however, by considerable independence; he several times deliberately opposed the policies and acts of President Wilson.

Soon after I had announced my support of Governor Wilson for the Presidency, I was asked by William F. McCombs and William G. McAdoo to meet with them regularly once a week at luncheon at the Railroad Club in New York to plan the strategy of the campaign and I did so. McCombs had volunteered to become the manager of the preconvention boom and to collect the necessary money and he was remarkably successful at that. McAdoo's sole claim to fame was that he, an unknown lawyer from the South, who had succeeded in reviving the plan for a tunnel under the Hudson and, thanks to improved engineering methods, had succeeded in building it, had been able to enlist Wall Street support for his Hudson and Manhattan Railway enterprise. He had much more managerial ability and a wider range of vision than McCombs, who was lame and always in delicate health. McCombs's pluck in sticking to his job, and working himself almost into a state of complete collapse, was a measure of his sincerity and his determination to succeed. Both men wanted rewards for their services. Mr. McAdoo's statement in his autobiography, that he never sought the Cabinet position which Mr. Wilson offered to him,[5] caused profound amusement to me, Jim Kerney, and the other survivors of the group that worked for the Wilson nomination, for we could each recall Mr. McAdoo's having come to us to ask our aid in persuading Mr. Wilson that he should become Secretary of the Treasury, an office in which McAdoo unquestionably displayed great ability but neither tact nor selflessness. He was one of the least valuable of Mr. Wilson's advisers on questions of policy for his advice was rarely actuated by principle, usually by political intuition. I enjoyed my association with both men in those early campaigning days and have kept my respect for McCombs and admiration of his courage.

Knowing that Governor Wilson was in a politically fluid state so far as his opinions were concerned, much pressure was brought to bear upon him by liberals to induce him to go still further than he had. On the occasion of my visit to him on August 13, 1912, to which I have already referred, I held forth on four of my pet subjects during the luncheon at the Country Club to which he invited me, his brother, and Tumulty. One of them was the Negro problem. The Negroes were with reason much afraid of Wilson's candidacy, fearing what would happen to them if a Southern white man were seated in the White House. I pointed out to the Governor the importance of the Negro vote in certain pivotal States and urged him to make some kind of a statement that would reassure Negro voters everywhere and help those of us who were trying to wean the Negroes away from their stupid and useless devotion to the Republican party for their own interest. For the Republican leaders, knowing that they always had the Negro voters safely in the bag, forgot all about them between elections. I told the Governor of the 5,000 Negro children in Atlanta, Georgia, who were walking the streets without hope of an educa-

[5] *Crowded Years*, by William G. McAdoo, Boston, 1931, p. 177.

tion and predestined to ignorance, vice, or crime. That very week a seventeen-year-old Negro girl was to be executed in Richmond for murder. "They are killing that girl this week," I said, "because being a child of a disadvantaged race and compelled to live in horrible slums, more or less of an outcast, she has had no chance to be anything else than what she is."

This made quite an impression upon him and, my notes say, "he told me with a great deal of feeling" that the "worst phase" of his policy of accessibility to all citizens who called on him in the State House was that he could not help "the poor and the victims of injustice" who found their way to him because he had no power to do so. He declared that he would speak out against lynching, "every honest man must do that," but that he did not wish the colored people to think that he could do anything about the lynching evil if he became President because "the President has no power in the matter. If I become President, I shall be President of all the people." He would appoint no man to office because he was colored any more than he would appoint one because he was a Jew or Catholic but he would appoint colored men on their merits. "The only place," said he, "where you and I will differ is as to where the entering wedge shall be driven." I arranged for him to receive a colored bishop and give him an interview; the Governor insisted that the bishop misquoted him and was much disturbed about it. A promised statement for the press as to his views on the Negro never materialized.

All in all, the roll of reforms achieved by Mr. Wilson as Governor and his advisers, with George L. Record, the Republican Progressive, outstanding among them, is remarkable. New Jersey advanced more in two years under Wilson than during any other governorship—that office has now fallen back into the hands of fools, nonentities, or cheap politicians. Wilson's legislation was progressive where not radical—the very sort of thing against which Wilson had inveighed. Yet Wilson himself was most concerned during his entire term in Trenton with his chances for the Presidency. Indeed, Kerney records [6] that he never really wanted to

6 Kerney, *op. cit.*, p. 43.

be governor, that his ambition was always to enter the White House. Hence he gave a great deal of time and thought and advice to McCombs and McAdoo and their planning, and once wrote me (December 9, 1911) a most appreciative note about my share in it. He was inordinately wrapped up in himself and his future and the lack of consideration for others which so often characterized him manifested itself constantly, as when he summarily discarded Mr. Record, after the latter had rendered great service, because he was told that consultation with this Republican was hurting him with his own party leaders.

Long years of living on small professorial salaries had made Wilson extremely penurious. He resented bitterly the provision in the New Jersey Constitution which made the governor forfeit his salary if he was absent from the state for even a day and he could not be soothed, when he had been off campaigning or vacationing, until the acting-Governors, Ernest R. Ackerman, and John D. Prince, generously endorsed the pay checks over to him, in violation of the intent of the Constitution.[7] Wilson came to consider it his right to be driven into the State House by his neighbors and to resent it if they were not on time and he frequently forgot to thank them adequately. On the other hand, his correspondence abounds in charming, graceful notes of acknowledgment and gratitude—often instigated by those never-sleeping advisers who gave him his political education. In his fight against Senator Smith's re-election he once paid tribute to a squad of public-spirited young Catholics who had fought and bled for him and well merited his praise. This was occasioned by the warning that Smith was threatening to inject the religious issue and to explain their falling out as the attack of a narrow, bigoted Presbyterian upon a powerful Catholic. With or without praise these young men and a number of others were drawn to Wilson's banner irresistibly and excused his oddities on the ground that, as Nugent once put it before their break, "the Professor lived in a sphere so

[7] *Ibid.*, pp. 139-41.

far above them" that they could not enter.[8] Like everyone else
they were charmed by Wilson when he did unbend and sought to
play the comrade, for none could be more delightful, and they
were at all times thrilled by his eloquence and his great ability.

The former never stood him in better stead than at the famous
dinner of the Periodical Publishers' Association at the Bellevue-
Stratford Hotel in Philadelphia on February 2, 1912. The leading magazine and newspaper publishers of the country had been
invited to hear the foremost candidates for the Presidency and
to pass upon their fitness, notably La Follette and Wilson—La
Follette at this time was making a strong bid for the regular Republican nomination. There was an enormous attendance and I
had the good fortune to be placed at one of the small tables right
in front of the speakers' table so that I was in the best possible
position to observe what took place—a complete rout for Senator
La Follette and a triumph for Woodrow Wilson. About an hour
and a half before we were to take our seats I sent my card up to
Governor Wilson's room. An assistant secretary appeared and
asked me as a personal favor to abandon my plan to see the Governor. "I know," he said, "he'll see you if I take your card in to
him. The trouble is that we have not been able to get him to sit
down and formulate what he is going to say tonight. You know
how tremendously important this dinner is. He ought to be resting
quietly and thinking about his speech but we cannot get him to
do so." Of course I agreed to do as I was asked, yet more than
half an hour later I saw the Governor in the lobby talking to a
group of men. As he had to dress he could not, therefore, have
had any adequate time for rest or contemplation.

Fortunately he talked before La Follette. He speedily showed
how groundless were those secretarial fears. He spoke without

[8] It was Nugent who, on July 21, 1911, publicly announced that he knew,
after all, the sphere of Wilson, for he toasted him in the presense of militia
officers in these words: "I propose a toast to the Governor of New Jersey, the
commander in chief of the militia. He is an ingrate and a liar. I mean Woodrow
Wilson. I repeat, he is an ingrate and a liar. Do I drink alone?" He did not.
Kerney, *op. cit.*, p. 149.

notes as was his wont and occupied exactly the right time. I noticed how nervous he seemed before he spoke. That was usually the case—he was never at ease until his part in the program was over.[9] Never was he in better form, more truly eloquent. He made one of his great speeches, and swept everything before him. The audience, largely composed of Republican reactionaries, was thrilled by him and his enormous success was enhanced by what followed. This occasion did more to advance his candidacy than would have months of routine press agent publicity. Naturally this success cheered McCombs, McAdoo, and myself, for we had fully realized how vital this event was.

For La Follette, on the other hand, this dinner was an unmitigated disaster. From that night on, any hope of his obtaining the regular Republican nomination was at an end; the editors of the country were almost unitedly against him. Various reasons for what happened have been advanced. Being friendly to the Senator, and in a strategic position to observe, I believe that Don C. Seitz of the New York *World,* who was toastmaster, was right in attributing La Follette's extraordinary conduct to his being under the influence of liquor, which is the more extraordinary because the Senator was not a drinking man. He had carefully prepared his speech on the train coming over from Washington and read it to his secretary and found that it was within the time limit given. He had, however, been suffering from intestinal trouble and was ill and weak. He took his place late and, feeling very miserable, asked a waiter to bring him some brandy. I saw an ordinary water tumbler with a dark liquid in it placed before him and saw him empty it—it was nearly one-half full. He had not eaten much and the stimulant took an immediate effect. It did not make him drunk but confused him and seemed to deprive him of a realization of what he was doing and saying. It was an accident which might

[9] Carl Schurz, who was one of our greatest orators, once asked me in my early speaking days if I had been frightened when I spoke a day or two previously. When I said "no," he replied emphatically: "Then I know you made a poor speech. If you are not frightened you cannot make a good one. That has always been my experience."

have happened to anyone in the same circumstances but for him it had dire consequences.

At first his speech went very well but then he became confused and repetitious, dropped his manuscript, and talked extemporaneously. He got madder and madder and proceeded to attack his listeners, saying that he knew what kind of men they were, just how reactionary and eager to exploit the public, and how all in front of him were in a conspiracy against him. Curiously enough, he singled me out, who was one of his best friends in the audience, and directed many of his vitriolic remarks at me. He spoke for hours and completely wrecked the dinner. I left, exhausted and pained beyond words, at quarter past one in the morning. People began to leave early and sometimes he denounced them for going out. Seitz was extraordinarily delinquent as chairman. He should have stopped La Follette after he had talked an hour instead of allowing him to ramble on. The audience frequently indulged in catcalls and hisses and requested that he sit down and shut up. This only infuriated him the more. Wilson left as soon as he could. The other speakers were never heard from; they had lost their great opportunity. Wilson alone profited by the occasion. The powerful Periodical Publishers' Association never attempted another such dinner.

To William Jennings Bryan, Woodrow Wilson owed his nomination as everybody knows. Wilson's dislike of Bryan had been intense, quite equal to Grover Cleveland's dislike, not to say hate and distrust, of Wilson.[10] There were some difficult hurdles to be jumped before Bryan could be brought into line, as, for example, Wilson's letter to Adrian Joline made public early in January, 1912, in which he had voiced the wish that something might be done "to knock Mr. Bryan once for all into a cocked hat." This publication naturally offset the tribute paid on April 5, 1911, to Bryan by Wilson, in which, among other things, he said that "we

[10] For a long time I possessed a copy of the letter written by Grover Cleveland to Prentiss Bailey, editor of the Utica *Observer*. Cleveland had violently opposed Wilson in the fight over the undergraduate clubs, and in this letter declared that Wilson was without a vestige of intellectual honesty.

have come in at a very much later time to reap the reward of the things that he has done. Mr. Bryan has shown that stout heart which, in spite of the long years of repeated disappointments, has always followed the star of hope, and it is because he has cried 'America, awake!' that some other men have been able to translate into action the doctrines that he has so diligently preached." At the Jackson Day dinner Wilson again paid a tribute to him. The credit of winning Bryan for the Wilson cause has been claimed for Colonel House and others. Kerney thinks that the major credit belongs to the first Mrs. Wilson. Ellen Axson Wilson was an unusual woman. She made no impression of forcefulness and was certainly not in the least aggressive, but she knew her husband from the ground up and he was devoted to her and to his daughters. Her influence upon him was excellent at all times and her premature death was a misfortune for the whole country—there are those who believe that she would have kept the country out of war had she lived, as to which, however, one may be entitled to doubts. But there can be no question of the tremendous aid Mrs. Wilson was to her husband, and of how excellent her judgments usually were. It was she who planned a private dinner with Bryan after she had been convinced that the capturing of Bryan was absolutely essential to her husband's nomination. The Reverend Charles R. Erdman of the Princeton Theological Seminary brought Bryan to Princeton on Sunday afternoon, March 12, 1911, and through him Mr. Bryan and the Wilsons came together. Afterwards Mrs. Wilson said to Mrs. Erdman: "That dinner put Mr. Wilson in the White House." [11]

As the convention approached, Champ Clark became Wilson's only dangerous rival. Bryan specially disliked Clark because of a mistaken belief that Clark was intemperate. The intemperate man was Bryan himself—not with wine but with food which, incidentally, resulted in his unexpected and needless death. His unfair linking Champ Clark during the Baltimore convention to Wall Street went far to defeat Clark after the Missourian had received

[11] Kerney, *op. cit.*, p. 163.

a majority of the delegates' votes. There was a time at Baltimore when everything seemed lost; McCombs himself thought that the end had come. At that moment McCombs's appearance was perfectly shocking. He had had no sleep for nights, had put every ounce of his scant strength into the battle, and as I look back it seems a miracle that what he went through did not cost him his life. Finally the tide was turned when Bryan made it clear for whom he stood and threw his votes to Wilson. I was not present when the end came, having been completely knocked out by my own labors at the convention and its dramatic excitement and by one of my recurrent migraine headaches. My joy in the nomination was greater than that I have ever felt over any political happening but I have long since come to believe that it would have been better for the country had Champ Clark been nominated. He had not the political vision or inspiration of Wilson, of course. He was a professional politician but he had the merit of standing fast in his beliefs and I share his family's opinion that if he had been chosen President—as he would have been had he been nominated (any Democrat would have been elected)—this country would never have gone into the war. At this writing we do not yet know whether the American Republic as such will survive our entrance in 1917 into the European hostilities.

With the election won the scramble for office began. I was one of those overrun by friends and swamped by letters asking my aid in getting their names before the President-elect. Mr. Wilson asked my advice as to some of his Cabinet appointments and I gave him the name of Congressman James L. Slayden of Texas for Secretary of War and called his attention to the admirable tariff speeches of William C. Redfield, whom he appointed Secretary of Commerce; I had for a time a business association with Mr. Redfield in the Home Trust Company of Brooklyn. Mr. Wilson appointed him, only to find out in a very few weeks that Mr. Redfield had no contributions to make, after which he thoroughly ignored him. Mr. Wilson was, of course, committed from the start to offering the Secretaryship of State to Mr. Bryan. Some of the other appointments dragged so much that Lindley Murray

Garrison was not asked to become Secretary of War until four days before the inauguration. Tumulty has told the story of how Garrison came to be picked [12] and it is worth citing here as a clear example of the fact that what most of us teach to our children, namely, that the highest honors in our national life go to men who have earned them by conspicuous service, is the veriest nonsense.

As the inauguration approached Tumulty became alarmed over the vacancy in the slate. Finally he pointed out to Wilson that they had not picked a single man from New Jersey, the State of which he was the head, which had given him his springboard into the Presidency. Wilson agreed that the Secretary of War must be a New Jersey man. The next question was where should they find him. They could not think of anybody but Tumulty got a list of the members of the New Jersey judiciary and Bar, opened it at the beginning and ran through the letters a, b, c, d, e, and f, without results. Under g he found Lindley M. Garrison who was a lawyer of excellent standing and was then vice-chancellor. Wilson had never heard of him and did not know that he was an outstanding equity judge in Jersey City. Garrison came to the State House when summoned the next day and was quite stunned by what Wilson offered to him—he knew no more about the army than the man in the moon. In this haphazard way Wilson obtained the services of one of the four ablest men in his Cabinet, whose rugged personality, as will later appear, became a thorn in Mr. Wilson's side. Three other members of his Cabinet Mr. Wilson had *never seen* until they were introduced to him at the inauguration! Such is Cabinetmaking in the United States.

McCombs's disappointment when Wilson passed him over in making his Cabinet selections and chose McAdoo was pitiful. He *was* the original Wilson man; he had given everything that was in him. Although Bryan at the end secured the necessary delegates, it was McCombs who assured there being any delegates at all and any publicity whatever for the Wilson boom. He was not actuated by the expectation of a reward but he would have been

[12] Joseph P. Tumulty, *Woodrow Wilson as I Know Him*, New York, 1921, p. 138.

less than human had he not been ready to receive recognition of his services. Moreover, his was a much finer character than McAdoo's. He was really heartbroken when he was told that the President-elect gave him only his choice of a diplomatic position —any one he wished save that to the Court of St. James's. It was all the harder because he had vigorously denied the talk that Wilson was an ingrate. The truth is that McCombs was not of Cabinet caliber and physically was probably not able to endure the demands of the position of Attorney General—even if he had had the legal equipment for that position. His anger and disappointment would not let him accept any lesser place and so he died with a broken heart.

When I saw all the bickerings and jealousies during those months I was more than ever glad that I was without officeholding ambition and had no favors to ask. Tumulty regrets to this day that I did not ask for a diplomatic post, which he insists I should have received although I made no large financial contributions to the campaign. Those to whom Mr. Bryan assigned the leading posts after Wilson had personally selected Walter Page, Thomas Nelson Page, and Henry van Dyke for London, Rome, and Holland, respectively, were chiefly men who had bought their offices by large campaign contributions—precisely as has been the rule under every successor to Wilson. Mr. Bryan had only the professional politician's desire to reward the faithful but this time the disposal of those high diplomatic posts to friends and rich contributors cost the country—and Wilson himself—dear. Neither the President nor the Secretary of State could have foreseen the World War but the fact is that soon after the war began Mr. Wilson found himself completely dissatisfied with four of his leading ambassadors, Walter Page, William G. Sharp in Paris, James W. Gerard in Berlin, and Frederic C. Penfield in Vienna, the latter having achieved this position (after previous useful diplomatic service) by reason of his having for his second wife one who was considered the richest woman in America. Opinions as to the worth of Gerard's services are divided. There are some in the service today who rate him highly.

Whether the President realized the extent to which Walter Page had gone in betraying his country's secrets to the government to which he was accredited, and playing the British game, I do not know. I presume not or even he must have recalled him. But here we come to another one of Wilson's extraordinary weaknesses. He would not remove a man he had appointed or ease him out after he had discovered that the appointee was a failure or a misfit. Whether the reason was that he felt he could not admit that he was fallible and had erred in his judgment, I do not know. It is the only one I can think of. Whether it was this or not, his attitude was not one to make for efficiency in government, from which the failures should promptly be removed. The case of Secretary Redfield is in point. Wilson did not, as has been said, have any use for him a few weeks after the first inauguration but he let him stay on for eight years. Anyone who was in Washington during those eight years can cite case after case. Much as Wilson disliked Secretary Garrison I do not think that he would have asked for his retirement. He had a perfect opportunity on his second inauguration to replace those ambassadors whose failure to give satisfactory service had been one of the reasons for the unprecedented dispatching of Colonel House as an unofficial ambassador to Europe but he did not utilize it. As long as we put ambassadorships up for purchase and sale we shall have similar happenings and the country is suffering as I write and will suffer therefor.

Throughout his first Administration Wilson was rigid in keeping Big Business at arm's length. Never before in my memory had the White House refused to receive the most powerful business men in the United States. They were literally outcasts. One day Thomas Lamont lunched with me and told me that Wilson had refused to receive any member of the firm of J. P. Morgan & Company, which was a brand-new experience for the firm. He said: "That's all right if we are devils or improper persons to associate with but what puzzles us is why, if contact with us is contaminating, we are being called upon by the State Department to help it advance its Central American policies by floating some loans. We are either one thing or the other. We are either respectable business men with whom the government can do business or we are not fit to associate with; we can't be both at the same time." I agreed with him and laid the matter before Tumulty in the White House the next day. He flared up and said he would lay the matter before Wilson but that he was sure the President would never have anything to do with J. P. Morgan & Company and would call Bryan off. He was correct but when the war came the outcasts were welcomed with open arms and the President entrusted extremely important things to them.

As a whole the Wilson administration got off to a remarkably promising and effective start. Again the theorist professor from Princeton, whose *New Freedom* was severely criticized in England as being "a maze of words" with only a few suggestions as to how those words could be translated into deeds, showed the professional politicians that he could get practical things accomplished—and quickly. At the outset he made it clear that he meant business and proposed to live up to campaign promises. Having called Congress into special session in the month following his inauguration, on April 8, he startled Congress and the country by appearing in person before the House of Representatives and reading his tariff message. This procedure was almost universally welcomed, foreshadowing, we of *The Evening Post* hoped in print, that seating of the Cabinet on the floor of the House for a question hour which Wilson had years before advocated in his *Congressional Government*. The message was, however, more than a mere demand for revision of the tariff. It called for the doing away of "a set of privileges and exemptions from competition behind which it was easy by any, even the crudest, forms of combinations to organize monopoly; until at last nothing is normal . . . but everything thrives by concerted arrangement."

The words that Wilson used then are as necessary for the public to keep in mind today, notably this statement: "We must abolish everything that bears even the semblance of privilege or any kind of artificial advantage, and put our business men and producers under the stimulation of a constant necessity to be efficient, economical, and enterprising, masters of competitive supremacy, better workers and merchants than any in the world. . . . It is best, indeed it is necessary, to begin with the tariff. . . ." Congress responded with amazing speed. The House promptly passed the Underwood tariff measure and the Senate followed suit in the following September after making numerous changes. It was an astounding success. More than that, the President had the resource and boldness to urge a currency bill and, in the face of the universal belief that it was impossible to do it, succeeded in getting the plan tolerated, discussed, and a bill framed which, when finally passed in December, 1913, became the Federal Reserve Act and completely remodeled the banking and currency system of the nation. No other President had done as much in peace time in so short a period. The New Jersey reformer was making good.

Chapter XIV. Last Years of Peace

SOON after the inauguration I broke my promise to the President never to ask a favor of him. My excuse was that it was nothing for myself that I asked but his approval of something which to this day I consider was a most constructive and useful proposal. On May 14, 1913, I submitted a printed plan for the appointment by the President of a National Race Commission modeled on President Roosevelt's Country Life Commission and President Taft's Industrial Commission, which was to be financed by private subscriptions to the extent necessary. The objective was "a non-partisan, scientific study of the status of the Negro with particular reference to his economic situation." It was to include an inquiry into the Negro's physical health and efficiency, homes and property, work and wages, education, religious and moral influences, his citizenship, legal status, and his participation in government. I proposed this on behalf of the National Association for the Advancement of Colored People, of whose board of directors I was then chairman. There were to be fifteen members, with Jane Addams as the head.

I pointed out to Mr. Wilson that such an inquiry would be of great service to the white South as well as to the Negroes; that a situation in which millions of people were living on the border line of destitution in the slums, which were breeding places of disease and vice, ought to be intolerable in civilized communities and that there was no adequate co-operation between the races. I cited to him a remark of Charles W. Eliot's that the vital statistics of the Southern cities were worthless because they did not take any, or any adequate, account of happenings among the colored people. He seemed at first entirely nonplused and said, "Well, what do you wish me to do about it? You do not expect me to answer today, do you?" "Of course not," I replied. "I am only laying this before you for your consideration. I am sailing for Europe in two or three days and shall not return until July. When I get back I shall ask you for another appointment and for your decision." The President expressed the greatest interest in the proposal and said he was ready to appoint the commission if it became clear that his relations with the Senate and the House would permit it. I reported on my return to New York that my interview with the President was the most satisfactory I had ever had with him.

That made more astonishing the situation which I found on my return from Europe in July. When I asked to see the President again to get his answer I met with his flat declination to receive me. I inquired at once whether *The Evening Post* had been criticizing him during my absence and found that on the contrary the editors had praised him uninterruptedly. I called at the White House and had a long talk with Tumulty about the Administration's hostile attitude to the colored people which had developed during my absence. The Negroes were up in arms because Secretary McAdoo had begun his policy of segregating Negro clerks from the white in the Treasury, the President had replaced Negro officeholders with white, and Mr. Bryan had appointed white men as ministers to Haiti and Santo Domingo, thus breaking a custom of many years' standing, according to which colored men were invariably appointed to these positions. I had had a letter from Booker Washington in which he had said that he had never seen the colored people so "discouraged and embittered" at what was going on in Washington. I felt deeply concerned, I told Tumulty, because I had given repeated assurances to the colored people during the campaign that if Wilson should be elected they would have nothing to fear. Tumulty was entirely sympathetic, particularly when I pointed out to him the political consequences and assured him that the time had come for the Administration to show its hand and be honest and above board. If it intended to take the Hoke Smith-Vardaman position, and exclude the Negro from all participation in political life, it ought to say so and then we who felt differently would cut loose and attack.

I applied several times for the promised appointment with Mr. Wilson, in vain, but I did get a graceful letter from him explaining why he could not see me. On August 19 he wrote, "Because you are an understanding friend, I took the liberty of sending you word the other day that it did not seem possible to arrange a satisfactory interview at present. I would not venture to do this with anyone who I knew would not instantly comprehend the situation. I was not jesting when I said that I had a one-track mind and just now the complications of the Mexican situation are so many, and my absorption in it and the currency matter so constant, that I knew it would be a mere form to put my mind through if I were to seek an interview with you just now." This was followed by three letters dealing with the colored people, their segregation, and the race commission. The latter, on August 21, he flatly declined to appoint. He found himself "absolutely blocked by the sentiment of Senators; not alone Senators from the South by any means, but Senators from various parts of the country." He had become convinced that there would be "a feeling of irritation [in the South] . . . because of the feeling that there is some sort of indictment involved in the very inquiry itself." On August 29, he added: "You remember I wrote you some weeks ago that I honestly thought segregation to be in the interest of the colored people as exempting them from friction and criticism in the departments, and I want to add that a number of colored men with whom we have consulted have agreed with us in this judgment." On September 22, he was hopeful that "by the slow pressure of argument and persuasion the situation may be changed and a great many things done eventually which now seem impossible. But they cannot be done, either now or at any future time, if a bitter agitation is inaugurated and carried to its natural ends. I appeal to you most earnestly to aid in holding things at a just and cool equipoise until I can discover whether it is possible to work out anything or not."

There our relations remained, in a highly unsatisfactory state until John P. Gavit, who was then our Washington correspondent, took the matter into his own hands without consulting me. He had no trouble in getting to the President and told him frankly

that he could not afford to put himself in the position of refusing
to see one who had been as loyal and helpful a supporter as I,
who had no personal ax to grind, and was deeply concerned in this
matter by reason of my official connection with the National Association for the Advancement of Colored People. The President
acted immediately and invited me to lunch with him on October
7, 1913. This was one of the most remarkable interviews in my
entire journalistic career and I immediately recorded it in fullest
detail. After the luncheon, at which only the President and Mr.
Tumulty and I were present, Mr. Wilson took me into an adjoining room where we talked for an hour. He allowed me to tell him
with the utmost frankness where I and the Association stood. He
repeated that his reason for declining to appoint the Race Commission was that he feared to antagonize the Southern Senators.
In time he hoped to win their respect and confidence to such a
degree that the day would come when they would vote to confirm
a Negro nomination. He stated that he would never appoint any
colored man to office in the South "because that would be a social
blunder of the worst kind." He admitted that the colored people
were deeply outraged by Mr. McAdoo's policy. "I fully realize
that because I get it on every side. Even Mrs. Wilson's life has
been threatened; I do not think seriously, but she is now always
guarded." He declared, however, that there was really no discrimination along race lines but that there was a social line of
cleavage which, unfortunately, corresponded with the racial line—
a disappointing bit of pettifogging.

I tried to impress upon him that both he and Mr. McAdoo
were "but atoms on the current of our national life." He said: "I
do not understand what you mean." I explained to him that his
administration would soon pass but that if his policy did not change
precedents would be established which might injure the colored
people for generations to come. When I told him of some particularly outrageous discriminations he said: "I will draw the teeth
of that; I will put a stop to that sort of thing." Then I said to him
that I was being charged with failure to do my duty in not protesting publicly because of my friendship for him. "Of course you

must not do that, Mr. Villard," Mr. Wilson replied. "I see your position clearly and I would not have you for anything shirk it; I understand perfectly." Finally he said: "I say it with shame and humiliation, with shame and humiliation," he repeated, "but I have thought about this thing for twenty years and I see no way out. It will take a very big man to solve this thing." I told him that I had given him a constructive suggestion in the Race Commission and another in an article on "Jim Crow" which I handed to him. I said that we of the National Association were perfectly certain that there were solutions available for this problem but that they must be based on justice, fair play, and giving the Negro his rights.

Nothing came of it all and when it was clear that the President did not propose to act I took the stump against the segregation policy and the mass meetings I addressed in Washington, Baltimore, Boston, and elsewhere were the most thrilling in all my experience. In Washington 3,000 people were turned away and formed an overflow meeting; the 2,000 people in the church rose and cheered me for three minutes—proof enough that they did not share Mr. Wilson's and Mr. McAdoo's contentions that segregation was in the colored people's interest. John Haynes Holmes, as usual, struck exactly the right note and roused the audience to a high pitch. I read a letter from McAdoo in which he declared that my speech, which I had sent him in advance, contained "numerous erroneous statements." Said he: "There is no 'segregation' issue in the Treasury Department. It has always been a *mischievous exaggeration*." (Italics mine.) This was a measure of the whole inadequate and weak reply. When I read out his assertion that he could not be a truer friend to the Negro than by promoting friendly relations through the removal of causes of friction in his Department the audience booed, hissed, and jeered. I told all of these audiences that the President's "philosophy is wrong, his democracy gravely at fault. He has given us beautiful and worthy sentiments in his book called *The New Freedom*. But nowhere do we find any indication that his democracy is not strictly limited by the sex line and the color line."

I am happy to add that by December our campaign had taken effect. Word went out from the White House that the segregationists must take the back track. *The Evening Post* stated its hope that the rumor that a return to former conditions was under way all along the line would prove to be true, in which case "President Wilson will not only have the approval of his own conscience but will distinctly and notably strengthen himself with the people of the whole country." None the less not one thing was done by Woodrow Wilson or his Administration to ameliorate the condition of the Negro. "The slow pressure of argument and persuasion" which he had promised changed nothing, if it was exerted. The colored people were left much worse off than when Wilson took office, for the precedent had been set; for the first time the American democracy had officially told the world that there were two classes of citizens under its flag. The supreme wrong came in 1917 when the Negroes of the South, who were denied all participation in their government, multitudes of whom were deliberately kept illiterate and deprived of every civil right and personal liberty, were drafted to go to France "to make the world safe for democracy"! What hypocrisy! What injustice! They were forced to die for the country which was still for them what Wendell Phillips had called it in Abolition days, "a magnificent conspiracy against justice."

One hearty laugh I got out of this episode. A Cincinnati newspaper announced that "the three most prominent Negroes in the United States, with the exception of Booker T. Washington, are the signers of a letter of protest against the policy of the national administration with regard to Negro employees of the government. . . . It is signed by Moorfield Storey, W. E. B. Dubois [*sic*] and Oswald Garrison Villard . . ."! I have at various times in my life been dubbed a "pink," a "red," "white," "yellow," "green," and "blue," but that was the only time that I earned the adjective "black." It recalled an experience of my grandfather's in London. Invited by Sir Fowell Buxton to meet a group of distinguished Englishmen, the host was overcome to discover that his guest, whom he had not met previously, was white. Sir Fowell's excuse, that he had thought that only a black man could have pled so eloquently for the freedom of the slaves, seemed to Mr. Garrison the finest compliment ever paid to him.

It must not be thought that my absorption in politics, the Negro, my other causes,[1] and my outside writing dimmed my joy in my profession or limited my activities with *The Evening Post* and my close attention to the details of its management, despite other important and often engrossing business affairs. Even the writing of my *John Brown, Fifty Years After,* a stupendous task, made possible from 1907 to 1910 by Katherine Mayo's enthusiasm in collating the material and rare skill in interviewing the survivors of the John Brown period all over the United States, was done on Wednesday afternoons, Saturdays, Sundays, holidays, and occasional evenings. The *success d'estime* of that book filled me with an amazement that has never passed. It was twice reviewed in one issue of the *North American Review,* by Henry Watterson and William Dean Howells. John T. Morse, Jr., the distinguished editor of the "American Statesmen" series, whom all beginners looked up to, lauded it warmly in a long article in *The Atlantic Monthly.* That stirred Ellery Sedgwick, for so many years the *Atlantic's* able editor, to a remarkable prophecy. "I am sorry for you," he wrote me. "After such praise you will probably never write another equal to it." Commenting on this William Dean Howells said: "Sedgwick is right in the sense that there are only three really dramatic figures in American history, Washington, Lincoln, and John Brown, and it would be hard to do something new and dramatic about the first two."

Much as I was drawn to historical writing, journalism remained my first love. I cannot truthfully recall that any desire for the power I may have exercised kept me in journalism. It was chiefly

---

[1] One of these interests was the establishment of the New York State Police. Moved by the fact that in a previous year no less than ninety-one women had been raped upon the unprotected highways of the Empire State, I took the lead in 1914 in calling the first meeting (at the Colony Club) to organize the work of persuading the Legislature to act, in which enterprise Katherine Mayo played a most important part.

the thrill of getting the news, of being in touch with and recording the daily kaleidoscope of public life at home and abroad as
well as the opportunity to champion reforms that fettered me. I
still cannot hear of a disaster like that of the *Hindenburg* without
being possessed by the desire to be at the telegraph instruments
or the teletypes, to receive the news hot off the wires. I suppose
that most veterans of my time will agree with me that the greatest
of peace time "stories" was the sinking of the *Titanic* on April
14-15, 1912. That had in it every element of stark, overpowering
human tragedy—pathos, superb courage, heroic resignation in the
face of death. Gross incompetency and criminal mismanagement
there were, too, and some cases of cowardice. Still it was, all in all,
a triumph for the human spirit. No one who had a hand in getting
out the issues which bore such tidings can ever forget those hours
or be free from the desire to be a part again of such journalistic
emergencies. In this case the newspapers were taxed to the fullest
to portray what happened.

Only once in my journalistic life has anyone ever attempted to
bribe me. It will hardly surprise when I affirm that it was a German ambassador who sought to buy me. Of course it was not
Bernstorff; he was too much the gentleman and had too much
sense and decency for that. It was Herr Von Holleben, who was an
especial favorite of Theodore Roosevelt's and a member of the
latter's "Tennis Cabinet." Nobody but a German would have been
as crude. At least he came right to the point. He had just returned
from Germany, he told me at my office. In Berlin he found that
his government was not happy over its treatment by the American
press. It wished to have one daily that would present its point of
view and its facts honestly. He had heard that *The Evening Post*
was not doing well financially, at least having a very hard time,
and, if this arrangement were entered into, extremely satisfactory
financial terms could be worked out immediately. It took my dull
brain some moments to grasp the purport of what he was saying
but it did not take much longer to put him in the elevator bound
for the front door of the building. It was so characteristically German! A French ambassador would have asked me to dinner at

least half a dozen times, showed me great attention, wined me, and presented me to many pretty women before saying in the most delicate way possible that he was *so* sorry to hear that *The Evening Post* was having financial difficulty—could he perhaps do something to help?

When the World War came on I could at least claim to be a seasoned journalist and I needed to be, for no American journalist had a heavier load to carry than I with my pacifism and my German birth and ancestry. I soon realized what this would mean, but when the Archduke Franz Ferdinand was assassinated we of *The Evening Post* were as slow as anyone else to recognize that a fatal train had been fired. It seemed to us only that "the real concern of European chancelleries in the presence of the Austrian tragedy is more with personal and dynastic changes which may follow in Vienna than with any possibility that Austria will be shaken out of her orbit. . . ." Not until its last issue in July, when war was at hand, did *The Nation* realize that events were pending which would forever shake all Europe out of its orbit of that day. In that we were no different from our fellow-craftsmen. From the moment war began the whole current of American life was changed and Mr. Wilson's great advances toward the New Freedom checked and finally stopped. The shadow of European events overhung everything—the markets, our sea-borne trade, the Treasury, the federal revenue.

The tremendous task of repatriating stranded Americans taxed the powers of the government at once and made most exciting reading. In the face of that horrible catastrophe it was practically impossible to focus public attention on domestic affairs. It is the truth that the process of domestic reform, reorganization, and modernization was postponed for nineteen years until Franklin Roosevelt became President. The war strain put such a severe pressure upon Mr. Wilson, besides shifting the burden of his interest from home affairs to those abroad, that he himself began to weaken. His shortcomings were intensified, his tendency to compromise accelerated, so that in reviewing his first four years we who had been his ardent champions were compelled to say of

MRS. HENRY VILLARD (*center*) LEADING THE WOMEN'S PEACE
PARADE, AUGUST, 1914

his speech accepting his renomination that, while it was the most
brilliant document he had ever penned, "he cannot expect that the
numerous blunders and disappointments of his administration will
be forgotten."

We stressed particularly "the arrogance with which, without
adequate consultation with party leaders, he has singlehanded
changed the historic policies of his party." Still, after war came,
the President tried to push his reform program, just as he had
upheld the national honor in obtaining from Congress the abroga-
tion of our treaty-breaking exemption of American ships from
paying tolls in the Panama Canal. The Clayton Antitrust Law
was passed October 15, 1914; it not only marked a step forward
in the control of monopolies but moved Samuel Gompers to call
it "the Magna Charta of American labor"—another one of its
many Magna Chartas. Early in 1914 the Chicago *Inter-Ocean*
had said that Wilson's visible control of Congress was "greater
than that of any other President within living memory." There
is no doubt that his first two years had made American politics
more interesting, not to say exciting, than they had been for a
generation. All the more was the pity that the European catastrophe practically stopped American progress.

As soon as Germany entered the war and invaded Belgium I
and the staff unqualifiedly committed both our daily and our
weekly to the side of the Allies. I stress this because I still find
references by alleged historians to my supposed tenderness toward
the Germans.[2] Never was there a more unanimous decision by all
concerned. I myself wrote a leading editorial called "The Real
Crime Against Germany" which alone should have protected me
from any such charge.[3] It contained this passage:

The Nation has always entertained and expressed the highest admiration for the German people, but never for the Germany of the Kaiser.
We have never believed that a people of essentially noble quality should
be subject to the will of an autocratic king or emperor, however enlight-

[2] Cf. F. L. Paxson, *Pre-War Years, 1913-1917*, Boston, 1936, p. 191.
[3] *The Nation*, August 13, 1914.

ened he may be, or however ardent a guardian of peace during a long period of years. Never have we upheld the Germany of the mailed fist, of the autocracy of militarism; against its excesses, its encroachments upon civil rights, its assertion that it constitutes a sacrosanct caste superior to any other, we have protested in season and out of season.

After reviewing the Germany of high aspiration and noble ideals, the Germany "to whose spiritual leadership every nation the world over is deeply in debt," the Germany of Schiller, Goethe, Kant, Fichte, Schubert, Schumann, and Wagner, I said that this war into which the finer Germany had been plunged was "nothing short of a crime." And I wound up with this sentiment: "For ourselves we can only say that the one consolation in it all is that, if humanity is not to retrograde unspeakably, absolutism must pay for this denial of Christianity. Out of the ashes must come a new Germany, in which democracy shall rule, in which no one man, and no group of professional man-killers, shall have the power to plunge the whole world into mourning." It does not seem to me today as if I could have been more emphatic and I at once brought down upon myself the antagonism of the Münsterbergs, the Von Machs, and Dernburgs.

The Evening Post was as well prepared to meet this emergency as our slender finances permitted. We were fortunate in our managing editor, John P. Gavit, who had been our Washington correspondent during 1912-13 after long service with the Associated Press in Albany and in Washington and as superintendent of its central division with headquarters at Chicago. There never was a cleaner or more competent journalist or one who could inspire greater affection and devotion in his subordinates. We especially utilized our foreign exchanges, including the German as long as the English permitted us to have them, and so printed a good deal of news that the other newspapers did not handle. Editorially Mr. Ogden gave a brilliant lead. Naturally we speedily felt the shock of the war in our finances and our advertising. On the other hand, the circulation responded to the earth-shaking events.

The first reaction of the public was against the whole military system in Europe and a recognition—before the passions engendered by the war began to becloud people's judgments—that this was at the bottom of the conflict; that you could not build up huge military rivalries without insuring an inevitable explosion, a truth as obvious then as in 1939. Within a few days a strong committee of women was formed, of which my mother became chairman, for the purpose of giving expression to the sense of outrage of American women at the unholy slaughter daily reported from Belgium and Alsace. On August 29 several thousand women paraded down Fifth Avenue from Fifty-Ninth Street to Union Square with my mother at their head. There were no bands; there was dead silence and the crowds watched the parade in the spirit of the marchers, with sympathy and approval. The President had also approved, for the organizers, in complete sympathy with his public statements in the early days of the conflict, had courteously asked him for his consent. He was especially pleased by the decision of the paraders to carry no flags except the peace flag and to have no set speeches at the conclusion of the parade, but brief informal addresses were made to all who would listen.

It was universally agreed by most of those who witnessed the parade, including hard-boiled newspaper men, that a more impressive demonstration was never witnessed in New York. The silence, the dignity, the black dresses of the marchers—those who did not have black dresses wore black arm bands—the solemnity of the crowds, all of these produced a profound effect upon the beholders. The press was not yet biased enough to ridicule it. What is more remarkable, the parade had the support of some of the most conservative women's organizations such as the National Council of Women and, amazing to relate, the Daughters of the American Revolution contributed $25 to the costs of the parade. Mrs. William Cummings Story, the President General, joined the committee with warm approval of the "practical character" of the undertaking. A little more than a year later the Daughters took the position, ever since held by them, that to be a pacifist is to be a pro-German, or a pro-Bolshevik, or a pro-something else which they do not like. Contrary to their usual custom of opposing parades on Fifth Avenue on Saturday afternoon, large dry goods stores contributed to the very small amount needed to make it a success.

I took advantage of the prevailing feeling against militarism to found a "League to Limit Armaments" because there was an immediate outcry from our jingoes and militarists that we must follow in Germany's footsteps and militarize. I obtained an amazing response to my call for support. On December 18, 1914, the League was organized at the Railroad Club. Nicholas Murray Butler, Bishop David H. Greer, George A. Plimpton, Charles C. Burlingham, George Foster Peabody, Adolph Lewisohn, Horace White, Hamilton Holt, Lillian Wald, and Carrie Chapman Catt were among the twenty-four who signed the invitation for the first meeting and recorded their opposition "to the exploitation at this time of the so-called military unpreparedness of the United States." We felt that "there has been presented to the United States an unexampled opportunity for constructive moral and political leadership in the work of the world," and we put ourselves squarely behind the President who had just said to Congress: "This is assuredly the opportunity for which a people and a government like ours were raised up—the opportunity not only to speak but actually to embody and exemplify counsels of peace and sanity and the lasting concord which is based on justice and fair and generous dealing." Eighty-three persons attended that meeting, with President Butler in the chair. He spoke eloquently against those who urged America "not to maintain the traditional American policy but to depart from it." No one could have made a better or more powerful antipreparedness speech; to him it was not a "gathering of protest so much as I conceive it in terms of offering constructive leadership in a great forward movement." We were still some time away from his complete yielding to the god of war by driving out members of his faculty who dared to continue to hold his 1914 views when we entered the war. Bishop Greer, who never surrendered, also bore strong testimony and so did George Foster Peabody and others.

Among those who joined the League were two men who also

later turned their coats completely. Newell Dwight Hillis's dreadful anti-German speeches, repeating the worst of the war atrocity lies, remain the foulest disgrace to the cloth of the entire struggle; were there a Devil he must have reveled in every war utterance of that noted divine who could not even remember the injunction not to bear false witness, to say nothing of some of the other Commandments. Newton D. Baker was one of the first to accept membership in my League and expressed himself warmly in favor of it. Yet as soon as he became Secretary of War he surrendered wholly to the militarists, yes, even outdid them, and so far from seeking to limit armaments he was by 1919 urging upon his countrymen the very worst feature of European militarism, universal military training. That once great liberal and democrat then and there began his rapid descent into the camp of the enemy.[4]

In 1916 I became a member of the board of directors and executive committee of the Associated Press, having been first elected on April 25, 1916, and later re-elected. I had been a member of this organization from the time that I joined *The Evening Post*. I greatly enjoyed my association with my fellow-directors, with the general manager, Melville E. Stone, and Frank B. Noyes who has only just (1938) retired from the presidency after thirty-eight years of devoted service. It is hardly an exaggeration to say that I was one of a very few liberals who ever joined that board. Mr. Noyes at a recent dinner in his honor stated that he always respected me and my views while never being able to agree with any of them. However, I flatter myself that I had a certain ameliorating influence upon the board, as, for example, when I induced it to issue a warning to all the members following the severance of the diplomatic relations with Germany. It urged that the utmost care be taken to guard against rumors of every description; "unverified stories of disturbances or demonstrations

---

[4] Trained in the noble school of Tom L. Johnson in Cleveland and one of his successors as mayor, Newton Baker turned corporation attorney after the war, defended the very forces that he and Johnson had attacked, and died without the regard and often the respect of his closest associates in his reforming days, some of whom united in publishing a pamphlet reviewing his apostasy.

incident thereto must be avoided and statements of military movements or other military aspects of the situation should be confined to the facts and no attempt made to construe or interpret
the reason therefor." None the less color constantly crept into the
dispatches which was, I suppose, unavoidable in view of the national hysteria. It is a curious fact about the Associated Press that
its very strength is also its weakness. Its organization is theoreti-
cally ideal in that it is a nonprofit-making, co-operative society
with all members contributing their news. That means, however,
that the head office cannot rise above the joint standards of the
members. As a matter of fact for years the profit-making United
Press was a much more liberal news gathering agency than the
Associated Press, with a wider vision, a more catholic taste, and
far greater sympathy for the underdog and the oppressed and for
the problems of labor in general.

These views of mine as to the Associated Press I have set forth
at length elsewhere.[5] I must, however, pay tribute to the workers
in its service. There must be exceptions, of course, in any such
organization but in all the twenty-one years of my membership I
found very few cases, indeed, of anything suggesting corruption.
In 1911 I was appointed chairman of a committee to investigate
the service, as there were many charges going round in progressive circles as to its integrity and freedom from corporate influence. Here again the service cannot be different from the standards of the members. As the bulk of them are large corporations,
whose managers are closely affiliated with Big Business and are
dependent upon the advertising of great business enterprises for
their success, it is inevitable that their points of view and tendencies
should generally be conservative if not reactionary. As everyone
knows, the number of really liberal and politically independent
newspapers is small. I was given an excellent committee comprising a Harvard classmate, Frederick Roy Martin, of the Providence
Journal as secretary, later general manager of the Associated Press,

[5] *The Nation*, April 16 and 23, 1930. Reprinted as pamphlet under the title,
The Press Today.

with Bruce Haldeman of the Louisville *Courier-Journal,* Victor Murdock of the Wichita *Eagle,* and the veteran Samuel Bowles of the Springfield, Mass., *Republican.* We held a number of sessions and examined twenty-one witnesses. We unanimously reported that "the statements and insinuations affecting the integrity of the Associated Press and its reports are unjustified."

We did find that there had been errors of judgment and we notified the directors "that the social relations of the general manager [Melville E. Stone] with the individuals prominent in powerful financial circles, and likewise his acceptance of decorations from foreign governments without objection from the board of directors, had not unnaturally aroused unjust suspicion of the independence and impartiality of his administration of the news service." We were convinced that Mr. Stone had not been influenced by these things, that he had been devoted to the interests of the Associated Press, and had been indefatigable in developing and strengthening its service. Nevertheless we believed that the head of the Associated Press should "by his personal conduct and relations give no ground for a suspicion of his independence and incorruptibility as the agent and representative of the press."

We begged the directors and general manager to defend the independence of the Associated Press from any governmental control "direct or indirect, conscious or unconscious," and asked that all statements given out in Washington by officials should, when printed, be clearly earmarked as official or semiofficial. Our report asked the most rigid opposition by the Associated Press to "attempts of executive officers, department and bureau heads [in the government], to make favorable reports or the absence of criticism a condition precedent to the giving of news to the Associated Press." Since this recommendation was made during the Republican administration of Mr. Taft it is of special interest in connection with the prevailing charges that the Roosevelt administration has similarly sought to influence the news or to control it in the interest of a Roosevelt dictatorship.

One extremely dramatic episode marked the committee's inquiry. Frank B. Kellogg of Minnesota, later Secretary of State and sponsor of the wholly abortive Kellogg Peace Pact, had made his reputation by successfully conducting the United States government case against the Standard Oil Company. It early came to our ears that Mr. Kellogg had made the most serious charges against the Associated Press, and particularly against Melville Stone, and we finally succeeded in getting a copy of a letter written by him on October 29, 1908, to George Thompson, the owner of the St. Paul *Dispatch*. This letter included these statements: "I am very busy these days taking testimony in the Standard Oil case. Your friend Melville E. Stone is controlled absolutely by the Standard Oil people. He will not, of course, send out any reports of the testimony that he is not obliged to, at least that is my opinion from all that I have seen. I told Don Seitz of the *World* and Hamlin of the *Tribune* and the man on the *Times*, and they have had special men at the trial, and as you will see from the enclosed clipping, they have published some of the testimony I have been bringing out. But from Chicago not a word came out against the Standard Oil. It is astonishing that that concern can control the Associated Press."

The committee called upon Mr. Kellogg at the Ritz-Carlton Hotel in New York. I asked him whether he had ever made any criticisms of or charges against Melville Stone and the Associated Press in connection with the Standard Oil. He emphatically denied that he ever had. It was an extremely painful moment when I handed him a copy of his letter to Thompson and asked him to explain it. The room was dimly lighted and he took it over to a large table lamp and seated himself with the light full upon his face. I do not think any member of the committee ever forgot that scene. All that he could say was that he had completely forgotten the letter and that he must have believed it when he wrote it. He then reiterated his position and stated that his opinion that the Standard Oil completely owned Stone and the Associated Press was also held by his associate counsel and by "other prominent men." After a most thorough and painstaking investigation the committee came to the conclusion that Mr. Kellogg was entirely mistaken and that his reference to the general manager was inexcusably reckless and wholly unwarranted by the facts. The Standard Oil, for example, was on record at the same time as being strongly of the belief that it could not obtain a fair hearing from the Associated Press for its side of the case. Mr. Kellogg stated that the reports carried by my *Evening Post* had been entirely satisfactory, beyond any criticism, yet in more than fifty per cent of the reports we had relied exclusively upon the Associated Press service which Mr. Kellogg criticized.

We found that the New York hearings had been covered by perhaps the most reliable man in the Associated Press, who would certainly never have been selected had there been a desire to color the testimony. This reporter gave us his word that no instructions of any kind had been given to him as to how to handle the story. We did, however, discover that the press agent of the Standard Oil, Captain P. C. Boyle, who was also a member of the Associated Press representing the Oil City, Pennsylvania, *Derrick*, had disbursed Standard Oil money to the reporter of the City News Association, which was entirely distinct from the Associated Press—not to purchase any favors, he said, but just in order to "secure accuracy of reporting." It was a great joke on me that some of that money had found its way to a minor employee of *The Evening Post* but after considering the circumstances as gravely as possible the committee absolved me and my paper of any corruption! That was the nearest I ever came to running down any Associated Press wrongdoing. I must add that on learning the facts Melville Stone promptly gave Frank Kellogg a very few hours in which to retract his statements or to face a libel suit for $100,000 damages. Mr. Kellogg withdrew his statements.

For one thing the Associated Press has deserved the strongest censure. Discovering that the Hearst newspapers which were members of the Associated Press and his International News Service, were deliberately stealing the news of the Associated Press and giving it to those of his papers which were not members, it brought suit against Hearst and carried the case up to the Supreme Court of the United States. The Court upheld the contentions of the Associated Press. In other words, Hearst was found guilty of everything with which the Associated Press charged him. When the case was first decided in our favor by a United States District Court in New York City, I demanded that Hearst immediately be expelled from the Associated Press. I was told that that could not be done while the case was pending, but that action would be taken just as soon as the case was concluded. When it did come to a triumphant ending the directors did not have the courage to expel the man whom they had convicted of theft of the news, violation of his pledges as a member, and other serious offenses. I have never received any adequate explanation of this failure of the directors to live up to their plain duty. One does not usually convict men of thieving and then continue to associate with them and let them benefit by an extremely valuable association.

Chapter XV. I Turn Washington Correspondent

ON the morning of Friday, May 7, 1915, my work was interrupted between ten and eleven o'clock by two telephone calls. Both were from the Wall Street district and both speakers asked excitedly if it was true that the *Lusitania* had been sunk. I answered that it was not and scouted the idea. They insisted that it had been. In each case I rang up the Associated Press to be sure. The A.P. also felt that it was a silly rumor. But at one o'clock there came the dreadful flash that horrified us all, changed the whole aspect of the World War and our own relations to it, and announced the most sensational disaster in marine history: *"Lusitania sunk by German submarine."* When the *Titanic* sank the news was also apparently known in New York hours before any announcement was made and diligent official inquiry failed to give any explanation of this. I admit that these two happenings have made me more inclined to believe in the supernatural or, at least, thought transference, than anything else I have been cognizant of; somehow or other the hundreds who were dying on the *Titanic* and *Lusitania* appear to have made those disasters known across the Atlantic. Even the fact that the Cunard Company withheld the news for some time, according to a story in the *Times* the next day, does not explain the *Lusitania* phenomena.

This tremendous event caught us of *The Evening Post* in an unhappy position in Washington. We had loaned our regular correspondent, Edward G. Lowry, to Ambassador Page for service in the embassy in London, and were relying chiefly on the Associated Press for our Washington news. John Gavit and I immediately put our heads together. We tried in vain for the veteran Francis E. Leupp, who had served us so well there for years, but he was unavailable and so were a couple of others. I urged Gavit to go; he was the logical man as he knew all the ropes and was *persona grata* in the White House. For family reasons he could not leave. We were at our wits' ends when suddenly he turned to me and said: "Why don't *you* go? You can do it better with your Washington contacts than any outsider we can pick up." The suggestion took my breath away; after considerable discussion I reluctantly acceded with the proviso that I should go only for a couple of weeks, or until we could find someone else. Those two weeks lengthened into ten months during which time I was a full-fledged Washington correspondent and engaged in what was indubitably the most interesting experience of my newspaper career, at least on this side of the Atlantic. My stay in Washington was as exciting as it could possibly be.

As I was the first managing owner of a metropolitan daily to be his own Washington correspondent my articles attracted much more attention than I had expected that they would, probably more than they deserved. No one was more surprised than I that I could acquit myself in this new field without discredit. Because of my reputed closeness to Mr. Wilson and his Cabinet my dispatches were read with especial care in newspaper offices all over the country and constantly quoted. Indeed, I was astonished to find my views, and notably a series of sketches of the Cabinet members which I wrote, taken very seriously—one of these sketches set off fireworks as I shall presently show. So far as Mr. Wilson is concerned, the truth is that I saw him only rarely and never was on anything approaching an intimate footing. He never sent for me or talked with me informally about politics and affairs. If I influenced him during this period it was through my letters in *The Evening Post* and my daily contacts with Joe Tumulty, for whom I retain to this day a great liking and respect, and a sense of gratitude for his kind and helpful reception of me, his confidence in me, and the many helpful tips he permitted me to use.

It is a curious fact that I had not been two days in Washington before I supplied the President through Tumulty with a phrase which brought down upon him a storm of abuse and denunciation.

The words "too proud to fight," embodied in his Philadelphia speech of May 10, were mine. When they were denounced as craven and cowardly Tumulty came to me in a state of great alarm. I explained that when I gave him that phrase—without the slightest idea that it would be offered verbatim to the President— I had qualified it by the words "because there are other and better ways of settling international disputes than by the mass killing of human beings." As my words appeared they were without the context and it is undeniable, as James Kerney has pointed out, that "it was not the happiest language to flash to the country three days after the sinking of the *Lusitania* when jingo Americans were lustily demanding German blood." [1] Subsequently the President modified the phrase, but the damage was done.

Tumulty was not the only the cushion between the President and the press, he was also the liaison officer without whom all the correspondents would have been badly served in the White House, or not at all. Indeed, the President's contacts with his "wireless antennae of public opinion"—as he first called the press men—became less and less useful until they were finally dropped altogether. He felt it a degradation that a man of his stature and office should be subjected to cross-examination by a group of news writers, which cross-examination, it must be admitted, was often hostile and meant to entrap. So we all got much of our news and most of our inside tips from Tumulty and after knowing him well we could read a great deal from his aspect and manner and between the lines of his statements. He was not only a rare interpreter of public opinion with a real sense of news and news values but he was often—not always—a surprisingly wise and farseeing coun-

[1] Kerney, *op. cit.*, p. 351. Wilson's actual words were: "There is such a thing as a man being too proud to fight. There is such a thing as a nation being so right that it does not need to convince others by force that it is right." I have been credited by Ernest Sutherland Bates in his *Story of Congress, 1789-1935* with being the author of the phrase "peace without victory" but that is, I believe, an error. Mr. Wilson's "we have no quarrel with the German people" was, it appears, taken from an editorial by A. G. Gardiner in the London *Daily News* of August 8, 1914. See Irene Cooper Willis, *England's Holy War*, New York, 1928, p. 87.

selor on questions and issues, sometimes as to foreign affairs where
one would not naturally have expected him to be competent. His
sense of humor and the Irish in him made him generally successful in his dealings with the politicians as well as with the newspaper men. He himself was an extremely skillful politician, which
means that he was at all times ready to compromise.

When I arrived in Washington the day after the sinking of the
Lusitania I found the capital in a state of excitement such as it had
not known since the blowing up of the *Maine*. Several members
of the Cabinet, including Lane and Garrison, were urging our
immediate entry into the war and the jingo journalists, the war-
mongers, and the followers of Leonard Wood and Theodore
Roosevelt were in full cry. I was, however, able to say with
authority in my first dispatch that "there will be no war as a result
of the *Lusitania* sinking unless Germany starts it." I reported that
there was an almost unanimous opinion in official circles that the
situation called not for mere words but action, "not war, of course,
but action which will convey to Germany in unmistakable terms
the righteous indignation of the American people for a violation
not only of international law but of the fundamental decencies of
civilization." The President, I soon learned, had shut himself up
and refused to see any of his Cabinet. They hoped for a Cabinet
meeting at once and, failing that, sent him letters as if he lived
far away—Lane telephoned. On Sunday the President emerged
from his seclusion to play golf, partly in order to reassure the
public by not departing from his regular routine. He secluded
himself again as soon as he returned from the links and the
Cabinet did not see him until the meeting called by him on
May 11.

It was much to Mr. Wilson's credit that he refused to be stampeded into hasty action and that he insisted upon calmness and
time for careful deliberation. A statement issued by Tumulty the
day after the tragedy stressed the words "deliberation" and "firmness" in announcing that the President was considering the problem "very earnestly but very calmly." Four days after the disaster
I telegraphed that "a policy and line of action have already been

decided upon," and that everything "sustained the theory that the
President came into the Cabinet meeting with a statement written
down, which was submitted to the Cabinet for approval." That
was the way Mr. Wilson worked. His Cabinet was not there for
consultation or deliberation with the President but merely to pass
upon his views submitted to it by him with the expectation that
there would be a prompt vote of complete approval. Only a
minority of the Cabinet was brave enough occasionally to dissent
or go counter to the President's views, for the members realized
that if they did so often they would lose what influence they had
with the Chief Executive—some had none at all.

While drafting the *Lusitania* note Mr. Wilson sat in his shirt
sleeves behind a locked door upstairs in the White House and typed
away upon his portable typewriter as was his habit. It was, a
Washington wit said, a new and lofty kind of shirt-sleeve diplomacy. He first made shorthand notes or wrote them out and then
himself typed out the whole note; his first draft was not finished
until Tuesday morning. It is true that one passage in the first note
to Germany was a direct product of the pen of William J. Bryan
and that there were other suggestions of Cabinet members embodied in the final draft. But it is a fact that he did not talk to any
adviser except Colonel House, and Secretary Lane by telephone.
When he appeared before the newspaper men at the weekly press
conference after the Cabinet meeting he was like "a man who had
dropped a heavy burden. . . . It was manifest to all at the conference that the President was in an exceedingly cheerful frame
of mind." This was my eye-witness testimony for I was given
permission to attend the press conferences and received also the
courtesy of the press galleries. My office was in the old Home
Life Building and we shared it with the Chicago *Daily News*, with
whose Washington correspondent, Leroy T. Vernon, I spent many
happy hours. He more than anyone else aided me in acquiring the
technique of the job and kept me from numerous mistakes and
I gave him whatever inside information I obtained. For many
years he was one of the most solid and trustworthy correspondents

in Washington, with a compelling sense of the dignity of his work and of his profession.

The *Lusitania* note dispatched, President Wilson left Washington on the night of May 14, bound down the Potomac on the *Mayflower* en route to New York to review the fleet and to get some rest and change. On the whole I thought his *Lusitania* note excellent and as restrained as could have been expected under the circumstances. But the more I pondered the situation the more I became convinced that unless the President showed an equally firm hand in dealing with the British the note would fail to produce the effect that it ought to in Berlin. The British violations of international law, their deliberate interference with American trade and shipping without warrant, had greatly exasperated the business men in New York and importers and exporters everywhere. American ships bound for neutral ports were often taken into Falmouth or Kirkwall by British cruisers and detained there from one to six weeks with what losses to shippers and shipowners can be imagined. Just after I arrived in Washington, Cone Johnson, the Solicitor of the State Department, had addressed a group of protestants from New York in a corridor of the State Department and had declared publicly that the British had "violated every canon of international law." The British fleet was maintaining a veritable blockade of the harbor of New York, often stopping and boarding ships just outside the three-mile limit, thus repeating a course of action which in the years leading up to 1812 helped to bring about our second war with the mother country. When the *Lusitania* was sunk Great Britain was actually blockading Norway, Sweden, and Denmark against the United States, an example of this being the detention of twenty-four cotton ships all bound for Scandinavian or Dutch ports, this in violation of assurances from the British embassy in Washington that all cotton for which contracts of sale and freight engagements had been made before March 2 would be allowed to pass, provided the ships sailed not later than March 31, unless the British government bought their cargoes at contract price.

Toward the end of May representatives of the packing industry came to Washington to see if something could not be done to expedite payment for $15,000,000 worth of American meat products consigned to neutral countries but at that time being detained in British harbors. As the government failed to accomplish anything, the Southern cotton and the Western copper men later joined the packers in protesting, the cotton men asserting that the South faced bankruptcy unless a fair price could be found for cotton and putting upon the British embargo the responsibility for the collapse of cotton prices. But the worst British outrage was the seizure of several vessels flying the American flag as they came out of New York harbor bound from that port for Norfolk to load coal. They had previously been German-owned but they had hoisted the American flag because they had been certified by the Commissioner of Navigation as having been purchased by American capital and being 95 per cent owned by American citizens. The British fleet actually took some of these ships into Halifax harbor, it was stated in Washington, merely because those ships had previously been German-owned. Anyone can imagine what the effect upon the country would have been if the President had announced this and given the British government forty-eight hours to release those vessels. No vigorous action was ever taken; if there had been, both England and Germany would have understood that the United States was not only really neutral as between the two sides but capable of extremely vigorous action.

With some of these things in mind I called upon Robert Lansing at his residence on Sunday evening, May 16. At that time counselor of the State Department, he received me in the most friendly manner. I told him that I thought I knew the German character about as well as any American could after my years of residence there and my constant reading of German political history and two German dailies. On the basis of this knowledge, I said I felt that excellent as the *Lusitania* note was it would not bring the German government to terms as effectively as we all wished if there were not correspondingly strong action against Great Britain. While it was true that the British had not taken American lives in violation of international law and in a particularly brutal and cowardly fashion, as had the Germans, they had none the less sinned gravely. I reminded him of Cone Johnson's words and I asked him if the time had not come to show that our government was determined to hold the scales even by sending the sharpest kind of a note to London.

To my surprise he replied that Mr. Johnson had not exaggerated; that the conduct of Great Britain was unbearable. It had promised in writing not to put cotton on the contraband list and now had done so. He was entirely of my opinion that this was the moment to act and in no uncertain manner. "In fact," he said, "I have drafted just such a note in as strong language as I could write. Did you meet a messenger leaving this house as you came in? No? Then you must have just missed him. He has gone from here to the train to put the note into Mr. Wilson's hands in New York tomorrow morning. I hope it will be dispatched at once." I could not begin to express my gratification for the more I thought about the situation the more convinced I was of the profound effect that such a note would have in Berlin, as well as in London. I then took my courage in both hands and asked him if he did not think the time had come to make some publication about this note and whether I might do so in *The Evening Post* the next day, protecting, of course, the source of my information. To my joy he said: "Yes, I think it should be done. You may go ahead, with discretion." It was thus that I obtained another of the important "beats" of my career and one that stirred the British government not a little.

The next day I carefully wrote the story, notified John Gavit that it was coming, and directed him to hold it until the last edition and then play it up as much as possible. It carried the head, "England's Turn Next to Receive a Reminder." The dispatch began: "Unless all signs fail, it is to be England's turn next. There is at this writing an excellent prospect that shortly—very shortly— perhaps within seventy-two hours, she will be haled before the Presidential bar of justice to receive from Mr. Wilson information as to just how this government feels in regard to her violations of international law and practice. It goes without saying that when this is done the information will be imparted in a note that will not fall behind that to Germany in vigor or skill. The friendly tone will be there, too. . . ." I added that: "It is felt in unofficial circles here that the government, to maintain its self-respect, must act as vigorously in this matter as it did in the *Lusitania* affair. It has right and justice on its side. . . ."

The dispatch made a sensation. Every managing editor in New York called his Washington office to inquire why I had been allowed to scoop the town in that way. A horde of correspondents rushed to the State Department, to Mr. Bryan, and Mr. Lansing. Mr. Bryan denied all knowledge of it. Mr. Lansing looked the reporters straight in the face and without blinking told them that he could not imagine how Mr. Villard had conceived such an idea! I never blamed him for that; under the circumstances he was bound to protect himself and it was not the first time in our history that a journalist had been made use of to fly a trial balloon and if necessary to take the consequences of doing so. We had constantly to risk our reputations for accuracy and truth telling. Naturally the correspondents got nothing out of Tumulty and were assured by him that he knew nothing about it—I doubt if he did. They were very much puzzled; I had not been long enough there for them to size me up but at least I had the reputation, I think, of being a responsible and not a sensational journalist.

The effect in England of my "beat" was immediate. On the following Friday the New York papers carried a long statement issued by the London Foreign Office "to correct what the Government believes to be a misunderstanding of Great Britain's attitude toward American ships and American cargoes in other neutral bottoms." It declared that there were only three American ships then held up but admitted the detention of thirty-six neutral vessels of which twenty-three carried American cotton, which cotton had been, or shortly would be, it said, purchased by His Majesty's government. It admitted there were great delays in dealing with other shipments but blamed this largely on the "exorbitant terms insisted upon by the representatives of American packers." Its tenth point was that the published American trade returns gave "little substance" to the "repeated complaint as to injury suffered generally by American trade in consequence of interference due to British naval measures."

Our traders did not share that optimistic view and all summer kept the State Department in a turmoil. An interesting side light is the fact, now authoritatively brought out by a British admiral,[2] that during all the time the British government was thus harassing American trade, for fear lest our cargoes of cotton and meat be resold by the Scandinavian countries to Germany, the crews of British ships were regularly landing goods on Scandinavian docks which were taken directly to Germany. In March, 1916, "all the wharves in Copenhagen were choked with cases of tea, a large part of which was from our colonies en route to Germany"; [3] "Germany received all she required to the end of the war through the prodigal supplies of coal from her foolish and gullible enemy [Great Britain]." [4] Not until about the time the United States came into the war was this direct British provisioning of the enemy checked. But this is only one of numerous pieces of war-time stupidity or crookedness on the part of the Allies.[5]

The day after my "beat" the morning newspapers carried general denials of my story which did not worry my editorial associates in New York because I had notified Gavit of the source of my information, and I followed my first story with reaffirmations

[2] Rear Admiral M. W. W. P. Consett, R.N., *The Triumph of Armed Forces,* London, 1923.

[3] Consett, *op. cit.,* p. 213.

[4] Consett, *op. cit.,* p. 128.

[5] In one case a Norwegian schooner sailing from Brest carried nickel purchased by the Krupps from a French firm *direct to Hamburg* after being stopped by a French warship. The story of the safety of the Briey iron mines from French bombers is familiar. Eduard Bernstein declared at the German Socialist Congress in 1920 that a *quarter of a million tons* of German steel were exported *from Germany to England in 1915,* that is, during the war! See *The Nation,* April 3, 1920, p. 412, for the facts as to the Briey mines. See also the *Journal Officiel* of the Chamber of Deputies, January 24, February 1 and 8, 1919, and the hearings of the Briey Commission of the Chamber. There is also a book, *Briey,* by M. Gustave Tery.

of it despite the denials. On the following Tuesday when I entered Mr. Bryan's conference with the newspaper men he asked me to please remain after the others had gone. I did so. Taking me to a window he said: "Mr. Villard, you are in a very serious situation. You have either stumbled across a governmental secret to which you had no right or you have betrayed the confidence of someone. You can choose either horn of the dilemma. I hope that I may feel that the disservice you have rendered the government can be explained by the fact that you have only been acting as a Washington correspondent for a short time and do not understand the conditions and the ethics governing the obtaining of news in this city." He spoke with great feeling and evident anger. I kept perfectly cool and replied to him that as it happened I did not have to choose either horn of the dilemma, that there were other possibilities. I added: "Mr. Bryan, as for my newspaper ethics and standards, they are known of all men because they are daily illustrated in *The Evening Post*. More than that, I have been sending correspondents all over the world for the last eighteen years and I challenge anybody to say that these men have ever violated ethical canons while they were in the service of *The Evening Post*, or have ever had any instructions from me to do else than abide by those canons. I know very well what the news-gathering conditions in this city are, and neither you nor anybody else can give me the slightest instruction therein. I beg you to believe that I have nothing on my conscience whatsoever in connection with that story, and I stand by it." Mr. Bryan then calmed down, took a different tone, and we had a talk which had a remarkable outcome.

He complained bitterly about the conduct of certain pressmen, notably the Hearst journalists. I had watched him and them again that morning and felt humiliated for him and for the country by the figure which he cut. The Hearst men were insufferable, shooting one question after another at him which he did not know how to parry or to stop. Some of the questions were diabolically clever and no more capable of being answered than the familiar poser: "Have you stopped beating your wife?" For example, Mr. Bryan was at that time appearing weekly on the Chautauqua circuit to eke out his income—a highly improper and undignified performance. One of the pressmen asked him where his next show would be and whether he would appear before or after the Swiss bell ringers and Japanese tumblers. I described this scene in my correspondence by saying that Mr. Bryan reminded me of a clumsy old buffalo trying to ward off attacks by a pack of young and agile hounds.[6] When he spoke to me of his press difficulties I asked him whether he had not considered taking up the matter with the standing committee appointed by the correspondents entitled to enter the Senate and House press galleries, which committee was, in a sense, a censor of the conduct of the pressmen, or at least was the only approach to anything of the kind. He replied that he had not but would think about it. I assured him that I would also keep it in mind, talk with some of the correspondents, and make suggestions to him the next time we met. We shook hands quite amicably; that was not the situation the next time we came together.

To return to Mr. Lansing's note, Mr. Bryan was strongly in favor of its being sent and, when the President did not act upon the note, on the ground that it might complicate our relations with Germany or even seem to weaken our attitude toward that country, since the sending of it might be interpreted as a yielding to Germany, everybody in the State Department was profoundly concerned, as the German newspapers were daily demanding that we should hold the scales even. Mr. Bryan himself, in an address to the German-American Friends of Peace at Madison Square Garden on June 25, after his resignation, declared that he had felt that the government ought to repeat "its insistence that the Allies shall not interfere with our commerce with neutral countries." He further put it thus: "The difference on this point [between himself and the President] was a matter of judgment and not a matter of principle. My reason for desiring to have the matter presented to Great Britain at once was not that Germany had any right to

[6] When Mr. Bryan said good-by to the pressmen on resigning, he likened himself to an "old hen" trying to safeguard her chicks under her wings, in his case diplomatic secrets, while the news men played the role of chicken hawks!

ask it but because I was anxious to make it as easy as possible for Germany to accept the demands of the United States and cease to employ submarines against merchantmen."

Nothing moved the President. The Lansing note, despite accumulating proof of further British aggressions, lay upon Mr. Wilson's desk from May until the following October. When it was sent it was weak and emasculated. In June I telegraphed that the administration was "merely waiting for the proper time to forward a message of some kind." But the proper time never came in Mr. Wilson's judgment. There was always some reason in connection with the Germans to prevent our taking the stand we should have for the sake of international law itself without regard to the rights and wrongs of the conflict then raging. It is to me undeniable that our failure to fight for the sanctity of international law at that time is one of the reasons why, at this writing, international law—if any still exists—is a joke, and I know that my view is upheld by high authorities, by men deeply versed in the history of international law and diplomacy.

I felt then, and feel now, that this was a turning point in our own attitude toward the war, this and the rescinding of the prohibition of loans to the Allies; that if that note had been sent and strongly backed up we might have kept out of it. The failure to send the note undoubtedly gave the lie to our pretensions of being neutral in the conflict, which Berlin sensed as well as some of us in Washington. We know now that several of the Cabinet had abandoned all pretense of neutrality even before the sinking of the *Lusitania,* but it was the President's failure to live up to his own proclamation and remain neutral that finally insured our going in. He, too, yielded more and more to British propaganda; his lack of knowledge of Europe and his strong Anglo-Saxon background made it easy for him to drift in that direction. In addition there was the great handicap of his not having in Berlin as our ambassador a man whom he respected, of a larger caliber and greater ability than Gerard.

On my arrival in Washington I naturally took advantage of my friendship with Count Von Bernstorff to get his view of the situation and what news I could out of him, and even ventured to lunch with him at the Shoreham (once at a table next to Lansing), for which breaking of bread with the Ambassador I was duly reprimanded by George Harvey in the *North American Review*. I was impenitent because I felt it a journalistic duty to keep in touch with Von Bernstorff and soon it developed that I could be of use as an intermediary. My notes of a luncheon with the Ambassador at the embassy on May 15, just after the sending of the President's first *Lusitania* message, cover four long typewritten pages. I warned him of the historic readiness of our people to go to war if they believed that a humanitarian principle was at stake and assured him that the unanimity of support given to the President was beyond any precedent. He admitted the gravity of the situation and agreed with my statement that war would not only mean ruptured relations "but an intensely bitter feeling against Germany, German culture, and German influence in the world, the end of which no living man could hope to see." He stated that it would take a week to get Berlin's reply to Wilson's note and that he had sent suggestion after suggestion to his home government.

He was not without criticisms of Washington for its failure to compel England to stop its flagrant disregard of the rights of neutrals and for permitting England to buy the cargo of the steamer *Wilhemina* instead of insisting upon her going to Germany to uphold the legal principle involved, but he agreed that all these things were now ended by the *Lusitania* tragedy. He explained to me that the appearance of the so-called "*Lusitania* advertisement," warning Americans to keep out of the submarine war zone, on the day she sailed, had been a pure coincidence as he had not wished the advertisement to appear at all and had kept it "in that drawer over there for two months," until a peremptory order from Berlin demanded immediate publication. He added with deep emotion that if there had been the slightest German expectation of the *Lusitania*'s being sunk he should be hanged from the lamp post nearest to the embassy, for he had given letters of introduction to two young passengers on her, both sons of friends of his, Lindon

Bates, Jr., and Herbert S. Stone,[7] and to have done so without warning them, if he had known that they were going to their deaths, would have been a fiendish act.

He did not see how war could come unless we desired it. I assured him that in my judgment Gerard would be on his way home in ten days if Berlin did not give assurances of the safety of American lives at sea. He admitted the emotional character of the American people and regretted that Berlin did not recognize it. He denied all knowledge of any German-American organization for secret or military purposes and, in response to a question, declared that he and Berlin had both guessed that the British fleet had deprived them of the services of 40,000 reservists, that is, one army corps of Germans temporarily resident in the United States. Finally, I impressed upon him as emphatically as I could my belief that the whole stupid and abortive pro-German war propaganda must cease. He replied that he agreed and that he was sending Doctor Dernburg, who had just made a most unfortunate speech about the *Lusitania,* home at once. "The Ambassador," my notes end, "made a wry face when I told him that Professor Münsterberg of Harvard had telegraphed his congratulations to the President on the tone of his note. 'That man,' said Von Bernstorff, 'always wants to get into the front.'"

The next day, on May 16, he wrote me, asking: "What would you think of the following proposal coupled with arbitration of some kind? We propose to give up submarine war if England will obey international law. We further propose to give up the submarine war temporarily to leave time for you to renew the above proposal to England." I at once consulted Lansing and others, made careful notes, and with Lansing's approval replied to Von Bernstorff as follows:

Of course I cannot speak with a shadow of authority, but from the impressions I have gathered I am very sure that this country would not

---

[7] Herbert Stone was the son of Melville Stone of the Associated Press, the last man Von Bernstorff would have wished to offend. Mr. Stone kept up his personal relations with the Ambassador and held him guiltless.

permit the government to arbitrate the principle at stake in the *Lusitania* case or the loss of life. I believe that I can say, too, that no proposal that has a *condition* attached to it is likely to be acceptable, particularly if that condition involves our exerting pressure or making a demand upon England. As I told you yesterday, I gather that the administration proposes to say a word to England in due course. But the two matters are quite separate and must be settled separately. The question to which our government expects a yes or no answer is simply whether your government will give specific assurance that the established laws of war will be upheld so far as they affect American citizens on neutral or belligerent merchantmen. . . . Have you thought, however, of suggesting that Germany will agree not to attack any passenger steamers if England prohibits the sending of arms and ammunition by them? I have excellent reason to believe that this would strike a favorable note with our government and people. If quite convenient I shall be happy to see you at four tomorrow.

The next day and thereafter these exchanges of views continued with the full knowledge of our authorities. Naturally the Ambassador had been greatly encouraged by my "beat" announcing that our government would proceed against England. He was entirely sincere in his efforts to keep the peace, not only in his official capacity, but because of his tremendous desire to remain in the United States. Gradually he became more and more outspoken as to the stupidity of his own government. After the German reply to our *Arabic* note, which he would not defend, I noted that "his profanity as to Berlin would have struck a warmly responsive chord in the heart" of the bitterest anti-German. He was never so happy anywhere else as in Washington and when I met him in Berlin in March, 1919, he at once asked me most earnestly whether I thought he would ever be allowed to set foot in the country in which he had spent his happiest years; I am sure that this ban is a continuing grief to him.

As the days passed, it seemed to me utterly ridiculous that the President and the Ambassador should be in the same city and be handling questions fraught with such terrible possibilities by means of letters or through intermediaries without ever meeting.

I thought that if they were two business men engaged in large and conflicting undertakings they would certainly have explained in person their differing points of view. I maintained that their meeting could not injure the progress of the negotiations and might actually be productive of a great deal of good. I laid these considerations before Tumulty, to whose common sense they appealed, with the result that the Ambassador was at once invited to meet the President, on June 1. The outcome was entirely satisfactory. As I learned from the Count within fifteen minutes after his return from the White House, the President was extremely cordial and friendly and they discussed the inhumane aspects of the submarine war with mutual satisfaction. I telegraphed: "It is possible to say that a long step in bringing about a better understanding between the United States and Germany on the issues now the subject of diplomatic negotiations between those countries has been taken." While the Count had no particular suggestions to make beyond his offer of good will and the expression of his own earnest desire to find a way out, the conference had one or two immediately practical results.

In the first place the President made it clear that he could not understand the failure of the German note to touch upon the humanitarian side of the *Lusitania's* sinking and stressed the fact that he was less concerned with the legal aspects than with the issue of humanity and justice. This Count Von Bernstorff immediately wirelessed to Berlin with good reactions. Next, the Ambassador made the President understand the difficulty of his own position. For weeks he had been able to communicate with his government only at some risk and had not received any replies to his cable messages and therefore did not know whether they had been received. This, he pointed out, impaired his usefulness as the honest mediator he was trying to be, and the President promised that the obstacle would be effectually removed so that both governments would have the benefit of Von Bernstorff's views and recommendations. This was done. It made it possible also for Germany privately to communicate to our government the information it had at hand in regard to the questions as to which, in its reply, it asked further information. For a time it looked as if the meeting of these two men would really mark a most happy turning point in the relations between the two countries. But the Berlin government was hopelessly stupid and without understanding of the American point of view and character, while it deliberately ignored our enormous military possibilities. Count Von Bernstorff grew in disfavor with the Berlin Foreign Office because of his ardent championship of the American attitude. As he himself testified before the Reichstag inquiry into the war, when he finally reached Berlin after getting his dismissal, he sat around for several weeks before he was given an interview with anybody of importance.

Naturally the Ambassador was grateful to me for my mediation. He had done me the honor soon after the outbreak of the war to say that I had done more harm to the German cause than anybody else in the United States, over which remark I often smiled when the accusations of pro-Germanism were showered upon me from so many quarters. What he meant was, he explained, that they had counted upon my German birth and inheritance to make me stand by them and he felt that the influence of *The Evening Post* was very great; he was aware how the paper was read and followed by other editors the country over. I thought him agreeable, sincere, and honest, but when all the facts came out I could not help feeling that he had deceived us all, including the State Department which assured him, when his military and naval attachés, Captain Von Papen and Captain Boy-Ed left, that the Administration had nothing against him. In his memoirs he declares that he knew nothing about the "illegal acts of secret agents sent to the United States by the military authorities." [8]

Still I do not see how the Ambassador could have lived under the same roof with his attachés and not known something of what

[8] For an opinion that Von Bernstorff was really part of this wrongdoing, see *The Enemy Within*, by Captain Henry Landau, New York, 1937. On the other hand the New York *Sun* said of Count von Bernstorff when he left: "No man has been in a more delicate position; none, it may be, could have comported himself more discreetly," February 4, 1917.

they were doing in violation of all diplomatic decency, in procuring men to commit acts of sabotage against industrial plants in the United States and Canada. They were spending enormous sums in the business of deliberately committing crimes and making criminals when they were the guests of this country. Surely Von Bernstorff must have sensed it even if he was not a part of what was going on. It has always seemed to me that it would have been the duty of a sensitive and honorable man to hand in his resignation or ask to be recalled. That would have meant the loss of his career and would have been hard to explain to his American friends since he could not have given the reasons for it; doubtless it would have seemed as if he were quitting when he and his country were in a desperately tight place. His love of the United States and his desire to spend the rest of his life here undoubtedly came into play also, but he certainly would stand higher today and perhaps be living in this country if he had chosen the more honorable course, even to the extent of ending his diplomatic service. Today he is an unhappy exile in Switzerland, being too democratic, perhaps too Americanized, to accept the Hitler regime.

When I next espied Secretary Bryan he was walking rapidly from the White House offices toward the front entrance to the White House. Remembering that I had promised to tell him what conclusions I had arrived at about his relations to the pressmen, I hurried after him. My mind having considerable one-track quality, I began abruptly by referring to my promise to make suggestions. I said: "In regard to the trouble that you are having with the press conferences, I have talked with a number of the best correspondents here and they feel that it would be well for you to turn the whole matter over to Mr. Lansing and so get rid of the whole bother." To my utter astonishment Mr. Bryan turned upon me in a fury, overwhelming me with a torrent of indignation and abuse and leaving me utterly speechless. Before I could say more than one or two stammering things he turned his back upon me and hurried on toward the White House. He had declared that he would be very much obliged if I kept my advice and my opinions to myself, that he did not wish them, and that if it came to a matter of breeding and education he begged to inform me that he was a better educated man than I could ever think of being and, as for breeding, there was no comparison between that of his family and mine, that I had clearly shown myself to be destitute of the characteristics of a gentleman.

When I could pull myself together I tried to understand what had happened. It then came to me that I had mortally offended him by an article that I had published about him in *The Evening Post* on May 17, in which I had written, besides many words of praise and acknowledgment of his ability, his devotion to principle, his sincere democracy, and his willingness to make any sacrifice for his party's and country's cause, this unfortunate sentence: "He is obviously lacking in taste, breeding, and knowledge of the world, despite his traveling," besides saying that his weakness as Secretary of State was largely due to his "lack of education." I have always deeply regretted writing it, not only because I never wished to hurt Mr. Bryan but because it was not my custom to make a personal attack of that kind. It sounded snobbish and ill-bred on my part and he was justified in taking exception to it, though hardly in the way that he did, especially in view of the fact that I had praised him for the greater part of a column and a half.

What made the matter worse was that he misunderstood what I was saying to him. His mind did not carry back to our previous conversation. So he went straight into the White House, saw the President, and said that I had not only insulted him in my article but had asked him to resign and turn over his office to Mr. Lansing and he demanded to know if I reflected the President's feelings. That afternoon I met several people who told me that the White House wished to see me at once. I called my office and got confirmation of it from Mr. Vernon, who said that I must go straight to Tumulty. I did so. Tumulty informed me that the President had asked him to ascertain from me immediately just what had happened and whether it was true that I had advised Mr. Bryan to resign. When he heard the whole story Tumulty burst into roars of laughter. Ever since he has made a great yarn out of what he calls "the greatest encounter in history between two battling pacifists," and much more of the same content.

I asked him to tell the President that I never had the slightest thought of suggesting that Mr. Bryan should resign and that I should not have had the impudence to say so to him if I had so thought. But, when Bryan actually resigned on June 8, the story got around that I was in considerable degree responsible for his leaving the Cabinet. That he was wise in resigning I know now; at the time I supported the President and felt that his resignation embarrassed the government unnecessarily. I wrote that the Berlin newspapers would be able to break the effect of the second *Lusitania* note by simply headlining it: "The Note That Mr. Bryan Refused to Sign." I do not mean that Mr. Bryan should have resigned at the moment that he did; but obviously the parting of the ways had come. His resignation is altogether to his credit.

Never, however, did a greater storm of abuse and vituperation burst upon a public man, except that the attacks upon Senator La Follette in 1917 were greater. Those on Bryan were so venomous and 90 per cent of them were so unwarranted that they increased my regret that I had written what I did. He was unfortunate in that he did not, or could not, present the case for peace and expose the dangers and weaknesses of the President's policy as well as that should have been done; at least he was then so unpopular that the people would not listen to his presentation. I am sorry that he could not have lived until today and seen how, twenty-two years after his resignation, the country adopted as its policy most of the measures that he urged before our entry into the war. Today it is written on our statute books that in the event of war abroad the President must forbid the sale of arms, ammunition, and giving credits and loans to the belligerents. He would have seen the President of the United States issue an order forbidding American citizens to travel on Italian ships during the hostilities between Italy and Ethiopia, except at their own risk, and ordering Americans out of the danger zones in Spain and China. It was for advocating precisely these things that Mr. Bryan was most abused.

He was portrayed as a coward, a traitor,[9] a contemptible American who would not insist upon the rights of American citizens to go anywhere at any time and to do business anywhere at any time with the certainty that the flag of the United States would follow and protect them wherever they went and whatever they did, and, if they lost their lives, would revenge that loss in the blood of our own soldiers and that of the wrongdoers.

For all his shortcomings I believe that Bryan will stand much higher in American history than anybody realized in 1915. No one can accuse him of having failed in loyalty to the President; he was devotedly loyal. From the time he entered the State Department the President considered that department to be his own domain and formulated and directed our foreign policy even before the World War began. Mr. Bryan accepted the situation and co-operated to the fullest extent where other men would have chafed or felt that they were being supplanted. I held at the time that this self-abnegation and readiness to risk having himself portrayed as a nonentity, a mere figurehead, a blunderer, was proof of genuine greatness of spirit. After the Cabinet meeting at which he announced his resignation, six of the members lunched with Bryan at the Shoreham Hotel—the President not attending. I heard from several present that there was not one man there who was not deeply moved by the parting and did not regret it. Bryan, despite all differences of opinion and background, had their hearty respect, regard, and even affection; it was a great pity that this was not made clear to the public at the time. Bryan did lack knowledge of the world and often could not and did not preserve his dignity, but he remains a far finer and more lasting figure in our history than George Wickersham and others of the opposition who made the nastiest and most unfair attacks upon him.

I am happy to add that I made my peace with Mr. Bryan and that he forgave me for my mistake. He kept in touch with me during the remainder of the fight to keep the country out of war.

---

[9] Thus the Louisville *Courier-Journal* said of Bryan on June 12, 1915: "Men have been shot and beheaded, even hanged, drawn and quartered for treason less serious"!

WAR EXTREMES:
DROW WILSON AND
TOR GEORGE W. NOR-

Harris & Ewing

Once he wrote me that he would "go anywhere at any time if there was any reasonable prospect of being able to accomplish anything but unless the President is sympathetic with the plan nothing can be done." He was right; it was and is all in the hands of the President, just as President Roosevelt stated in his speech at Chautauqua on August 15, 1936. There Mr. Roosevelt pointed out the great truth that no matter what neutrality and other laws might be passed they would be of no avail unless the President and the Secretary of State should be determined to keep the country out of war if there was danger of our going in, and should be strong enough to resist the terrific pressure which would be brought to bear upon them to fight. Mr. Wilson could have kept us out of war but he had neither the foresight nor the courage nor the understanding to prevent the reversal of his original policy of forbidding loans to the belligerent countries and of stopping the sale of arms and ammunition and American travel on British ships. He allowed the country to become so tied up with the British war machine that only a man with the backbone and courage of a Grover Cleveland could have stood out in 1917, and then only if such a man had really been neutral and had undertaken to instruct the country as to the misconduct of Great Britain toward us and the real war aims of the Allies as revealed in the secret treaties.[10] I have always cherished a message that I received from Mr. Bryan through David Lawrence in January, 1916: "Tell Villard that the Lord does not require us to win—He simply requests us to do our duty as we see it. We can never tell in advance what we can do—we can only tell by trying. If after trying we find we have failed we have nothing to regret."

When Mr. Bryan resigned Tumulty asked me to make suggestions as to his successor and said that the request came directly from the President. My first choice was Moorfield Storey, the Boston lawyer, who in his youth had been secretary to Charles

---

[10] It must not be forgotten that as early as October 26, 1916, President Wilson said: "I believe that the business of neutrality is over." Ray Stannard Baker and William E. Dodd, *Public Papers of Woodrow Wilson*, New York, 1927, Vol. 2, p. 381.

Sumner, who was honorably unpopular at Harvard, of which he was a graduate, because of his criticisms at times of the conduct of the university, and in Boston because of his espousing of unpopular causes. He was an independent all his life and had supported Mr. Wilson but he was not conspicuous enough and was well advanced in years. Finally the President selected Lansing, my second choice, perhaps rather by default, or because he felt, as I did, that no one else could step into the office so steeped in knowledge of what was being done up to that time. Of course I did not know then that Lansing wanted us to get into the war. He resolutely set his face against any negotiated peace and when the Pope made his peace offer in 1917, Lansing, *without even taking time to study it,* told two ambassadors who came to see him that the United States could not consider the proposition.[11]

[11] David Lawrence wrote me on August 16: "I guess Lansing didn't expect the news of his reception of the ambassadors to get out because here they want to give the impression of careful consideration, etc., though they are absolutely set against any peace."

Chapter XVI. Wilson Humbles Berlin

AS the summer wore on the tension increased, for the German replies to Mr. Wilson's first and second *Lusitania* notes were not satisfactory. German ineptness, failure to face the issues frankly, to recognize the humanitarian aspects of the disaster, and to admit the dreadful mistake made kept the official world in a state of keenest anxiety, save for those who wished the country to go to war. Not until July, when the *Nebraskan* was sunk, did the Germans show a different spirit. In that case, without any parleying or pettifogging the German government promptly admitted its liability, regretted the error of its submarine commander, and asked for the bill, in striking contrast to its previous attitude when American ships were sunk. On July 16 Lansing and Von Bernstorff had a long interview. I was able to lay before *The Evening Post* readers in advance of the meeting what was going to happen there, namely, that the Ambassador would press his plan for American mediation in the submarine and blockade problems. He felt that the representatives of the three nations, Germany, England, and the United States, should meet to settle all the issues involved in this submarine warfare, provided, of course, that Great Britain would consent to yield somewhat in the matter of what the Germans called the extralegal blockade.

Mr. Lansing and the President could not be moved though the proposal seemed to many an excellent one and assuredly worth trying. No avenue that might lead to peace should have been left untried. The Ambassador complained to me constantly that the American officials and public failed to understand that Germany considered "her submarine blockade less a new kind of warfare than a reprisal," that most of the international law textbooks considered all reprisals as illegal or extralegal, and that the Germans were ready to give up these reprisals if the reasons for them,

279

namely, Great Britain's extralegal blockade and illegal interference with neutral trade, could be ended. One trouble was that by taking months to eat humble pie and to yield to the American point of view in the case of the *Lusitania*, and by quibbling, the German government now stood in its own light. Had it promptly cleared up its relations to the United States, and had it settled all the other cases as promptly as it did that of the *Nebraskan*, Mr. Wilson could have had no further excuse for failure to address himself to England or to proper mediation, if asked.

The third *Lusitania* note, which took us much nearer to war, was much the ablest and most vigorous of the President's series and it brought the matter to a head. It surprised his Republican and militaristic critics by the severity of its tone, its declaration that the second German note was "very unsatisfactory," and that our government was "keenly disappointed" by Berlin's failure to disavow the *Lusitania* sinking and to accept the American contention that no condition of a war permits a belligerent to modify the laws of war and then to offer reparation. Berlin was sternly warned that any sinking similar to that of the *Lusitania* would be regarded as an "unfriendly act," that is, something closely akin to a *casus belli*. Von Bernstorff was so distressed by the iron of the President's reply that he assured me he would not have been astonished if he had received not a reply to the note but just a cablegram recalling him and closing the embassy. He would doubtless have agreed with a man long connected with Wilson when the President was at Princeton, who observed to me: "When Mr. Wilson strikes, he strikes hard and often unexpectedly."

The note was published on Saturday, July 25. The afternoon before I met the President on the Union Station platform in Washington as he was walking up and down waiting for the train to leave. I had just been reading a confidential copy of the President's note. I at once expressed to him how much I liked it. He was plainly greatly pleased by my praise, saying that he hoped the whole press would approve and how earnestly he wished that the note would at least achieve our purpose of getting satisfaction from the Germans. We talked on for several minutes, I trying to draw him out as to how far he would go with Germany, when he said to me these unforgettable words: "I know what is in your mind, Mr. Villard, but you need have no anxiety. As long as I am President this country will not go into that war." Soon after the conductor called "All aboard." The President entered his private car which was taking him to Cornish, then his summer home, and I climbed into the Pullman which was to drop me at New London for a week end with my family at Black Point.

Naturally I was greatly elated by the President's statement. He said much the same thing to me on another occasion but this one stands out in my memory because of the place and the grave crisis the country was in at that moment. I had not then come to distrust his assurances. His words enabled me to give an optimistic color to my dispatches when they related to our staying out of war, and to stress the very grave difficulties he had in finding means to bring Germany to book and to make her yield to us. The next four weeks were grave ones while everyone wondered what Berlin would do. Then came, on August 19, the sinking of the *Arabic* and it looked as if the end of peace with Germany were at hand. Suddenly the skies cleared. Von Bernstorff wired Mr. Lansing on August 24 begging him to withhold action in the *Arabic* case until he could hear from his government again—a procedure so unusual as to startle and to amaze official Washington which regarded that message in itself as tantamount to a disavowal of the sinking of the *Arabic*.

Only one week later the Ambassador sent a note to Lansing reading in part: "With reference to our conversation of this morning, I beg to inform you that my instructions concerning our answer to your last *Lusitania* note contain the following passage: 'Liners will not be sunk by our submarines without warning and without safety of the lives of noncombatants, provided the liners do not try to escape or offer resistance.'" He added that he hastened to inform our government of the above "because this policy of my government was decided upon before the *Arabic* incident occurred." Mr. Lansing promptly accepted the statement at its face value, giving the following comment to the press: "In view of the clearness of the foregoing statement, it seems needless to make any comments in regard to it other than to say that it appears to be a recognition of the fundamental principle for which we have contended." The peace party in Berlin had triumphed. In this country every real lover of peace acclaimed the event but the war crowd was distinctly disappointed and so were some of those who spoke for England and wanted us drawn into the hostilities.

I was so jubilant that I wrote an article declaring that the President by his ability, steadfastness, and determination had brought Germany to her knees "by sheer force of moral indignation nobly expressed in the name of the greatest Republic in history." I went further. I smashed the traditions of 114 years of *The Evening Post* by printing Woodrow Wilson's picture on the first page with these words under it: "This is the man who, without rattling a sword, without mobilizing a corporal's guard of soldiers, or lifting the anchor of a warship won for civilization the greatest diplomatic victory in generations"—for which I was considerably razzed at the time.[1] Indeed, this radical departure almost brought about a revolt in the office and I had to overrule Gavit to get the picture in. After twenty-three years I still feel that that was an extraordinary achievement of Mr. Wilson. The Germans have only themselves to thank that their surrender in August, 1915, did not definitely keep us out of the war. Unfortunately it was only a respite. More ships were sunk; the seesaw with war and peace on either end went up and went down. Our hopes of peace rose and fell until finally war came. But by October of 1915 the situation was ameliorated so that we were for a time out of the woods. We who were for peace at all costs could breathe with some freedom again.

[1] At the St. Louis convention which, ten months later, renominated Wilson, Senator Ollie James phrased it thus: "Without orphaning a single American child, without widowing a single American mother, without firing a single gun or shedding a drop of blood, he wrung from the most militant spirit that ever brooded above a battlefield the concession of American demands and American rights."

During that whole summer Woodrow Wilson was under an almost unbearable strain. Even when he was supposed to be resting at Cornish he was under the harrow, for he never could have been without awareness of the crushing responsibility which was his. He was compelled to keep in closest touch with what was going on in Washington and in Europe.[2] It is only just that I record again that Mr. Wilson contributed enormously to the calm preserved by the country by keeping himself under complete restraint and refusing to make speeches tending to inflame the public. Neither he nor any of the Cabinet sought in that highly emotional summer to make political capital out of the crisis. He took no advantage of the cry that went up from a part of the press that now every patriot must stand by the President. Indeed, in those months he wholly subordinated himself and his future to the task immediately in hand. It is an interesting fact that even after the sinking of the *Arabic* the plain people of the country were not becoming excited over the German situation despite many warlike outbursts in the press.[3] The White House mails were not full of letters dealing with the crisis or demanding that we go to war. That was left to the professional patriots, the jingoes, the profiteers, the munitions makers and those newspapers like the New York *Tribune* which daily spat venom at Wilson and all who worked for peace.

Among the most bitter and brutal criticisms was that of Theodore Roosevelt at Plattsburg on August 25. Then a broken and beaten politician, on the eve of the President's winning his tremendous diplomatic victory, Roosevelt declared:

The man who believes in peace at any price or in substituting all-inclusive arbitration for an army and navy should instantly move to China. If he stays here then more manly people will have to defend him, and he is not worth defending. To treat elocution as a substitute for action, to rely upon high-sounding words unbacked by deeds is proof of a mind that dwells only in the realm of shadow and sham.

[2] But in all those twenty-five days no visitor crossed his threshold to discuss public affairs.

[3] See my dispatch in *The Evening Post* of August 24, 1915.

Altogether Roosevelt's speech was well calculated to give the greatest satisfaction in Berlin. Its crass brutality and cave-man savagery got under my skin. One did not have to agree with President Wilson's course but it did seem to me that one might have some little feeling for the tremendous difficulties of the situation and the responsibility which the President had to face; one did not need to be a barbarian. I especially resented the time and place of the attack upon Mr. Wilson. Finally my feeling led me to Secretary Garrison's office and my meeting him for the first time. That interview produced some news.

I went into the Secretary of War's office boiling with anger, being taken in by Vernon and another correspondent. Mr. Garrison did not get my name. After the others had asked for news I inquired with a good deal of feeling in my voice whether he had read the news from Plattsburg in his morning newspaper. "Not carefully," he replied. I said that he must have noticed the attack by a politician upon the Commander in Chief of the Army, President Wilson, and that that politician had been invited to Plattsburg Barracks by the major general commanding there, Leonard Wood, and that the attack had been made in the presence of regular officers and enlisted men in addition to members of the Citizens' Training Corps. I begged to ask him whether that attack made for military discipline and respect for authority, and whether it had the approval of the War Department. If the War Department was of the opinion that this happening was improper, I desired to inquire whether it proposed to take any action in regard to the officer responsible for this happening. Secretary Garrison, who seemed a little bored when we first came in, raised his eyes from the papers before him and took a good deal of notice when I began to talk and shot those questions at him. He replied, very slowly and deliberately, that this was obviously an important matter and that he was glad to have his attention called to it; that he could not say anything then because he had only been in his office for ten minutes and must consider the questions carefully. As soon as I left the room he had a secretary overtake one of my companions to inquire who I was.

Above: THEODORE ROOSEVELT JUST AFTER HIS
WOUNDING AT MILWAUKEE. *Below:* ROBERT M.
LA FOLLETTE AND HIS NAMESAKE, THE PRESENT
SENATOR

As I was lunching at the Shoreham that day the head-waiter asked me if I were Mr. Villard. When I said yes he gave me the penciled note which lies before me. It reads:

DEAR SIR:
   You asked me this morning regarding the Roosevelt speech at Platts-burgh. I had nothing then to say thereon. I will have copies this after-noon of my action in the matter. The information will be self-explanatory and will answer the questions you put to me.   Yrs
                                        LINDLEY M. GARRISON
To Mr. Villard

That afternoon the severe rebuke administered to General Wood was handed out. I was soon connected with it and roundly attacked by a part of the press; but I knew the army too well not to know that I was right in considering it a gross breach of discipline. Obviously, if any general could invite politicians to come and at-tack his superiors we would have the army in politics with a vengeance, and my many army friends agreed with me that the incident should not have been passed over, especially with Leonard Wood.

   Not until years later did I learn from Hermann Hagedorn that General Wood had warned Roosevelt on his arrival in Plattsburg against any indiscretion, had actually edited Roosevelt's speech in advance of its delivery, and that the address he made to the officers and men was entirely innocuous and without criticism of the Presi-dent. Mr. Hagedorn continued:

   After Roosevelt had parted from Wood, however, and stepped on the train, he was surrounded by correspondents and talked to them freely. The press confused the two speeches and Wood received a re-buke. His aide, Captain Kilbourne, begged him to explain the matter to the Secretary of War, but he refused to do it, not wishing, apparently, to pass the buck to Roosevelt.[4]

I find it hard to believe that General Wood sacrificed himself and allowed this black mark to remain on his military record merely

[4] Letter of May 12, 1930, to the author.

. . . And yet there is a virtuous man whom I have often noted in th
company. . . . Now I remember me, his name is Falstaff. . . . Him
keep with, the rest banish.—King Henry the Fourth.

A CESARE CARTOON OF THEODORE ROOSEVELT
FROM "THE EVENING POST" OF JULY 12, 1916.

out of love for one who was so well able to take care of himself as Roosevelt. Surely the general should have notified Secretary Garrison of the facts or at least have had the record corrected when he became an active candidate for the Presidency.

Later on Secretary Garrison and I became well acquainted. I liked him and I think he did me. On army matters we were as far apart as the poles and I opposed his great military expansion plan in one article after the other, but always with respect for the man and with admiration for his ability, his courage, and his forthrightness, which soon led him to resign from the Cabinet. He stood right up to the President and I am certain that he would have made a far, far better wartime head of the army than was Secretary Baker. But his temperament and that of the President were bound to clash. He had too much character and personality and he never agreed, when he took the so unexpectedly offered secretaryship, to be a yes man to anybody. During the war he would have kept the generals in their places and would not submissively have taken their orders. On the other hand, he would not have opposed any projects for the thoroughgoing militarization of his country.

When Mr. Wilson returned to Cornish at the end of August he was again completely tired out. Indeed his health in this momentous summer was a cause for great alarm to his physician, Doctor Cary Grayson of the navy, a year later an admiral by Mr. Wilson's appointment. This fact about Mr. Wilson I learned from Doctor Grayson himself. He asked me to lunch with him at the Shoreham. We talked only about the President; I learned some surprising things. He explained that he was greatly worried about the President's health. "I am going to tell you," he said, "something known only to two or three persons besides myself. In the early part of his administration the President was seriously ill. I am prouder of the fact that I pulled him out of that illness, and that no intimation of it ever got out, than of anything else in my whole professional career. Now I am worried about him again, chiefly because of the lonesome life he has been leading since Mrs. Wilson's death. He does not go out except occasionally. He sits by himself. He does not see enough young or old people, there is no gaiety around him and, in addition, he is carrying this frightful burden of his job. I feel that something must be done about it if there is not to be a serious breakdown and I want your help. I want you to join Joe Tumulty, Colonel House, and me in going to the President and telling him that for the sake of his health he must alter his mode of life. You can help us render a great service if you will."

I told him at once that I wanted to help, of course, but that my joining the group would be a great mistake, that I was on no terms of intimacy with the President such as he, House, and Tumulty were, and that I was certain the President would strongly resent it if I took part in making any such representations. I told him how much I had been regretting that the President did not gather a group of young men around him to inspire them with his ideals and to fire them with the desire to become future protagonists of the New Freedom and leaders of the party, but that I had not thought of this as a means of helping the President, only the party and the cause. Naturally I was astounded at Doctor Grayson's statement that Mr. Wilson had been in such ill health as to be in peril of his life; none of us had suspected it. Even so, I could not go along. "Why," I said, "the President does not even like me and I practically never see him." "You are quite mistaken," Doctor Grayson replied. "He has a very high opinion of you and constantly reads extracts from your writings to us and cites your opinions." I insisted that I was right. As we parted we agreed that I would go along with the others to call upon the President if Tumulty and Colonel House were of the same mind as Doctor Grayson and also asked me. I never heard again from Doctor Grayson on the subject. Almost immediately thereafter Mrs. Galt came into the picture—here Doctor Grayson was the intermediary, doubtless for the same reason that led to his talking with me as he did. He was determined to keep the President fit for his task and he succeeded until the fatal trip West in 1919.

It was true that the President's mode of life was unnatural and Doctor Grayson was only doing his duty in seeking to alter it.

Whereas at Trenton, where people could see him and talk to him and he was gracious and affable to them when they did so, in Washington he became less and less accessible. Congressional visitors and volunteer workers for him were no longer welcome. Some of his strongest and most loyal supporters were denied a word with him. I met an official whose vitally important reports would have created a sensation if published. They were constantly before the President who profited by them but in three years this man had never had a word of praise or blame from the President and had seen him but once. As I wrote in 1916,[5] Mr. Wilson seems "never to ask what he can do for others, particularly for those who have worked for him with complete and devoted enthusiasm. Their homage is accepted; but it never occurs to Mr. Wilson that there might be a reciprocal obligation. He never realizes how much a friendly hand clasp, a pat on the back, a word of wholehearted praise would do for one laboring by night or day in his service or that of the party." Or, for that matter, what such kindnesses would have meant to himself as well.

Always his test was not what he could do for the other fellow but what that fellow had to give him and in answering that question he felt himself upon an Olympian height looking down. He made great trouble for Tumulty through his refusals to see people because they had, in his judgment, "nothing to give" him. One such case was that of the Governor of a Western State. Visiting Washington he went to the White House and as a state executive asked for an interview with the President. Tumulty promised it at once. Mr. Wilson flatly refused. Probably he asked the usual question, "What has he to give me?" Tumulty argued, implored, beseeched—in vain. The President allowed him to get out of the hole as best he could. The Governor left Washington thoroughly incensed. Not very long after, at the request of a foreign legation, the President asked this same Governor to reprieve a citizen of that country sentenced to death at the hands of the firing squad

[5] *North American Review*, September, 1916, "The Mystery of Woodrow Wilson."

then in use in that Western State. There were grave doubts as to this man's guilt; it was believed that he was sacrificing himself for another. The Governor sent a sizzling reply, as vigorous a slap in the face as any President ever received from a high official. He was told to mind his own business and not to interfere in the affairs of a sovereign state. The firing squad did its work and I have always wondered whether the life of that man might not have been spared, or at least lengthened, if it had not been for Mr. Wilson's inexplicable rudeness. Anything that could have been done to humanize the President and warm up his relations with other beings would well have been warranted.

The President's second marriage did not, however, bring about that change for which so many of us hoped. He drifted further away from his friends and the realities. The news of the engagement came as a shock to his old associates who had known and loved his first wife and it made the President unpopular with women all over the country. Tumulty sensed that this would be the case and so he broke the force of an event which had profound and unhappy consequences, unforeseen at the time, for the President and the country, by simultaneously releasing two other pieces of news—one that the President had been converted to woman suffrage, and the other that Mr. Wilson had now been finally won to large armaments. Tumulty had told me in confidence several days before of the suffrage flop as we were driving aimlessly around Washington to cool off. He said: "I know something that will make you the happiest man in this country but I can't tell you yet." I asked him if I had ever violated his confidence. He said no, but I had to tease him as if he were a coy schoolgirl before he finally swore me to secrecy and revealed the news. To his astonishment I not only did not jubilate but felt downcast. "Naturally," I exclaimed, "I am glad to have him out for suffrage but where does it leave *him*? Is he going to change his mind on everything? Don't you see that everybody will attribute this not to conviction but to the fact that he wants re-election, must win the suffrage states, and cannot allow Theodore Roosevelt to have a monopoly of the suffrage support?"

Those were the only reasons for the change. He was no more convinced than before that woman suffrage was the right thing. I first spoke to him on this question when at lunch with him at the Trenton Country Club on August 13, 1912, when I showed him a letter from a Massachusetts woman saying that he was losing thousands of votes to Theodore Roosevelt because of this issue. "I have no doubt it is true," he commented, and then added that he was not like Roosevelt and could not change his opinions in order to get votes. "I cannot do anything," he said. I replied: "You certainly cannot change now, unless you are converted, without putting yourself in Roosevelt's class." "That is it exactly," he responded. Yet here he was three years later, finding himself quite convinced. I could never believe it. He liked, as any proper man should, pretty women and their company but he never had respect for their intellectual accomplishments or believed them else than quite inferior to men. Women no more than blacks figured in his vision of a really democratic society.

At the end of August I came in for much notoriety because of the publication in the New York *Tribune* and many other newspapers of dispatches to the effect that I had supplanted Colonel House in the President's confidence and regard and was now the controlling factor in the White House situation, which was represented, of course, as a great misfortune for the country. It was part of a three- or four-day attack upon Mr. Wilson and was an attempt to break the friendship between Mr. Wilson and Colonel House, besides making it appear that the President had succumbed to my unworthy and craven pacifist point of view. It was also a clever effort to end my alleged intimacy with Mr. Wilson. I was at Black Point recovering from an indisposition due to over-fatigue and my failure to appear at the White House offices as usual was at once taken as a sign that the intrigue had been successful. Leroy Vernon wrote me that some of the authors of the attack were newspaper men who desired to "even up personal scores because of your work here. The papers handling this attack have either been left behind with conspicuous regularity during the last few months or have been guilty of wild faking and lost caste here." I was relieved to have him add: "I see no reason why either you or Tumulty should be embarrassed in the slightest degree by what has occurred. The general opinion here, based on knowledge, is that you played the game squarely and fairly." The Washington *Star* came to my aid by saying that I had been in the capital "working on good stories" for my newspaper, had taken my "chances with the reporters and correspondents," given my views to governmental officials when asked, and that I had not seen the President "when other newspaper men were not present."

That was the truth. Indeed, nothing could have been more ludicrous than this whole yarn but it was well calculated to make the President more than ever wary of me. A month later, when I wrote asking to see him so that I might lay certain views as to preparedness before him, he did not even trouble to write his declination. There was justification for this for he had already begun to change his attitude on this question as on so many others, and had closed his mind. It would have been a waste of time. Tumulty promptly and correctly issued a denial of the Villard-House story, saying that it was "fantastic" and that the Colonel stood just where he always had been in the President's regard. As for Colonel House, he wrote me on September 2—sincerely or insincerely: "I did not need your assurance to know that you had nothing whatever to do with it. I hope you will not let it interfere with the splendid work you are doing in Washington. I cannot recall when anyone has served the country at a critical time better and I would regard it as a public misfortune if you allow anything to interrupt it."

Tumulty then once more saved the President from a bad blunder. In his anger Mr. Wilson peremptorily ordered the correspondents responsible for the attack barred from the White House. When Tumulty announced this edict to a number of the correspondents there was a roar of protest. They argued with Tumulty that it would do much more harm than good and that he had other and more effective ways of handling such a situation. The order was held in abeyance and soon "forgotten" by Tumulty as he had "forgotten" numerous other peremptory orders of his chief.

The sensation did not, however, die down immediately. Colonel Harvey devoted a whole article in the *North American Review* to it with a full-page picture of me. The article was spiteful, of course, for he was attacking Mr. Wilson in every issue as he had been ever since the President's refusal to make him our ambassador in London. The Colonel had a grand time standing by Colonel House as First Assistant President and nominating me for Second Assistant President with Colonel Henry Watterson as scorer, and again insisting that it was I who had forced the "Chautauquan Secretary of State" out of the Cabinet. But the reason for the Colonel's malice against the President was so well known, and his humor so forced, that comparatively few people were impressed by it. Before long he had to switch from the *North American Review* to *Harvey's Weekly*—which became a solo performance.

An amusing, and for me professionally very useful, result of all this publicity was that wherever I went in the government offices doors flew open before me; I was rarely kept waiting, not even by Cabinet officials. On the other hand, I was pestered by people with axes to grind who were sure that I could get President Wilson to come to their aid within twenty-four hours. One tragic incident also resulted. At a great dance at Lenox, Massachusetts, where my wife and I were visiting, I was suddenly approached by the Austrian Ambassador, Doctor Constantin Dumba, who was in a pitiful state of distress and begged me to come and talk with him in a small room which happened to be unoccupied. A few minutes earlier he had received the news that compromising letters from him had been found by the British in the luggage of an American correspondent, J. F. J. Archibald, when he was searched on a steamer by boarding officers. Archibald, who was on the German pay roll, had offered to take these letters over and deliver them in Vienna and neither of them had thought that passengers on ships stopped in British waters, or landing in England, would be examined—Captain Von Papen was just as stupid when he was expelled from the country and took with him a lot of correspondence that also proved very damaging.

Doctor Dumba told me that the letters would probably be published the next day and besought me for my good offices. This scene with that broken diplomat, in evening clothes and wearing his decorations, with the dancers in the ballroom close at hand whirling past while he more and more realized that he faced disgrace and the bankruptcy of his long public life, was as dramatic and as tragic as ever I saw upon the stage. I felt so sorry for him that I said I would visit the State Department to see if there was any hope of saving him but I told him that it seemed to me fatal and I reminded him of what had happened to Sackville-West. He was utterly crushed and it was all the more stunning because he had been getting on better in Washington than Von Bernstorff, partly because he represented a less important country. When I read the letters in the newspapers the next day it was plain that his jig was up and it was impossible for me to say anything about him at the State Department beyond the regret that so apparently decent a person had been doing the things he had. The letters not only reflected upon President Wilson, they revealed the fact that Dumba, too, had been hiring men to sabotage American munitions plants, to arrange strikes, and to commit crimes.

How those veteran European diplomats could have been so stupid I cannot understand. Von Bernstorff was bright and clever, yet he never suspected that his telephone was tapped and his every conversation recorded by government agents, or that secret service men followed him to New York and elsewhere and kept a complete diary of his every movement, even recording all his visits to a woman friend in the metropolis and noting when he entered her house and at what hour he left it. One would have thought that any tyro would have been on his guard at such a time but apparently they thought that the United States Government would be above underhand and illegal work of that kind—illegal so far as tapping the telephones was concerned. All of these men had grown up in the fetid atmosphere of European chancelleries where everybody was spying on everybody else and purchasing state secrets right and left. So it seemed all right to Dumba, Boy-Ed, and Von Papen to engage in the dirty work that they were ordered to do and yet they felt badly when they were caught at it and sent home. Von Bernstorff's carelessness is the more remarkable because whenever he left Washington he was hounded by reporters—often three taxis full of them pursued him when he went to New York. He was nagged there to distraction and given little peace or privacy, which was in marked contrast to the respect with which he was treated by the Washington correspondents.

Those summer months cemented my friendship with Secretary Franklin K. Lane although we, too, were in hostile camps, for he was most eager to have us enter the war. I never could understand how so great a liberal and humanitarian could be as inconsistent as he was. He wrote to the editor of the New York *World* in 1917: "But the war will degrade us. That is the plain fact, make sheer brutes of us, because we will have to descend to the methods which the Germans employ. So you must go somewhere else for your uplift stuff." Yet he wrote with pride that his son had killed one German and bombed others and he wanted to end the war with American troops far into German territory and he did not care how many thousands of additional American lives that would cost. When Mr. Wilson sent Pershing after Villa, Lane wrote to the President: "My judgment is that to fail in getting Villa would ruin us in the eyes of all Latin America. I do not say they respect only force but, like children, they pile insult on insult if they are not stopped when the first insult is given." Of course we did not get Villa and today our influence in Latin America stands higher than ever before because of the Good Neighbor policy and the cessation of those bloody and brutal attacks upon Haiti, Santo Domingo, Nicaragua, and Mexico which disgraced the Wilson Administration.

When the Russian revolution came along Franklin Lane calmly contemplated our spending "a million lives" to put it down, but that sacrifice, he said, "will prove to us the value of law and order." Yet this same bloodthirsty man penned one of the finest descriptions of what the ideal America ought to be, wrote one of the most beautiful tributes to the American flag ever recorded, and knew well that the call for radical changes in the United States was due to bad government, politics, and corruption. He was obsessed with the fear that Germany would win the war and believed that if she did we should have to keep a million men in arms on the Canadian frontier and devote as much as 30 or 40 per cent of our national income to national defense which is just what we are doing, after having won the war, in the fiscal year 1938-39, if we figure our normal budget at approximately three billions of dollars.

While we fought over these differences of opinion I none the less profited greatly by the breadth of Lane's point of view and his clear and accurate judgments of his associates in the government, and notably Mr. Wilson, which he freely gave me. He was under no illusions as to the President who, he said, was not frank enough, was too selfish and opinionated to be popular with the American-born citizen. He wrote to his brother: "It is hard for him [Wilson] to get on with anyone who has any will or independent judgment." Lane was constantly tempted to resign when balked by the President, as were Lansing and Houston in addition to Garrison, but after we got into the war Mr. Lane felt that he could not leave lest his resignation give encouragement to Berlin. When the *Lusitania* sank he, as stated, rang the President up on the telephone and did not ask permission to send him his views as to what should be done but demanded this as his right and Wilson had to accede. When I wrote a long article reviewing Wilson's handling of the Mexican situation and putting it in the best possible light—much more favorably than I could possibly write about it now in retrospect and in view of later information—Lane went over my manuscript and made most useful suggestions. He was always warmhearted and impulsive and I have never ceased to regret his premature death for, with all his faults and inconsistencies, he was a great American, and an admirable administrator—of whom we never have too many.

Had those three belligerent men, Lane, Lansing, and Garrison, stood for mediation and been determined to find a way of stopping the war before it caused the ruin that it did, I believe they could have influenced the President to move in that direction. In the early days of the war the President would have been glad to act and he let it be known that he was ready to renew his early offer of mediation which was so promptly declined, but he could not be won for a neutral mediation conference because, for one reason, he wanted to be the sole mediator when the end arrived. Efforts to stay the slaughter broke down in the face of the fear of the bureaucrats of each country lest any move toward mediation show undue weakness. Hidebound, tied up with red tape and tradition, and often slaves to mere phrases, totally undemocratic and remote from the aspirations of the people, the European governments and their diplomats fought blindly on without making in that summer of 1915 any serious efforts to end the bloodshed. At first there could be no mediation because Germany was on top; then the Allied victory in the summer of 1915 was brushed aside as being merely the entering wedge; Germany must be further humbled before there could be any inquiry as to whether there was not some satisfactory basis of settlement. I wrote then that "to one dull human in the ranks it does seem as if it would do no harm at least to inquire; after which, if necessary, the slaughter could go on as before."

Jane Addams and other able women came to Washington to urge the calling together of the neutral nations but the State Department would not consider the matter at all. When Doctor Aletta Jacobs of Holland and Professor Emily Balch interviewed Secretary Lansing at the end of August, he ridiculed the idea of "continuous mediation." It had never been done and all a mediator could do anyhow was merely to offer to mediate and then withdraw. He was scandalized at the idea of the United States proposing terms of peace; that was meddling in other people's affairs and the United States could never for a moment consider *that!* All that they could get out of him was that the United States would not resent, or object to, or put obstacles in the way of such a neutral conference and would not refuse to send delegates if it seemed to be a practicable undertaking. When Professor Balch brought up the disinterested action of the United States in making peace between Japan and Russia, Mr. Lansing showed intense feeling and bitterly condemned the settlement which Theodore

Roosevelt had helped to engineer, declaring that it had done much harm.

He then shocked his visitors by voicing the today obvious truth, that treaties and international agreements would be broken by the nations whenever the pressure to break such agreements was strong. An individual, he said, might sacrifice his existence to keep his word but a person in power, responsible for a nation, would not do this and he "did not know that he blamed that decision." The two women reported that what Mr. Lansing "said to us was on an unspeakably lower moral level than what was said by any European statesman with whom we talked." [6] It was impossible for me to understand this inhumanly callous attitude of men like Lane and House and Lansing and those in power everywhere; they never seemed to have any human feeling or moral sense about causing the slaughter or failing to stop the slaughter of millions of men.

One new and attractive figure came upon the State Department scene in September when Frank L. Polk of New York City, who had been Corporation Counsel of the City of New York, was appointed Counselor of the State Department. I was present when Mr. Lansing introduced him to the newspaper men; we were all astounded at the ease with which Mr. Polk took over his new duties and not only those of his office. The day after Mr. Polk appeared Mr. Lansing went off on a long vacation and turned over the whole department to this newcomer who had never been in the diplomatic service nor in any way connected with the State Department, this happening in the midst of one of the gravest international crises the country had ever known. We newspaper men refused to believe that Mr. Polk had not had three or four weeks' warning of his appointment and burned much midnight oil in "boning up" on the status of our international troubles. He at once seemed "to have all our foreign affairs at his fingers' ends and his straightforwardness and frankness in answering questions make him a very satisfactory man to do business with." I com-

[6] From the manuscript notes of the conversation in my possession.

mented at the same time upon the many fine younger men whom
Mr. Wilson had brought to Washington, such as Thomas Ewing,
the Patent Commissioner; the Assistant Attorney General, Charles
Warren; the Assistant Secretary of the Navy, Franklin D. Roosevelt; the Assistant Secretary of the Treasury, Andrew J. Peters of
Massachusetts; and Carl Vrooman, Assistant Secretary of Agricul-
ture. Two others, Joseph E. Davies of Wisconsin, now Ambassador
to Belgium, and the Solicitor General, John W. Davis, were also,
I noted, standing out because of their ability and efficiency.

Colonel House during all this time was playing his pathetically
incompetent role. On May 30, 1915, he confided to his diary
(which any real friend of his would not have edited but suppressed): "I have concluded that war with Germany is inevitable
and this afternoon at 6 o'clock I decided to go home on the S.S.
St. Paul on Saturday." He, like Page, took it to be quite consistent
with our policy of neutrality to show his most private dispatches
to Sir Edward Grey and obsequiously accept the latter's instructions without resenting Sir Edward's constant reflections upon the
United States because it did not go to war to please the British
foreign minister. House came home "to persuade the President not
to conduct a milk-and-water war but to put all his strength, all
the virility, and all the energy of our nation to it." But when he
got home he changed his mind; then it appeared to him that we
probably would "drift into" the war. He vacillated from day to
day but in one thing he was steady and consistent—he was all
things to all men. To the preparedness people he was all ears and
approval; to me he gave it as his belief [7] that the President's preparedness program was never intended to go through and in his
judgment *never* would. When I and others like Jane Addams and
Emily Balch went to see him we came away believing that he was
on our side—and with justification. But we know now that he
was as cordial and encouraging to those who advocated the exact
opposite of what we did.

On September 25 another turning point was reached when the

[7] In New York, October 28, 1915.

Wilson Administration reversed its position of August 14, 1914, forbidding loans to belligerent countries.[8] As Walter Millis correctly puts it: "Our neutrality was at an end." The ease with which loans to belligerent powers were forbidden by Congress in 1935-36-37 shows how easily Mr. Wilson could have obtained such legislation but the President had yielded to the bankers as well as to the militarists. He had written to me that he would join neither antipreparedness people like myself nor "go the whole hog" with the militarists, but now he threw himself into the arms of the latter. The preparedness propaganda was gaining ground like wildfire chiefly because of Hiram Maxim's abominably false and misleading *Defenceless America* and the shocking moving picture based on it called *A Battle Cry for Peace*, a lurid portrayal of the conquest of America by Germans;—Mr. Maxim's brother was supplying enormous quantities of rapid-fire guns to the Allies. All of this could have been offset or stopped by a firm character in the White House unmoved by political considerations.

A protest against the disloyalty of the influential German-American Alliance made by me at Stockbridge was well received by audience and press. That Alliance was anticipating the Nazi leagues by demanding the teaching of German in every public and private school in the country and asserting that all German-Americans should vote and act as one cultural and political unit instead of submitting to the melting pot. Franklin Lane, for all his belligerency and our diverging views, took the occasion of my leaving Washington to write me that he was sorry to hear of it "but I know you have earned a rest. You may take this satisfaction with you, that a more useful three months to your country and your reputation as a journalist could not have been spent."

[8] See Lansing's incredibly cold-blooded letter of September 6, 1915, to President Wilson urging that the loans be made "for our own good," in order to avoid a "critical economic situation" and asking whether we should let our declaration of "the true spirit of neutrality" stand in the way of our saving the bankers from the inevitable consequences of their doing business with the Allies. This letter was first brought out by Senator Nye on December 26, 1935. Lansing either did not have, or suppressed, a conception of what this would do to us in relation to the war.

J. RAMSAY MAC DONALD, THE AUTHOR, AND ISHBEL MAC DONALD
AT CONCORD, MASS.

President John H. MacCracken of Lafayette College, in awarding me an honorary degree during that vacation, declared that I had "placed conscience and ideals above wealth" and given "voice to our hopes and desires that the America of tomorrow shall be greater and better than the America of the past." Little did they realize in how brief a time the man to whom they referred would be shown up to the country as a craven pacifist, a traitorous pro-German who at heart really desired not only the subjugation of America but the raping of all its women by a victorious foreign soldiery.

Chapter XVII. We Drift into War

ON the morning of November 24, 1915, I was summoned from the breakfast table to the telephone to hear that Henry Ford, the automobile manufacturer, whom I had not met, wished me to come at once to the Biltmore Hotel as he had something of the greatest importance to communicate to me. When I reached the hotel and Mr. Ford's presence, I found Rosika Schwimmer there, as well as Louis Lochner and others of the Ford entourage. I was told at once the astounding news that, acting on the suggestions made to him, Mr. Ford had chartered the steamer *Oscar II* to take a party of distinguished Americans to Europe in order to bring about the end of the war by rousing the neutral nations to a joint offer of mediation. Mr. Ford at once asked me to go along and explained that he had summoned me in order to aid him in presenting the news to the press.

The invitation left me almost speechless; I could only say that I should be glad to consider it and that, as a means of advertising the idea that the war should and could be stopped by reason and arbitration, I thought the chartering of the ship a master stroke. I saw at once, however, that everything would depend upon the way that it was done, the standing of the persons who would make up the party, and whether the neutral nations would take the matter seriously. I was shown the names of those already invited by telegraph and found them unexceptional. I was also, then and later, told the less than half-truth that telegrams from foreign governments gave the assurance that the move was welcome and would be dealt with seriously. Here was the great mistake of the entire enterprise. There was, I am convinced, no intent to deceive anyone. But those who counseled Mr. Ford, and Ford himself, misinterpreted the purely polite expressions of good will from neutral governments as something vastly more than they actually signified. It will be recalled that the voyagers were not informed as to the real tenor of those messages until a revolt on the *Oscar II* compelled their being shown as the ship neared the European coast. Only then did they learn of the absence of any definite plan of procedure or genuine assurance of neutral governmental co-operation.

After getting the news I asked Mr. Ford what he wished me to do as to the press, as a large parlor near by was rapidly being filled by pressmen, women, and photographers. He said he wished me to stand by him while he made the announcement. I asked if any statement had been prepared and typed to be given out. There was none. I warned him that the press would be largely hostile and that all of us who were working for peace were constantly being misinterpreted or misrepresented. He waved that aside and airily said: "Oh, I always get on very well with the boys. All you need is a slogan." I said, "Yes, Mr. Ford, what kind of a slogan?" "Oh," said he, "something like—'we'll get the boys in the trenches home by Christmas.' What do you think of that?" I thought privately that it was crazy. When I got my breath I replied: "Mr. Ford, there are said to be at least ten million men in the trenches. You have chartered one of the slowest steamers on the Atlantic and she is not to sail until December 4. If you succeed in stopping the war the day you arrive, which will probably be December 16, it would be physically impossible to march or transport those men home by Christmas." "Oh," said Mr. Ford, "I hadn't thought of that." Thereupon, after cogitating a moment, he said, "Well, we'll make it, 'we'll get the boys out of the trenches by Christmas.'" "It would be possible," was my discouraged answer, "if you obtained an armistice over the holidays, to have them sitting on the tops of the trenches by Christmas." This was the genesis of the famous phrase that went around the world and has almost become part of the language. It disheartened me no end for I knew it laid the enterprise open to ridicule; it was already evident to me that he had no clear conception of what it was all about, what the war conditions were, or what he was undertaking. Indeed, it gave me a doubt as to his general intelligence, which was subsequently confirmed more than once.

After that Mr. Ford again refused to have any statement written out so I sat and waited. More reporters came and soon ten o'clock arrived. They were reported to be getting restless and I already was so for I had pressing work waiting for me at the office. Finally I told Mr. Ford that I should have to leave if the interview did not take place at once. Thereupon all his brashness in regard to the press vanished. It was evident that he dreaded the interview. He pushed me into the parlor ahead of him and there ensued a scene so extraordinary that I have no parallel to it in all my experience. It ran thus:

Mr. Ford: "Well, boys, we've got the ship."
Chorus of reporters: "What ship, Mr. Ford?"
Mr. Ford: "Why, the *Oscar II.*"
Chorus: "Well, what about her? What are you going to do with her?"
Mr. Ford: "Why, we're going to Europe to stop the war."
Chorus: "Stop the *war?*"
Mr. Ford: "Yes, we're going to have the boys out of the trenches by Christmas."
Chorus: "My, how are you going to do that?"
Mr. Ford: "Well, we're going to Holland and all the neutral nations."
Chorus: "And then what?"
Mr. Ford: "Well, Mr. Villard will tell you all the rest."
Mr. Villard: "No, Mr. Ford, I cannot do that [I, of course, knew nothing] but I can explain that the idea is to seek by a delegation of important Americans to induce the neutral nations to join together to offer mediation to the nations at war."

Thereafter the cross-questioning was participated in by Mr. Lochner and, I believe, Miss Schwimmer. The newspaper men thought it "a whale of a story" and fled to their offices to ridicule the whole proposal. *The Evening Post* was almost the only newspaper to treat the peace voyage seriously and respectfully. I left for my office also—not, however, until, against my advice, Mr.

Ford had informed the reporters that he had given me $20,000 with which to establish a bureau of the Union Against Militarism in Washington to fight against Mr. Wilson's preparedness program, provided it raised a similar amount; I had asked that the announcement be postponed but he went ahead. "We want to know just why preparedness is necessary," Mr. Ford affirmed. "I shall take an active part in the inquiry immediately on my return from Europe. I will give Mr. Villard all the aid and assistance I can. If $20,000 is not enough he can have more." After that experience with Mr. Ford it did not take me long to decide that I had more important things to do than going on the *Oscar II,* and one of these was the fight against the preparedness agitation. It is worth recording for the light it throws upon Mr. Ford that, although the committee raised $27,000 from other sources to match the $20,000, it never received one cent of Ford money. I did my best to collect it, appealing to two of his secretaries and to Dean Samuel S. Marquis, who at that time was supervising Mr. Ford's charitable gifts, but in vain. They could not deny the facts nor Mr. Ford's own published statements; the only apparent excuse was that I had resigned my office on the committee lest I be accused of being a lobbyist and so forfeit my press gallery privilege.[1]

The opening of Congress on December 7, 1915, brought official proof of the President's surrender to the advocates of preparedness. In the previous summer House and Tumulty had won the President to this position; the Colonel had then become convinced that the President "was lost unless he got on the band wagon of preparedness." [2] At the same time Tumulty had discovered that the Republican party had only two available issues left for 1916, the tariff and preparedness and, with pitiful inability to understand how far-reaching would be the consequences of the President's going over to the military party, had at once decided that the President should cut the ground from under the Republicans

[1] This was not an isolated instance of a broken pledge, as Dean Marquis knew when he wrote his revealing book *Henry Ford, An Interpretation,* Boston, 1923, after quitting his service.

[2] Walter Millis, *Road to War,* Boston, 1935, p. 209.

so that they would have no issues left in 1916. The President was now most eager for renomination; as far back as February, 1913, he had written a letter to A. Mitchell Palmer, not published until 1916, in which he had treated the Bryan-sponsored, one-Presidential-term plank in the Baltimore platform as merely a bit of buncombe, although in accepting the nomination he had stated (like Franklin Roosevelt in 1932) that he stood squarely upon the entire platform. He notified Mr. Palmer—before his first inauguration—that he was ready to run again if his party and public opinion desired him. It is my firm belief that if Congress had passed in March, 1916, a bill for universal military service the President would have signed it; nothing would have been allowed to stand in the path of his ambition.

When Congress convened the President assured it that the time had come to arm. This was in direct contradiction of his position a year earlier when he had told his congressional hearers that America must not become "an armed camp"; that the country should keep cool and await the outcome of the war before taking counsel as to what further steps for safety should be taken. In 1915 he made proposals intended to set 725,000 Americans to drilling each year and his naval program was described by his party's leader in the House as "the most stupendous and costly in the history of any country in peace times." The President declared this program to be merely an acceleration of a policy which certain naval experts—unnamed—had had in view for some time. This was in contradiction of his address to the New York Chamber of Commerce in the previous May when he had laid down the sound American principle that matters of policy should never be determined by military and naval officers whose sole duty it is to carry out the policies formulated by responsible civilian officials. Thereafter his reversal was rapid. In January and February he undertook a cross-country pro-preparedness campaign. When he reached St. Louis on February 3, he was so affected by the applause of his audience that he demanded "incomparably the greatest navy in the world," which words were subsequently modified in the official text to read "incomparably the most adequate navy in the world," which, as Walter Millis remarks, means the same thing—"if it means anything." The following June he headed the preparedness parade in Washington carrying an American flag, and thus completed his robbery of the Republicans' preparedness clothes; the Democratic National Convention soon after abandoned the historic Democratic position on the tariff and went far to the Republican side of that issue.

Secretary Garrison was not, however, satisfied by this conversion of the President and resigned his office on February 12, 1916, because the President would not support his plan for a Continental Army of 400,000 militiamen and oppose the efforts of the National Guard to defeat the scheme. Mr. Garrison's proposal was not downed until the army bill was finally licked into shape in the joint conference committee. The Senate had accepted it; the House defeated it by only thirteen votes, 203 to 190. Then, as today, there was not the slightest effort by Congress to study the military situation intelligently or scientifically; [3] but there was a rush to vote $358,158,361 for the army and $239,632,757 for the navy for the fiscal year 1916-17. "When this measure becomes a law," Congressman Claude Kitchin, the leader of the Democratic House, said prophetically, "thereby putting the arms of the munitions makers into the Treasury to the elbows, with their heretofore undreamed of profits at stake, we can hardly conceive of a power in the nation strong enough to extract them. I fear that the big interests behind this program, with their tremendous and irresistible influence, and their infinite ingenuity will find or make a way to persuade or force the controlling factors of both parties to make perpetual the surrender to them of the Federal Treasury and to place permanently at their mercy the taxpayers of the country."

Claude Kitchin was the bravest of the brave, but there was ob-

[3] For example, the preparedness advocates would not listen to the truth that the German battleships did not jeopardize us because they were without coal capacity to cross the ocean. Secretary Daniels aided in the hue and cry until after the war. In May, 1919, on returning to New York after having seen the German battleships before they were sunk at Scapa Flow, he announced that their bunker capacity proved that they were built for fighting in European waters only. *The Nation*, May 24, 1919.

viously something wrong with him. He could not understand, and publicly said so, why, when the three-year Republican naval program had, on the advice of the weather-vane Secretary of the Navy, Josephus Daniels, been denounced by him and others in Congress as "criminal extravagance and waste," it suddenly became correct and proper two months later when the Secretary and President decided to flop for it. "If such a program was wrong and extravagant then, it is wrong and extravagant now . . ." declared Kitchin,[4] upon whose clear and honest head there descended from then on an avalanche of foul newspaper abuse and, on the part of the New York *Herald*, complete misrepresentation, through an entirely fabricated interview, until his health and career were wrecked. If ever a patriot was murdered by the press it was Claude Kitchin.

During the whole winter of 1915-16 I was almost more concerned with the antipreparedness campaign than even with my newspaper work. I spoke constantly and usually in the face of increasing hostility[5] and misrepresentation, noting the growing effectiveness of the British propaganda and the greater difficulty of making it clear that we peace lovers were fighting not to aid the Germans but to keep this country out of war and from being militarized. At the Gridiron Dinner early in December I was goodnaturedly represented as a recruit in the Plattsburg officers' training camp. Two days later at a large dinner of the Economic Club of New York, at which David Jayne Hill, Norman Angell, Admiral Peary, and my old chief, Professor Hart, were the other speakers, I abandoned my usual arguments to read an imaginative "Letter from Berlin" which purported to be the rejoicing of a German officer at the arming of the United States, together with a picture of a German general's wife denouncing the whole military system on the receipt of the news of the killing of her fifth son. This piece was not relished by the audience, although a most

[4] Professor A. M. Arnett, *Claude Kitchin and the Wilson War Policies*, Little, Brown & Company, Boston, 1937, p. 103.

[5] The New York *Times* declared, after the President's first speech for preparedness, that thereafter no dissent would be allowed on any platform!

bitter attack upon German militarism, but it was widely reprinted, was made into a one-act play and had been accepted by Nazimova when the nearing of our own entry into the war made it no longer possible to produce it.[6]

As the spring came on the preparedness issue overshadowed every other domestic one, ranking almost with the troubles with Mexico and the continuingly difficult relations with Germany. The country was still by no means united for preparedness. I had, for example, one audience in Philadelphia which overwhelmed me with its applause and united approval. In the Middle West our speakers were astounded by the cordiality of their reception. They found a deep-seated feeling against militarism and the preparedness movement, as another form of special privilege. The people felt that it was backed by the same influences that controlled the railroads, trusts, and similar aggregations of capital. On the other hand, in the East, encouraged by the President's flop, the preparedness campaign waxed in intensity and bitterness and reached its crest in New York City on May 13, when 135,000 persons, many of whom had been ordered to march by their employers, paraded from morning until long after dark, at least 20,000 of them women.

On June 23, I had a memorable encounter with members of the Virginia Bankers' Association at the Hotel Chamberlin at Fortress Monroe. The dining room was full of officers in uniform, in addition to the membership; many of the audience were noisy and some overstimulated; there was a wretchedly inefficient toast-master, and it was stiflingly hot. I had not been speaking for more than four minutes before I sensed the menacing hostility of most of the listeners. Never did I face a harder task; I discarded about a third of my manuscript and finally sat down conscious of complete failure. Instantly there was an uproar and a man who was unsteady on his pins confirmed my feeling by moving that as a result of my speech the association go on record as favoring a

[6] "Nothing more powerful in the way of satire has come out of the war than this piece of literature." *Commerce and Finance* in reproducing it, February 23, 1916.

regular army of 500,000 men and 50 more battleships! He was noisily seconded by a number but the toastmaster refused to put the motion. My hosts were obviously greatly distressed and not mollified when some of the diners, chiefly women, came up to speak of what they called my "bravery," as if I might have been expected to run away and refuse to play.

At Middletown, Connecticut, when I re-entered my hotel after the meeting, I noticed a noisy crowd at the front door. When I asked the reason the clerk said: "They are waiting for a pacifist fellow from New York who is making a speech over at the college." I went to my room, moved a rickety bureau before a rickety door, and slept soundly and quite undisturbed. These were experiences that came to all of us dissenters and made us certain that worse was to come, just as it increased our faith in the righteousness of our cause since we did not ourselves feel compelled to intolerance and bitterness. On May 8, President Wilson received a considerable delegation of our group; I did not join it as the President had refused to see me to discuss the preparedness issue and I did not wish to antagonize him by going with the others. He assured them that he thought that New York State was going too far with its compulsory service bills but beyond that made the most unfavorable impression.

Mr. Wilson told the committee that he thought 250,000 men were too many for the army but asserted that arming largely was not a matter of principle but one of pure expediency, that the country was not in danger of being militarized but that it might be. His facile mind drew a distinction between universal military training and universal service. Then he took the mistaken ground, which has ever since been the basis of our naval policy in relation to other countries, notably under Secretary Hull, that we cannot lead in the direction of international disarmament unless we have considerable forces to disarm, and he waved aside the historic success of American diplomacy when we were unarmed with the statement that the "world has changed since 1895." When the committee returned to New York one of the leaders telephoned to me that the President had not given them "one frank, honest, or ingenuous word. You were right; the President has undergone a grave moral deterioration." Until this time Colonel House had assured me that the President's preparedness program was merely a shrewd political maneuver and not intended really to be put into effect, but this time I was not fooled.

In April I astonished my wife by saying to her that I was no longer going on with my Washington correspondence—I had already been working in David Lawrence as our Washington correspondent. He resigned from the Associated Press to join us, thus beginning a career which has carried him far, not without its ups and downs, and with the result that he has now become one of the foremost conservative columnists. There were two reasons why I told my wife that I was no longer going to the White House: the first was that the approaching arrival of our second son made me naturally wish to be at home; and the other was that by then I had completely lost faith in Mr. Wilson. I pointed out there had been no quarrel between us, no breaking off of relations, that our friendship continued, but that despite what he had said to me I was certain then—in April, 1916—he would put us into the war. In that case I should have to take a position of complete antagonism to him and I wanted to stop my regular visits to the White House offices while relations were as good as they were. That did not mean complete cessation of my visits to Tumulty, with whom I constantly corresponded; it meant that I could no longer cooperate with or uphold the President himself.

By that time, or a little later, Mr. Wilson had changed his mind on the initiative, referendum, recall, woman suffrage, the tariff commission, tariffs for revenue only, a permanent diplomatic service beyond politics, the merit system in the Civil Service—from the beginning of his administration he forgot that he had been for years a vice-president of the Civil Service Reform Association and its staunch upholder—on Tammany Hall, on Bryan, on a Continental Army, on preparedness, and then finally, child labor legislation. As for the latter Senator Borah was able to show that Mr. Wilson described this legislation in his *Constitutional Government* as unconstitutional and as "obviously absurd extravagance," carrying a congressional power to regulate commerce beyond the "utmost boundaries of reasonable and *honest* inference." If it is only a narrow man whose mind is closed to new ideas, and if a big man does not fear inconsistency, Mr. Wilson by this test was obviously one of the broadest men this country has produced.

During all of that year the blundering in Mexico continued. We neither got Villa, dead nor alive. The entire militia was called out, for what reason no one yet understands unless it was to be a training of the National Guard preparatory to our going to war in Europe. Where Mr. Wilson's handling of this situation was not opera bouffe it became ruthless murder.[7] For example, at two-thirty o'clock one morning Bryan, Tumulty, Daniels, and Wilson decided to intervene in Mexico merely to prevent a German steamer's delivering her cargo at Vera Cruz lest the munitions which composed it be used against us.[8] We had no legal right whatever to stop this ship; we were not at war with Mexico or threatened with war. One of our admirals who witnessed the intervention told me subsequently that "it was as brutal a slaughter as ever disgraced our flag." It cost the lives of four hundred men, women, and children, chiefly boy naval cadets between the ages of twelve and sixteen years. When the bodies of the American dead from Vera Cruz were brought to the Brooklyn Navy Yard the President, who had ended their lives illegally, solemnly mourned their heroic and utterly uncalled-for deaths. Naturally the President failed then or at any time to tell the American people that, despite all this criminal waste of life, *Huerta got those munitions!* No just man, I assert, can read that record and not be convinced of the inefficiency and moral irresponsibility of Daniels, Bryan, and Wilson in dealing with Mexico. Finally, Mr. Wilson was rescued from the mess by our drift into war with Germany

[7] See General Smedley D. Butler's eye-witness accounts of our forcible interventions in Lowell J. Thomas, *Old Gimlet Eye*, New York, 1933.

[8] For Tumulty's prideful account of this see his *Woodrow Wilson as I Know Him*, pp. 150-53. Mr. Wilson's order to Admiral Mayo was: "Take Vera Cruz at once"—without the slightest stopping to inquire what that would cost in lives.

which allowed him to withdraw Pershing, the unsuccessful, from Mexico to become the successful and honored head of the army in France.

During this time the attacks upon *The Evening Post* grew steadily, because of my activities, because we were not anti-German enough, and because we were not deluded by the crass war propaganda. One day I got a letter from two ladies in Stockbridge denouncing me as pro-German because *The Evening Post* had not reported a speech there by a Canadian sergeant who told of a comrade's being crucified by Germans to a barn door. I replied that the sergeant had not told that story in New York City or it would have been reported and I asked for his address that I might obtain his statement. I did not get it but his yarn was extremely effective in inducing young Americans to enlist in the Canadian army which was his purpose. Later I regretted not having kept the names of those ladies in order to have the satisfaction of sending to them the cold-blooded admission in Parliament after the war of Sir Sam Hughes, the Canadian Minister of Defense, that there never was any truth in that yarn but that he had approved of its being widely used for recruiting purposes. What are honor and truth to a statesman?

My refusal to believe those stories of the Belgian children with their hands cut off stamped me clearly as a traitorous pro-German. Nothing else that I know of illustrates so clearly the flight of reason from the herd mind and its utter gullibility in war time. When people told me about those babies—who surely ran into millions—I asked for evidence and got none. I explained that babies with their hands cut off could not live for more than a very few minutes unless there were surgeons present to tie up the arteries, apply dressings, and offset the shock; that I could not see what the Germans had to gain by it when they needed every doctor and nurse and all their surgical supplies for their wounded. This logic earned me only snarls and vicious looks. Then I made matters worse by stating that by my orders our London correspondent had visited a number of hospitals and found no record of any such case; that I was sure Hearst would pay at least $100,000 for pictures of handless babies.

Once I thought I was really on the trail. At a dinner party a woman assured me that Helen Gould had sent for two Belgian children who turned up on the dock in New York minus hands. "At last," said I, "I'll write to her at once." I did so and got the usual answer that it had not happened to her but to someone else, President Bush, of the Missouri Pacific Railroad. So I wrote to President Bush, who in turn assured me that it had not happened to him but that it had been told to him at a dinner party by a very charming woman, whose name he had unfortunately forgotten, as having been not her experience but that of a very dear friend of hers. That was as close as I ever got to a handless Belgian baby [9] and I was not the least surprised when Sir Philip Gibbs told me after the war that during his four years at the front he had never seen or verified an actual German atrocity beyond those horrible crimes against humanity which *are* war, and take place in all armies.[10]

As the time for the national conventions in 1916 came on, the President, Tumulty, and House became more and more impressed, despite the success of Wilson's preparedness speeches, with the desire of the bulk of the people beyond the Alleghenies not to be drawn into the hostilities. Hence the decision during the campaign to sound the note, "He Kept Us Out of War," side by side with a vociferous stressing of what the President had achieved in

[9] "I was told by Cardinal Gasquet that the Pope promised to make a great protest to the world if a single case could be proved of the violation of Belgian nuns or cutting off of children's hands. An inquiry was instituted and many cases examined by Cardinal Mercier. Not one case could be proved." Colonel C. A. Repington, *The First World War*, Boston, 1920, Vol. 2, p. 447.

[10] Busch, the biographer of Bismarck, records how our General Philip H. Sheridan shocked Prussian headquarters during the war of 1870 by saying to the German generals: "The proper strategy consists in the first place in inflicting as telling blows as possible upon the enemy's army, and then in causing the inhabitants so much suffering that they must long for peace and force their government to demand it. The people must be left *nothing but their eyes to weep with over the war*." (Italics are mine.) See Doctor Moritz Busch, *Bismarck*, London, 1898, Vol. I, p. 171.

arming the country on land and sea. There has never been any doubt in my mind that it was that slogan which re-elected Mr. Wilson. After we got into the war and charges were freely made that the President had won his re-election by false pretenses, it was alleged on his behalf that he had himself never pressed that point; [11] it was not known until years afterward that the speech of former Governor Martin Glynn at the Democratic National Convention, which contained the "kept-us-out-of-war" phrase, had been passed upon and edited in the White House by Wilson himself.

I reported for *The Evening Post* all three of the national conventions, the Republican, the Democratic, and the Progressive. There was tremendous enthusiasm in St. Louis for the President, notably when Senator Ollie James delivered his tribute to him; only one delegate refused to make it a unanimous renomination. But the desire for peace was the outstanding feature of the convention. When Governor Glynn undertook to slur over the hanging of some American seamen by the British the crowd shouted: "What did we do?" "*We didn't go to war*," roared the former governor of New York. Then "men jumped up in their seats and danced about the aisles and waved American flags, shouting like schoolboys and screaming like steam sirens." [12] Thereafter Ollie James emphasized the same note. The party of the war makers then in office thus put itself squarely on record against the country's going to war. In Chicago, the Republican convention was far more interesting because it was not absolutely certain who the choice would be, though Hughes was from the beginning the outstanding candidate. For Theodore Roosevelt these two conventions were a fearful disaster. He tried, behind the scenes, with Senator Penrose particularly, to negotiate a compromise so that both wings of the party might unite upon him. When that became impossible he broke the hearts of his devoted followers in the Progressive convention which was meeting simultaneously with the Republican.

[11] Tumulty, *op. cit.*, p. 185, n. 8.
[12] Millis, *op. cit.*, pp. 318-19.

I sat in the former on the fatal day. It was a tense moment when Raymond Robbins, the presiding officer, stepped out of a telephone booth to give to the delegates the recommendation he had just received by telephone from the Colonel himself—and informed the stunned listeners that "T.R.'s" compromise candidate was his old ally and chum, the chief Republican Old Guard reactionary, Henry Cabot Lodge! This suggestion being rejected by both conventions, the Progressive delegates nominated Roosevelt, being tricked into doing so by their own leaders. Victor Murdock of Kansas assured the convention that the Rough Rider would stand by the party and lead it to victory, but the newspaper men and the dominating leaders were aware that if Hughes were nominated by the Republicans the Colonel would not stand; he never could have faced certain defeat. On the spot, immediately after the nomination, $100,000 was raised to start the campaign and a call issued for a Woman's Progressive League to aid the cause. Then, just before five o'clock, the hour fixed for adjournment, Raymond Robbins read the Colonel's letter declining the nomination and at once adjourned the convention which had already put through a resolution that the National Committee should have the right to fill vacancies on the ticket.

Only twice in my life have I seen men weep in a public assembly. Around me men of the frontier type could not keep back their tears at this self-revelation of their idol's selfishness, the smashing of their illusions about their peerless leader. Then the Colonel went back to the "thieves and robbers" he had so ardently denounced from 1912 to 1915, and the Progressive party was betrayed and slain. I telegraphed that: "On its tombstone History will write: 'Created by Theodore Roosevelt for his own purposes and killed when it suited him.' In all the sizable graveyard of the third parties of our political history there lies none done to death so cruelly and so casually." Theodore Roosevelt then and there committed on a smaller scale the same kind of crime as did later Woodrow Wilson. Roosevelt inspired great masses of his fellow-citizens to battle for justice and progress, took them up on a high mountain, showed them the Promised Land, fired them with a belief in his own inspired mission, and his own divine leadership, and then basely let them down. Woodrow Wilson's dupes were the masses all over the world who craved life, liberty, perpetual peace and self-determination. From that moment in Chicago the Progressive party was dead and the fight one merely between Wilson and Hughes, with those liberals who could vote for neither casting their ballots for Eugene Debs, the man in Atlanta Penitentiary who, in his character, his devotion to principle, and his readiness to perish if need be for his beliefs, towered even in his prison cell head and shoulders above the President and Mr. Hughes.

We of *The Evening Post* and *The Nation* tried our best to support Mr. Hughes. I called upon him on June 27, in the Astor Hotel, soon after his nomination, and told him frankly that we were undecided but most friendly to him and that we would await his utterances in the campaign before finally deciding whom to urge our readers to support. I was much impressed with the outline that he gave me of his proposed strategy during the hour and a quarter of my lunch with him. He showed then his old fearlessness, his courage, and his independence. He seemed like the Hughes of the early days of his governorship but when it came to the question of militarism and the opportunity of the United States to mediate abroad at the close of the war, I noted at the time that "he does not know what you are talking about." I added, however, "None the less, he spoke very strongly against our getting into the war and criticized Wilson severely for maneuvering the country into a position where war may be a necessity." Unfortunately Mr. Hughes, whatever the reasons, did not live up to the outline of his campaign that he gave me. He became weaker and weaker as the election neared. "All along the line," we wrote on the eve of the election, "the voters in doubt about supporting Wilson find no satisfaction in the thought of turning to Hughes." Two weeks previously we had said that Mr. Hughes's campaign had been a woeful disappointment to his friends and admirers, that he had left the country cold.[13] We admitted frankly that we

[13] *The Nation*, October 19, 1916.

had no answer to the riddle of Mr. Hughes in that campaign and I have heard none since to satisfy me. It was not merely his sad blundering when he reached California on his swing around the country that defeated him. The inspiration, the force, and the power which made him such a great figure in the years of promise when he was governor were somehow lacking.

Thanks to the astuteness of David Lawrence, *The Evening Post* was the only important newspaper which did not concede the election of Mr. Hughes on election night. Mr. Lawrence, who had traveled across the country for us during the campaign, had become convinced in California that Wilson would carry the State and so wrote in one of his letters, and added later that he believed California would decide the election in Wilson's favor. That extraordinary prophecy gave him a national reputation. Just before we were going to get out our final extra, as we were being besought by the Associated Press to state whether or not we conceded Wilson's defeat, David Lawrence called us up and begged us under no circumstances to affirm Hughes's election, pointing out that California had not been heard from. I took his advice and we were duly elated when, unlike the *Times* and the *World*, we were on record the next day as not having been misled by the early returns which sent Mr. Hughes to bed believing that he would be the next President of the United States. After the election I satisfied myself by careful inquiries in California that it was the women's vote which had carried the state for Wilson and that they were largely influenced by the slogan, "He Kept Us Out of War." I have never believed that if Hughes had become President he would have kept us at peace; the tremendous forces within the Republican party which were eager for war, and their close alliance with the Big Business interests, together with the great manufacturers who were making millions out of the struggle, and the influence of the pro-British leaders in New York, like Joseph H. Choate, would, I think, have led Mr. Hughes to find that Wilson *had* maneuvered us to a point where the country could not keep out of the war.

All through the summer the fight to keep us at peace went on.

On August 30 some twenty-seven members of the Neutral Conference Committee called upon the President at the White House, urging upon him once more the summoning of a conclave of the neutral nations to offer mediation and to insist upon the stopping of the war which was becoming ruinous to all Europe. My mother was one of the leaders of the delegation and on that day entered in her diary: "He received us most graciously but turned us down without compunction." It is undeniable that this movement, behind which should have been placed the whole force of the American government, had been brought into wholly unmerited contempt by the pitifully inept handling of the Ford crusade. Colonel House remained steadfastly opposed to the conference plan and so was Mr. Lansing. Yet it was one avenue to peace [14] which should have been explored again and again, for the stake was the saving of millions of lives and billions of wealth. Mr. Wilson's failure to try this is the more difficult to understand because it would have given him that opportunity to lead toward peace that he so craved. The Allies were so largely dependent upon supplies from the neutrals that if the latter had spoken firmly with one voice they would have had to listen, and Germany, too, because of her dependence upon supplies coming to her from England and the neutral countries through Scandinavia.

On December 9 the Woman's Peace Party, in convention assembled in Washington, fairly laid siege to the White House, my mother again in the front. Then, on December 12, our hopes ran high when the German Chancellor handed a peace note to our chargé d'affaires, Mr. Grew, and announced to the Reichstag that he had done so and that the Central Powers were ready "even then" to enter into peace negotiations. This spiked the guns of Mr. Wilson who had been meditating a peace note for some time. On Friday, December 15, he none the less came into the Cabinet meeting with the note in his hand. The Cabinet opposed it and the President said it must be that note or nothing. In it he asserted

---

[14] Mr. Millis terms it "one of the few really generous and rational impulses of those insane years." Millis, *op. cit.*, p. 245.

that both sides had in mind objects "virtually the same, as stated in general terms to their own people and to the world." After specifying those objects, the President suggested an immediate comparison of views as to the terms which must precede "the ultimate arrangements for the peace of the world." The note aroused the bitterest antagonism among the intense pro-Ally sympathizers in this country and among the Allies who had certainly no desire to let the world know what their real objectives were. It was further noteworthy as the beginning of the rift between Colonel House and the President, for it was the only important action that the President had taken in international affairs without consulting Colonel House, the reason being that he already knew that the Colonel was opposed to this action. It was a marvelous opportunity for the Germans but, while they were delighted with the President's note, they again muffed it and before long their military leaders were calling for the renewal of unrestricted submarine warfare.

On January 22 the President made what seems to me the greatest speech of his entire career; at least no other has been so justified by subsequent events. If ever a man was given a vision of the future, and the power to prophesy it, Woodrow Wilson was then. These are the words that will always be imperishable:

They [the implications of the assurances of both parties to the war] imply, first of all, that it must be a peace without victory. It is not pleasant to say this. I beg that I may be permitted to put my own interpretation upon it and that it may be understood that no other interpretation was in my thoughts. I am seeking only to face realities and to face them without soft concealments. Victory would mean peace forced upon the loser, a victor's terms imposed upon the vanquished. It would be accepted in humiliation, under duress, at an intolerable sacrifice, and would leave a sting, a resentment, a bitter memory upon which terms of peace would rest not permanently, but only as upon quicksand. Only a peace between equals can last. Only a peace the principle of which is equality and a common participation in a common benefit. The right state of mind, the right feeling between nations, is as necessary for a lasting peace as is the just settlement of vexed questions of territory or of racial and national allegiance.

Had Woodrow Wilson but lived up to these words the whole world today would be a happy and prosperous orb; there would be no Hitler and no Benito Mussolini. Instead, we have the Treaty of Peace resting "not permanently, but as upon quicksand"—actually disappearing in the quicksand which Woodrow Wilson saw in his mind's eye.

This utterance, too, profoundly angered the Allies. It should have been followed up even when the news came that the Germans in their utter folly and madness were beginning the final, unlimited submarine campaign. What swung the President over then into forgetfulness of those great, prophetic words is something that no man has yet explained. I have asked Tumulty and a number of others who were among the President's closest advisers. There are theories but no facts. Aside from the action of the Germans, it is thought that the President was finally influenced by a revelation as to the desperate situation of the British treasury and had been given facts about the submarine sinkings in contrast to the false statistics published by the British government; the former showed that Germany was winning the submarine war. There are others who insist that the President forgot all about peace without victory because he decided that if we did not go into the war he could not play the part in the peacemaking upon which his heart had so long been set. It will remain a mystery and the key to it will never be found.

From then on the tides which had been running so strongly for peace were reversed. The President, having made up his mind, pursued his end with the most rigid determination, with intense bitterness toward all in Congress who dared to hold to the view which he had held so short a time before. On March 4 he made his attack upon "the little group of willful men," namely, eleven Senators who, he said, representing no opinion but their own, had rendered the great government of the United States helpless and contemptible. He threw to the wolves of the press and of politics these patriots, who had placed their consciences and their judgments above their own welfare, who had decided that they must live up to their oath of office as they interpreted it, to vote according to

their best judgment in a tremendous and what was to prove a disastrous crisis for the American people. They were La Follette of
Wisconsin, Stone of Missouri, Norris of Nebraska, Lane of Oregon, Gronna of North Dakota, Cummins of Iowa, Clapp of Minnesota, Works of California, Vardaman of Mississippi, O'Gorman
of New York, and Kirby of Arkansas—a true roll of honor. They
were called traitors, Iscariots, Germany's allies, and much worse.
They had defeated the Armed Neutrality Bill but none the less the
President announced, on March 12, that naval guns and gun crews
would be put on American ships whether the Senate so voted or
not. Lane and Stone went to early deaths; others were retired
from public life promptly but La Follette and Norris, by their
undaunted heroism and courage, survived to see their attitude on
the war justified by the events. On the twentieth anniversary of
our going into the war the man to whom the press associations of
America gave the greatest space and paid the greatest attention
was George W. Norris, and after him the House survivors of the
antiwar vote.

As for the battlers for peace, they fought right down to the last
ditch, not always with wisdom and with nothing like the knowledge and understanding that would be possible today. Even as late
as April 2, a pacifist army, led by David Starr Jordan, arrived in
Washington, only to be repelled by armed guards at the State
Department and to achieve nothing in the halls of Congress. There
was a new organization, the Emergency Peace Federation, which
spread throughout the country; its "Keep-Us-Out-of-War" committees held hundreds and hundreds of meetings throughout the
United States. Our Edward G. Lowry, who had temporarily returned from London and was studying public sentiment in the
Middle West, found that the people were opposed to going to
war but that they would follow the President. At least two separate polls were taken of Congress, one as late as the end of March,
and both confirmed the fact that, if there could have been a secret
ballot, a large majority would have voted against our going to
war; but the President's assault upon the eleven willful men de-
terred most of them from voting as they thought right. Tumulty

himself is authority for the statement as to one of these polls.[15] One of the peace groups engaged a former army officer to question Congressmen as to their genuine beliefs; he came to the same conclusion. It was the perfect illustration of the fact that the President has usurped the war-making power and that he can maneuver the country to the brink of war and then, by rousing public passion, force the Congress to do his bidding.

Only a relative few of the peace-loving hauled down the flag when war came. A session of the American Union against Militarism produced a most dramatic scene. In the midst of a discussion of what our policy should be, Rabbi Stephen S. Wise said that he felt the time had come for a re-orientation of the pacifist point of view and that he wished to read us extracts from a sermon he intended to deliver the next Sunday. It bowled us over for it was a complete yielding on every point, an acceptance of the war as highminded and all for the best—a complete reversal of everything he had stood for. He asked us to state our frank opinion one after the other and he got what he asked for. Crystal Eastman, Walter Fuller, Lillian D. Wald, Amos Pinchot, Agnes Leach, L. Hollingsworth Wood, Mary W. Ovington, Norman Thomas, I and others told him exactly what we thought. Never have I heard such plain, straightforward language; never have I seen a man so flayed to his face. When my turn came I reminded him that in several public sermons he had penned the finest tributes to my grandfather's nonresistant doctrines yet published, that he had declared his allegiance to them, and I said that if he read that sermon I should never wish to speak to him again.

During this ordeal by fire the perspiration ran in streams down

---

[15] "My authority for the straw vote in Congress, as quoted in the *Good Housekeeping* article, was Joe Tumulty. . . . It was in answer to my resentment that Wilson had not already declared war, and the vote was, I understood at the time, taken in December, 1916. I may add that my own wide acquaintance in Washington during that period seemed to verify Mr. Tumulty's statement. Outside of the Eastern coast there was practically no enthusiasm for the war until Mr. Wilson finally declared that a state of war already existed between the German Empire and ourselves." Letter of Mary Roberts Rinehart to the author, January 8, 1938.

the rabbi's face. When it was over he remarked that it was evident that he could not deliver that sermon and that he would not do so. A few weeks later the sermon was delivered, with modifications, and thereafter the rabbi became one of the war's great supporters. He took a job in a shipyard—with that fanfare of publicity which, quite by accident, surrounds his every move—and was duly photographed at work, carrying his dinner pail, and nobly giving his week's wages to some poor woman in need of aid. Of late years he has again recanted, has confessed that he made a mistake in 1917, and has said that he will never, never, never have anything to do with the next war to free humanity. I wonder—if that war should be one to save the Jews from Hitler!

When the vote was taken in the House, fifty Democrats, thirty-two Republicans, one Independent, and one Socialist voted against war.[16] In the Senate Gronna, La Follette, Lane, Norris, Stone, and Vardaman stood out until the end. I was alone in a room in the offices of the Associated Press when a boy brought me a bulletin reading that Wilson had gone before Congress to ask for a declaration of war. It had long been inevitable but the blow was terrific none the less. It came nearer to unmanning me than anything in my life. For I knew, as I knew that I lived, that this ended the republic as we had known it; that henceforth we Americans were to be part and parcel of world politics, rivalries, jealousies, and militarism; that hate, prejudice, and passion were now enthroned in the United States.

A week later I wrote a letter to Joseph Tumulty:

You have had my sincerest sympathy during these trying days. . . . I know how you must have been suffering mentally and morally, and I can, I am sure, wholly enter into the feelings that must have been yours. To see your beloved chief congratulated by Henry Cabot Lodge, warmly endorsed and called upon by Theodore Roosevelt, and acclaimed with joy by every munitions maker, every agent of Big Business and all the evil forces combined against whom he has fought for

[16] "I really believe that there were a number of others who would have voted against the resolution if they had dared. . . ." Robert Lansing writing to E. N. Smith of Watertown, N. Y., April 7, 1917.

American democracy until recently—all this, I know, must have caused you profound concern and unhappiness. Believe me, I am ready for any concentration camp, or prison, but I am *not* at war and no one can *put me into war*—not the President of the United States with all his power; my loyalty to American traditions and ideals renders that impossible. We shall see what we shall see, but what I should like to know now is what shall we newspaper men say who supported the President's speech of January 22, in which he said: "It must be a peace without victory. . . . Victory would mean peace forced upon the loser, a victor's terms imposed upon the vanquished. . . . Only a peace between equals can last. . . ."?

Chapter XVIII. The War Madness

SO the great tragedy had come. The country was in the war, in the war it was to win and to lose. The fundamental foreign policy of the republic—to remain aloof from the jealousies, intrigues, and wars of Europe—was thrown overboard. Again the dream of empire, of being the dominating world power was upon us. In the White House Woodrow Wilson more than ever saw himself the dictator of the peace. He at once became the dictator at home with unlimited control of the country's finances; the dictator of the press; the dictator of the farms; of all business, or nearly all; soon of the transportation; and dictator as to who of our youth should live or die—greater power by far than had ever been Abraham Lincoln's. This, we were assured, was proper, for the country was now actually fighting for its life as well as for the democratic doctrine in the world, for everlasting peace, and nobody and nothing must stand in the way of the holiest and noblest crusade since the quest of the Grail.

From the moment we embarked upon that crusade it was marked by a bitterness, a vindictiveness, a rage against all who opposed it, which in themselves should have given pause to those who really believed that out of such passions, out of wholesale murder, would come an all-cleansing spiritual victory. Most of those who dissented and refused to recant, as Rabbi Wise had recanted, and take service with Mars, felt the full force of governmental disapproval or hostility and popular hatred. That was not surprising; we expected misrepresentation, contumely, even persecution, precisely as the conscientious objectors awaited their prison sentences. I am proud to say that I never heard one of our group complain or express self-pity. For a time some of the peace societies suspended all operations, well aware that they were watched and spied upon. Moreover, we were in the war and those of my faith certainly did not want the Germans to win and hoped from our hearts that, if the war must be fought to a finish on the battlefields, our troops would speedily end it. The last thought of any of us would have been to put obstacles in the way. We were determined, however, to ward off the militarization of the country in so far as lay within our power and we were ceaseless in our efforts for a peace of justice and the remaking of the world into a sensible, decent whole. I personally did my uttermost to keep *The Evening Post* and *Nation* free to print as judicially as possible all news of significance, and even to report the undercurrents abroad which did not find their way past the cable censorship.

It was not an easy course to steer, especially as the staff was almost wholly pro-war—intensely so—and much worried lest the pacifist owner get himself and them into serious trouble. There was real fear that the government might move against me or the newspaper, notably when the Burleson censorship was established. That fear was needless; the record soon showed that the Post Office Department was concerned only with arresting small-town editors, suppressing foreign-language publications or little far-Western newspapers, in other words terrifying helpless fry who could not strike back. Since the government knew that the bulk of the people beyond the Alleghenies was not in favor of going to war, the bitterest and most unscrupulous campaign of lies to make Americans hate, to rouse their passions to the boiling point, and to suppress criticism was launched—with the sanction, of course, of the President. Some of the worst speeches of the war were formulated under Mr. McAdoo and sent out by the Treasury in connection with the Liberty Loan campaign. Some of them stopped at nothing. For instance, I heard a passionate and dynamic speaker for one of the Liberty Loans explain in a theatre that he wanted our money—and was going to have it whether we wished to give or not—not for the Red Cross or for the Y.M.C.A. or any field hospital but just to kill Germans, kill them by day and night until there were none left. "The Germans," he said, "are the snakes of the human race and must be stamped out. No, I apologize to the snakes and to the animal kingdom. There is nothing in it so low and vile as a German." It did not seem to me that those in the audience who gave the speaker money did so enthusiastically or even willingly. But that was far less important than the fact that this arousing of blind mass passion worked wholly against any intelligent appreciation of what the war aims ought to be and what kind of a peace should be obtained.

Individually we dissenters soon had the conventional experience of learning who were our real friends and who were not. I soon discovered that half of mine were afraid that I would land in prison and that the other half was afraid that I would not. It was amusing to see how many men got up and left the room if I went into a club and how many others had become too shortsighted to recognize me. Amos Pinchot chuckled with joy in telling me how he had heard one of two men in the washroom of the University Club, who were unaware of his presence, say: "By God, it's come to a pretty pass when a man has to be in the same club with Amos Pinchot and Oswald Villard!" Once I met Talcott Williams on the street. In his most unctuous manner he said: "It must be terribly hard for you. I hear you have seventeen first cousins on the German front line." "That," I replied, "is news to me. I wonder where they all came from. Neither of my father's sisters had children and he never had a brother." This was typical of the attitude of many men, even intellectuals. It was beyond their comprehension that anyone could refuse to agree that the war was the greatest of moral undertakings, bound to result in the regeneration of the world. They could only explain my attitude by my German blood. They thought I was crazy because I revolted against the whole idea that good could come out of the slaughter of millions.

One day a member of the board of directors of the Philharmonic Society came to tell me, the president, that in the board's judgment the time had come for a new head, that "pacifism and music would not mix in war time." The directors' action was entirely proper and the message was tactfully delivered. I should have handed in my resignation when the war began, for the Philharmonic then needed money more than ever as the costs jumped up with the war time and I could not have raised a dollar; indeed, my continuance as president would have cost the society much support. So the directors turned to Clarence Mackay and to other rich and influential persons for the aid that they needed. The society, too, was charged with pro-Germanism and found it necessary to print on its programs in large letters that it had bought Liberty bonds. Before very long one of the most useful women directors led a vigorous fight to prevent the playing of any German music during the war—even Beethoven was to be banned lest its rendering encourage the Germans and dishearten our troops in the trenches! [1] Every concert had to be opened or closed with the poverty-poor music of "My Country, 'Tis of Thee." The national anthem was worn threadbare in those crowded months and if familiarity breeds contempt it must have sunk low in popular esteem.

When I resigned I naturally recalled how on January 17, 1917, on the occasion of the seventy-fifth anniversary of the society, I had addressed the audience in Carnegie Hall and had boasted that our art and our orchestra were unaffected by prejudice, even in the face of war. How soon had this been proved false! On my resigning, the *Musical Courier* declared that in its judgment it would be hard to find another president "to devote himself to the welfare of the organization as unselfishly and enthusiastically as Mr. Villard did at all times, and to fight its battles as stoutly and successfully against financial discouragement and against the insolent attacks of its malignant enemies, chiefly newspaper men trying to manipulate musical quality for their own ends"—pleasant words but giving a picture of my work that I could not recognize and did not merit. Indeed, as I reread these words it is obvious that they were the invention of some other virulent pro-German seeking to enthrone the Kaiser in the White House.

Looking back on those war years it seems to me that I got off

---

[1] Even the passionately anti-German Owen Wister protested. He denounced this policy as "a mistaken patriotic sentiment." Most of the German symphonies, he pointed out, were written by men who had not shared the spirit of modern Germany. "They wrote the most beautiful music in the world; to banish it from our programs is to make bricks without straw." *The Nation*, November 30, 1918.

very easily. We dissenters suffered most, however, through the pain we caused members of our family. Our children were not spared; my little daughter was constantly asked, with that refined cruelty of which children are often capable, whether she was not ashamed of her pacifist, disloyal and traitorous, pro-German father. One day she burst into my room and in great excitement asked: "Daddy, have I *got* to believe as you do about the war?" "Certainly not, Dorothea, you must believe what you think is right and some day when you are old enough to understand I will tell you just why I have taken the position that I have." "Well, then, I believe that the Germans ought to be killed—all of them—and I am going to say so!" That relief helped a lot to carry her over this most difficult period. At Black Point my elder son, then aged six, manfully fought his way through that first summer of the war, often with his fists.

What caused that summer colony to boil over, however, was the fact that we actually possessed a lovely brown dachshund whose name, worse luck, was Fritz. One of the ladies called upon my wife to inform her that that was too much. The community, she said, found it hard enough to stomach my pacifism but a German dog, by name Fritz, was more than they could stand. Two days later I took Fritz to Thorwood for sanctuary because our children reported that the poor beastie was actually in danger of being stoned to death by neighboring children who were quick to take their cue from their elders. As I stood with him on the platform of the station I heard two of my neighbors say: "Well, I see the Kaiser's leaving us at last," and "it's high time, indeed." Such was the mentality of well-bred men and women in that summer of 1917 when all the country, we were told, was rising in one glorious, elevating, idealistic symphony of patriotic devotion to country and mankind. Needless to say that during that time I found unvarying support from my wife and mother, who never flinched through all those arduous days.

Incidentally the messenger who brought the protest to my wife was a member of one of the most fashionable New York churches and a devout worshiper of Jesus. One day the news came that a young relative of hers, an aviator, had singlehanded bombed and destroyed a German submarine. Her joy and pride were unbounded; he had made good and distinguished himself; he had sent forty-five Huns to one of the most terrible of deaths. They were enemies and that was that. Why not? The Commandment, "Thou shalt not kill," was just then in a moratorium—with God's blessing—and the Scriptures were in cold storage. God was pleased that those forty-five young German "snakes" had been annihilated. As for their parents and families, why, no well-bred patriot thought of them. The amusing thing about this lady was that a distinguished ancestor, of whom she was most proud, was bitterly hated and nearly run out of the United States because he opposed the country's going to war with England in 1812!

Naturally the yarns about me grew day by day. It was reported that I had said that I would not defend wife or daughter if they were attacked by raping Huns; that I had declared that I would fight the conscription of my two sons in that war—their ages of one and six years were not mentioned; that I had affirmed that I would not succor a wounded man if I came across him! I was reported to be in daily communication with the Kaiser—doubtless by the kindness of the Army Intelligence corps and the Department of Justice. The story about my attitude toward the wounded grew out of my opposition to the perversion of the Red Cross into a partisan adjunct of the Allied and American armies, instead of its being permitted to retain its original function, for which it was organized by Clara Barton, as an international, nonpartisan, peaceful organization extending its aid to both sides in every conflict. These experiences were, however, but pin pricks beside the pain of being unable to throw oneself into the stream of war work, to share that utterly mistaken and misguided popular enthusiasm.

For one like myself, who had for some years been in the heart of things, it was hard to see the tremendously reinforced tide of national life sweeping by while one remained stationary on the bank, as it were, and to have the feeling that one must not only refuse to participate but that the great mass of one's fellow-citizens would not wish one to take part. The sense of intellectual isolation was complete save when with spiritual comrades. We fled the brass bands and the parades; uniforms became almost unbearable, less because of their relationship to the war than to the future. Some of the dissenters became apathetic. I could not, for the pain and disappointment were too keen; but I cannot recall having had doubts, not even when the Portland *Oregonian*, for one, railed (August 1, 1918) at the conscientious objector who "sets up his own individual opinions of right or wrong conduct against the opinions, the experience, and judgment of all others. He and his conscience are everything and the voices of the past, the present, and the future, so far as they are phrased by others, are as nothing. He alone is right, he alone may interpret the divine will; he alone may say what should and should not be done—by him at least," thus ignoring the fact that, historically speaking, the world had been chiefly advanced by just such men. We held firm not because we were egotists but because we knew that the great wave of national emotion was largely artificial; deliberately cultivated by the government propaganda; that it was an appeal to base human traits; that it could not be honest and therefore could not succeed, could not evoke great literary and artistic creations, and could only impoverish American promise.[2] It was this certainty that made the lot of the dissenters hard rather than the aspersions upon their courage or their motives. Not one of them but would have welcomed the chance to make any sacrifice to advance the genuine welfare of the America they adored.

I had hoped from the beginning to enter some nonmilitary governmental service. Here, as at other points, the dissenters were divided as to how far they could go. It was obvious that one could not escape participating in the war, try as one might, for every railroad, theatre and concert ticket, every stamp purchased and all taxes paid contributed to the war. I, for one, freely bought Liberty bonds and conformed otherwise where I conscientiously could.

[2] The San Francisco *Argonaut*, intensely pro-war in 1917, has recently written: "How mad the world was then may be seen from one fact alone, to wit, that scarcely a book was written anywhere during the war period that is worth reading."

As president of the Dobbs Ferry Hospital, for whose initial construction I and one other had raised the funds, plus a bequest from
my father, I took the lead in offering its services to the government and, so far from being indifferent to the needs of wounded
soldiers, contributed freely to relief agencies, specifying, however,
in the case of the Red Cross, that my gift should be earmarked
to be used only for reconstruction in France. Once it appeared as
if a way had opened for me to serve the government directly, for
Herbert Hoover asked me in Washington one day to become a
member of his inner council in the Food Administration, pre-
sumably in charge of publicity. I returned to New York and did
my very best to free myself to join him but the financial situation of *The Evening Post* was becoming so precarious that I could
not leave for there was, unfortunately, no one in the office or in
my family connection to whom I could turn over that phase of
my responsibilities.

When the war began John Gavit suggested that the Villards
withdraw publicly from *The Evening Post* and turn it over to the
staff but that would not have been in keeping with the family tradition. Whatever else may be said of us, we don't run under fire.
I accomplished what I wished to—keeping our great paper from
becoming, like all the others, a Hun-hater and suppressor of news,
and if I had achieved nothing else than publishing the secret
treaties I think that I was justified. I am proud of the fact that
I wrote thus to the president of the bank from which *The Evening
Post* borrowed money: "It is true that *The Evening Post* has not
adopted the policy of approving this war. It was opposed to our
going into it and believes that it forebodes disaster to our American institutions, which are to us priceless. . . . We have not hesitated to print criticisms of the Allies, believing it to be the duty
of a newspaper like *The Evening Post* to dispense evenhanded
justice even in war time." That the paper suffered by this attitude
and my connection with it is true. Advertising contracts were can-
celed and only the war excitement maintained the circulation.
Everybody forgot the stand we had taken against the Germans
the day they entered Belgium and how on February 1, 1917, we

had said: "Having begun the European war by an act of perfidy the German government now seeks to end it by an act of criminal insanity." But readers, as well as friends, were neither remembering nor reasoning animals at that time. Had I been willing to join the mob it would have been easy to refinance *The Evening Post*. I could then have taken Mr. Hoover's job and thus ended all the doubts as to my loyalty. Needless to say I have no regrets— especially when I look at the world in 1939.

Soon after the war began I asked Tumulty to get the President's consent to my submitting to him a memorandum of a policy for the government to follow in relation to the conscientious objector. I explained that I had knowledge of the English procedure and that I wanted to make constructive suggestions for dealing with these men in the best way for themselves, their families, and the government. I was partly moved to this by my old friend, General Enoch H. Crowder, the Judge Advocate General, who told me, when I asked him what the army's policy would be, that he had not decided but that his younger associates were urging that the objectors be shot out of hand as had been done, it was reported, in the German and Austrian armies. President Wilson at once agreed to my proposal so I returned to New York and called on Roger N. Baldwin [3] for aid.

Mr. Baldwin, one of the true moral heroes of this country, and one of its devoted servitors, eagerly undertook the preparation of the memorandum in which he had a personal stake since he knew that he probably had years of imprisonment before him because of his refusal to serve. After I had amended his plan I sent it to Tumulty. In return I received a note from him enclosing one of the little typed memos which Wilson attached to papers he had passed upon. It reads:

Dear Tumulty: Please thank Mr. Villard of *The Evening Post* for his memorandum which you sent me about the conscientious objectors. It contains a great deal that is interesting and sensible, and I am sure

[3] "Mr. Baldwin has lived only to serve others." *The Nation*, November 9, 1918.

that it will be read with as much sympathetic appreciation by the Secretary of War, to whom I am sending it, as by myself.

The President

C. L. S.[4]

For some weeks Baldwin and I were in the seventh heaven. We thought that a rational policy would be adopted. But Baker never paid the slightest attention to this action of the President; the court-martials gave sentences up to fifty years and the horrible tortures of the dissenters in camp and prison began, notably at Angel Island in San Francisco harbor, where men were spread-eagled and otherwise sadistically punished.[5] None of this would have come to pass had Baker followed our suggestions for our plan was to settle the men on the land in farm camps in order to raise food for the army; nearly all of them would have accepted this service or some alternative. Instead they were left in the hands of the army officers who made every effort to break them spiritually and physically—some of the objectors have never recovered to this day from the ill-treatment then received.

Another constructive opportunity occurred when a Japanese imperial commission, headed by Viscount Ishii, arrived in the summer of 1917 to co-ordinate war activities. I then still labored under the impression that the Japanese honestly desired friendly relations with us and the rest of the world, including China, and it seemed as if the time were most propitious for the removal of all causes for friction and misunderstanding between the two countries. I therefore entertained the commission at a dinner in the St. Regis Hotel to which there came 125 guests, representing 60 of the leading American newspapers and magazines, thus giving to

[4] C. L. Swem was the President's confidential stenographer.

[5] For the full story, see Norman Thomas's "Conscientious Objector in America," New York, 1927. At Leavenworth Barracks "during the first week they stand with their hands crossed at their breasts, during the second week they hang by their wrists." *The Nation*, December 7, 1918. Among those thus tortured were Evan Thomas (a brother of Norman Thomas), Howard Moore, and Francis Henessy. They were hung by their hands from early in November until December 6, when this treatment was stopped by Secretary Baker who finally officially admitted these military atrocities. *The Nation*, December 28, 1918.

Viscount Ishii and Ambassador Sato an opportunity to speak directly to our most important journalists. Don C. Seitz, John Dewey, Controller Prendergast of New York, and I also spoke. Ishii warned us against hostile German intrigues in the Far East and in the United States for the purpose of embroiling our two countries. He declared that there was a fundamental difference between our Monroe Doctrine and Japan's attitude toward China: "In the first, there is on the part of the United States no engagement or promise while, in the other, Japan voluntarily announces that Japan will engage herself not to violate the political or territorial integrity of her neighbor and to respect the Open Door and equal opportunity, asking at the same time, other nations to respect these principles."

His remarks were telegraphed all over the United States and made a most favorable impression. I wrote to him in October, 1937, just twenty years later, to ask him how he could reconcile that official pledge—he spoke for his government—with the undeclared war, the horrible and bloody aggression in China in 1937. My letter was not deemed worthy of a reply. It is of interest to note that immediately upon the arrival of the Japanese delegation in 1917 the press of the country was asked by Secretary Lansing not to comment on the negotiations in progress in Washington, nor even to speculate as to just what the Viscount took up with our government. It was a clear-cut case of controlling the press but, as I told the Viscount at the dinner, "To this injunction we have loyally given heed," and the negotiations took place under controlled conditions. I have lately been asked [6] how one as sensitive to encroachments upon the freedom of the press as I assented to this. My answer is that I did resent this at the time and privately protested and that we did not concede the right to abandon our freedom of editorial comment. But it was war time and we were given to understand that if the negotiators were undisturbed by the reporters great progress could be made in solving all the outstanding issues between the two countries. How deluded we all were!

[6] By Professor Daniel J. Gage of Bucknell University Junior College.

Although the country had been told there would be no conscription, by June it was adopted and it was elaborately explained to the people that this was after all the most democratic way of dealing with the situation and that Abraham Lincoln had instituted it during the Civil War. The truth was that the army had been planning for it from the beginning and, as General Hugh Johnson has now boasted, had not only prepared the scheme but had actually violated the law in preparing to put it into effect. Moreover, the results of the volunteering showed clearly that the American people were neither overwhelmingly in favor of the struggle nor eager to have their sons fight in the European trenches. Thus was violated what had always been considered, except for the brief period during the Civil War, the fundamental right of American youth to decide whether to give their lives in the service of their country or not. It meant the strangling of the most precious thing in the world, the conscience of the individual, and it opens the way for future infractions of the liberty of the citizen such as universal enforced labor service, an idea which has met with considerable favor since the success of the Civilian Conservation Corps, and the examples set by Mussolini and Hitler, with many American military officers hoping that if that can be put over the way to universal military service will be cleared. The war-time conscription is even used as a justification for compulsory military drill in peace time in many American schools and colleges. In the main, however, the conscription was put over in 1917 with amazingly little friction [7] and with unquestioned ability and has established one favorable precedent. The almost overnight establishment of the selective draft boards showed how quickly new machinery for taking a referendum on such an issue as war and peace could be set up.

As the first war summer dragged on mob violence appeared all

[7] Even the liberal *Survey* printed an article in its issue of December 28, 1918, in which the author wrote that "conscription was necessary, we had to conquer the awful savages and make sure that they cannot murder, torture, ravish and enslave again." The author, a well-known social worker, is still alive to contemplate, as so many others, his complete folly in war time.

over the country. In New York City soldier mobs, with the consent and approval of Mayor Mitchel, broke up Irish and Socialist party meetings—which was one of the causes of his defeat for re-election despite Administration aid. A partial list of the mobbings came to 124 cases between April 1, 1917, and May 1, 1918, yet in only two cases were mob leaders prosecuted and in only eleven cases did the authorities proceed legally against the victims. Whites and blacks were lynched and many tarred and feathered. By April 24, 1918, the Department of Justice reported that 3,465 persons had been convicted or had pleaded guilty to interfering with the operation of the draft, while 181 had been acquitted. Under the general war statutes, 228 additional had been prosecuted and 89 acquitted. By June 8, 1918, the department had prosecuted 1,180 other persons under the Espionage Act, of whom 210 pleaded guilty, 143 were dismissed, 125 were convicted, and 31 acquitted, the remaining 672 cases pending at that time. In addition, 787 were prosecuted under other criminal statutes and, under the act making threats against the President a criminal offense, sixty persons were prosecuted. Those nearly 6,000 cases speak volumes for the alleged unanimity for the war of the people.

Many of the convictions were outrageous miscarriages of justice, later set aside by higher courts. Thus, the officials of the International Bible Students Association in Brooklyn were sentenced to eighty years' imprisonment for an alleged violation of the Espionage Law. The judge, being a loyal patriot, denied them bail, and they were nine months in a penitentiary before they finally obtained bail from another judge. Two months later the judgment was reversed because "they did not have a fair trial." On May 5, 1920, the government dismissed the cases and vindicated these victims of judicial hysteria. The sentences passed were incredible in their severity. In New York three men and one young girl were sentenced by a United States judge to 285 years in jail for circulating legal handbills criticizing our intervention in Russia, which, the court held, obstructed the draft. For saying in an angry moment that he hoped "the government would go to hell," a citizen of Lansing, Michigan, received twenty years in jail and was fined $10,000. A bad prophet, who said that the Kaiser would win the war, got off with six months in prison. For saying truthfully that the Russians "had more right to feel bitterly against the Americans in Russia than we had against the Hessians in 1776," a New York Assemblyman was indicted for "uttering disloyal, scurrilous, and abusive language about the military and naval forces." [8]

In Los Angeles the Reverend Robert Whittaker was sentenced to six months in jail and fined $1,200 for saying that under certain circumstances he would prefer the ideals of the Bolsheviki to those of the Merchants' and Manufacturers' Association; the Reverend Floyd Harden received a similar sentence for saying he preferred to die with his own blood on his hands rather than with that of a brother! The Reverend Herbert S. Bigelow of Cincinnati, at this writing a member of Congress, was kidnapped and horsewhipped by a mob "in the name of the women and children of Belgium," and left helpless on the banks of the Ohio River; he was long in recovering. Large employers took advantage of the prevailing hysteria to move against their workingmen, particularly if they were members of the International Workers of the World. In Bisbee, Arizona, more than a thousand workers, women, and children were driven from their homes into the waterless desert, and one of the chief officials of the company involved, long the head of one of the great charities in New York, defended this procedure to me. Some of those thus treated were among the 93 members of the I.W.W. sentenced to serve an aggregate of 800 years and fined $2,500,000; their torturers went unwhipped of justice. During all this time the Republican politicians were abusing the President in language which would have landed obscure persons in jail for fifty years. Thus, Mr. Roosevelt said that the President was guilty of "trickery, treachery, and bad faith."

The war spirit greatly encouraged our national lynching habit. Mary Turner, a colored woman, was hung in 1918 merely for saying that if she knew the murderers of her husband, who had

[8] For these and many other cases, see *The Nation*, November 9, 1918, p. 546.

just been lynched, she would have warrants sworn out for them.
She was in the eighth month of her pregnancy; her clothes were
burned from her; her unborn child was cut out of her body and
stamped to death as the mother dangled head down from a tree
and she was then riddled by hundreds of bullets. White supremacy
and nobility were vindicated once more! Our officials were too
busy saving us from the raping Huns to say one word about this
proceeding or to punish the fiends who butchered Mary Turner
and her child; after all they were just "niggers." [9] Nothing could
have been more ironic than the drafting of our Negroes to save
the world for democracy when all over the South they were denied every vestige of democracy, taxed without representation,
refused a seat in the legislature or any local governmental body,
and often denied common schooling.

On January 25, 26, 28, 1918, I published in *The Evening Post*
the famous secret treaties. I shall treat later on of Mr. Wilson's
denial that he knew anything about them until he reached Paris.
These vitally important documents were found in the Russian archives when the Bolsheviki took over the government and were
promptly published in full in all of the then existing Russian
dailies. Every effort was made by the Allies to keep them out of
the United States and to prevent our officials from reading and
understanding them. Our great press associations were either too
ignorant to appreciate their value, were unaware of the opportunity for one of the greatest scoops on record, or were too subservient to our government to undertake the publication; not even
when I published them were they carried by the Associated Press.
One day a man walked into my office with a note from Amos
Pinchot saying that the bearer had a matter of the utmost importance to discuss with me. He was a Russian, apparently a sailor or
stoker. He produced far from fresh copies of a Vladivostok newspaper containing the secret treaties in full; from their appearance
the papers looked as if he had worn them ashore between his skin

[9] Between Armistice Day and May 15, 1923, thirty-four Negroes were burned
alive.

d his undershirt. He asked a moderate price, received it, and
parted, leaving upon my desk the means for me to render what
ould have been the greatest public service of my journalistic
reer had the officials in Washington been aware of their duty
their country and if the editors of the United States had had
fficient intelligence and knowledge of what the war was all about
appreciate the tremendous significance of these documents, re-
aling as they did the hidden policies and the sordid bargains of
ur hypocritical Allies.

I had the treaties translated and the accuracy of the translation
as never questioned. Then, in order to obtain the widest possible
rculation for them, I offered them at low rates to the leading
wspapers of the country. Only nine took them. They were the
hicago *Daily News*, St. Louis *Post-Dispatch*, Milwaukee *Journal*,
hiladelphia *Inquirer*, Pittsburgh *Press*, Baltimore *Sun*, Richmond
ews-Leader, St. Paul *Dispatch*, and, partly, the Hartford *Times*
d Buffalo *News*. If there were others which recognized the sen-
tional character of what I offered them, their editors probably
lt that there was too much dynamite in the publication or that
ey might get into trouble with the government, and they also
iled to understand what a service to their countrymen they could
nder by the publication.[10] As it turned out, nobody in Washing-
n asked us any questions about the publication or how we got
e documents (I promptly forgot the Russian's name and did not
k him where he was living). The censorship officials were cer-
inly not clever when they failed to understand the importance
these documents and the light in which they placed the Allies.
o one who understood them could thereafter claim that the
llies had clean hands or that they had played fair. At the Peace
onference the whole fight centered on how far Mr. Wilson could
t aside the underhand bargains contained in those documents.

[10] For a full statement of Ray Stannard Baker's deliberate and misleading be-
dling of this incident, slurring over the facts, and attributing the publication
"a small group of radicals in New York," see my exposure of him as an his-
rian in *The Nation* of February 14, 1923, under the title, "Ray Stannard
ker's 'Honesty.'"

Full Texts

of

Secret Treaties

As revealed at Petrograd

The sensational "secret diplomacy" disclosures made by Trotzky when the Bolsheviki came into possession of the Russian archives

---

Reprinted from

𝕿𝖍𝖊 𝕹𝖊𝖜 𝖄𝖔𝖗𝖐 𝕰𝖛𝖊𝖓𝖎𝖓𝖌 𝕻𝖔𝖘𝖙

More Than a Newspaper—A National Institution

Price

TITLE PAGE OF THE SECRET TREATIES PAMPHLET PUT ON SALE ON
NEWSSTANDS, PARTICULARLY WIDELY IN NEW YORK AND WASHIN

Two pleasant events lightened for me the strain of the second ar year. Early in 1918 I was invited to take part in the semi-ntennial of the University of California at Berkeley and to make a address on "The Press in War Time," and it was gratifyingly ated that the invitation was extended at the request of a number the faculty. That was an invitation not to be declined and, de-ite the critical situation of *The Evening Post*, I left for Cali-rnia early in March, stopping over at New Orleans. There copies *The Evening Post*, which showed an amazing change of edi-rial tone after my departure, overtook me. The infamous Treaty Brest-Litovsk had been made public; it quite upset Mr. gden's balance. In Berkeley my reception was all I could ask. Iy address on the press in war time drew a large and apprecia-ve audience. My enjoyment of my visit was, however, marred y the news from France. It was the hour of the successful break-g through of the Germans on the Amiens front and the rout of e Fifth British Army. Nobody in California seemed to realize e gravity of the situation, least of all the San Franciscan dailies. s I traced on my map the rapid daily advances it seemed as if thing could prevent the Germans from reaching Amiens and tting France into two parts.

At dinner at Mills College one evening I was asked by some structors there, before the talk scheduled for me, what I thought the military situation. I told the truth—that at that moment e Germans were winning the war; that the outlook was most arming since never before had they broken through in such umbers and taken so much territory. I should not have said this. ne of the instructors then asked what would happen to us if Ger-any won. I naturally replied that we should have to make the est of it. This was repeated, doubtless with much embroidering, d reached the ears of President Ray Lyman Wilbur of Leland tanford, Jr., University. Although he had been present when Ierbert Hoover showed his confidence in me by asking me to be e of his closest aides, Mr. Wilbur, without even stopping to ask hat the facts were, reported me to the Department of Justice for ditious utterances! He defended himself when I demanded an

explanation of his conduct by saying that he was bound (und
President Wilson's appeal to the people) [11] to report to the prop
authorities any information which came to his ears which seeme
to him to indicate disloyalty.[12] I could not refrain from writing
him that his action without investigation was far from the duty
a patriotic citizen and comparable only to the action of a meddl
who repeats gossip to while away the time. I should add that
never heard from the Department of Justice. Such was the spir
of the time and so warped were the judgments of men in hig
positions! My attendance at the June commencement of the Un
versity of Missouri and my delivery of the commencement addre
were unmarred by any unpleasant happening.

During my trip to California, and on my return to New Yor
it became increasingly plain that unless financial aid could be ol
tained somewhere I should not be able to retain *The Evening Pos*
The indicated deficit for the fiscal year was $120,000. I let son
sympathetic friends know and they readily subscribed $75,000
year for a period of three years. It was not enough for, in add
tion to everything else, it had become clear that the shop must l
unionized and that that alone would add $75,000 to the pay rol
I was quite ready for the unionization for I had come to reali
that, happy and contented as our printers and pressmen were,
was impossible for them to remain the only nonunion shop an
moreover, I had become convinced that they ought not to do
whatever the defects and shortcomings of the unions. In additic
to this was the growing disaffection of the editorial staff. When
returned Mr. Ogden offered his resignation in an undignifie
whining, and unmanly interview. I asked him to remain until
had decided what my own relationship to *The Evening Post* woul
be. Had I known how near to the end of the war we were I shou

[11] This was one of the worst of Mr. Wilson's blunders for it was the excu
in every community for men and women to vent their spite against neighbors
those with whom they had quarreled. This resulted in grave injustices, in t
hounding of innocent persons, and loading the authorities down with endl
rumor and gossip. This appeal of Mr. Wilson also gave the lie to the asserti
that the people were unanimously behind the war.

[12] Mr. Wilbur's letter to the author, September 30, 1918.

ave tried to fight on, but there was then no prospect of an early
essation of hostilities. Moreover, my estimates of what the finan-
al needs would be were later proved to be extremely conserva-
ve.

After much heart searching I decided to offer to the staff the
rivilege of selling *The Evening Post* to an owner of their own
hoosing. They were profoundly grateful and one of the veterans
aid: "You may be sure, Mr. Villard, that we shall not take it
o the corner of Wall and Broad Streets." Unable to find a pur-
haser themselves, the group asked the aid of Charles Dyer Nor-
on, then of the First Securities Company, who generously gave
. He speedily found a buyer but told me that there were certain
easons why the name of the purchaser could not be revealed until
he sale was concluded. Quite unsuspecting I placed myself in
Mr. Norton's hands only to find that the new owner was Thomas
V. Lamont; the dear old paper *had* gone to the corner of Wall
nd Broad. I resigned as director of the Associated Press, pur-
hased *The Nation* and other assets from myself and the other
ockholders, and bade farewell to the men with whom I had
orked so happily for so many years. I had given to *The Evening
Post* the best of my younger years, all the idealism, the good will,
nd the devotion of which I was capable, never drawing a salary
f over $3,600 in order that others might have more, striving in
very way to make the office a happy one and the conditions of
abor of the best, even to the extent of erecting the building at
o Vesey Street at an eventual heavy loss to myself and family.
But I had failed in my task and this chapter of my life was at an
nd. I am happy to add that when I left I received an engrossed
esolution of regret signed by all the members of every depart-
nent, and nothing has given me greater pleasure than the voting
o me by *The Evening Post* Alumni Association of the gold medal
nnually awarded for the best service in journalism of a former
taff member of *The Evening Post*.

As we walked away from *The Evening Post* building after the
nal papers were signed, Lamont generously remarked that he
was sure that I had all the qualities needed by the successful editor

of a weekly. It was very hard not to reply in kind but I could not honestly say that he seemed to me the ideal owner of *The Evening Post*. He imitated my father in appointing three trustees to insure editorial freedom to the editors. They were Theodore Vail of the American Telephone and Telegraph Company, Henry S. Pritchett, president of the Carnegie Foundation, and Ellery Sedgwick, editor of the *Atlantic Monthly*. He made at the outset one of those bad mistakes of judgment of which the ablest business men are so often guilty. He entrusted the management and direction of the paper to Professor Edwin F. Gay of Harvard University. There was no question as to Professor Gay's great ability, his high standing, and the fact that he had troops of warm and devoted friends, but he was a pure theorist without any newspaper training and he appointed to two of the most important positions men also totally without newspaper experience. William O. Taylor of the Boston *Globe* tells of being approached one day by a man who asked if he might see the *Globe's* pressroom. "Certainly," said Mr. Taylor, "but why do you want to see it?" "Because," was the reply, "I have been appointed superintendent of the pressroom of the New York *Evening Post* and I want to be able to say that I have been inside a newspaper pressroom!" Professor Gay was prophetic when he said to me on taking over the paper: "I shall either make the greatest success in New York journalism or the greatest failure."

On his return from China in 1920 Mr. Lamont discovered that the deficits of *The Evening Post* were well over $2,000,000—so it was reported at the time—which made me think that I had not done so badly after all. Although Mr. Gay was at that time making considerable progress, Mr. Lamont turned the ownership over to a group of thirty-one public-spirited citizens, headed by William Church Osborn, which gave rise to the witticism that it was "no longer a Post but a picket fence." They, too, were unable to make it succeed; it came back to Mr. Lamont, who sold it at an amazingly high figure to Cyrus H. K. Curtis of *The Saturday Evening Post*, after which its descent was rapid; its lost all vestige of distinction and ability and the deficits piled up until it was finally

rned over to the present owner, J. David Stern. Mr. Ogden was
ropped or left very soon after Lamont took over; as already said,
e then became editor-in-chief of the New York *Times,* a news-
aper with an editorial viewpoint in many matters diametrically
pposed to ours, and served it faithfully until his death a few
ears ago.

Chapter XIX. The Nation's Rebirth

WITH the sale of *The Evening Post* completed I turned all my attention to *The Nation*, of which I had been the nominal editor since January, 1918, after the resignation of Harold DeWolf Fuller, the fifth editor. Mr. Fuller left *The Nation* because he found himself no longer in sympathy with the restrained war policies of the paper; he took with him the regard and good will of us all. Henry Raymond Mussey had been carrying it on in the interim, and now became managing editor. He had resigned from Barnard College as a protest against Nicholas Murray Butler's treatment of those of his professors at Columbia who were so mistaken as to believe that what Mr. Butler said about peace in peace time he also meant and stood for in war time. In his character, ability, and devotion to principle, Henry Mussey measured up to the high standards of my predecessors in the editor's chair; a tremendous worker, he was beloved by all who came in contact with him. The alteration in *The Nation* which then took place caused acute pain to many of the old readers, of whom it was jestingly said that many perished from shock and heart failure. As a matter of fact several thousand of them stood by; so did many of the old contributors, and I was especially gratified that Edwin L. Godkin's only son, Lawrence, heartily approved the change and gave me emphatic support as long as he lived. For every old reader who stopped his subscription four or five new ones joined us.

The general belief, however, among the war-mad, the reactionaries, the war profiteers, and the general public which did not read *The Nation*, was that we had suddenly gone violently "red," crazily pacifist, and openly pro-German, while the new adjective "bolshevik" seemed expressly invented for the purpose of tagging the editors of this wicked sheet. As I look over our issues for the remainder of the war period, it is hard to understand how any

FOUR "NATION" EDITORS

Top Row: ERNEST H. GRUENING (PHOTO BY CONSTANT), DOROTHY VAN DOREN

Lower Row: ARTHUR H. WARNER, MARK VAN DOREN (PHOTO BY J. A. FITZSIMMONS)

ody could possibly have objected to them. They were intelligent
nd well written and certainly as loyal as anyone could ask, unless
 was disloyal to stress incessantly that the war was less impor-
nt than what kind of a world order would be left after it was
ver. No one rejoiced more, or with more pride and sincerer
leasure, than we did in the American achievements in France and
ne magnificent progress and success of our troops. But the red tag
as firmly attached to us and was not to be removed even though
 great journalist, Henry W. Nevinson, after one of his periodic
isits to the United States, described our *Nation* in an article con-
ibuted to a London daily as "what we in England should call a
onservatively liberal weekly."

Those were stirring months and called for incessant labor. I was
ptain and supercargo, purser and recruiting officer, and I had
ne complete satisfaction of molding my historic journal according
o my exact wishes and beliefs. In restoring news features, adding
nore departments, in printing more foreign correspondence, and
 other ways I was merely returning to the original policy of *The
Jation,* as in fact the paper had been doing under Lamont, Paul
:lmer More, and Harold Fuller; it was not until after the com-
ination with *The Evening Post* in 1881 that it had become more
nd more a purely literary journal. In October, with the financial
id of some devoted friends, notably Mrs. Henry Goddard Leach
nd Mr. and Mrs. Francis Neilson, I inaugurated an International
Relations Section of sixteen pages which appeared fortnightly; the
rst issue contained articles by John Bassett Moore and T. G.
Iasaryk, the future President of the still unborn state of Czecho-
lovakia. In addition to contributed articles this section contained
he texts of important diplomatic documents or others of interna-
onal interest, furnished with suitable introductions and explana-
ory notes. We also printed summaries of the foreign press, ex-
racts from magazine articles dealing with international affairs, and
pecial book reviews.

This was our substantial contribution to the need for public dis-
ussion of what was happening abroad, of the host of new and
ifficult problems confronting our country, and of the possibility

of international co-operation and unity. As we stated in the ar
nouncement: "It is more than ever important that what is bein
done or said in other parts of the world regarding these interna
tional problems should be fully, faithfully, and impartially pre
sented and candidly discussed. For the world outside the Unite
States it is important that the best public opinion of Americ
should be both accurately and widely known." This section wa
I later learned, the inspiration of the publication by the Ne
York *Times* of *Current Events*. We were not able to continue
very long on so elaborate a scale—my deficit for the first year c
the new *Nation* was more than $100,000—but it helped greatl
to give us a standing among all scholars. We created for this sec
tion an advisory council of fifteen distinguished men, among ther
Gilbert Murray, Joseph Reinach, Sir George Foster, and André
Louis Chevrillon abroad, and James Harvey Robinson, John Bas
sett Moore, Stephen P. Duggan (who was most co-operative), th
American Winston Churchill, Henry Goddard Leach, Frank Van
derlip, Jacob H. Schiff, and Rómolo Náon, the Argentine ambas
sador in Washington. It was in charge of William MacDonald a
associate editor and of Freda Kirchwey, then and always the mos
faithful and devoted and loyal of editorial lieutenants.

The staff was rapidly recruited, the first accession after Musse
and MacDonald being the brilliant Albert Jay Nock, later th
creator and editor of *The Freeman*, the best written weekly ye
to appear in the United States, a publication which thoroughl
merited a permanent place in American journalism. Others wh
sooner or later joined the staff were Lewis S. Gannett, Hendri
Van Loon, (briefly), Arthur Warner, Ludwig Lewisohn, Ernes
H. Gruening, Lincoln Colcord, Arthur Gleason, able and winning
Suzanne La Follette, Buckner Kirk, Norman Thomas, Georg
Soule, Stuart Chase, Marian Tyler, Raymond Gram Swing, Mabe
Barrows Mussey, and the four Van Dorens, Carl, Irita, and Mark
all three in turn sterling literary editors, and Dorothy, able an
keen and long a valued editorial writer and editor. For a tim
William Hard acted as Washington correspondent. One of ou
greatest finds was Joseph Wood Krutch, now professor at Colum

a, whose literary essays and dramatic criticism won him imme-
iate fame, as had Ludwig Lewisohn's previously. John Macy,
oo, joined the staff for a time and later Henry Hazlitt—to my
reat satisfaction for he had been one of *The Evening Post* staff
nd I knew his fine qualities and temper, though he seemed too
onservative to suit some of his associates. All in all it is a remark-
ole roster and never as a group, I believe, surpassed. It was a
appy and congenial family despite the fact that we were all
narked individualists, and the spirit of youth actuated it. Yes,
ven the older members. It was a rare privilege to work with so
nfaltering and courageous a group in those embattled years—
ven though they were at times restive in the traces—and a joy
o see how they appreciated their untrammeled opportunity to
xpress themselves and to watch them graduate into greater and
reater usefulness.

To single out any one of them would be invidious, yet, since he
s no longer living, I may be permitted to pay a special tribute to
rthur Warner. He, too, had been with me on *The Evening Post*
nd had spent two and one-half years of the war period in Paris
vorking for the Paris edition of the New York *Herald* and the
London *Daily Mail,* so that he knew exactly what the war was
ke and how little hope for the future it afforded and was eager,
s he would have said, to come aboard our craft. One advance-
nent I did resent: Lewis Gannett's going to the *Herald-Tribune,*
or it seemed to me that of all others he was the best fitted to be
ny successor, by temperament, training, ability, inheritance, and
nowledge of Europe. To the Van Dorens I shall always be bound
y ties of deep affection; Carl and Mark brought to us a mid-
vestern freshness, optimism, realism, and cheer and contributed
reatly to the sanity and gaiety of our editorial council. Ernest
Gruening also stood out. He had had splendid training in daily
ournalism as managing editor of the Boston *Traveler* and the
New York *Tribune.*[1]

[1] I also constituted a board of contributing editors among whom were J. A.
Hobson of England, Anatole France, F. W. Foerster of Germany, H. L. Mencken,
Robert Herrick, and Heywood Broun.

If there was sometimes talk about the rapid turnover of the staff, that never worried me. I have always been of the opinion that a staff that is static too long is bound to go to seed and there is surely no greater tribute to an editor than to have other journals, and universities, recruiting their forces from the men and women he has selected because of their promise. It is true that there was some disappointment in the group that *The Nation* was not to be run as a co-operative editorial enterprise. It was inevitable that I decided finally that I must be the head and have the last word. I still do not believe that this was due solely to a dictatorial quality in me. In my judgment no publication of this type or any daily journal can be run successfully without one responsible head. Otherwise it is impossible to avoid editorial weakness, undue compromising, and deadlocks. During all my years with *The Nation* and *The Evening Post* the public and press held me responsible and would never have believed that I was not wholly in accord with or did not approve some of the editorial positions taken. By and large the *Nation* staff was amazingly of one mind on all the fundamental issues.

As for our "radical" and dangerous platform, it seems far from such now. In the first issue of 1918 I published reconstruction proposals which comprised the following diabolical suggestions for the post-war peace: (1) immediate and radical disarmament of all nations and the abolition of universal conscription; (2) abolition of all tariffs and the establishment of free trade; (3) the acceptance of Abraham Lincoln's doctrine that "no man is good enough to govern any other man without that other man's consent" as the only sound guiding principle for the readjustment of national, international, and racial relationships; this carried with it a referendum in Alsace and Lorraine as to their future status; (4) the establishment of an international court and international parliament. "Can we not all agree," I wrote, "that if none of these four principles is accepted when the war ends, then the unparalleled sacrifices of the war will have been largely for nothing?" This question time has thoroughly justified.

Our domestic platform we worked out gradually. We were for

he democratic organization of industry and were even then for
ld age pensions and unemployment insurance. We could not
tomach Samuel Gompers and most of the other leaders of the
American Federation of Labor but we were for the development
f a sounder and more intelligent leadership, for greater sincerity
nd efficiency in organizing labor everywhere, and for the estab-
ishment by federal law of the principle and right of collective
argaining on the part of all labor, for which the workingmen of
America now owe undying gratitude to Franklin Roosevelt. We
vere for taxation reform, for a real budget, a liberal immigration
olicy, and the control of natural resources for the benefit of all
he people. We also desired a Constitutional Convention to vote
ation-wide initiative and referendum, a Cabinet responsible to
Congress and a popular referendum prior to the country's going
o war. The most shocking thing in our platform was government
wnership of railroads and recognition of the fact that, whether
ne desires it or not, the government will sooner or later take over
uch basic industries as oil and coal, both of which Washington
nd several of the States are now regulating, with a governor
f the great coal State of Pennsylvania insisting that that industry
nust be taken over at once by the federal government.

In 1918 we were specially concerned to get the United States
nd the Allies out of Russia—the Russians themselves soon at-
ended to that. Next to the after-the-war peace the freedom of
he Russian people to control their own soil and to build their own
ew institutions seemed to us most important, and this without
elation to the eventual success or failure of Communism. The
ntire transformation of the social life of the 140,000,000 Rus-
ians was what fascinated us and I, for one, believe that, bad as
nything under Stalin may be, the 160,000,000 Russians of today
re vastly better off than under the Czar—an impression confirmed
y a visit to Russia in 1929. Even today there survives a basis for
aith that this tremendous country with its extraordinarily tal-
nted, great, and really constructive people will yet work out a
emocratic salvation. We reprobated the Wilson administration
nceasingly for its usurpation of the power to declare war which

the Constitution places solely in the hands of Congress, and asked
whether our invasion of Siberia and the Archangel regions was no
war—there we Americans burned villages and killed Russians because Mr. Wilson was so inclined, not because the American Con
gress had so voted.

Our interest in Russia was not, however, the reason for my
clash with the war censorship which took place on September 13,
1918, when we were suddenly notified that our issue of September
14 was unmailable. Utterly dumbfounded, we seized copies and
ran them over. The leading editorial was a severe attack upon the
Department of Justice, based upon the conservative, pro-war
Tribune's denunciation of it for having arrested in New York and
near by towns within two days no less than 75,000 young men
merely in order to ascertain whether they were draft evaders—
less than 3 per cent were found to be such. As our article was but
tressed by the fact that the President had ordered an inquiry into
this scandalous and high-handed action, and as it quoted from the
privileged utterances of two United States senators, we could no
see that that article could possibly be the offending one. The nex
editorial was a criticism of Samuel Gompers's being sent to Eu
rope to report on the conditions of labor there. It was from the
pen of Albert Nock who wrote that "the public will get from him
[Gompers] at his best merely the kind of information that a sturdy
partisan drummer, traveling continually in an atmosphere of sheer
bagmanism is able to furnish; and with all that the people can do
nothing." Obviously that could not be the trouble. The other two
leaders were harmless for they dealt, the one on the possibility of
a united labor party, while the other praised highly the pending
revenue bill. We then examined an article by Stuart P. Sherman
entitled "Carlyle and Kaiser Worship." This certainly was in
nocuous and so we were stumped. The New York postmaster
Mr. Patten, could throw no light on the matter. He had merely
received orders from Washington to impound the issue.

I took the night train to Washington with our counsel, Mr
Wherry, in order to discover what it was all about. I reached Sec
retary Lane by telephone at breakfast time and he asked me to

ome to his house at once. He carefully looked over the articles
nd showed how much cleverer he was than we by putting a finger
n the Gompers article and saying: "This is what they are after."
t seemed incredible that we had come to such a pass that an
merican newspaper could not criticize Samuel Gompers but Mr.
ane insisted. Then, when I asked for his advice, he said: "Go
traight to the White House and demand to see the President.
)o not let yourself be put off by Tumulty or be satisfied with
eeing him. You are an American citizen, your constitutional rights
ave been infringed, and you have a right to know from the Presi-
ent himself if he stands for this. Villard, this is an extremely
nportant matter—of vital interest to the press and the country
nd you must go to it."

When I reached the White House I found Tumulty so incensed,
nd so profanely desirous of helping, that I did not insist on see-
1g the President although I told Tumulty I might yet demand
his right. He replied: "Well, first you go down and see that old
oll weevil from Texas in the Post Office Department. Tell him
vhat you think of him and if you can't get satisfaction from him
ome back and let me know." Mr. Wherry and I had a long wait
1 Mr. Burleson's outer office and the old boll weevil finally re-
used to see us but sent his solicitor, Mr. Lamar, instead. Lamar
ame right out with the complaint. It was the Gompers article.
aid he: "Mr. Gompers has rendered inestimable services to this
overnment during this war in holding union labor in line and
vhile this war is on we are not going to allow any newspaper in
his country to attack him"—thus giving the most perfect proof
f the lengths to which a censorship, intended by Congress only
o prevent the publication of vital military news or seditious arti-
les, had already been stretched. Argument with one of his small
nental caliber soon proved to be impossible. There was no com-
non meeting ground and he did not care what the law said or
lid not say. Finally he made this offer to me: "If you will tear
ut that page, which you can easily do, I'll release the issue."

I flatly declined. If memory serves, I told him that that had
never been done in our forty-eight years of *The Nation's* history

and could not be done then. He refused to yield and I told him
that I should have to go over his head. Mr. Wherry and I adjourned to the Hotel Raleigh for lunch; a few minutes later Mr.
Lamar and others took seats at an adjoining table. When we had
finished I returned to the White House offices and told Tumulty
what the boll weevil had and had not done. He again said, "Leave
it to me," and I did. At the Cabinet meeting the next day, according to dispatches in all the newspapers, the President himself
brought up our case and, after hearing Burleson's defense, overruled the boll weevil and ordered *The Nation* released. It reached
our subscribers nearly a week late; it had been on sale on the newsstands during the whole time and it sold like hot cakes when the
news of its being held up appeared. As is always the case, this
bout with the censorship boosted our circulation greatly and got
us a lot of publicity, pleasant and otherwise, but not a single New
York daily came to our aid or championed the cause of the freedom of the press until the fight was won. Then the *World* said:
"This action is as creditable to the President as the original action
was discreditable to the bureaucrats of the Post Office Department,
who seemed determined to set up an intellectual reign of terror in
the United States." It added: ". . . we regard Mr. Gompers as
a most useful and patriotic citizen but it is certainly not sedition
or treason to declare in print that 'the opinion of a Cornish miner
or a Lancashire overlooker would help us more to an understanding of labor than any number of observations from Mr.
Gompers.' "

Of course men of the type of Burleson and Lamar could not
but resent the President's rebuke and seek to get even. Lamar
promptly countered by publishing a dispatch from an anonymous
newspaper suggesting that all other newspapers "refrain from
printing these seditious utterances of *The Nation*." To which the
World retorted: "To say that this is asinine would be gross flattery; yet the episode is wholly characteristic of bureaucratic methods in dealing with public discussions of issues relating to the
war." My own reply was emphatic. I telegraphed to Lamar: "No
seditious or treasonable utterance has ever appeared in *The Nation*

or ever will. I resent the base libel on me personally but I resent
more deeply the infringement of the right to criticize policies of
the government, a right which is guaranteed by the Constitution.
How far this right can be limited by arbitrary action of executive
officers is the whole issue between us—and no other." Emboldened
by Lamar's action an obscure deputy attorney general in New
York State, by name Becker, sought to curry favor in Washington
by giving out an affidavit from an enemy alien who was then interned at Fort Oglethorpe, Georgia. This man swore that *The
Nation* and the *New Republic* were the periodicals "most popular
among the Germans and Austrians interned there." Search of our
circulation lists speedily showed that in all the internment camps
we had only two subscribers and of course we were not allowed
on sale at any one of them. I doubt if any other official ever
stooped to such pettiness to do an injury. I was ready to take this
case to the Supreme Court of the United States if the President
had not acted as he did.

It is needless to add that other publications which were also
victims of the Burleson-Lamar malignity and asininity [2] did not
get off as well as we. At the outset Mr. Burleson informed the
press that every Socialist paper in the country was in danger from
him, not because it was Socialist but because of the doctrines that
it taught! No paper, he declared, would be allowed to affirm that
this was a capitalistic war—thus demonstrating beyond all question
his misconception of his task. He who was there merely to prevent sedition and treason openly avowed his determination to control public opinion. As was the case so many, many times, this
statement went without rebuke from the President, whose defenders alleged that he had not seen it. So Burleson went on and

[2] On one occasion Lamar remarked: "You know I am not working in the dark
on this censorship thing. I know exactly what I am after. I am after three things
and only three things—pro-Germanism, pacifism, and 'high-browism.' I have been
watching that paper [The *New Republic*] for months; I haven't got anything on
them yet, but I shall one of these days." Until the Espionage Act was passed
Lamar had only had routine office matters to handle, yet the freedom of the
American press was placed in the hands of one of such limited experience, vision,
and ignorance of Americanism.

actually suppressed the little publication *Unity* in Chicago for what? *For publishing a poem of Robert Browning's!* And the *Freeman's Journal,* published in the interest of Free Ireland, suffered for printing figures, facts, and arguments which the Democratic House leader, Mr. Kitchin, had freely used in drawing the then pending financial legislation. Burleson declared to two clergymen editors, whose international views he did not like, that they could not edit any publication that he would pass. Naturally we made the suggestion that a board of press revision be constituted at once and composed of Herbert Croly, Doctor Albert Shaw, and William Allen White, but again the President was too busy to consider the matter. Our readers stood by us magnificently but one San Francisco reader wrote us that he hoped we should be suspended indefinitely, "for you are the most dangerous because you are the ablest journal (in an intellectual and literary way) published in this country." This whole censorship business was a clear illustration of the way the administration did not allow its right hand to know what its left hand was doing. Throughout the war Mr. Wilson with his Cabinet heads "rode off in all directions."

For the rest of the war we continued to praise the administration wherever we could. We thought Wilson's Liberty Loan speech in New York on September 27, 1918, "undoubtedly one of his very great utterances. Not that we can agree with him that the war is now or ever was a peoples' war in the sense in which he uses the phrase, but he has again sounded a noble note of warning to the nations of the world as to what must come out of this titanic struggle if the world is in the remotest degree to profit thereby. . . ." We similarly highly commended Lansing's reply to Germany on October 26 and ardently defended the country from the charge that everything at home was breaking down, charges so freely made by the Republicans. We felt that the country was making marked diplomatic progress, that the strategic initiative in the diplomatic as well as in the military field had passed to the Americans, but we never for a moment forgot to stress the fact that the hope of a democratic peace rested wholly with Wilson. Despite the so frequent limping of Wilson's own democracy, we none the less felt as the fall came on that the faith of liberals was steadily growing that we should arrive at a settlement of the world disaster worthy of the stupendous sacrifices made, even though public opinion and editorial expressions in our press were about of the character and temper of those in France and England in 1915. When the President, however, made his great blunder in demanding the election of a Democratic House and putting it upon an avowedly partisan basis, we lashed out as vigorously as possible. It was not, we said, enough in Mr. Wilson's view to be a patriot; it was necessary also to be a Democrat if one's patriotism was to be counted for righteousness. It was plain, we thought, that he had accomplished something by his bungling appeal: "He has opened the gates of discussion in Congress and the country and any attempt to close them hereafter will put him and his party in jeopardy." Under no illusions whatever as to the Republicans, we none the less wholeheartedly rejoiced when the returns showed that the Democrats had lost the House.

Of one thing we were certain and that was that the war had showed the falsity of one charge against which we had always protested—that the American people were utterly lacking in discipline. We knew that Americans were impatient of unnecessary restraint and that this was combined with independence, self-reliance, and quickness in meeting emergencies. These we valued far more highly than the docile subordination of the peoples in the regimented countries. Criticisms of our record in the war rested upon weaknesses of organization, and executive and administrative failures, and not upon any lack of mass discipline. We could not overlook the continuance of intolerance and the illegalities of executive officials everywhere, which certainly smacked of a lack of respect for law as well as of a failure of administrative discipline. Still, we felt that the history of the first year of our military participation in the war offered incontrovertible proof of the essential unity and the democratic discipline of our people. Acknowledging all our errors and weaknesses, regarding as we still did our entrance into the war as the greatest blunder the American people could possibly have made, we none the less felt that with all our errors and weaknesses "our faith is confirmed in the general correctness of those methods of education and toleration and co-operation which we have employed, as opposed to the force and repression and compulsion which many would press upon us, as the lesson of a war for liberty." Finally, we were convinced that what America needed was, of course, neither the discipline of arrogant Prussianism in Washington nor the discipline of battlefields but the discipline of a world of free peoples. All of which is as true today as when it was written.

When the finis of those dreadful war years came so suddenly with the false armistice, the editors of *The Nation* were at lunch with the Bishop of Oxford, one of the outstanding peace men of Great Britain, exchanging views with him as to what the new world would be like. We, too, were carried away with astonishment at the tremendous popular jubilation and enthusiasm; so dominant had been the note of prosecuting the war to the bitter end, so strident were the appeals of Theodore Roosevelt and the jingoes that we should sign the peace at the point of the bayonet in Berlin and nowhere else, that the hysterical outburst of happiness took us completely by surprise. When the rejoicing was all over and the real armistice had been proclaimed we were able to take stock of our situation. The new *Nation* had then only been about four months under way but we felt that we had made a place for ourselves. The outlook was certainly not discouraging. Our net sales were running about 11,000, a figure which *The Nation* had not reached since 1877.[3] With the immediate danger of interference from Washington at an end we felt more than ever free to labor for a just peace, knowing full well that the stigma of pro-Germanism would continue to be attached to anyone who ventured to say that now the war was over the Germans ought

[3] H. L. Mencken explained this in these words: "Villard, when he took it [*The Nation*] over . . . began printing the truth. The effect was instantaneous. His circulation increased four- or fivefold in a few months. His paper became a sort of super-newspaper. By the simple device of trying to be honest he made an enormous success." Baltimore *Evening Sun*, March 16, 1920.

to be treated as decently, humanely, and wisely as the North had treated the conquered Southern armies after Appomattox.

I must not fail to add here how greatly we were aided and stimulated by our immediate competitors in the weekly field. For a time during the war and immediately afterwards the *New Republic* was regarded by many as the mouthpiece of Woodrow Wilson; it was considered bad form in some official circles to be seen without it and its circulation climbed to about 45,000. It was believed that Walter Lippmann and the *New Republic* had won the President to our participation in the war in order to shape the peace and that Lippmann had written the fourteen peace points. For this belief the *New Republic* paid when the League of Nations and the peace treaty crashed and the disillusionments as to its policy came—in addition to the loss of Herbert Croly. Its circulation and influence sank rapidly until under Bruce Bliven's able leadership it received a new impetus. But the service rendered by the *New Republic* in making people think about the after-the-war problems cannot be overestimated. Mr. and Mrs. Willard Straight's generosity in supporting this weekly for so many years and giving absolute freedom to the editors constitutes a public service for which Mrs. Elmhirst (as she now is) deserves far greater recognition than has been accorded to her. But her generosity and her failure to demand that the paper make both ends meet have proved a complete obstacle to the journal's establishment on a paying basis; in this respect the *New Republic* has illustrated both the strong points and the weaknesses of the endowed newspaper.[4]

As the plans for the Peace Conference unfolded and Mr. Wilson announced his intention of proceeding to Paris himself, as he had planned to dictate the peace ever since the beginning of 1915,

[4] Curiously enough, it was I who engineered the first meeting of Leonard Elmhirst, then an impecunious English student at Cornell, and Mrs. Willard Straight. Once when I was speaking at Cornell he welcomed me and explained that the building devoted to foreign students was falling to pieces and needed at least $75,000 to avoid foreclosure. Where could he get it? I replied: "I know just one person big enough and generous enough to do it—Mrs. Straight," and later brought about their meeting—with such remarkable results.

it became clear to us that *The Nation* must be represented in Paris and the staff felt that I should be the one to go. We doubted, however, whether I would be permitted to attend. It was Senator Lawrence Y. Sherman of Illinois who opened the way. On November 21, 1918, he denounced the Wilson Administration for misusing its right to grant passports, insinuating that it had witheld permission to go to Paris from, among others, me and Gifford Pinchot. He was more than willing that I should leave the country. He hoped I would stay away "at least until he changes some of the sentiments he has heretofore entertained. . . ." When I read this the next morning I at once telegraphed to the Senator that he was in error so far as I was concerned, that I had not applied for a passport and so had not been denied one. I then telephoned to Frank Polk, still Counselor of the State Department, and asked him if he had seen Senator Sherman's attack. "Of course," I said, "I have already telegraphed to the Senator that he is mistaken so far as I am concerned but I should like also to be able to tell him that you are not intending to withhold a passport from me." He had not seen Sherman's speech but replied: "Certainly not. If you would like to go we should be delighted to have you. Your point of view ought to be represented at Paris. We need all shades of press opinion there. Put in your passport application and if you have any trouble let me know and I'll see that you get it."

That determined me to go but there were still various obstacles in my way. Passage was difficult to obtain; at length I got a stateroom on the Castle liner *Balmoral Castle*, sailing December 2, which I shared with Edward Hungerford, the historian of the Baltimore and Ohio Railroad, the author of other books, and a recognized expert in railroad publicity and exhibitions. The passport was long in coming. I had to go to Washington three days before sailing in order to obtain it from Frank Polk's hands; the Army Intelligence bureau had held it up. Back in New York on Saturday I engaged in a mad rush to get the French and British visas. The French vice-consul kindly agreed to affix his stamp at his residence far uptown after official office hours. He was courtesy itself and everything went well until he asked me where I was born and for my father's birthplace. When I told him that we were both born in Germany he laid down his pen and, with genuine regret, said: "Then I can do nothing for you, for my country at the outset of the war passed a law that no German-born son of a German-born father may enter France during the war."

In vain I pointed out that the war was over; that my birth abroad was accidental; that my father was an American citizen when I entered this life; that the French government had officially stated it would accredit to the Peace Conference any American correspondents the Government in Washington might designate and that I had been invited to go by the State Department. He was entirely sympathetic but could not be moved; he pointed out that the state of war would legally continue until a treaty of peace was signed. He kindly permitted me to call Ambassador Jusserand from his home. The Ambassador, who had been for many years a most valued contributor to *The Nation* during the editorship of my uncle, was also sympathetic and promised to cable his government immediately and ask for an exception in my case.

On Sunday morning I called upon the British visa officer at his apartment. I found him an insolent bounder in a major's uniform. He cross-examined me at great length on my alleged hostility to Great Britain and informed me that he objected greatly to the way I had edited *The Evening Post* and demanded to know why I had sold that journal. I made no headway until I explained my attitude in full and assured him that I had committed both *The Nation* and *The Evening Post* to the side of the Allies the day the Germans entered Belgium. Well, why had I been born in Germany? What finally won him was my telling him that during the Venezuela episode in 1895 *The Evening Post* sided with the British and broke with President Cleveland! When he put his stamp on my passport he asked if I had a car at the door. When I said yes, he remarked: "That's fine, I have some important business downtown." I took him to his destination, for which I was not thanked. I have always regretted that I never had the opportunity to meet this gentleman again and tell him just what I thought of him.

When the time for sailing came, Ambassador Jusserand had not heard from Paris. He, therefore, advised me to go to London and get into touch with the French consul general there to whom he would communicate any word he might receive. I gladly followed his advice.

When we sailed the *Balmoral Castle's* appearance hardly suggested that peace had come. A six-inch gun was mounted on the stern wheelhouse and alongside of it were piles of projectiles. The low rear deck was cluttered with temporary washrooms and locker rooms for troops as the ship had been for three years carrying men from New Zealand and Australia to France. The deck entrances to the first-cabin quarters were enclosed by wooden partitions so that no light could possibly be seen. The ship's whole appearance was rather seedy, as of a vessel worked continuously with little time for overhauling. Half the accommodations on this voyage were given over to women—girl vaudeville entertainers from the Broadway booking offices and canteen workers. This surprised us as we had thought the war was over and the troops returning. The women were berthed on the starboard side and all the men on the port; the latter were also chiefly war workers. To my delight Simeon Strunsky was on board, bound for Paris to represent *The Evening Post* at the Peace Conference. There were some Englishmen and families of English officers—the first children, we were told, allowed to cross the Atlantic on an English ship since the loss of the *Lusitania.* A Japanese family added to the motley collection of humans.

The beginning of the voyage was auspicious; on our third day out I sent to my family the first private wireless message transmitted from the *Balmoral Castle* in four years. I reported very smooth seas. The next day storms began and by Sunday the wind was of hurricane velocity and the seas of a grandeur and a height I had never before seen. We had to alter our course to run before the wind, passing one steamer hove to, while another wirelessed us of the loss of the chief officer and a seaman overboard and the wrecking of her steam steering gear. The *George Washington* reported all well and the weather not too bad but added, sig-

FOUR MORE "NATION" EDITORS

Top Row: JOSEPH WOOD KRUTCH, FREDA KIRCHWEY

Lower Row: LEWIS S. GANNETT (PHOTO BY BEN PINCHOT),
CARL VAN DOREN

nificantly perhaps, that the President and Mrs. Wilson had breakfasted alone—conditions not stated. From far and near the ships
said that now the war was over and the submarines had gone it
was time for nature to behave herself and give them a chance.
The *Balmoral Castle,* having been built for the South African trade
and not for the Atlantic, had a very handsome ladies' cabin and
library combined, on the promenade deck, right next to the lounge
and writing room at the head of the main stairway. The ladies'
cabin, like the lounge, had large and unprotected windows. At one
o'clock we were boarded by a tremendous, overtaking sea which
swept over the stern and smashed into the ladies' cabin through
the windows on the starboard side as if they had been of paper,
wrecking every bit of furniture on one side of the room. The torrent flowed down two decks below and seeped into two of the
holds. It crashed into the dining saloon just underneath as the
members of the first service were sitting down to dinner.

When the ship was struck I said to Hungerford: "Let's go. I
have been at sea often enough to know that something serious has
happened." We rushed out. Near our stateroom was a small space
at the foot of the stairs in which were the children's and nurses'
dining tables. As we got there a perfect Niagara came down to us,
more than enough to terrify the women and children. The youngsters rose automatically and simultaneously, with a precision they
might have shown after weeks of drill, climbed up on their chairs,
turned round, and sat down on their soup plates. As soon as possible Hungerford and I ascended to the dining-room deck where
everything was in a state of complete wreck and confusion with
the drenched passengers hastily seeking their staterooms, and then
went up on deck to see the damage done there. Then a call came
for all male passengers to form a bucket line and we were soon
at work on the lower deck, ankle deep in the icy Atlantic waters,
bailing out the ship—again something new in my ocean experience.
Some fool, without authority, added to the confusion and fright
by passing the word: "All women on deck with life preservers
on." Whereupon there arose from their bunks people so utterly

seasick that they had never expected to walk again and forgot to be seasick, at least until the storm had blown itself out.

By four o'clock the water was out of the pantry and dining saloon and kitchen, the tables were again set and most of the wreckage cleared away, when, just at the moment that the baffled members of the first table were again taking their seats, the ship reeled under another crash and worse was upon us—two terrific seas in succession. One entered the port side of the library, wrecked the rest of the room and also poured down into the dining saloon. The other carried away the heavy wooden wall outside the main entrance and injured three passengers and four of the crew. Two women, seeking air at the entrance door, were washed out on deck and then washed in again, one of them unconscious. The stern deck was swept clear of all the washrooms and the piles of ammunition washed off onto the deck below, where they rolled around until the crew could capture and get rid of them—a scene for Victor Hugo. Three seamen volunteered to stay in the stern wheelhouse and did so with the water frequently up to their necks. So we of the bucket brigade went to work again and only one small sea came to interfere. The stewards gave up thought of dinner; they passed sandwiches to us as we worked, the women helping.

At last we cleared the saloon and pantry again, and some of the passageways, and had a chance to get dry clothes and boots—the men's staterooms were free of water while those of the women were thoroughly soaked, with ankle-deep water on the floor. We were proud of the way our countrymen pitched in, of their characteristic good cheer, and ability to extract fun from any situation. But gradually indignation rose. The ship's officers never came near us to reassure the frightened passengers, most of whom had never been to sea before, or to minister to their comfort, or to speak to the three injured women. True, the captain inspected but he did nothing; the insolent purser told passengers who complained to write to his government and lifted not a finger. The story spread that the doctor would not visit one woman because she was only seasick and that was not an illness he was required to treat.

When evening came and it appeared that the officers were not

concerned as to what became of the women and children whose
staterooms were flooded, Miss Mary Agnes Irvine, the fine cool
head of the women's group, and others formed a committee and
turned men out of their staterooms right and left. At ten o'clock
I found a poor mother and three children—eleven weeks on the
road from Burma—with no place to sleep, so we aroused another
group of tired but cheery men and sent them to the smoking room
to sit up all night; Hungerford and I had given our stateroom to
three girls. In the midst of all that excitement a baby boy was
born and this time the doctor stood by.

Tuesday, when the weather became threatening, we turned and
ran for eight hours straight back toward New York in order to
head into another following storm. Turning back upon our course,
we were again struck by a sea which sent two of the crew to the
hospital, with a broken arm and leg, respectively. The next morning a committee of passengers had a talk with the captain, to whom
we had sent a complaint as to the failure of his officers to show
some decent interest in the condition of his passengers. He showed
very clearly that he was no disciplinarian; indeed, he seemed old
and tired. We persisted in our complaint until the chief officer
came to me and asked me if we would not withdraw it. "Otherwise," he said, "it will have to be forwarded to the Board of Trade
and the officers and men will be deprived of their Christmas leave
because of the inevitable investigation; it is to be our first leave in
two years."

I asked him whether, if he had been captain of the ship, she
would have been handled as she was. He looked embarrassed for
a moment. Then in a very frank and manly way he said that she
would not have been, that we were justified in our complaints, and
that all he could do was to offer his apology; the crew was worn
out by its incessant service. His apology seemed to be all that the
committee needed and the complaint was torn up. There was no
doubt that the stewards and the crew did their best. Many of them
wore wound stripes and had had ships sunk under them; the
smoking-room steward told us that he had lost his six brothers
and his father in the war and been severely wounded himself.

Finally, the first officer, like the captain, asked us to send in a request to the company that the ship be withdrawn from the Atlantic trade and this we did.

When the pilot boarded the *Balmoral Castle* off the Mersey, on Friday the thirteenth, his first question was: "Did you meet a German submarine that didn't know the war was finished?"—so battered was our appearance. We were three days behind time, to the especial sorrow of the journalists on board who had hoped to reach England in time for the closing days of the Khaki Hang-the-Kaiser election. When we reached the dock at Liverpool the passengers were told to report to the boarding officers in the smoking room for their respective permissions to land. As I stood in line I was approached by a steward who said I was wanted elsewhere. In another room sat a group of four officials from Scotland Yard. On the table before them was a red-ink list of names of eight suspects; mine headed it. As there were others being examined I wandered around, wondering what was going to happen to me, when I suddenly encountered the first of a number of extraordinary pieces of luck that marked this trip to Europe: I ran into the man above all others to help me in this emergency—an old and warm friend. It was my classmate, Thayer Robb of New York, in the uniform of an American captain.

From the beginning of the war he had served Scotland Yard in connection with Americans and American problems, later being commissioned in the British army and then being transferred to the American when we got into the war. His regiment having been severely cut up in the Argonne, he had been sent back to England to become the American disembarkation officer at Liverpool. We fairly fell into one another's arms. When I told him of my situation, he said: "Leave that to me," and taking me right to the Scotland Yard group he said to them: "Gentlemen, Mr. Villard is one of our most distinguished American journalists. I have known him for more than twenty-five years. I vouch for him absolutely and make myself personally responsible for him. Please give him permission to land." The disappointment of those Hawkshaws at the loss of their prey was so obvious as to be laughable but they were unable to protest and asked me only a couple of perfunctory questions.

Robb accompanied me on shore and there the hours slipped by for some reason or other. The 11.30 train went without us. It was two o'clock when we left. Strunsky, Hungerford, Ernestine Evans, the journalist, and Miss Buckner Kirk of the Red Cross, whom I had already determined to add to *The Nation's* staff as soon as she got back to New York, were in one compartment. Our chief topic of conversation was whether we should get to London in time for the closing meeting of the campaign which Lloyd George was to address; a rumor that it was an afternoon meeting depressed us greatly. London at last! Three quarters of an hour late but still time to drive directly to the hall. There on the platform stood Herbert Horwill, the London correspondent of *The Nation*. "The meeting is over," he said, "Lloyd George has had his final say but you are in time for the polling tomorrow."

Chapter XX. England During the Armistice

LONDON in this post-war period was, of course, a London changed but a London whose streets were amazingly crowded with people. The throngs were largely made up of returned officers and the lesser ranks; every other man was still in khaki and the many women in uniform—startling to us in their revealed stockings, short skirts, or trousers—added much to the colorful appearance of the crowd. Dashing chauffeuses, driving motor-cycles with able-bodied officers in the sidecars, demonstrated the topsy-turvydom of war. Constantly one met, in the maimed and disfigured wounded, grim reminders of the massacres that had been going on, to an extent that we never remotely approached in the United States. One even saw men wearing complete masks— perhaps permanently—unlike those worn by the numerous men in officers' uniform, who, to the government's disgrace, sang or played musical instruments in the streets and begged for money. Some of these wore signs reading: "Demobbed and No Work to Do"; "This is the Way Our Government Rewards Us for Doing Our Bit." The nights were gloomy for the streets were still barely lighted. There were few motor cars or taxis for the petrol supplies were very low, so that getting about was slow and difficult.

We pampered Americans suffered greatly from the cold, damp-ness, and constant rain, and the almost total lack of heating but we were ashamed to complain when we thought of what the men in khaki had lived through. I did remark in a letter home that when we went to the Old Vic to see an exquisite fifteenth-century miracle play of the Nativity the management had made the usual mistake of letting the furnace go out and turning on the cold storage machinery, so that we were each happy indeed to buy a penny hot baked potato from a vendor and to consume it as we walked to the bus line. I reported that the weather had been unusually good: "That is, it has not snowed; nor rained more than three times a day; and not rained all day more than two days in a week." Strunsky and I, who shared two bedrooms and a bath at the Savoy Hotel, were able, on request, to get an electric heater turned on when we were compelled to use our typewriters. The management was unfortunately clairvoyant for invariably the heat went off as the last pages were written and our hands then returned to their customary numbness. Our wits never were adequately thawed out. On that we were agreed when we read each other's articles before going outdoors to get warm.

At the large hotels the food was good but the bread was lumpy, the butter meager, the sugar entirely lacking. In the small and cheap restaurants the staple was "sausages and mashed." Chocolates were in enormous demand. Here, too, there was a false and misleading prosperity. The fashionable restaurants were jammed to the doors; never had there been so much buying for Christmas; the stores could not handle the trade. Now that the war strain was over everybody seemed ready to spend all they had. There were many, many profiteers, with any amount of money to squander. People of all ages were dancing-mad—another natural reaction from an almost intolerable strain. We soon learned how great the effect of the German air raids had been and how much larger the loss of life and property damage than the world had been allowed to know. What the sirens, the antiaircraft guns, and the explosions of the German bombs took out of those persons who had small children to shield could hardly be described. When the New Year came in, and we heard at midnight the Boy Scouts blowing the signal "All Clear" on their bugles for a last time, we could somehow share the deep emotion of those around us.

Yet we were astounded to find that, for all their suffering, the people we met had little of the hate and bitterness so prevalent at home—especially the soldiers and returned prisoners. I met a number of the latter, including a group at the office of a Red Cross captain who rejoiced in the patriotic surname of American; I found no one to complain of ill-treatment except, of course, that the food was abominable. The men always added: "We got as good as they

did." The first one I met was a handsome boy officer in a train for
Birmingham. His uniform and everything about him were brand-
new. As I looked at his rosy cheeks and perfect condition I thought
he must be just out of a training camp. When one of the other
officers asked where he had been when the Armistice came, he
blushed and said that he had been two years in a German prison
camp. "And you look like *that?*" I burst out. He explained that
the prisoners had been fortunate in getting regular shipments of
food from home. Every officer in this group—I was the only
civilian—was absolutely without bitterness against the defeated
foe. Captain American's job was to interview the released American prisoners just as soon as they arrived and to take down their
statements stenographically. It was an interesting fact that those
statements made to an official in uniform were not recognizable in
the interviews with them which appeared in the newspapers the
next day and in the letters they wrote to their homes. That was
the reason why, Captain American explained, he was so careful
to interview them before they saw anybody else. "By the time
these men reach home," he said, "the horrors they have been
through will be appalling."

How tolerant the British were of dissenters appeared when Mrs.
Philip Snowden told me that, in 1918 alone, she had spoken at
fifty peace meetings, only two or three being interrupted. Snowden
himself, although daily vilified by the jingo press, assured me that
he had never had an unpleasant word said to him in public or in
Parliament or anywhere else, and Ramsay MacDonald testified
somewhat similarly. It was not until later that some soldiers
brutally assaulted the crippled Snowden in the lobby of a theatre.
I told Mrs. Snowden that in the United States she would have
been assaulted at her first peace meeting and jailed on attempting
a second. No one in London could understand the bitterness in
America or the severity of the sentences given to conscientious
objectors, to Debs, or those accused of pro-Germanism. One remark was: "We did our propaganda work too well."

No one could have been given a warmer and friendlier welcome
than I received in London from friends new and old. It con-

trasted so sharply with the atmosphere of suspicion and hate I had left behind me as to be almost overwhelming. I found the Liberal and Labor friends I met wholly united on several points. I recorded that "they hate Lloyd George with a deadly hatred, feeling about his lack of principle as I do about Wilson's, only one hundred per cent more so. They all believe some kind of revolution inevitable here; the only difference is as to when it will come." Next, they were all clear in their minds that whether the war was lost or won would depend solely upon the Peace Conference. They unitedly placed all their hopes upon Woodrow Wilson, in whom they saw the savior of the world. They felt this so deeply that they resented any suggestion that he might prove unequal to the task. I discovered this when I spoke at the 1917 Club, then a brilliant organization, formed in the year of the Russian Revolution to fight for liberal and just principles in the peace and for a better world. It was my first appearance before a British audience and I was badly frightened by the distinguished people crowded at the tables in front of me. The men and women I most admired in English life were nearly all there, among them MacDonald, the saintly George Lansbury, J. A. Hobson, Lord Haldane, H. W. Massingham (the very able and lovable editor of the London *Nation*), Lady Courtney, the Snowdens, Mildred Minturn Scott (an American by birth, sister of Mrs. Amos Pinchot), the Pethick-Lawrences, Lady Barlow, and Mrs. Despard the fiercely democratic sister of Field Marshal French who at seventy-four had just been defeated for Parliament.

I felt compelled to warn this group against having too much faith in Wilson and told them of some of the things he had tolerated or approved: the outrageous censorship; the torturing of conscientious objectors; the first suppression of all dissent in war time in our history; the abandonment of his liberal program; his veering steadily to the right; and his monstrous and bloody conquest of Haiti. I stressed, of course, the value of his ideals and his admirable program but told them of his readiness to compromise. The applause when I sat down was merely dictated by politeness to a foreign guest. Lady Barlow, next to whom I sat, could not conceal her disapproval. "You must have had a personal quarrel with Wilson," she remarked. We have often referred to that since and to my justification by what took place in Paris.

Francis Hirst, then the able editor of *Common Sense*, who had forfeited his editorship of the *Economist* because of his espousal of Lord Lansdowne's wise proposals for a negotiated peace, invited me to dine with Sir John Simon and himself. They asked me many questions about Wilson which was not surprising because the London papers gave precious little news of America. Sir John said: "You sound like a carefully prepared legal brief, written by an American lawyer, which points out all of Wilson's weaknesses and tells how they can be played upon and utilized. It is being circulated among our peace delegates for their edification." Rather stunned by this treason to a just peace, I asked Sir John if the author was James M. Beck, then in London. He replied: "I neither affirm nor deny." It is but fair to add that subsequently Mr. Beck absolutely denied any knowledge of any such document.[1] I could not help wondering if anybody was coaching Wilson as to the weaknesses of his coming adversaries. I thought Sir John "plainly very able" and more conservative in his forecast of trouble to come than Hirst, who looked for disaster in two years.

That dinner was noteworthy if only because of Sir John's vivid and dramatic description of how he and the other members of the Cabinet sat at the Prime Minister's residence, 10 Downing Street, on the night of August 4, 1914, and listened to Big Ben striking eleven o'clock, the hour set for the receipt of Germany's acceptance of the English ultimatum. As the clock struck, the war was on: a million Englishmen were at that instant doomed to early death; millions to indescribable suffering. Simon was opposed to England's going to war but, unlike Morley and others, stayed in the Cabinet until conscription came, when he resigned in protest. His subsequent speeches against its being made permanent would have

---

[1] I have lately heard that Lord Northcliffe ordered his New York correspondent to supply the fullest possible analysis of Wilson, his habits, associates, weak points, etc., everything of value to enable the British delegation to take his measure.

earned him at least forty years in Atlanta Penitentiary if delivered in the United States. Sir John's career since then has belied the promise of those earlier years and has lost for him the regard and respect of many of those who admired him in 1918. It would be hard to find a much worse Foreign Secretary than he was; none the less, he seems more of a Cabinet fixture than anyone else and is at this writing Chancellor of the Exchequer, his fifth Cabinet office.

I had been only three days in London when I was invited to the *Nation's* weekly staff luncheon at the National Liberal Club where, in addition to the staff, I found Hirst, J. H. Whitehouse, Lowes Dickinson, and C. Roden Buxton. If there ever was a finer and more sensitive soul than Lowes Dickinson's I have yet to discover it. But my affection went out especially to Massingham. My admiration for him as a man and editor grew until his death. His *Nation*—he told me he had stolen the name from mine when in 1907 he took over *The Speaker*, remodeled, and re-christened it —set a standard I could not hope to attain. He carried on his paper with the aid only of H. M. Tomlinson, now famous for his books, a business manager, and his able secretary, Gertrude Cross, whereas we had a large and expensive staff of assistant editors. English journalists have never been able to understand this.[2]

Massingham and his successors, however, were in a position no American editor could hope to approach. He was surrounded by gifted and highly trained writers, all of them experts in certain fields, whom he had only to call on the telephone in order to obtain a first-class article, admirably written and rarely requiring the slightest editing. It seemed to me that Massingham lived in an editor's paradise when he had such writers as the Buxton brothers, Henry W. Nevinson, L. T. Hobhouse, Hirst, Dickinson, George Bernard Shaw, S. K. Ratcliffe, J. L. Hammond, H. N. Brailsford, Augustine Birrell, Robert Lynd, Robert Dell, Delisle

[2] C. P. Scott of the *Manchester Guardian*, whenever he saw a list of editors of an American daily or magazine, would say: "I wonder what on earth they all find to do." J. L. Hammond, *C. P. Scott of the Manchester Guardian*, 1934, pp. 318-19.

Burns, Hobson, Charles F. G. Masterson, Bertrand Russell, Graham Wallas, Wilson Harris, MacDonald, Sir Sydney, now Lord, Olivier, H. J. Laski, Leonard Woolf, H. G. Wells, and still others to call upon. That there are so many admirable writers in all the camps in Fleet Street is surely a triumph for the English university system. It is rare, indeed, that a manuscript reaches the editor of any American journal which has pretensions to style that does not call for much revision, even to spelling and punctuation, unless it comes from England. In the New York *Nation* office it has long been a cynical joke that the worst manuscripts come from our college professors.

To meet such kindred souls as I have described has always been one of my happiest and richest experiences—I have encountered them in nearly every country though not in such numbers as in London. Somehow I cannot believe that Tories, or Rotarians, or Imperialists can feel anything like the same deep satisfaction in contacts with their kind. For one thing, there is the joy of being instantly on the footing of an old comrade or friend; we can take many things for granted at once. Our conversation does not start from the usual beginnings; we do not have to probe to ascertain just how we feel before reaching real communion. To be opposed to war; to hold no hate for any peoples; to be determined to champion a better world; to believe in the equality of all men and women; and to be opposed to all tyrants and all suppression of liberty and conscience and beliefs—when one stands on this platform, one has a ready key to priceless friendships. We may not see these friends often; when we do, we begin not just where we left off, but where we left off plus all the joint experiences given to us since we last met by our keen mental and moral participation in the world's events. We are up-to-date in our emotions when we begin to talk. I have a friend in Europe today from whom I hear irregularly; no one need tell me how Ethiopia burned into his soul, how he suffers for Spain by day and night, and how earnestly he has opposed every Hitlerite aggression on his fatherland. He is one of the fellowship of those whose country is the world, with which fellowship, I insist, there is none to compare.

Two week ends out of London resulted in valuable new friendships. In Birmingham my Quaker host of the distinguished Sturge family, friends for three generations, introduced me to "a very interesting young man, John Drinkwater, who runs a small repertory theatre and has written an effective play on Lincoln." After the performance we had tea and discussed his play with him. Lincoln was acted by a player with a strong Irish brogue, while Frederick Douglass, the gifted Negro orator, who in real life was an excellently educated and highly cultivated man, independent and outspoken, with some of the best white blood of Maryland in his veins, was made up as a typical vaudeville darky of the subservient waiter type, speaking a language no American Negro ever used. Nevertheless, thanks to the earnestness and sincerity of the author and actors, the play was extremely impressive in that English setting; they unquestionably caught the spirit of Lincoln. In the years that followed I tried in vain to interest Drinkwater in the great drama of John Brown.

At Street, in Somerset, in the hospitable home of Mr. and Mrs. William S. Clark (she the daughter of John Bright), also warm and sympathetic friends of many years—now four generations—I met General J. C. Smuts whom I had been most eager to know. He had been one of the Boer leaders I admired, and his rise in the war from an ex-enemy of England to a lieutenant generalcy in her army and to a seat in the inner British War Cabinet was surely one of the most romantic of the World War. I found him simple and modest in bearing and altogether impressive if not exactly distinguished-looking. His keen eyes were kindly, his complexion fresh and ruddy, his manner most friendly; the grandchildren of the household ran to him with the utmost affection. At dinner the first evening his hosts, who were his warmest friends in England, as their children still are, were surprised how much their guest talked of public men and affairs. He, too, asked me many questions about the United States both then and the next day, and about Woodrow Wilson whom he still rates above Lincoln and next to Washington in our history. General Smuts was particularly interested in our Negro problem because of the serious color difficulties in South Africa, in the handling of which he has denied democracy and made his greatest blunders.

General Smuts talked to me very frankly. He thought Pershing and Haig very much alike—excellent generals technically but wholly without imagination or statesmanship, and he could not conceive of Pershing as a Presidential candidate. He told me, also, of his two long talks with Wilson in London in which he had warned the President that he must not be deceived by the apparent cordiality of the French statesmen. He was quite blue about the prospect of a clean peace for which no man fought more bravely and determinedly up to the last moment than he. Indeed, he did not make up his mind until the final morning to sign it, which he did with a long and earnest protest. According to his recent biographer, Sarah Gertrude Millin, it was he who inspired Keynes's *Economic Consequences of the Peace*. General Smuts certainly had a clear understanding of the failure of the treaty. In his statement given to the press after he signed he said: "This treaty is simply the liquidation of the war situation in the world. The spirit of new life, the victory of the great human ideals for which the people have shed their blood and their treasure without stint, the fulfillment of their aspirations towards a new international order, and a fairer, better world are not written in this treaty, and will not be written in treaties. 'Not in this mountain, nor in Jerusalem, but in spirit and in truth,' as the Great Master said, must the foundation of the new order be laid." [3]

He saw that a new spirit of generosity and humanity born in that great hour of suffering and sorrow could "alone heal the wounds which had been inflicted on the body of Christendom." It is sad to read today that he added: "In this treaty, however, two achievements of far-reaching importance to the world are definitely recorded. The one is the destruction of Prussian militar-

[3] Sarah Gertrude Millin, *General Smuts*, Boston, 1936, Vol. II, p. 256.

ism; the other the institution of the League of Nations.[4] As I write these words we have a militarism in Germany worse by far than that of the Kaiser, while the League of Nations is a pitiful and disintegrating failure. Mrs. Millin says that her hero's character is "even more difficult, complex, and contradictory" than Wilson's. She adds: "His platitudes jostle his profundities. His cynicism laughs at his idealism. He is dependable and also incalculable. In the midst of all his higher truths—high above ordinary heads and also sometimes above mundane use—suddenly a chunk of earthy sense. Accident? Knowledge? Genius? That is what puzzles South Africans." [5] However true or untrue this characterization may be, my admiration for General Smuts remains high despite the fact that his ideals broke down in dealing with the colored races. I honor him especially for his friendship for, and championship of, the Jews.

On the Monday morning after our week end General Smuts and I and Miss Alice Clark traveled to London together. His frank conversation made the hours pass with amazing speed. To my happiness I succeeded in obtaining from him the right to publish in America his draft of a proper League of Nations. I was the more elated because the Associated Press had been telegraphing to him repeatedly from Paris asking for this document. Its publication as a special supplement to *The Nation* was extremely useful and a great help to our circulation. Much of the General's proposed League was embodied in the present Covenant, but some things which ought to have been in were omitted—as that conscription should be abolished and all making of munitions and armament factories be nationalized and subject to the League's inspection. He also proposed an international military and naval force. And yet he, with the rest of them, believed that the prime

[4] Some of Mr. Wilson's best friends on the *George Washington* begged him on the homeward voyage to send out a similar message to the peoples declaring he had done his best against the forces opposed to him; that he knew the treaty contained evil things which must be changed. He refused.

[5] Millin, *op. cit.*, Vol. II, p. 164.

ministers or foreign secretaries of the Great Powers should dominate the Council of the League.

Of course, I did not miss either of Mr. Wilson's triumphal
drives through London. It seemed very odd to see him and Mrs.
Wilson going by in one of the historic state carriages with four
horses and cocked-hatted and white-wigged coachmen, footmen,
and outriders—a far cry from the simplicity of life in Princeton
and Washington. The crowds were not always large or vocal
though there was often cheering, but the profound respect and regard with which the men removed their hats and the women bowed
and waved were beyond mistaking. Those receptions certainly,
and even more the greeting in Manchester, warranted him in
thinking that he was speaking for the peoples of the world.

But his English visit began with a bad blunder—bad though
unavoidable; he could not decline the invitation of King George to
stay at Buckingham Palace. That meant that he was surrounded
by official Englishmen whom he least needed to see. His residence
there cut him off from almost all contacts with the liberal and
labor groups who were his real friends and supporters and had
much to give him—he did receive one large labor delegation and
insisted on seeing C. P. Scott of the *Manchester Guardian*. It
would have been a real education for him to have had a long talk
with Robert Dell, the former Paris correspondent of the *Manchester Guardian*, who had been expelled from Paris for writing
the truth about the several times in 1917 when the Allies could
have made an honorable peace—probably a much better peace than
we know now—and how they concealed from the President what
was really going on. No one knew the inside of what had happened
in France as he knew it, and none could better have prepared Mr.
Wilson for the obstacles he was to encounter. Incidentally, Robert
Dell was one of a number of dissenting Englishmen who asked
me, the instant we met: "Why, *why* did you Americans have to
come in and spoil the whole business?"—meaning a sane and negotiated peace. The masses in England, as well as the middle class
and all the Liberal and Labor elements, did not share this point

of view. They were profoundly grateful that we had come in and that Wilson had crossed the Atlantic.

In all my journalistic experience I have never attended a meeting so moving and reverential as that in the historic Manchester Free Trade Hall on December 30, at which Mr. Wilson spoke. I am sure that if it had been Christ Himself returning to this earth, His reception could not have been more impressive or awe-inspiring. When that great crowd rose to its feet as Mr. Wilson appeared, there was an atmosphere around me—yes, all through the hall—that defied description. Reverence, profound gratitude, the feeling that there stood the savior of the world, the creator of a new and better universe—all of these feelings were expressed on every countenance. Never have I noted elsewhere such complete unanimity of sentiment or such a reverential spirit outside of a church. It would have taken very little more for that audience to have gone down on its knees to Wilson. Any man so welcomed might have been forgiven if he had been carried away by his emotions, but his entrance was too quick, probably, to enable him to grasp the situation. The speech that he made was by no means one of his greatest but it satisfied those who had come to do him honor.

Earlier that morning he had been driven around the city. We newspaper men had been allowed to accompany him on the boat which took him down the Manchester Ship Canal. The banks were lined by cheering throngs; there was all the enthusiasm that anyone could ask. At one point we came abreast of what looked like an ordinary merchant vessel. Suddenly there was a whistle and in sixty seconds there was a transformation before us—the innocent tramp was changed into a warship. It was one of the "mystery boats." Bulwarks fell out and revealed men and guns—indeed guns rose up from the hold in all directions—and false hatchways similarly vanished to reveal gun crews at attention. I glanced up at the bridge above us and there stood the President waving his hat, cheering, evidently as thrilled as a boy. It was all too spectacular and stage-like to make us realize what this display connoted. I thought then that the President looked very tired and when I asked Admiral Grayson if I was right, he said: "You are. I shall have to make him rest very soon." But he did not show fatigue when he spoke in Free Trade Hall.

I stayed over in Manchester to call upon C. P. Scott, who had made the *Manchester Guardian* the bravest, most fearless, and outspoken, yes, the best, daily in the world and found him rejoicing over the return of his son from a German prison camp—the son destined to succeed him for a few months in 1932 and then to be drowned so needlessly and cruelly at Windermere—and like the others most eager to talk about Woodrow Wilson and the chances of his success. The tributes Mr. Scott paid to Mr. Wilson would have humbled any man. Mr. Scott was especially fine in demanding that the Allies get out of Russia and leave that country to work out its own solution, as to which Mr. Wilson had not spoken up to that time. Mr. Scott helped to inspire the great campaign, then being organized by the Liberals and Laborites despite their overwhelming defeat in the election, to hold meetings all over the country in behalf of the Wilson program, especially the Fourteen Peace Points. Indeed, all England seethed at this time with this question of the peace, with the bitter-enders demanding the complete subjection of the German people and convinced that Lloyd George would have the Kaiser on the gibbet by Whitsuntide. They helped Lloyd George to believe that the election had given him *carte blanche* to do anything he pleased and steeled him to the making of the bad peace, the responsibility for which he now places on others.

To see English public opinion at work then was a highly instructive experience but a disheartening one, for it became apparent that it was just as difficult to deal with the reactionaries in a small and compact country like England as in our own enormous and so diversified republic. The liberal elements, including Mr. Scott, were then quite fearful that the completeness of Lloyd George's victory would strengthen the direct-action forces and lead to serious labor troubles. They were much concerned over the mutinous conduct of large bodies of the returned troops, like those at Folkestone, where thousands paraded, defying their officers and bearing signs reading: "We Will Not Fight in Russia" and also demanding their immediate discharge. Not one word of these demonstrations was printed in the London press but the Cabinet knew of them and the danger of their spreading all over the country. Undoubtedly these demonstrations, together with the outspokenness of the Liberal and Labor press, plus Wilson's refusal to go along, kept England from the folly of a hopeless holy war to purge Russia of the Bolsheviks.

When the New Year came in I felt I could make no better use of the day than to devote part of it to visiting a friend, Hubert W. Peet, a conscientious objector, in the hideous Pentonville prison. He was allowed to see his wife only once a month and permitted only two short letters during that period. Knowing him to be a Quaker, a man of deep religious convictions and high spirituality, I expected to find him calm and serene, for I remembered hearing how cheerfully my grandfather and the other Abolitionists and the early Quakers had borne their various incarcerations. Mr. Peet showed clearly how grave are the effects of imprisonment even upon men whose consciences are clear, who are guilty only of obeying their consciences and following in the footsteps of the Savior. The severance from all family ties, the complete change in one's habits and work, the deadly routine of endlessly sewing upon mailbags, which was Mr. Peet's task, the intellectual isolation, all took a heavy toll. He did not, of course, complain or express the slightest self-sympathy but the strain on his nerves was evident enough. Thus all over England and in the United States were men of the very finest type martyred even when not tortured by the shocking cruelties practiced in Alcatraz and at Fort Leavenworth. No one could foresee, on that New Year's Day, 1919, that in fifteen years no fewer than thirty-five of those British conscientious objectors would have seats in the same Parliament. The badge of dishonor turned in their cases to honor. So stupid and so wasteful of precious human material are governments!

Not until the turn of the year did I obtain permission to enter France. A letter from Jusserand told me that it had been granted;

the French Consul was not so advised. He had forwarded an application soon after my arrival but later told me that I need expect no reply for five or six weeks. I then wrote in despair to Melville E. Stone in Paris and besought his aid. He responded, as always. I do not know what he said to Clemenceau but he wrote to me that Clemenceau had agreed to let me in because he, Clemenceau, had been assured that I was now completely cured of my "furious pacifism"! It took me some time to make up my mind to go under that circumstance. I decided that it was not my fault if he had been deceived. On January 9 I boarded a dirty little steamer at Southampton and found it crowded with Y.M.C.A. men and Y.W.C.A. women who had left New York on December 28. I wrote that the latter were less attractive than my fellow-voyagers on the *Balmoral Castle*, that they looked singularly sallow after the beautiful complexions of the Englishwomen, and that their shrill American voices grated as if I had been long away from home. After a rough crossing that night we passed through the deeply flooded valley of the Seine and there was Paris, so fraught with the destiny of mankind.

Chapter XXI. The Fatal Peace Conference

DAY by day the Peace Conference was deferred. With hundreds of the most difficult problems the world had ever faced pressing for settlement or decision, somebody postponed the conference—Wilson, Clemenceau, Orlando, one after the other, until Mr. Wilson's departure for home was only four weeks away. Men might die by the thousands and women and children starve, but the conference must be postponed. Finally, on January 13, there was a dress rehearsal in the meeting of the leaders of the conference as the Supreme War Council. But it was not until January 18 that the conference was officially opened by President Poincaré in a plenary session in the dreadfully overornate Louis XV room, with its numerous heavy candelabra, in the Quai D'Orsay. I had had the luck to be one of the American correspondents to receive cards for the first meeting with the understanding that it was probably the last to which some of us could get access because of the limitation of tickets due to the lack of space.

As I entered the room assigned to the journalists, which opened into the conference room, an American newspaper woman fluttered up to me: "Oh, Mr. Villard," said she, "are we not among the most fortunate of mortals to have been selected to view this occasion about which historians will be writing for a thousand years to come?" I answered her without enthusiasm and, as I looked later upon the assembled potentates, I felt neither exaltation nor enthusiasm. True, it was a magnificent spectacle of the complete officialdom of the Allied world. There were all the statesmen most talked about save for half a dozen Germans. There were the most famous of the victorious generals of the war of attrition just ended. There were men, like Poincaré, who helped to bring on the war and were unable or unwilling to stop it or to negotiate a peace. There were the chief diplomats of the school whose follies and failures had made war inevitable, some of whom had been especially active in luring us Americans into the struggle. Of course if one cared for spectacles one could ask nothing more remarkable. There were uniforms without number, unending gilt and braid, and so many decorations for successful killing that they speedily became a commonplace. All the pomp and circumstance of government were on view. Chamberlains, lackeys in livery, waiters in dress suits, a guard of honor at the doors with officers in dress uniforms in control of all—yes, a magnificent performance. As for the speeches, I recorded that, but for Woodrow Wilson's, they were dull and uninspired and got us nowhere.

That day William Allen White cabled to his syndicate that he had found me asleep in an anteroom. My eyes were closed; I was trying to think what to write, how to describe what was going on, how artificial and even repellent the whole scene was to me. Even the graceful speech of President Wilson, who was plainly the only possible barrier between a peace of folly, rapacity, and vindictiveness, failed to dispel my deep depression. I knew Woodrow Wilson, knew his cowardice, knew his egotism, knew his readiness to compromise, and to persuade himself that surrendering to your opponent was, in a tight place, the height of political skill, and so could not from the start put the slightest faith in his holding out alone. Moreover, whenever I looked into the conference room I could only see that of all the millions of mothers and wives who had given of their beloved there was not one present; not one of the private soldiers who had borne the brunt of the fighting and had poured forth most of the blood, and no single representatives of the masses who had paid the price of the stupidities, the follies, the blunders, and the crimes of the statesmen and the generals there assembled. The victors, yes, but none of the victims under their own flags. How could any thinking man exult or see in this gathering the dawn of a new world and of perpetual peace?

Great territories involving the lives of millions of black men were to be turned over to new masters, yet there was hardly a dark skin visible. Worst of all, for the first time in modern history, a great peace was to be written without a single representative of the defeated peoples in the council chamber. We did not know then, or even suspect, that this policy would be continued until the Germans were brought to Versailles, placed behind barbed wire like wild animals, and told to sign on the dotted line.[1] Did Wilson's words of January 22, 1917, "a peace dictated by the victors will be as writ in water," recur to him? Plainly not. At that moment he was at the high-water mark of his life. His most cherished ambition was realized. He was the foremost figure among the peacemakers. He, Woodrow Wilson, was making over the world. Yet already he had surrendered; his measure had been taken. Within a short time all pretense that this was to be a peace *conference* was at an end. On January 28 I wrote home that "the small nations are quite vigorous in their protests against the way they are being ignored in the committees and there is much feeling against the dominating leaders as Strunsky and I found out when we called upon Venizelos." A month later the Big Ten—gradually whittled down to the Big Four—had taken over the whole show and nobody talked any more about this being a conference to lay down the general policies of territorial settlement, the terms of military and naval disarmament, to found the League of Nations, and to let a subsequent gathering work out the innumerable details. The peace of vengeance writ in water was in sight.

The President's first yielding was on his "open covenants, openly arrived at." When word reached the American journalists that we were all to be excluded from the sessions of the Peace Conference and from the private meetings of its bosses, there was the bitterest indignation. A lot of us went to Ray Stannard Baker, who was the commission's press representative, to protest. He actually turned pale before the onslaught. He was told by some

[1] Cf. Harold Nicolson's comment: "During January, February, and the first half of March—for a period, that is, of more than ten weeks—the rulers of the world were completely unaware whether the treaty which they were discussing was to be negotiated or imposed." This question was shelved as "too painful to raise immediately, as something which would settle itself." The similar failure to decide whether the treaty should be preliminary or final Mr. Nicolson considers one of the vital mistakes of the conference. Harold Nicolson, *Peacemaking, 1919*, London, 1933, p. 96, *et seq.*

of the representatives of dailies that they would cable home demanding their recall and would "show up" Wilson, House, and the entire proceedings. It would be absolutely hypocritical, they rightly said, to shut out the press after Wilson's assurances that everything was going to be open and aboveboard. Mr. Baker promised to take the matter up at once with Colonel House but he did not commit himself to a vigorous championship of our freedom to report. As we walked away William Allen White, who had been among the most outspoken of the protestants, made a remarkable prophecy. "That settles it," he said. "That finishes the conference and Wilson. Lloyd George and Clemenceau will now take him upstairs into a private bedroom and fool him to death" —only the word he used was much less elegant than "fool." The result was, as I have indicated, the admission of some correspondents to the few open sessions of the conference and some, but quite inadequate, efforts to tell us what was going on.

Sometimes I was tempted to feel as did Madame Vandervelde, the English wife of the Belgian Socialist, minister and delegate, who frankly said to me: "I wish that all the leading men of the conference could be guillotined—except Wilson—for they are standing between us and a rational world." How true those words became! "Their deaths," she truthfully added, "would save those of many others." She had found, as I did, that wherever she went in French and foreign official circles there was nothing but scoffing at Wilson and derision for the League of Nations and the proposed system of mandatories. Indeed, it was because of their utter cynicism as to these new political devices and methods that the French were so determined to render Germany weak and forever to remove the menace of German militarism without any Frenchman of great influence being aware that this was a golden opportunity to remove that menace forever by generosity, by kindliness, by good will toward a beaten foe, by a determination once for all to make impossible, by humane methods, the recurrence of so horrible a disaster to both countries. All the statesmen knew only the road to vengeance, to severest punishment, to bitter humiliation, to humbling their enemy in the dust, and as always is the case with statesmen who do wrong, their excuse was that they were merely obeying the wishes of their vengeful constituents. As late as November 6, 1937, Colonel House repeated the moth-eaten contention that "various clauses were included in the peace treaty which were necessary to satisfy popular prejudice." This is nonsense. Some clauses were included by Woodrow Wilson in the face of the protests of his own economic advisers and of the British delegation.

Never was there a greater falsehood than this one. If the statesmen had but asked their soldiers they would have learned that the men who had dared and suffered were without desire for post-war revenge and wished fair, just, and merciful treatment for the adversaries they respected, whose prowess they admired. As in England, I met in Paris officer after officer and enlisted man after enlisted man who spoke in high praise of their former foes. Indeed, I noted on January 20 Melville Stone's telling me of two American officers who had just come from Coblenz and had said to him that they felt that they had been fighting on the wrong side! Walter Lippmann, back from two weeks with our troops in Germany, Frederic C. Howe, and numerous others told me of the bitterness of the army against the French because of their dislike of French methods of life and lack of cleanliness and because they believed that they were being exploited, cheated, and over-charged at every turn.

Already the Allied armies on the Continent were beginning to murmur and disintegrate, and in this atmosphere of unhappiness, unrest, mutual dislike, intrigue, mad, selfish determination to get all the spoils possible at the expense of everybody else, the Big Four arrogated to themselves the right to make peace. Only Mr. Wilson pretended to live in another world. Said he on February 3: "The nations of the world are about to consummate a brotherhood which will make it unnecessary in the future to maintain those crushing armaments which make the peoples suffer almost as much in peace as they suffer in war!" In presenting the draft of the League of Nations Covenant to the third session of the Peace Conference on February 14, he slipped even further away from realities: "The miasma of distrust, of intrigue is cleared away. Men are looking eye to eye and saying, 'We are brothers and have a common purpose.'"

True, the President soon came to realize that he must use another tone. In his address to the second session on January 25, Mr. Wilson warned his fellow delegates: "We are not representatives of governments but representatives of peoples. . . . It is necessary that we should satisfy the opinion of mankind. The burdens of this war have fallen in unusual degree upon the whole populations of the countries involved. . . . We are bidden by these peoples to make a peace which will make them secure." There was a threat in his voice and manner which was unmistakable, in which he was justified. So exalted was his standing at that moment with the victorious peoples that he could easily have toppled governments by appeal over their heads to their electorates. But the hardened statesmen in front of him were little moved, no more than when he went on to say of the American delegates: "We would not dare abate a single part of the program which constitutes our instructions. We would not dare compromise upon any matter as the champion of this thing—this peace of the world. . . . You can see that the representatives of the United States are, therefore, never put to the embarrassment of choosing a way of expediency because they have had laid down for them the unalterable lines of principle." The listeners must have put their tongues in their cheeks. They well knew that the President had already yielded to expediency and to compromise and that he was interpreting his instructions from the American people as he and he alone thought fit.

But, aside from the inevitable forebodings that came from observing this and the critical state of Europe, which no political reporter could forget for many minutes, life in Paris was extraordinarily interesting and exciting. In addition to all the remarkable official personages, Paris was crowded with the elite of the world's journalism (excepting always those of the defeated nations) and with innumerable distinguished people who, on one pretext or another, had come to have a share in the making of the treaty or in helping to build a new world order. There were delegations from all over the globe, some from minorities and little States and territories that most of us had never heard of, many of these visitors bent on ascertaining if there was some Anglo-Saxon journalist who would listen to their tales of woe and their appeals to sympathy. Never, I fancy, were so many distinguished Americans in one city at one time. It was truly, as one journalist wrote, "a regular national convention of Americans." In the Rue de Rivoli there were more American uniforms than French and there was, for the French, a sting to the quip that the Paris stores were going to put up signs reading, "Ici on parle Français." Bishop Brent preached a sermon on January 12 in which he rightly declared that the French hearthstone had been trod often enough in the last four years; it was time strangers got out and left the French a bit to themselves. Well, our troops wanted to go, but not those Americans who had to do with the conference. It was too thrilling even in its hopelessness; the stakes with which the game was being played were the greatest in history, the dangers too titillating. The fate of humanity was centered there in Paris.

Some of the friendships I formed there lasted long. Ramsay MacDonald, who then appeared to me as an ideal figure, was one of the first to look me up, together with Mrs. Philip Snowden and Margaret Bondfield, all three being bound for the congress of the Socialist Second Internationale at Berne. If ever a man was in political outer darkness it was Ramsay MacDonald at Paris. When walking with him I often saw British officers in uniform cross the street to avoid passing him. I noticed that when he and I and Andrew Furuseth, then a leader of the American seamen, and that noblest and rarest of Christians, George Lansbury, and other kindred souls of the group that "had not gone along" in the war, went to dinner together, MacDonald was always eager to find a quiet back room in some restaurant where we would be unmolested and not spied upon. MacDonald was then at the height of his manhood and seemed the perfect knight errant who had risked and lost all for conscience's sake. No one imagined that he had any future. The election had deprived him and his best friends of their seats in Parliament. He seemed forever stamped as an outcast, a discredited pacifist—although as I now know he did compromise in his speeches about the war. Five years later he was Prime Minister of England.

It must never be forgotten that when Lloyd George at the outbreak of the war took MacDonald figuratively up on a high mountain and offered him a seat in the inner Cabinet on behalf of the Prime Minister if he would wholeheartedly co-operate, MacDonald declined. The government constantly spied upon him, even employed a very handsome woman to try to trap him by getting him to violate the law against communicating with the enemy by forwarding letters for her via Switzerland. It stooped low to try to jail him! But then he never stumbled. Nor was his bearing in Paris that of a beaten, or whining, or unhappy man, or one who wore the crown of martyrdom. It was all in the day's work then and the thing to do was to fight on, to wait and see. But when he reached the height of an Englishman's ambition and governed his country, that insidious moral paralysis which results from high officeholding, and the deadly social lobby in London brought about his downfall. A witty friend of mine has said that if you put a Socialist before an official roll-top desk for a few weeks he will be certain that the fate of the world depends on his holding on to that desk indefinitely. Ethel Snowden, J. H. Thomas —the list is long of those who have been gravely altered by the wiles and lure of the "nobility and gentry" and by holding high office. In Paris we were equals in adversity, absolutely certain of the correctness of our viewpoint, which was hourly being proved right by the folly of the peacemakers, and happy in our comradeship and our seeking to swim upstream.

Of all those at the conference, Fridtjof Nansen stands out as the greatest I met or observed. If ever there was a nobleman and a statesman it was he. Had the making of the treaty been but placed in the hands of Nansen, Smuts, MacDonald, and Branting of Sweden as the Big Four, the whole world would be utterly different today. Nansen was really what his admirers thought that Woodrow Wilson was, a genuine, inspired, and creative statesman.

He could be detached and neutral because he came from a small country which had not taken part in the war. He had tact and skill in dealing with others and he was entirely at home in the European scene. Yet there was a certain naïveté about him which was in curious contrast with these other traits—the naïveté of a clean soul. Though he was capable of tremendous indignation at wrongdoing, he always seemed to have himself in hand. His vision was broad, his knowledge amazing. He seemed to personify the unswervable purpose of Vikings discovering a new continent or seeking the North Pole.

Nansen's presence was superb; his frame gigantic and capable of any feat of Arctic endurance; his blue eyes were clear and unwavering; his integrity fairly shone out of them. His heart was overflowing with sympathy and kindness, for he had the power to feel the suffering of the individual, yet it, too, was also under control. Modest and unassuming, he worked steadily, behind the scenes and openly, always bettering conditions and making one constructive suggestion after another, like his "Nansen passport" issued by the League of Nations which has to this day been an immeasurable boon to hundreds of thousands of refugees who lost their countries and were adrift in the world. He was the "umpire" in the permanent commission to investigate all matters in dispute between England and the United States and he devised a plan for feeding the Russians which was slow to receive official approval because it was too wise and too humane. Of course he had what Wilson lacked most—European background and understanding; the use of several languages; a certain *savoir faire* that cannot be acquired by living in America alone; the intuition that comes from dealing for years with just the type of citizens, soldiers, and officials who assembled in Paris. If nature ever intended that there should be a king of men it had Nansen in view.[2]

[2] "Hero, adventurer, archangel—all in one—he set in motion the imagination of every man, woman, and boy. The curiosity he roused, the authority he enjoyed were immense. Moreover, his humanitarianism was backed by a great capacity for practical organization. With untiring energy he succeeded time and again in rousing the inertness of a war-weary world for the millions whose grim fate it was to wander the earth." Dorothy Thompson, *Refugees: Anarchy or Organization?*, New York, 1938.

Hjalmar Branting, later the Swedish Prime Minister, violently anti-Bolshevist at Paris, lacked totally the great personal distinction that marked Nansen. I wrote of him that he could make speeches in German, French, and English, all equally bad. He was, however, very proud of his linguistic achievements; at Berne, as chairman, he repeated his views incessantly, first in bad French, then in miserable German, and finally in halting English. But his heart was sound and in the right place for he, too, knew what the world needed. A Socialist, a labor leader, an ardent democrat, he was counted on as much as any man in Europe to reunite after the war the ranks of social democracy and he gave everything he had in him to this end. He became one of his country's representatives in the League of Nations, which he served with all possible ardor. Three times Prime Minister, he was a recipient in 1921 of the Nobel Peace Prize, which he had well earned. My contacts with him in Paris were relatively few but each one refreshed and encouraged and gave one strength in one's faith and hope for the future. It was a real misfortune that his gifts and his knowledge could not count in the making of peace.

I was much amused to find Thomas W. Lamont, whom Wilson had refused to receive in the White House, turning up in Paris as one of the President's economic advisers. Lamont's horns and hoofs had suddenly disappeared. He easily proved his worth and rendered his best service at the conference. At times he really had the ear of the President, who consulted him when his associate peace commissioners were not admitted to the Presidential presence. But that does not mean that Lamont's advice was always accepted. On the contrary, at vital points the President refused to take it when he should have been guided by it, as in the matter of handing over South Tyrol to Italy and the charging of war pensions against the Germans as "damage to the civilian population," to which Wilson, incredible as it seems, consented. He was always ready to accept information from his assistants to fill the void of his own complete ignorance of world affairs. But, as in Washington, acceptance of advice was a different matter.

As for the other American peace commissioners, Bliss, White, and Lansing were soon practically ignored by the President. At first all the American correspondents went to the ten o'clock press hour at which one or more of these three commissioners appeared. That press hour yielded less and less. At first it was not plain why. Gradually, however, it became clear that they told us little because they had so little to tell. The President again wronged himself by refusing to avail himself of the counsel and knowledge of these men. All three of them knew what was happening if the President did not. General Tasker H. Bliss, whose acquaintance I made in Cuba in 1899 when he was winning the highest praise from all who observed him, well merited the position he held in Paris. Henry White, while not a big man, had had a remarkable experience in our diplomatic service, notably in London, with the result that he had innumerable friends among the British delegation and their entourage. He was the only Republican commissioner and it was said that the President picked him because his was not an aggressive personality.

The years have not dimmed my admiration for General Bliss. He was, like General Smuts, that rare combination of statesman and soldier. In addition, he was a scholar and a humanitarian and there was nothing of the militarist about him. He always suggested to me the Civil War generals I had known and he certainly had nothing whatever in common with our present type of militarist generals. In appearance General Bliss was much more the student and scholar than the soldier but I am certain that, if anything had happened to Pershing, General Bliss would have proved himself not only a great organizer but also a great tactician and strategist. Before the armistice General Bliss represented the United States on the Supreme War Council and we could have had no finer plenipotentiary. From the moment he entered it his intellectual eminence was recognized by all and the soundness of his judgment served the Allied cause well, even though his advice was not always welcome to the Europeans.

What especially won my respect was the total absence of any egotism or "side," as the English say, in General Bliss. He was always as simple, modest, and unassuming as when he, at middle age still a lieutenant of artillery who had suffered severely from an archaic system of regimental promotion, was appointed Collector of Customs in Havana. He was utterly opposed to the trappings of militarism and knew well the effect of subordinating the civil life of a nation to the military arm. Like myself he was much disturbed in Paris by some proposals in Congress to establish a regular army of 500,000 men. As for the proposal to introduce universal military service in the United States, which is still the goal of some of our generals, just as Douglas MacArthur has introduced it in the Philippines, General Bliss abhorred it. Soon after we met in Paris he said to me, as my notes record: "If we go in for universal service and militarism we shall be as great brutes as the German militarists in twenty years." [3]

It was the President who did all the official talking for his colleagues and decided, without consultation with them, what the Americans should stand for. Colonel House was, of course, in high favor until the time came when he, too, was thrust into outer darkness and the "perfect friendship" smashed. If he tried to aid some of the correspondents, the truth still is that our press was very badly handled. Ray Stannard Baker was not enough of a daily journalist, was too timid, and too conscious of his loyalty to his official superiors to be very helpful. The President paid dearly for not keeping the American press informed and content for it gave him an increasingly bad press at home where he so sorely needed a good one. The hostile correspondents dwelt with acerbity upon the growing secrecy of the conference and the autocratic domination of the Big Four.

Harold Nicolson feels that the press of the world should have been forbidden to send those five hundred correspondents to Paris.[4] He would have had all discussions secret and only have issued official communiqués. He is mistaken. That would not have kept all the special writers away; they would have drifted in somehow and dug up what they could. Moreover, the world was en-

---

[3] Cf. Frederick Palmer, *Bliss, Peacemaker. Life and Letters of General Tasker Howard Bliss*, New York, 1934, pp. 215-39.

[4] Harold Nicolson, *Peacemaking, 1919*, pp. 123-24.

titled to a picture of what was going on and what the atmosphere of Paris was and, if the public had not been gradually prepared for the treaty and the collapse of Wilson, the shock of the sorry ending would have been far worse. But the game of telling journalists half-truths, or trying to keep them in ignorance, pays not at all. Soon our American journalists [5] were fed up and felt, as did I about my own work, that they were not doing themselves proud. I cannot imagine a worse punishment for some of the clan than to compel them to reread today their dispatches from Paris. An exodus home promptly began, some actually cabling for permission to return; a considerable group left on February 5, quite disgusted. After it became clear that the plenary sessions were farces, and that the whole thing was going to be decided by the Big Four, everybody ached to get into Russia or Germany and envied the dispatch of William C. Bullitt, now ambassador to France, Lincoln Steffens, and Captain Walter W. Pettit to Russia by the President as a commission to report the actual facts. As President Wilson on his voyage over had given out a radio message that any American correspondent who went into Germany would be disgraced and sent back by the first steamer, and as no visa to any neutral country adjacent to Russia or Germany was granted unless the applicant took a formal oath not to enter those countries, the two most interesting regions at that hour were closed to the press.

There were several reasons for this, but prominent among them was the desire to keep from the world, and especially America, the fact that, despite the armistice, the war blockade was being enforced and old men and women and children were daily dying in Germany for lack of adequate food. I have never been able to forgive Lord Robert Cecil for the part he played in this peace-time game of death by withholding food. He is one of the most religious of men and his zeal for the League of Nations as a step to the brotherhood of man is unbounded. But his Christianity was not ardent enough to make him publicly demand relief for innocent noncombatants who were too undernourished to resist dis-

---

[5] Among them were eight graduates of my *Evening Post*.

ease or survive deprivation. Had he, as the British Minister of Blockade, urged abolition of the embargo, the whole world would have listened. The godly Presbyterian from the White House also could not be induced to make a public stand against this indefensible cruelty to noncombatants; the screw of starvation was kept turned in order to compel the vanquished to sign whatever treaty might be drafted.

While the old and very young were being starved in Germany, life in Paris was outwardly gay and fast. The restaurants were crowded, particularly by American officers, and the women they escorted, some virtuous, many demimondaine. The jewelry shops were doing an enormous business and it seemed to me that there were more of them than on previous visits. The hotels were jammed—the peacemaking, if not the war, was extremely popular with *hoteliers*. To me the most distressing phenomena were the war profiteers, obviously extremely rich, who, precisely as in England, had made tremendous fortunes out of the blood and suffering of their countrymen and countrywomen. Champagne was plentiful; the lid was off everywhere. If you had money you could get anything you wanted. In the hotels we were not expected to have sugar, butter, and other luxuries, but if you could find the head waiter and were willing to tip well you could obtain whatever you wished. The reaction from war-time restrictions and the war strain made for license and the old moralities applied not at all. It was amazing to discover how slight the hold conventions really have upon us, how quickly personal standards go by the board if there is any excuse.

Some of the hotels were open houses of assignation. Within many of the others was liberty hall. Women of all nations were equally affected. There was one Canadian Red Cross nurse in the Continental who was always "so sorry" when she entered your room by mistake and then sat down on your bed to talk. Her inability, and that of a friend of hers, to find their own chambers, and their refusal to leave promptly those rooms they "accidentally" entered, finally led some of the visited to complain to the office, after which these two saviors of France disappeared. One American journalist, who had always seemed to me the tamest, most demure, modest, and utterly proper of women in the pre-war days in New York, said no to nobody in uniform in Paris and accompanied an Italian general on his travels with complete frankness and tremendous enthusiasm.

One could understand the multitude of French women who offered themselves, for they were usually destitute and some had lost at the front every man they had any interest in and cared no longer for themselves or their future. The daughters of the middle class had not been trained for business or industry; as the war factories demobilized the suffering grew and the easy road seemed the only one. I found the new American army conditions and the functions of our military police difficult to understand. Thus, traveling once with an American major we found ourselves opposite two young American officers in company with two of the worst-looking prostitutes imaginable. Their tawdry finery was filthy—as if they had literally lain in the gutter. I waited for a while expecting my companion to act—as he would have in the old army days. Finally I asked him if what we saw did not concern him. "Not at all," he said, "the military police will take care of them." Arrived in Paris the officers showed their leaves, bundled the women into a taxi, and disappeared. To see an enlisted man with the arm band "M.P." walk up to an officer, demand his papers, cross-examine him, and in some cases actually arrest him, was to me a constant source of amazement.

While the outward signs of extravagance were on every hand, underneath there was the greatest distress, save for some factory workers who had been receiving good wages and, in the case of the women, allowances for absent husbands. The middle class was ground down and the white-collar workers, too. Everyone outside of official circles wondered how long the revolution would be postponed. "If our government will only help us a little more we shall have revolution very soon," said a French Socialist. "Heaven knows I wish they would strike," I wrote home. "It is enough to make an anarchist out of anybody to see the world in such hands. The calm way they go on carving up Europe without consulting the Russians, Germans, Austrians, Hungarians, etc., is beyond words. No one knows where it will end. The Poles and Czechoslovaks, Italians, and others have about as much idea of making this a better world and ending war as the cows in New Jersey." How we liberals in Paris lamented at that time the atrocious murder of Jean Jaurès! Had he but been alive at that time the whole aspect of the French scene would have been changed.

In this mood of utter discouragement I, too, determined to leave Paris and, if possible, enter Germany. For this I had a personal as well as a professional motive. My father's sister still lived in Munich. She was largely dependent upon the income of a trust fund in New York which was, of course, not transmitted after we entered the war. I knew she could not live upon her tiny pension and was certain that at her advanced age the lack of nourishing food must be very serious for her. My wish to see her again and aid her went on all fours with my desire to view the new Germany stripped of its Kaiser, its autocracy, its feudal army, and apparently well on the road to republican institutions. The difficulty was how to get over the border in view of the Wilson fiat. Meeting Colonel House one day I had the inspiration to ask him if he was aware that the Second Internationale was meeting at Berne and whether he did not think that we should watch what took place there. He agreed and said: "Why don't you go?" I said I would if I could have his aid, for I knew that it would be extremely difficult for me to obtain permission to leave. "Go to my military secretary, Captain Van Santvoord," the Colonel replied, "and give him any letters you wish me to sign."

I went at once, drafted a letter for Colonel House's signature which asked the American Consul General to grant my visa for Switzerland and, on getting it signed, deposited it at the consulate together with my passport. Then the days passed. I had again to appeal to Captain Van Santvoord when it appeared that the army intelligence officers were holding up my visa. Altogether it took all of two and one-half working-days to obtain the American and Swiss visas and the French permission to leave. Finally on the very day that I had to leave for Berne I heard that my passport would be ready in the late afternoon. So far, so good. But the final hurdle, and the most difficult, was still before me. How could I avoid taking the prescribed oath not to enter Germany from Switzerland? For weeks I had racked my brain, consulted a few trusted friends, and especially Lewis S. Gannett whose part time assistance I had obtained on arriving in Paris. He had been in the Quaker war work in Paris and this association was the beginning of his long, most happy, and valuable connection with *The Nation*, and of our enduring friendship.

When the hour came for us to drive to the consulate for the passport he and I were no nearer a solution of our problem than we had been. Not until the taxi stopped at the consulate doors did the way out come to me. It was ridiculously simple. "Go upstairs, please," said I to Gannett, "and tell the official to give you my passport as I am not coming myself, and let us see what happens." Gannett went and I waited in trepidation. Five minutes passed and he appeared triumphantly waving the passport. "No questions asked," he reported gleefully. How the officials failed to demand the oath I have never understood. We dashed back to the Continental to give the news to Simeon Strunsky who was again to be my traveling companion. Armed with a letter from General Smuts, most cordially recommending me to all British officers, a similar one addressed to all Belgian officials by Minister Vandervelde, and one from Captain Van Santvoord, I boarded the night train for Berne, the happiest man in Paris. Thanks to that simple ruse at the consulate there began for me a most remarkable experience.

Chapter XXII. Real Peacemaking—and Then Bloodshed

"THOUGH no Socialist myself, if I had the power to decide on which conference to rest the future of the world I should unhesitatingly, and with real joy, decide for this simple conference with its plain membership," I wrote to *The Nation* on February 7, 1919, after observing the Second Internationale at work in Berne for two days. There were ninety-one delegates and at the sides of the none-too-large room the representatives of the press, who outnumbered the delegates, were crowded together at long tables. Here I found a conference with fullest publicity and real debating, without official domination, with officeholders at a minimum. Nobody in Berne was taking orders and the group met three times a day instead of convening twice in four weeks merely in order to ratify the acts of a handful of men. It was a gathering of victors and vanquished alike. This was the first time, I think, that Frenchmen and Englishmen, Germans, Belgians, Austrians, and Hungarians had met after the war, shaken hands, and sat down together with good will to see what could be done to put the world on its feet again. They were mostly without political responsibility at home and so were sincere, straightforward, and in deadly earnest in their desire to eliminate war and to contribute of their best to the making of a better and wiser world. Here were almost all the elements I had missed at the Quai d'Orsay—a number of women, men who had just doffed their privates' uniforms, and genuine representatives of the proletariat. There was not a lackey, not a uniform, not a decoration, not a title; no formality and no ceremonial. One President of a country was there, Kurt Eisner of Bavaria.

Unfortunately there was no Swiss representation, no one to

speak for the Italian minority group which had so bravely opposed Italy's sale of her sons to the Allies and, of course, no Americans. Indeed, with their usual contemptible muddying of the stream of hope and progress for the peoples everywhere, and their constant attacks upon all real workers for peace, Samuel Gompers and the professed Socialists, William English Walling and Charles Edward Russell had issued a broadside against this gathering in which they outdid themselves in vituperation. But no amount of detraction could conceal the fact that in that one room were many of the most striking and valuable personalities in all Europe. From Germany there were, among others, Edward Bernstein and the gentle Karl Kautsky, so soon to plunge into the task of collecting and editing the German war documents the Socialists found in the archives when they took hold. Among the spectators I met was Professor Friedrich Wilhelm Förster of the University of Munich, then Bavarian Minister to Switzerland, who had been allowed to teach in Munich throughout the war although he continuously declared that he opposed it and publicly said that Germany was wholly in the wrong. Another spectator was Doctor Wilhelm Mühlon, the former Krupp director, whose remarkable revelations as to German pre-war preparations for conquest did so much to arouse public opinion in the United States; with him I passed some delightful hours. There were then great hopes that Doctor Mühlon would play an important role in the new Germany; instead he has remained in private life in Switzerland, while Professor Förster is an exile in France.

But the outstanding German was President Eisner, to whom I was especially drawn because he had done in Bavaria in 1918 what my great-uncle Friedrich had accomplished in the Palatinate in 1848—deposed the King of Bavaria. I had expected to find a fiery revolutionist of the type of Gustav Koerner and the young Carl Schurz. Instead, Eisner was a bald-headed, black-bearded man inclined to stoutness, who looked like nothing so much as an absent-minded German professor of the type so long depicted by *Fliegende Blätter*. He had long been a Social-Democratic journalist, often jailed before the war for his political views, a Munich contributor to the *Frankfurter Zeitung* and later an editor of the *Vorwärts* and a constant frequenter of cafés. Arrested and imprisoned for high treason for urging a general strike in 1918, he was released in September, when he was nominated for a seat in the Reichstag. On the seventh of November he took part in a great popular gathering on the Haasenheide. It passed resolutions and then merely demonstrated before the royal palace. Eisner decided that the time had come to establish a people's republic in Bavaria. He put himself at the head of a small group of friends. As he later described it: "The Wittelsbachs had ruled Bavaria for eight hundred years. With eight men I drove them out in eight hours." This was hardly an exaggeration. That historic royal house fell to pieces at the mere suggestion of a movement against it. There was no defense; the Wittelsbachs fled like hares before the feuilletonist—deserted by their servants, their guards, and those they believed their devoted friends. Eisner took hold of the government, made a sergeant just back from the front his Minister of War, organized a number of returned soldiers, restored order and set up a republican form of government.

The speech that he made at the Second Internationale will always remain with me as one of the most remarkable and the bravest I have ever heard. It not only stamped him as a man of action and of the finest ethical ideals but it probably cost him his life. It was by all odds the most striking and dramatic utterance at the conference. To everyone's astonishment he began his speech, which was on a resolution for the prompt release and return of prisoners of war, with the frankest avowal of German guilt. He said that the resolution called for "protests against the retention of the German and Austrian prisoners," but that he could not protest. If he should essay to do so there would rise before him the memory of what Germans had done in France and Belgium. How could he, a German, protest against the proposals to retain the German prisoners and to compel their help in the rebuilding of the devastated districts when his countrymen had dragged French and Belgian men and women and young girls to enforced labor far from their homes? Germans were now, however, free

Above: KURT EISNER WALKING BETWEEN FRIENDS

Below: THE PLACE OF HIS MURDER THE DAY AFTER

to say these things and he wanted with all his heart to say them. He was willing to appeal for clemency for the German prisoners because, having been in prison himself only lately, he knew how terrible were those last days of waiting before release. He had worked in the prison camps about Munich and he graphically described the scenes he had witnessed while aiding sick prisoners during the dreadful influenza epidemic and declared that, although he had known what it was to face hostile barricades, nothing in his experience was as horrible as what he had seen in the camps. In justice to himself he must say that when the end came he did everything in his power to cut red tape and to expedite the return of the Allied prisoners to France. As for the proposed enforced German labor, he said that if France needed additional help he would favor the voluntary recruiting of German laborers. He was ready to appeal for such an army to German architects, builders, designers, and laborers, if they would be acceptable, to build up where Germans had so wickedly destroyed, and he would be willing to head it. The audience listened spellbound, the German majority Socialists and pressmen obviously downcast at this plain-speaking from a German.

Eisner spoke without the slightest attempt at oratory or histrionics, calmly and sincerely, and it was the braver because his political future was in the balance. Already there was in the offing a strike of officials against him. He did not dare stay in Berne and left the next morning. As he stood and said farewell to friends on the station platform, Strunsky and I watched him. He could not conceal his anxiety. Referring to the coming meeting of the new Landtag, which he had called to assemble and formulate a new government, he said: "In neun Tagen wird's mit mir aus"— "In nine days I shall be finished." His thought, of course, was that when the Landtag met he would be supplanted as President but on the fifteenth day the Angel of Death laid hands upon him.

When Friedrich Adler of Vienna took a seat upon the platform as one of the officials of the conference, a thrill ran through the hall. I found myself repelled as I looked upon the man who in cold blood had murdered Von Stürgkh, the Austrian Premier and tyrant, for I have never found assassins admirable whatever their motives and however just their cause. For years he had sat in his cell awaiting the executioner. As a woman alongside of me remarked: "He would have been dead long ago if Austria had had the courage to carry out the sentence." The pallor of those years of confinement still marked his countenance; the opening of his cell doors by a revolution he could not have foreseen must have seemed to him a miracle out of heaven. There were no other figures as dramatic as Eisner and Adler, but there were plenty in the room of striking distinction. The minute Ramsay MacDonald rose to speak, that rather noisy audience grew absolutely still. It was a tribute he could hardly have failed to notice.

I had looked forward especially to meeting Arthur Henderson at Berne but I was greatly disappointed in him, writing, "it is ridiculous to pretend that he has the material for a Prime Minister in him." As I added that "Ramsay MacDonald is true blue," I probably erred in my judgment of Henderson as well. His solid, sterling qualities were revealed to me in later years as well as the deep affection in which he was held by all members of the Labor Party. But an inspiring figure I never found in him. Mrs. Snowden and Margaret Bondfield graced the British delegation and Stuart Bunning made two admirable speeches while McGurk and Shirkie, pugnacious and determined to obstreperousness, were genuine representatives of British factory workers. They lent color to the scene and so did the French who roared at one another with a violence that was an agreeable relief from the tedious monotony of the double translation of every speech. The rivalry between Pierre Renaudel and Jean Longuet was well in evidence, and so was a professional Alsatian who did not show to the Germans the fine and generous courtesy and good will which distinguished the rest of the Gallic delegation and helped the obvious nervousness of the German delegation at the beginning to disappear rapidly in the sunshine of their friendly reception. All these delegates were living, pulsating human beings and not official automata. Their wellsprings of compassion and human sympathy were intact and not dried up by politics and the possession of temporal power.

Upon the platform near Friedrich Adler sat Branting, the too-voluble presiding officer, and with him Huysmans, the Belgian, whose keen, sensitive face was a joy to watch. Troëlstra, the Dutch leader, a man of obvious ability, stood out in his refinement and culture. In every row there were challenging personalities and among the spectators also. In the audience near the main door sat Rozika Schwimmer, no longer engaged in eager efforts to stop a world war but in her startling new role as Hungarian Minister to Switzerland, the first woman ever to hold a plenipotentiary diplomatic position. Of course there were difficult moments and here Huysmans knew just when to step in with precisely the elucidating word or the exact compromise necessary; a Belgian with deep feelings, he was wholly without bitterness. "It was extraordinary," I noted, "how personal differences were set aside for the sake of the Internationale; under such circumstances it could not fail." The only serious criticism of the conference was that it gave no clarion call to the younger generation. It approved the League of Nations, demanded an international court, the immediate abolition of all armaments and standing armies, and urged that the League should insist upon absolute free trade, free access to all countries, and the international control of all world thoroughfares. Of course, it voted that immigration should not be prohibited "in a general way" and that "workers shall have the right of free combination and association in all countries" and the right to strike. Is it not true that if the Paris Conference had taken this as its platform, and lived up to it, the world today would be sane and normal, happy and prosperous, without a Hitler or a Mussolini, and free from the threat of war?

The conference over, I met for the third or fourth time my good friend Herbert Parsons, the New York lawyer and Congressman, then a lieutenant colonel in the army attached to the Berne Legation. He looked at me quizzically and said: "How's this, Villard? All the other correspondents have been to the Legation to get their visas for their return to Paris. You have not come. I want you to understand [this in a very severe and menacing tone] that there is one thing that happens to anyone who seeks to jump the Swiss border and go into Germany—he has *got* to come and dine with me first!" Kind as he was, I did not dare admit what was my purpose, explaining only that I was going to Zurich to visit my Swiss cousin, Professor Emil Hilgard, before returning. But I gratefully recalled that kindliness when years later I read with great sorrow of the premature death of this fine American citizen because of an injury while maneuvering a bicycle with a motor wheel attached.

I lost no time in setting off for Zurich—Strunsky had already left for Paris radiant in the thought that he would be home in four weeks and taking with him three articles by me for *The Nation* and letters for my family, to be mailed in Paris. We had had comfortable rooms in Berne but they were icy cold and there was hot water only on Saturday, which did not help very much, however, for the bathrooms all had beds in them and were never unrented. Food was cheap but coal extremely scarce; there was one heavy snowstorm. In Zurich at the familiar Baur-au-Lac Hotel, there were all the comforts. I enjoyed there several long talks with Prince Alexander von Hohenlohe, the pacifist son of the former German Chancellor. Greatly relieved by the knowledge that I would not have to write, or be able to mail any articles for several weeks, I went with my cousin to Engelberg where I had established my family for the summer before the war.

I was astounded at the change. It was no longer a tourist resort but looked like a German garrison, filled as it was with hundreds of officers and men in uniform, convalescent from severe wounds or suffering from lung and throat troubles. I felt rather upset at being thrown among them. I still could not look upon that uniform and fail to remember all the misery it had brought upon the world and my feeling was intensified when I read in the newspapers the canard from Paris to the effect that the United States had agreed to maintain an army of 500,000 to be at the call of the League of Nations. For that, if true, would have meant the immediate militarization of the United States. But I was very nearly able to forget the misery of the world in the glory of those superb mountains under their blankets of heavy snow. I wondered why these German prisoners in a neutral country had not long since been sent home. The answer was the usual one, "The Allies will not have it." And so, because of the great humanitarians in Paris, these men were wearing their hearts out despite the beauty of their surroundings, beauty being no palliative for nostalgia.

Back in Zurich I made immediate preparations for my departure across the border. I had a soldier's trunk and I spent hours packing it with soap, thread, coffee, chocolate, crackers, cakes, and other supplies for my aunt. Never did any smuggler work harder than I on this my first plunge into crime—crime because the Allies had forbidden the Swiss to allow any traveler into Germany to take even a package of chocolate to succor the starving Germans. Every pair of my socks contained some useful article. My shoes did not need trees for they were stuffed with thread and soap. Not a shirt found its place until it contained bars of chocolate. My handbags received the same treatment; an innocent-looking soap case contained only spools of thread and needles, for these were especially lacking in Germany. The ulster that I carried on my arm, the overcoat and suit that I wore, had their pockets so stuffed that it seemed as if I must be an object of suspicion on sight.

Thus equipped, I went with my cousin, who throughout his life was very dear to me and all of my family, to the railroad station to check my trunk to Munich. With indescribable trepidation I watched the inspector open the trunk and examine its contents. The tray passed perfectly but my horror can be imagined when the tray was lifted off to expose three fatal coffee beans reposing on the stiff bosom of a dress shirt. "What is this?" said the inspector, looking at me. "Oh, just a little coffee," I replied, "for an invalid relative in Germany." "But that is strictly forbidden by the Allies." "Oh, in *that* case . . ." said I and I put my hand into the trunk and produced a bag of coffee and a bar or two of chocolate. It satisfied him and to my joy the trunk was closed, not to be opened again until I arrived in Munich. I then went to the train with my cousin to whom I had formally given the contraband taken from the trunk. But though he saw me to my coupé I did not dare take back what he offered me—indeed I hastily gave him some of the things in my pockets—to my lasting regret.

The train pulled out and duly arrived at Romanshorn where I was to take the boat for Bavarian soil on the other side of Lake Constance. Here we were all marshaled into a room for inspection of our hand luggage and here my downfall came. The very first bag revealed my guilt. In a loud voice the inspector demanded to know what I was about. In a minute I was surrounded by a gaping crowd and for the first time experienced all the feelings of a detected criminal. A heart-rending pile of coffee, chocolate, and much more grew upon the counter, but even at that a good deal was not discovered. The inspector then demanded my passport and disappeared with it. I stood there under the withering observation of an increasing crowd of travelers and railway employees. It seemed a very long time before the inspector and a gendarme re-appeared. I was publicly denounced and lectured. I gladly bore the public disgrace, however, for they gave me back my passport and told me that their superior officer, after careful consideration, had decided not to arrest me but to allow me to proceed. "Your name will, however, be put on the list of detected smugglers and instructions will be issued to all consular offices never to permit you to enter Switzerland again." I hoped my countenance did not show my gratitude and relief too clearly, gratitude for, among other things, the failure of the officials to search my person and overcoats. As fast as I dared I hastened on board the German steamer alongside the pier, where I fled directly to the men's toilet in fear lest the officials have a change of heart. My joy when I heard the paddle wheels turning and was able to go on deck and see the boat moving out into the lake, I can hardly describe. The road to Germany was clear.

When the steamer finally reached its destination, Lindau, and I again stepped on to German soil, I found everything verified which had been told me about the disorganization of that beaten country. Every vestige of the old discipline and respect for authority had vanished. The train for Munich was a wreck, the cars dirty, with broken windows and torn seats, worn out by their use in troop trains. Everyone fought like mad to get on board without the slightest regard for anybody else. Nobody paid any attention to the red-capped station master or any other official. There was a long wait before the train left, much behind time, and we lost more time all the way to Munich, where we finally arrived after midnight. My trunk had not made the train so I got a porter and started for the hotel recommended to me, not one of the large ones in which I had so often stayed but a sort of Y.M.C.A. hostel, the Baselerhof, diagonally opposite the Landtag building. "You will find," a friend in Berne had said, "that the Baselerhof is the quietest hotel in the quietest street in Munich—and it is very convenient." It was quiet enough in all conscience when I succeeded in gaining admittance. It turned out to be extremely convenient, miraculously so, for right there in that quietest street stark tragedy occurred; but when I arose the next morning all was still peaceful.

In the middle of the morning I was on my way to the railroad station bent upon retrieving my trunk. The large square before the station was strangely confused, many people standing around in excited groups; I had heard suspicious rumblings in the morning from that section of the city. Military patrols were parading ceaselessly to and fro, each comprising an officer and four or five men; here and there on the pavement reddish pools. I dodged between patrols; every door in the station was closed. I pounded on the one marked "baggage." It opened a few inches. "No entrance," said an official who peeped out. My foot was in the aperture. I insisted I must have my trunk. "Then come in quickly." The room was full; the shades of the windows drawn; no one had time or interest for me. A watcher at the window kept peering out under the shade. I waited and waited. Suddenly the lookout cried: "*Alle nieder, es wird geschossen*"—"Everybody down, they are going to shoot." In a minute I alone was standing, lost in astonishment at the celerity with which at least forty able-bodied men had thrown themselves flat on the floor. A surge of purely nationalistic feeling swept over me, the internationalist. A voice within me said in violent protest: "Why, you are an *American*; you *can't* lie down with those Germans." So far as the Germans were concerned nobody cared whether I stood or lay. Minutes passed. No bullets came through the windows; at last word from the lookout: "It's all over."

No trunk for me; no sign of it. I would be lucky, porters said, if I got it in three or four days, if ever, with people shooting up the town. I went back to the square. "What is all this excitement about?" I asked a policeman. "You've not heard?" "I heard some of the firing." "Well, we don't know why, but a train with six hundred sailors came without warning into the station this morning and they tried to take over the city. We beat them back. Some are dead; some still about; the rest have gone." I, too, stood at a corner to see what turned up. Next to me were two returned soldiers still in their torn and dirty field-gray. Soon a patrol came by. "Do you see him?" cried one of the veterans, pointing to a lieutenant. "He was the worst scoundrel of them all." Whereupon he leapt upon the officer, struck him in the face, and knocked him flat. The patrol went after the veterans as they tried to flee. The lieutenant slowly rose to his feet drawing his revolver, blood streaming down his face. He rushed at me and jammed the muzzle of the gun against my neck. "What are you doing here?" "*Amerikanischer Journalist, Herr Leutnant.*" "Then get to hell out of here," said he in the German equivalent. I went back a short distance and found the veterans, badly beaten by the butts of the guns of the patrol, lying on the sidewalk. The offender I helped to his feet when the patrol moved on; his tunic was soaked in blood to the waist. In two minutes I was back at the corner. No more excitement. On the way home I passed the new building of the Bavarian Supreme Court, a member of which my grandfather had been until the end of his career. The stonework was bullet- and shell-chipped, the ornamental figures mutilated. For lunch the hotel gave us incredible coffee which tasted like straw—nothing else. The soup was tepid water slightly flavored; there were some things I could not identify which passed for vegetables; and there was the Ersatz which went by the name of bread. I got up hungrier than when I sat down. Three years of this? Well, it was certainly not for me to complain.

I took the familiar way to my aunt's; I carried a small satchel filled, even without access to my trunk, with smuggled goods. We met with the deepest emotion for she had written me in 1915 that I must never set foot in Germany again else I should be dealt with severely for my disloyalty to my German traditions and ancestry in taking sides with the Allies. But whatever attitude she may have meant to take with me, blood and deepest affection proved stronger than national feuds. The agonizing past, with all its bitter, hateful differences, dropped away as she came, weeping, towards me. . . . I was the same, but she! War, suffering, and undernourishment had taken their toll. This pitifully thin, trembling, almost tottering woman hardly suggested the extraordinarily erect, vigorous, distinguished aristocrat who was my aunt; the one who was always beautifully gowned, always equal to any situation, whose title *Excellenz* seemed not a title but a description. The world she loved and adorned had crashed. She who had known royalty and courts was now like a pitiful child confused. Again and again she asked what it all meant, why this terrible disaster? They had been told for more than three years that victory was assured; why had all the world turned against them? Why had the Kaiser and the kings fled? The very ground seemed sinking beneath her feet. "Why, why, why?" she kept asking me, her nearest of kin.

It was on February 21 that things happened right in front of the quietest hotel in the quietest street in Munich. Upon that day the Landtag, which was to decide the fate of Kurt Eisner, finally met in its building diagonally opposite to the Baselerhof. I presented myself to the guard and demanded admittance. In vain. I must have a pass and the passes had all been issued. I asked to see the official in charge. His astonishment was great. A representative of the American press at this historic opening session of the first democratic Landtag in Bavaria— "Well, really, Mein Herr!" What papers had Mein Herr with which to identify himself? "Here is my American passport; here is my Paris pass admitting me to the Peace Conference as an American correspondent, here my visiting card." "But what is there to show that you are connected with *The Nation?*" I tried to explain a rather intimate connection; apparently it only made matters worse to have me declare that I was both editor and owner. Suddenly the official's face lighted up. Something about the name on my passport attracted him. "Are you by any chance," he asked very earnestly, "the son of Henry Hilgard Villard, the benefactor of the Palatinate?" I replied that I was. He rose to his feet, solemnly shook hands with me, and said: "I used to live in the Palatinate and your father's son can have everything here that it is possible for me to grant. This is your ticket to the journalists' box for the session already under way." I left the room fairly dazed by the extraordinary coincidence that this official should have been one of the few men in Munich still to remember my father's name and deeds; I seemed to feel his spirit watching over me.

The journalists I found in the box in the gallery, directly opposite to and looking down upon the platform upon which the officials sat, were astounded when I appeared. A colleague from America? Why, there were hardly three Americans in all Munich. The correspondent of the *Frankfurter Zeitung,* Doctor Fritz Wahl, kindly pointed out the various dignitaries. That minister on the right was a locksmith's apprentice only a little while ago. Timm, the Minister of Education, on the left was a tailor's son and long a public schoolteacher. Minister Auer, about whose head the storm was particularly raging, had left school at eleven to be a herdsman for eleven years. Yet this was aristocratic Bavaria. Then there was Rosshaupter, to whom the independent Socialists and Communists were as much opposed as to Auer; both were charged with being reactionaries and too kindly to the old order. Several women delegates came in. "Think of that in Bavaria," said my coach, "woman suffrage in hidebound, priest-ridden, old Bavaria. Then there is Professor Quidde, the chief of the Bavarian pacifists, of whose efforts to stop the war you must have heard in America. Now they are all here except Kurt Eisner." A moment later a very young man, as pale as a sheet, walked feebly to the platform. "That," said the voice by my side, "is Fechenbach, Eisner's secretary. What is wrong? Something must have happened to Eisner." At that moment a soldier dashed into our box; calling down to the platform he shouted: "Kurt Eisner is murdered; Kurt Eisner has been shot." And to prove it he held up the bloody eyeglasses of the liberator of Bavaria.

It is almost impossible to describe the scene when the house grasped the import of the news. Ever since I have felt that I could gauge the shock that there must have been in Ford's Theatre when the audience realized that Abraham Lincoln had been shot down. From every part of the house and the gallery came cries of "shame" and of horror. For a few minutes there was utter confusion. The galleries were more vocal than the members of the Landtag. Even the journalists joined in. "Adjourn, adjourn," they cried and then rushed for the telephones. Finally the temporary president called the meeting to order and in a cool, calm voice announced the assassination of the President and declared the meeting adjourned for one hour. The news that the assassin was the young Count Arco-Valley intensified the gravity of the situation. The bitter hatred of Eisner cherished by the middle classes, the aristocrats, and the officials, and carefully fanned by a capitalistic press, had vented itself. More than one of the journalists declared that there would be bloodshed that night and that bolshevism would come to Bavaria.

"I pity the anti-Eisner press tonight," said one, "there will not be a stone left in the building of the *Münchner-Augsburger Zeitung*." "You'd better get away," declared my Frankfurt friend to his wife, "things are going to happen." Here I was betrayed by my New England conscience. Remembering that I had a luncheon engagement with two leaders of the peace and suffrage movement, Anita Augsburger and Lida Heimann, I tried to telephone. The booths were all occupied by frantic newspaper men calling the capitals of Europe. I decided to go across the street to the Baselerhof and cancel the engagement. In five minutes I was back but it was too late—journalist passes were no longer of any avail. I and others stood about disconsolate, but a Viennese correspondent thought we should miss nothing and went off advising us all to stay indoors that night. "Tonight blood will flow." There was no doubt that this dastardly crime by the young aristocrat (never adequately punished for his atrocious act) would bring the impending class war to a head. What next in peaceful Munich?

The answer came quickly enough. An officer dashed out of the Landtag, crying out, "Auer is assassinated, Auer is assassinated—and Osel!" I had missed a most thrilling adventure. What happened Doctor Wahl described later: "You may thank your lucky stars that you were not there. The Landtag had hardly reassembled when a man walked in through a side door, reached the platform, lifted his right arm, and fired point-blank at Auer. An officer dashed at the assassin but was shot down. Then they began shooting from the galleries all around us. Auer is not dead but wounded—like Osel and a clerk. Well, we journalists then crawled out of that box on our hands and knees! I have seen terrible things at the front, and witnessed two attempts to assassinate kings, but I never saw anything like the panic and the terror and the flight and the generally promiscuous shooting."

Never shall I get over my disappointment that I missed that scene. But there was an aftermath that was personal to me. As I stood there watching the Landtag door before the news had been fully verified, a man with a terribly drawn, ashen-gray face, utterly repulsive, walked slowly out of the building. The soldiers gathered around him. I joined the group to hear what he said. My appearance was promptly resented. Said the man, pointing at me, "There's another chap I ought to get." Two soldiers turned, grabbed me, and marched me away. "You had better go home, something might happen to you here." They marched me across the street and turned me adrift near the door of the Baselerhof. The man of the dreadful pallor turned and walked off quietly with four soldiers. As he did so a journalist I had seen in the box rushed over to me and said excitedly: "See that man? He's the fellow who just shot Auer and the others and they are letting him run away!" He was a butcher, Alois Lindner by name, and he was not caught until months later; on December 14 he was sentenced to fourteen years in prison. The officer he had shot down, Major Jahrreis, was dead; he had faced enemy bullets for four years and had just returned to safety and a peaceful existence in his home.

That day I saw how quickly a city can die. By one o'clock business and traffic were paralyzed; street cars stopped running, disappeared as if by magic. The restaurants on the main streets hastily closed and the shops, one and all, pulled down their heavy roll shutters. No one needed to be told that trouble was at hand. In less than three hours the stage was all set for civil war. It was in the air. There was no need to call a general strike. Without consultation with one another the workers laid down their tools. As I went to lunch in the business center I met long processions of workmen, horribly pale, gaunt and lean, and ragged, so overworked, starved, and hungry-looking as to move any heart. Not knowing what my feelings were, many shook their fists at me as they did at every well-dressed man they met, shouting: "We'll get square with the aristocrats who killed our Eisner."

Proclamations came thick and fast; first one from the Council of Workmen, Soldiers, and Peasants declaring a Socialist Republic and announcing that the peoples' revolution was endangered and that a three-day general strike was ordered by the Committee of Eleven which took power. By four o'clock airplanes were flying over the city dropping handbills; bits of white paper proclaiming that everybody must be indoors by seven o'clock; bits of blood-red paper declaring a state of siege; anybody found on the streets after seven o'clock would be arrested. Another proclamation asserted that anybody who stole or pillaged would be shot on sight. Troops were soon moving in every direction; there were no afternoon newspapers; the telephone ceased and the telegraph offices closed. Twenty prominent men of the bourgeoisie and military were seized as hostages and put in an upper story of the Hotel Vierjahreszeiten a block or two away from the Baselerhof. They were notified that if there was another assassination they would all be shot against the nearest wall.

Every newspaper office was soon in the hands of troops. Great placards on some of the offices read: "Comrades! Don't shoot. This building is in the hands of the Council." Every workman over twenty years of age who was a member of a recognized trade-union was armed forthwith. Soldiers raided all the gun shops and entered private houses in search of arms. Great camions and trucks rumbled through the quietest street in Munich carrying arms, food, ammunition, and bundles of straw for the soldiers to sleep upon. The Landtag building became one of the chief fortresses. Other camions, with their exhausts wide open, patrolled the streets with machine guns mounted upon them manned by soldiers wearing trench helmets. The spot where Eisner fell between the Vierjahreszeiten and the Landtag building was speedily heaped with flowers. I found a guard of honor making people obey a sign which read: "Proletarians, hats off before the blood of Kurt Eisner."

All that day and the next women and children came and laid little handfuls of flowers on the sidewalk and every man uncovered. I saw three men roughly handled, beaten until the blood came, for having expressed pleasure at Eisner's death. What infuriated the people was their knowledge that in the clubs, at the university, and in all the well-to-do sections, men and women of property and privilege were saying openly that Eisner ought to have been shot, that he was nothing but a Galician Jew anyway and never a Bavarian. What right had such a man to upset the existing order? There were some who admitted that he was a man of peace and that he meant well, but they insisted that he had released terrible forces which were threatening to engulf all society and destroy civilization itself. But one got everywhere a wonderful feeling that the plain people on the streets had lost something infinitely dear.

There were no laggards when seven o'clock came. Reluctantly I went indoors to my room. It was not long before the machine guns began to speak; the crack of rifles was incessant. Every drop of journalist blood within me rebelled at my being confined. Repeatedly I went to the window fascinated by the spectacle across the street. A corner light shone down on as picturesque a group of soldiers and reserves as ever Detaille painted. But every time I looked out a soldier across the street threw his gun up to his shoulder and cried: "Close that window or I'll shoot," and my

head came in. But I still peeked through the curtain. The flashes
were plainly visible. Civilians came running by for cover. Finally,
in despair, I sat down to my typewriter to record the day's events.
The quietest street in Munich! And not twenty yards away as I
wrote men were being killed by their brothers!

Chapter XXIII. Civil War in Munich and Berlin

"I SHAN'T ever have to reread Carlyle on the French Revolution," I wrote three or four days later, "for I am living through a duplicate of it here. From Aunt E. I know how the aristocrats felt when the guillotine was working. Three nights ago a gang of men tried to break into her apartment house and fired a shot under her windows, escaping before the police came. Her fright is well warranted. There is disorder in every direction, thieving, burglary, murder—the natural result of four years of wholesale plundering and killing known as war. There is only money for two weeks in the treasury and nowhere to get any more; there is no coal, or very little; there are hundreds of thousands of idle men in Bavaria—it is all enough to make your hair stand on end. There will be starvation by May first unless the Allies act. Surely this country is paying for the sins of its rulers and, alas, its new rulers are going to be as brutal and ruthless as the old. I can see nothing ahead but anarchy." This was no exaggerated picture. Bavaria was tottering and headed toward a Soviet government. When I wrote we had been promised a railroad strike in addition to all the others; the Minister of War had offered me an airplane if that occurred and I wished to leave.

One piece of luck I had had at the Landtag meeting; I made the acquaintance of two young women whom I had previously encountered at a women's meeting. They lived in a hotel and their rooms were the rendezvous of several of the ministers and undersecretaries. It was there that I met the Minister of War and received from him the pass that enabled me to be on the streets at night. Even with that, moving about after seven o'clock had its excitements for you could not tell out of which doorway or courtyard a picket would suddenly emerge and grab you, sometimes with quite unnecessary roughness. All night long camions filled with soldiers dashed through the streets and they were not always careful about using their weapons; there were few nights when one did not hear some firing. One night I was out of luck, having forgotten to take my pass with me. A patrol seized me. Fortunately an officer came on the run. "Oh, it's that *Amerikaner*," he said, "let him go." Usually the presentation of my pass and passport won me a military salute and a barrage of questions about the United States and how we felt about Germany and what was going to happen to the world. Sometimes I stayed out most of the night to talk with these men. How they denounced their former officers! Stealing was one of the least offenses they charged against them. It was no wonder that the authorities were mustering out every bit of the old army and were forming a national militia and that no officer of the old regime dared show himself upon the streets in uniform. It made one proud of being an American to hear on all sides nothing but praise of our troops as fair and square and brave fighters and as the kindest and most gentlemanly of the invaders.

On February 25 came Eisner's funeral—a great proletarian outpouring. All the tradesmen closed their shops and the quarters of the well-to-do were entirely bare of men and women; the windows were shuttered. The long procession through the city, the great middle class and laboring class crowds, the masses of flowers, the dirges of the military bands, and above all the wonderful solemnity and dignity of the crowds themselves profoundly impressed me. All through the exercises airplanes flew overhead. In the streets there was an astonishingly small proportion of police and soldiers. My notes tell me that the services at the chapel in the cemetery were without prayer or religious ceremony. Gustav Landauer, one of the radical leaders, pronounced the oration and there were many brief speeches by representatives of some of the delegations which had brought the great wreaths heaped up in huge piles on the chapel floor. Then the coffin was taken to a neighboring building for cremation and Kurt Eisner had passed into history.

Eisner's family, the chief mourners, and the leading officials of the temporary government came and drove away in the royal carriages and motors, the former denuded of their silver trappings and royal crests. I returned in the magnificent motor of the former Bavarian Crown Prince, thanks to the Minister of War to whose use this car was now dedicated. As we left the cemetery we heard the church bells ringing a requiem for the agnostic who had just done the terrible thing of separating Church from State to the special horror of the Catholics, who would doubtless now cheerfully exchange Hitler for Eisner. We talked much about the serious situation of the country. Temporarily Bavaria's Socialist factions had come together, but what of the peasants? Controlled as they were by the Church, would they stand for more radicalism, or oppose it? I found the War Minister quite depressed. It was at this time that I met Ernst Toller, an eager, passionate youth, outstanding in his desire to build the perfect State in Bavaria, refusing at first to be stampeded by the Communists but later joining them.

Again I was in the journalists' box in the Landtag building, and this time I learned how it feels to be held up at the point of a revolver and stand with your arms upraised until you think that you cannot hold them up another second. This happened at a meeting of the Councils Congress, composed of delegates from the Soldiers', Workmen's, and Peasants' Councils, called together to reconstitute the dispersed Landtag. Suddenly there came into the hall on a level with the dais a group of armed men in uniform yelling, *"Haende hoch!"* Some of these invading gentry had a revolver in each hand and, as everybody recalled the tragic events in this same room a few days before, there were cries from all over the house: "Don't shoot!" For two or three minutes I again refused to conform by raising my hands. But when I was singled out by one of the men who pointed his gun straight at me and was ordered to put up my hands, I meekly complied. Doctor Levien and Kurt Muehsam, the two chief radicals, were seized at once by this group of reactionary noncommissioned officers, Levien being beaten before us all. Then he and Muehsam were taken out of the room. For twenty minutes his captors held revolvers at Levien's breast and forehead and told him to prepare for his end. He kept his nerve perfectly and played the role of Marc Antony so successfully that before he was reached by a committee of rescue from the Landtag he had been freed by his guards, who actually then pointed their revolvers at their own leader. With his head bound up and one hand badly swollen, Levien was cheered and applauded as he and Muehsam re-entered. "But, gentlemen," he said very earnestly, "one does not applaud a man who has just been beaten as I have been beaten. I hope we shall now go on with the order of the day." It was a magnificent exhibition of coolness and calmness and I recorded the fact that he could have proclaimed himself dictator of Bavaria that night had he so chosen.

Calling upon a young physician that evening I found Doctor Levien there, being treated, and got his story from him—the first real Bolshevist I had seen at close range. With his stained bandages he looked like a pirate chief, especially as he wore high Russian boots and a torn and tattered uniform which he had worn at the front with the German army. He was coarse and unattractive but his great power was evident. "Levien," I wrote, "was educated at two universities, has his Kant and Hegel at his fingers' ends, is master of three languages and three German dialects at least, and has a splendid library (his sole possession) in Switzerland, where he was studying when the war began." "Why do you not make yourself dictator?" one of those present in the physician's room asked Levien. "I should need four strong men to see me through," he replied, "and they are not to be had." He put his finger on the sore spot. Here, as in Berlin, there were no outstanding leaders of genuine personality.

In this, as in every other group I entered, one heard the bitterest denunciation of the press, which was held directly responsible for the murder of Eisner because of its misrepresentation, yes, deliberate falsification, of his Berne speeches. The temporary government set out to curb the press at once. For some days nothing appeared except a newspaper edited by the Council which stepped in when Eisner was murdered. It was planned to allow the press to reappear after a time but to curb it by official censorship, by establishing a state monopoly of advertising, and by compelling the press to print advertising at cost so as to remove all possibility of private profit in journalism. I noted then how similar were the world's problems: "When I left New York the radicals there found in the capitalistic press their real enemy. Good liberals, not extremists, in London filled my ears with indictments of the rich and powerful press of England; the same complaint, but little altered, is the special grief of the French radicals."

One morning I spent at the food bureau and became convinced that if the people of the United States knew what the figures showed—that there would be absolutely no food in Bavaria in three months' time—they would demand a cessation of the blockade. I was shown the ration for twenty-four hours and decided that it would not keep a chicken alive. Naturally everybody had to get more by hook or by crook. I was shocked by the wan and sickly faces one saw whenever there was a queue at the butcher's or provision stores or at a tobacconist's! Indeed, signs of despair, disintegration, and hunger were visible on every side. One morning at six I accompanied my aunt's cook to the market place in order to see just what the housewives of Munich could purchase there—it was necessary to go early because there was nothing left by seven. What I saw was beyond belief. There was practically no fruit and, of course, no potatoes. The women fought over things called vegetables but I could not identify a single one; they looked like roots out of a forest and bore no resemblance to anything I had ever seen that passed for food. In some of the restaurants one could get a fair meal if one had the price; they seemed to have underground connections with farmers. A chief occupation in all the cities at this time was going out into the country by train, by bicycle, by horse, or afoot, and hunting for food. Naturally the farmers held out for high prices but their lot was not a happy one. The invaders from the cities were worse than a horde of locusts; it often happened that the farmers had to arm themselves or they would have been stripped of everything.

Day by day my anxiety over this food situation grew and I was earnestly besought by an old friend, Frau Elisabeth Graul, who had come from Frankfurt to be with me, to do something about it, at least to notify the American delegation in Paris just how grave the situation was. It was a bad dilemma for me. If I revealed the fact that I was in Germany, it might have very serious consequences for me; on the other hand, every humanitarian instinct within me urged me to act. Finally I did so, telegraphing both to Colonel House and Herbert Hoover. I told them just how dangerous the conditions were and put on paper almost the only noteworthy prophecy I ever penned—that if food were not put into Munich there would be bolshevism there by the middle of April —it was on the 8th of that month that the Soviet government seceded from the Reich and held out for three weeks. Meanwhile I had the fortune to meet the famous General Von Hoffmann who was then hiding under an assumed name in a small hotel in Munich, not daring to show his head upon the streets. Had I told my friends of the revolutionary government about his presence I think he would have been arrested instantly. He was the author, or co-author, of the infamous treaty of Brest-Litovsk which had aroused such bitter feelings all over the world. In discussing the treaty with me he warmly defended it and declared that it was the only thing to do. I could not impress upon him the damage that it had done to the German cause throughout the world; like so many other prominent Germans he was either unable to evaluate what the loss of favorable public opinion abroad meant or he felt that Germany was in the mire so badly that a little bit more cursing did not matter. I tried to see him again but he had been smuggled out of town, for which I was very sorry. There are many people in Germany who believe that it was Hoffmann who furnished all the brains for Ludendorff and Hindenburg and won their Russian battles for them. His book, *The War of Lost Opportunities*,[1] is little known in America, but it is one of the most

[1] New York, 1925.

valuable contributions to the history of the struggle and shows clearly how the stupidity and shortsightedness of the higher-ups in the military hierarchy repeatedly threw victory away.

I also ran across the only American officials in Munich, Doctor Haviland H. Field, who was there as the representative of the American Peace Commission, and a young lieutenant I met on the street, who turned out to be the military courier for Doctor Field. The latter, an eminent biologist, had lived for years in Switzerland and was, therefore, thoroughly conversant with European affairs but his nerves appeared badly shattered by the happenings in Munich. Residing as he did, in the Vierjahreszeiten on the same floor with the twenty or more hostages imprisoned there after the shooting of Eisner, he was mortally afraid lest some other crime bring a mob storming into the hotel. "Just think how terrible it would be," he said, "if in raiding the hotel to get at those generals and aristocrats the mob should accidentally kill me. It would dreadfully inflame the relations between the United States and Germany." I ventured to suggest that he might move around the corner into the Baselerhof or into a suburb, as some Germans were urging him to do, but without result. A few days later he telephoned me and asked me to come to see him. He was then definitely of the opinion that he must leave at once lest there be a grave international incident and he asked me, since I was going to Berlin anyhow, if I would accept a commission to represent him on a tour of investigation into food conditions which he was to have made. I agreed to go to Weimar and Dresden on my way to Berlin and Doctor Field provided me with an official letter with instructions what to do and where to report and he duly notified the authorities in Dresden of my coming. For all of this I was extremely grateful to him since it gave me a sort of semi-official status and might, I thought, be useful in mitigating the punishment which I was certain awaited me on my return to Paris for my deliberate violation of the President's orders forbidding American pressmen to enter Germany.

My journey from Munich to Weimar instead of taking seven hours lasted for twenty-four, four of which I spent sleeping on

chairs in the station restaurant at Jena. The railway system was
shot to pieces. As on the trip from Lindau, the coaches were battered and dirty and in Munich there was the same crowding into
the cars to get seats. The aisles were jammed by people standing
or sitting on their luggage. There was, of course, no pretense of
keeping to a schedule. But, long as the trip was, there was never
a moment when it was not of profound interest. What more
astonishing piece of luck could I as a journalist have had than to
find late that night that one of my fellow-travelers had been an
officer of the guard on the train which took Lenin across Germany
and into Russia when he was set loose to begin his contribution to
world history? From this young man I got at firsthand the whole
story of the way Lenin and others were penned up in a car like
wild animals and never permitted to leave, and how the officers
and men were sworn to secrecy. No one was allowed to know who
was in the car or what the whole move signified. Even more thrilling were the conversations around me that went on all day and to
which for hours I was a silent listener. The minute the train left
the station in Munich the debates began. Why had Germany been
beaten? Was it true that the German army had misbehaved in
France and Belgium? How guilty was the Kaiser? Everybody was
a stranger to everybody else but that made no difference. No one
held back. Others crowded into the coupé to listen or take part
in the debate.

The most striking figure was a man who told us that he was a
peasant leader, a rather distinguished one I afterwards learned,
a man of deep religious feeling. It was he who wanted to know
why it was that the churches of the world had failed so completely. Why had the German churches blessed the war and told
them it was righteous and fine to kill their enemies when the
churches in France and England and Italy and the United States
had done the same thing? How could anyone respect churches that
behaved this way? How could any intelligent man believe that
God approved of the action and policy of these various national
churches? As for himself he was perfectly certain that, if war
came again and the churches repeated their actions, religion was

doomed. He would never again take part in a war no matter what or how occasioned, he who had done so much to rouse his people to the support of their government during the struggle just ended. For him the only way out was complete pacifism and disarmament. There was no disagreement. Then I spoke up and asked if an American might say amen. The astonishment was almost ludicrous. An American in Germany—in that train? They could hardly believe it, and when they found out that I was a journalist without hate, save for the war and the governments that brought it on, a torrent of questions poured over me which it took hours to answer. They ceased only as one by one my fellow-travelers got out, leaving me the opportunity to hear the lieutenant's story of his part in a great historic episode which the German government had as much cause to regret as any other incident in the whole struggle.

Weimar was jammed with soldiers, hundreds of troops brought from Berlin, together with many Berlin policemen—you could not enter the town or buy a ticket for Weimar at any station in Germany without showing an official *laissez-passer*. I had already ascertained that there was not much interest in Germany in the National Constitutional Assembly which was drawing up the constitution destined to be finally destroyed by an ex-house painter then doubtless still in his lance corporal's uniform. The Assembly was like the Paris Peace Conference in that its proceedings were much too long drawn out; it often proceeded as if it could discuss every proposal *ad infinitum*, just as if Germany were not on the edge of chaos and ruin and actually fighting the Spartacan movement to bolshevize the country. There was, of course, much unreason in some of the criticisms. The long-drawn-out negotiations in Paris made people feel that they were in the position of a criminal awaiting sentence and that there was no use planning for the future until the sentence was pronounced. The radicals were, of course, bitter that the Weimar convention had not proclaimed a Soviet Republic or at least socialized all German industries, as if that were possible. But I found some real reasons for criticism and discovered that the faults of the Assembly were largely the faults of the Ebert-Scheidemann government. I was amazed at the number of old men present, or of men more or less closely connected with the old regime, like the notorious Doctor Bernhard Dernburg, Count Posadowsky-Wehner, Doctor David, and others. I thought the *Journal de Genève* was not far wrong when it described the Assembly as "a sister of the defunct Reichstag," though I could not go so far as to agree that President Ebert was using "precisely the language of Wilhelm." Certainly the Assembly made no impression of vigor and force upon a casual observer like myself. I wrote that it was curious to hear in that Assembly "the old stories of terrible outrages upon women and children bobbing up again upon this side of the line from this new field of war [Poland]. The enemy always makes it his special business to outrage women and butcher children—no matter who the enemy is."

At Dresden I was received at the station by a group of officials who bowed low before me as if I really represented the destructive Big Four in Paris. They put me into one of the three automobiles of which Dresden then boasted and took me to the food bureau where I was again shown the official ration for a day—eight or nine unidentifiable morsels supposed to be food, which anybody could have swallowed at one gulp. Together they did not cover more than half the palm of one hand and on this a human being was supposed to exist for twenty-four hours. Not one pound of meat was distributed in Dresden during that week. Of course the people made getting other food their chief concern. They bought, bribed, and stole. Anyone whose second cousin's brother owned a farm some twenty-five miles away counted himself one of the most fortunate of men. The food officials knew this yet strove sincerely to make the people live upon nothing. They were an earnest set of men, borne down by the weight of their responsibility and actually unable to see anything ahead but the collapse of society if food did not come in soon. They told me that the returned soldiers felt the lack of food most for they had been well fed before the armistice.

The soldiers I saw on the streets there and in Berlin were mostly pale, weak boys who had not been to the front. In the hospitals in Dresden, as later in Berlin, I found many children with the swollen limbs and bellies of famine sufferers. Children six and seven years of age were the size of normal children of four or five and I was told that most births were of ten months' babies. One workman I met had lost two children from tuberculosis, from which his wife was then dying.[2] The effect of the undernourishment was most severe upon the middle class and especially the great group of small officials. Those I talked with told me of their utterly desperate condition; some of them were getting much less than tram drivers who were receiving more pay than a captain in the army. They all admitted the charge made by their superiors that there was a marked loss in their mental efficiency and alertness. A typist in the Dresden Foreign Office told me that she was appalled by her own inability to do a day's work, and a few days later a distinguished Berlin physician, who formerly worked all day and devoted his evenings to research, told me that he had to rest every afternoon for two hours because of exhaustion and that he was unable even to read at night. At the moment there was no fighting in the city—the War Minister had been assassinated some days before. Later things got much worse. As the officials drove me around Dresden it was hard to recognize that lovely old city, for it was shabby, dull, listless, half dead; the theatres mostly closed, the hotels, if open, almost empty, and it was hard to grasp the fact that the royal palaces were destitute of royalty.

Thanks to my "official" status I had a comfortable seat and much saluting from the conductor on my journey to Berlin. When I came out of the Potsdamer Bahnhof into the familiar Berlin streets, into a city afflicted simultaneously with a general strike and a civil war, I thought some holiday was being observed. The

[2] "The Allied and associated governments during the armistice killed hundreds of thousands of German noncombatants in cold blood, after victory had been won and assured to them." Count von Brockdorff-Rantzau's speech before the Peace Conference at the presentation of the peace treaty to the German delegation, May 7, 1919. "We are enforcing the blockade with rigor. . . . This weapon of starvation falls mainly upon the women and children, upon the old, the weak, the poor, after all the fighting has stopped." Winston Churchill in the House of Commons, March 3, 1919.

crowds on the streets were enormous, partly because the underground and the trams were not running. But everybody seemed to be on the go and the pressing into service of all possible vehicles as jitneys added to the holiday aspect. So did the innumerable fakirs and peddlers, mostly returned soldiers seeking to keep body and soul together. At the Leipzigerplatz the crush was worse and there camions, with their machine-gun crews wearing trench helmets, gave the first warnings that civil war was raging—camions with startling skull-and-bones insignia painted on them. It was difficult to recognize the city it was so shabby; apparently the stucco buildings had not been repaired or painted during the war. The public buildings and walls were covered with bills and proclamations, appeals to the electorate, and warnings against bolshevism. One of the latter represented a woman dancing with a skeleton and underneath was the line: "Berlin, do you not see that it is death that is your partner?" The neatest city in the world had dirty streets and many of them were torn up. The people as a whole looked clean but seedy.

As in Munich, I noticed that one of the greatest causes of suffering was the lack of soap, which made it impossible to keep clean or do much washing, and this the German women felt keenly for they have always been a clean people. "People," I wrote, "are obliged to wash the children with potash water and their skins suffer—but the Allies apparently think that giving the Germans soap and letting the German fishing fleet put to sea will adversely affect the settlement, or the League of Nations, or the boundaries of Jerusalem, or prevent them taking the place of the Lord as the dispenser of vengeance." It was no wonder that the people were in a state of nervous exhaustion. It was no wonder that all Berlin also was dancing-mad. Noske, the brutal Minister of War, made the mistake of forbidding dancing instead of being thankful for this emotional outlet. The concerts were crowded and so were the theatres. The complete uncertainty of the future, so many told me, made people determined to enjoy themselves until the crash came and this was particularly true of those who had just come back out of the jaws of death. Of course there was great moral relaxation. Just as all the moral laws were off in every country for soldiers returning from the front on leave, so now in the face of what seemed anarchy no one felt the slightest obligation to walk a straight and narrow path. It was also a normal reaction from the endless regulation of officialdom. I was told that during the war the various government bureaus had issued 30,000 orders or regulations, the violations of which were punishable by fine and imprisonment, so many that the effort to enforce them speedily broke down; no one could possibly keep himself informed as to what he might or might not do.

In the center of Berlin there was little evidence of the fighting going on yet in the neighborhood of the Leipzigerplatz there were killings, as when a car containing four officers came slowly around the corner near the Esplanade Hotel. Men sprang upon the running board and, before the officers could move, killed every one of them and made good their escape. But it was in the Lichtenberg district that the heaviest fighting was going on with field guns and mine throwers at work, too far away, however, to be heard in the Adlon Hotel and on Unter den Linden. For days the battle waged about the police headquarters and the general post office. Just before I left New York I had heard a good, kindly, Christian woman of high social standing, a pillar of her church, expressing her deep regret that the Armistice had come before a lot of German women and children had been killed by our American troops. She would have been satisfied had she been in Berlin then for women and children were dying in sufficient numbers if not at the hands of Americans. On March 12, they were still firing shells down one of the principal streets. That had been going on so long that people were not only accustomed to it but stood on the street corners to hear the shells go by. One of the latter turned out to be defective and exploded in a group of peaceful onlookers. Thirty went to the morgue or hospitals. An airman killed and wounded fifty persons of both sexes by bombing them, although they were merely idlers standing in front of some wrecked houses.

Still casual pedestrians and housewives with market baskets on their arms would stop to watch the fighting. Fear did not even temper the curiosity of the children. One day an insurgent leaned out of a window right over my head and took a quick shot at a sentry in the middle of the street. Nobody ran; on the contrary everybody stopped to see what would happen next and three little children were extremely vexed when told to run along and not to come back. Shots cracked about us constantly. Yet remarkably few people were hit despite the numbers in the streets. Of course I jumped at first when guns went off but it was plainly very bad form. You were supposed not to stop and look back and it was extremely poor taste to watch the roofs for snipers. So it has not been hard for me to understand how life went on during the bombardment of Madrid. In Berlin people certainly had a fatalistic attitude or were so deadened by four years of war and suffering and undernourishment as to have lost the capacity to care very much. If you spoke to them they said it was *schrecklich* and *entsetzlich* and then went their way, ready, whatever the risk, to stop and gaze anew at the wrecked houses, the smashed windows, the great battered department stores, from which millions of marks' worth of goods had been plundered, and the shell scars everywhere. Even when I left the fighting was going on. On my last day in Berlin I made a final effort to get a mass of mail that had accumulated for me at the general post office. I succeeded in stooping and dodging to within less than a block of my destination but I could not get any nearer and was assured that if I did reach the post office I would find it in a complete state of disorganization and chaos.

In the Kurfuerstendamm section of the city I found that part of the familiar street in which I had spent two such happy years as a boy was closed off by barbed wire entanglements and sentries with machine guns. One day four soldiers were killed here. As I crossed the canal at the head of the street I shuddered at the thought that it was near there that Karl Liebknecht and Rosa Luxemburg were thrown into the waters of that sluggish stream and drowned—a deed that explains many assassinations of officers of the old army, for the murderers of these two popular leaders were former officers. I still think that it was a stupid and short-sighted crime, to say nothing else about it, for those were two extremely fine spirits, whatever their political views, who would, I believe, have exercised an ameliorating power had they but survived.

As in Munich, going about in this quarter at night was serious business. Indeed the one time that I really felt alarmed for my safety was when I left a house in which I had spent an evening going over the military situation on the Polish frontier with a group of young officers charged with planning the German defense. My companion when I left was also a nephew, on her husband's side, of my Munich aunt. Colonel Rolf von Xylander and I had been lifelong friends, both having been in school in Berlin at the same time. He had resumed the wearing of his peace-time Bavarian uniform and I noticed that as we walked away he went close to the street edge of the sidewalk and that he kept a sharp eye upon the entrances to the houses which we passed. While I admired his courage in sticking to that uniform I heartily wished that he had preferred civilian clothes for the old uniforms were often incitement to murder on sight. We got safely out of the dangerous district, not, however, without being frequently challenged by sentries. The Colonel, who was the captor of Lille in 1914, has not changed his views about the desirability of a nation putting all its faith in its armed forces and is now a happy lecturer at the Berlin War College under the regime of Lance Corporal Adolf Hitler.

I had taken up my residence at the Fuerstenhof in order to be in a quiet hotel and to avoid the Allied and American officials at the Adlon. It wasn't always so quiet; the hotel was searched nights on several occasions and when you opened the door, in response to violent pounding, the soldiers came in with a rush and woe to you if you could not produce the proper papers instanter. But curiosity quickly overcame me and I wandered into the Adlon. The very first person I met was a gentleman I did not wish to meet, Count Von Bernstorff, because of my deep feeling about the role the ex-ambassador to the United States had played.

To my surprise the Count did not seem astonished by my appearance. "Oh," he said, "I knew you were here in Germany for I have been reading your dispatches about the food conditions in Bavaria." "My dispatches," I said, "why, I haven't tried to send any dispatches." "Well," said he, "our wireless station picks up every night the dispatches from the Peace Conference to the American press and a few of us get copies the next morning. I will send you the dispatches attributed to you telling of the bad food conditions in Munich." At first I did not know what to make of it; then I realized that he had told me a very welcome piece of news—that Hoover and House had given my dispatches to them to the correspondents for transmission to the United States; that I had helped them in the efforts they were making to get food into Germany.

Thanks in part to Count von Bernstorff and to others, I speedily got into touch with high officials who were most eager to talk with me as soon as they heard that I had been in Paris. The first question was invariably: "Is the treaty going to be as bad as the reports say and are we not going to be allowed to discuss it in any way?" I especially enjoyed my meetings with the Foreign Minister, Count von Brockdorff-Rantzau, with Max Warburg, with various officials of the Foreign Office and of the Deutsche Bank. Both Von Brockdorff-Rantzau and Max Warburg were having to decide whether they should go to Versailles and sign the treaty for Germany. Both declined. They asked me what policies they and their country should follow. I reminded them that our respective countries were still technically in a state of war and that therefore I could not advise them. I did say, however, that if I were a resident of Mars and victorious forces from a neighboring planet demanded that I sign a humiliating treaty depriving my country of territorial possessions I should absolutely refuse.

The difficulty was that all the German officials then and for several years after were too timid and fearful of what the Allies might do to them to take any strong stand. They were afraid that if Germany did not sign the treaty the Allies would march in and occupy all of the cities. I pointed out to them that the armies would disintegrate, reminded them of the mutinous conduct of the troops in England of which they had read, and assured them that the last thing the Allies wished to do was to keep large forces in Germany even if they could get men to stay there. Unfortunately the government of the republic then and later lacked the daring and the nerve of Adolf Hitler and resigned themselves finally to signing the treaty which made the downfall of the republic possible and insured the rise of Hitler. No government should have fallen so low as to sign the false statement that its country was solely responsible for the war and so give to its domestic enemies the argument that it had had no regard for the good name and honor of its people.

Among many old friends I looked up Frau Theodor Barth, the widow of the editor of the Berlin *Nation*, and a distinguished member of the Reichstag, and found her but a shadow of her former self, for she nearly killed herself by trying to live only on the government ration and so fell off to ninety pounds. One of her sons had been killed at the age of nineteen; the other had been a prisoner for three and a half years and was destined not to be released for many more months. Everywhere one ran into similar stories and here, too, fear of the future, fear of starvation and absolute destitution, dominated. The great capitalists and leading business men were mostly in hiding. Ludendorff had fled, Von Hindenburg was in retirement. The government had its hands so full in trying to keep peace and order that it did not act as quickly as it should have in dealing with the reactionaries and the men who had brought about the downfall of Germany. I did not then and do not now advocate the bloody ruthlessness of dictators, but it is a fact that Socialist governments have failed in various portions of Europe because they were not thorough in cleaning house. Every one of the old German generals should have been banished. No officer above the rank of captain should have been allowed to remain in the government's service and later on the officers who were concerned in the Kapp Putsch should have been rigorously dealt with and so should Hitler, of course, after his abortive Putsch of 1923. So with the socialization of Germany. With in-

MRS. MURIEL MAC SWEENEY, THE AUTHOR, AND
MISS MAC SWEENEY

credible procrastination the republic appointed a couple of committees to discuss and plan for socialization and put some of the Big Business men upon those commissions. The natural result was that socialization never came to pass and that the power of the business potentates was never broken.

But in March, 1919, there was much to explain the government's shortcomings. The Socialist leaders whom I met were obviously inexperienced in government; they had had parliamentary but little administrative training and had none of the extraordinary courage and power, not to say genius, of Lenin. It has been easy for Hitler and Goebbels and German Big Business to abuse the founders of the German republic. We must not forget that when the crash came those wicked, red Socialists alone were ready to step in, to pick up the pieces, and to hold Germany together—whence all but they had fled. Had they not done so there would have been chaos and anarchy in Germany and we and the Allies should have had to march to Berlin.

Chapter XXIV. The Collapse at Paris

HOW to get back to Paris from Berlin troubled me not a little. There were reasons why a return through the American occupied territory might not prove pleasant so I decided to try to go via Brussels and was successful in obtaining a German outgoing visa and also a Belgian one. To my satisfaction I found no difficulty in getting over the Belgian border.[1] Having some time to wait at the border station for the connection for Louvain and Brussels I made a rush to the nearest restaurant. I was ravenous for real food and felt like a king when I sat down to an omelette, real butter, real bread, and delicious cheese. I could hardly stop eating to talk to some men of the New York 165th Regiment, the old 69th, Irish, organization, who seemed to be there without any especial reason or destination. Even when I reached Brussels my hunger had not been alleviated. I bought a package of chocolate as soon as I left the train and wolfed it all down; in the comparatively brief period of my sojourn in Germany I had lost fifteen pounds. Yet, as I noted at the time, I had had a good deal to eat in Germany, far more than the average German; it did not satisfy or nourish.

At Brussels I immediately reported to Brand Whitlock, happy to shake hands again with one who had done so much for American prestige, with one of our diplomats who had distinguished himself and proved his entire fitness for his task. I told him I had come to surrender myself because of my entering Germany

[1] On the train from Berlin I met two former German officers going home for the first time since the armistice, one a law official of Cologne. The other denounced the severity of the rule of one of the Allied armies in garrison on German soil. The official replied: "We have no right to complain. They are only giving us a dose of our own medicine that we gave the Belgians and the French. I, for one, propose to stand it like a man with teeth clenched, knowing that we have no right to protest."

without permission. He laughed most pleasantly and said: "I'll have a visa for you for Paris from our consul in no time. I'll give you a letter and a courier to the French Consul and if you wish you can be on your way tomorrow." Then he asked me where I was staying. I said: "The Palace Hotel." He raised his eyebrows and whistled. "Pretty bad, isn't it?" "I've never seen anything like it," I replied, referring to the prostitutes who filled every chair in the reception hall and parlors and were most eager to welcome every arrival. They had been living with German officers and had now transferred their allegiance.

"Well," said Whitlock, "the conditions are so shocking, so bad for all the young officers who are coming in here, that I called a meeting of the Council of Ambassadors to see if we could not clean up the hotel. We made fine progress until we reached the Spanish Ambassador. He gave his views promptly: 'My royal master, the King of Spain, is the chief stockholder in the hotel. We do not want conditions changed. We think they are good for business.' The meeting collapsed then and there." "The joke of it is," Whitlock added, "that Cardinal Mercier is staying there!" When I met Hugh Gibson in Paris a few days later (at this writing he is again Ambassador to Belgium), he, too, asked: "Where did you stay in Brussels?" "The Palace." "Rather awful, isn't it? You know," he continued, "what I am going to do? I've got to go back to Brussels in a couple of days. Before I leave I am going to buy me a pair of girl's shoes and I'll put them outside my door at night with my boots. That'll be the only thing that will keep those harpies from breaking down the door and coming into my room!"

I went at once to the French Consul in considerable trepidation and found on the sidewalk a long queue of people, some of whom had been trying for days to get permission to enter France. But the visa official belonged to the two-hours-for-lunch club and had to have afternoon tea also and closed his office at five. I felt that I richly deserved the cries of protest which arose when the courier put me at the head of the line just outside the street door. I finally reached the official's desk just as he was quitting in no pleasant mood. I felt sure that I would get into trouble again if he read my passport and saw that I was the German-born son of a German-born father and noticed from the German stamp that I had come direct from Berlin. So with a profuse apology for delaying him I did a sleight of hand and laid a blank page of the passport open before him. Still grumbling, he read Brand Whitlock's letter and then, without examining the passport, stamped it where I held it open and let me go. My return to Paris the next morning was assured.

When I got back to the Palace the five o'clock tea dance was on. I went in—still hungry—and found the only vacant seat, at a table next to a buxom but extremely handsome Belgian woman who was the perfect type of a German blue-eyed, flaxen-haired blonde. Dressed in deep, but most becoming, mourning, she asked me if I was English. When she heard that I had just come out of Germany she was agog with excitement and, with a woman friend who was with her, asked innumerable questions as to German conditions, but not out of vindictiveness. She explained her mourning by saying that her only brother had been killed but two or three days before the Armistice; her husband, a Belgian captain, had fortunately come through unscathed. Despite her loss, she had only sympathy for the German women—unlike my New York friend. They were not to blame for the war, she said, and after all that she had been through she knew what they had had to endure. When the dance ended she asked if I would not accompany her to her home to meet her husband. He was especially interested in the United States and, in addition, all the officers were most eager to hear what was happening in Germany.

Of course I acquiesced. Her friend left us at the door of the apartment house. The captain, much smaller than his wife, greeted me most cordially and proved the correctness of his wife's statement by asking me one question after the other, especially about economic conditions in the United States; I got the impression that he was considering immigration. Finally, he excused himself on the ground that he had military duty, buckled on his sword, bowed, saluted, and left. He could not have gotten out of the house before Madame turned to me and told me without palavering that her husband was always on duty with his company mornings and that she would be happy to share her bed with me at ten o'clock the next morning. Never in my life have I been more astounded. She had seemed, if only by contrast to the low-grade prostitutes of the Palace, the embodiment of refinement and good breeding. Not the slightest suspicion had entered my mind; not one word that she had said had prepared me. When I got my breath, I assured her of my appreciation of the honor she had done me but as my train left at 7:30 the next morning I should have to depart then. Her exquisite complexion turned fiery red. "There are other trains to Paris, in plenty," said she. I explained that I had been in Germany in an official capacity and must report promptly to Paris. Inside of two minutes I was ushered out of the apartment; her rage was barely controlled.

Nobody broke into my room that night and I successfully made the early train, again without the slightest examination of my luggage. I stopped at Lille where the pleasant head of our Red Cross kindly put his Ford car at my disposal to take me all the way to Paris via Amiens, passing over many battlefields, the first that I had seen. Lille itself was so severely battered that I should have been deeply affected by it if I had not spent a night at Louvain on my way to Brussels. The sight of Louvain and of its striking memorial to victims of the sadism and utter brutality of the German general who ordered the shooting of so many innocent citizens as a "reprisal," and in order to "encourage the others" not to snipe at the German troops, filled me with a horror and indignation that were still with me when I reached Paris. That was the finest flowering of militarism. Unfortunately, Louvain was but one of many examples yet by no means all of the wrongdoing was on one side. But if I needed anything to prove to me that there never is and never can be a good war, Louvain sufficed. Unhappily, the new Germany is not only without contrition for such acts but is being taught by its latest false gods that ruthlessness and purgings and mass murders are the highest aspirations a race of Aryans can possibly have.

When I arrived in Paris I still was in doubt as to what my reception would be and for two days stuck pretty close to the Continental, writing article after article and long letters home. Then I ventured forth and attended the regular morning newspaper hour with the lesser American Peace Commissioners. Here a great surprise awaited me. I was late and Secretary Lansing was already answering questions. The minute he saw me he exclaimed: "Oh, you're back? I want to see you at once." In two minutes more he asked the correspondents to excuse him unless there was something important on their minds as "Mr. Villard has just returned from Germany." He took me into his office, broke several engagements, and cross-examined me at great length. I asked him if he did not think I should lay my observations before the President. "Most assuredly," he replied. I asked him if he would not help me to get to the President. He hesitated for one moment and then said: "I cannot. I have not seen him myself for more than two weeks. I cannot get to him nor can my associates, except Colonel House." He then unburdened himself as to the utterly erroneous treaty making. As he has since written, he declared that there was no teamwork, no concerted action, no program and no common counsel within the American delegation.

Taking out a bunch of keys he unlocked a desk drawer, drew out a diary with a lock upon it, unlocked it, and then read to me excerpts from the diary written a couple of months before the Armistice in which he had set forth his ideas of the dangers the treaty makers would face. It was an amazing forecast, coupled with a statesmanlike recital of how the beaten foe should be treated. It raised him in my opinion and I am still in hopes that this intimate diary will be published to help redeem his reputation from the recent tarnishing in the revelations of his eagerness to put us into the war for business reasons while ever pretending to keep the scales of neutrality even. Of this we knew nothing in 1919; I can still recall the thrill I received from his reading of his prevision of what should be done after the cessation of hostilities. When he ended our conversation he said: "Please go at once to Mr. White and General Bliss and say to them I think they should cancel any engagements they may have to hear your report." I went directly to them, feeling certain that I was not to be disciplined for my unauthorized entry into Germany and wishing I had frankly talked to the commissioners about it before going in.

Mr. White and General Bliss took the rest of my morning and the former said he would at once tell Lloyd George of my arrival and report. I called upon Colonel House and told him I had had some unusual experiences. He was quite uninterested and did not ask a question. I asked him to have the kindness to tell the President that I had returned and that I should be glad to report to him if he wished to see me. "The President," said Colonel House, "is extremely busy and only sees the most important people. I do not think he will have time for you." "I quite understand," I replied, "but I wish you would tell him nevertheless, as I wish to do him the courtesy of reporting my readiness to be of service to him." The Colonel promised to do this. For the next four days I was passed around from one official to another, dining among others with General Smuts who, as I have shown, was as well aware of what ought to be done as Mr. Lansing. His whole attitude again demonstrated his keen intelligence and high-mindedness. I spent some time with Lord Robert Cecil and the Associated Press cabled a complete summary of my experiences. The newspaper men thought that I had had the most exciting experiences of anybody; even William C. Bullitt and Lincoln Steffens, who had just returned from Russia, envied me. I was interviewed for the English and Paris newspapers. Indeed, I was perfectly astounded at the changed attitude toward me. Instead of being shunned or looked at askance I was sought after, much invited, and entertained. Apparently it sometimes pays to defy Presidential ukases.

Lloyd George responded to Mr. White's information by promptly inviting me to breakfast. There were also present Philip Kerr, now the Marquis of Lothian, Mr. Edwin S. Montagu, later well known for his work as Secretary of State for India, and Major Lloyd George, the Prime Minister's strapping son. It was my first meeting in Paris with Lloyd George and it lasted for an hour and a half all told. It resulted in his keeping the others of the Big Four waiting.[2] What he had most in mind was how far the Germans could be pushed and stripped before they would refuse to go along. I told him what the leaders had said to me, that they would never sign any treaty that alienated any German soil except Alsace-Lorraine. "What, for example?" he asked. "Silesia," I replied. Putting his hand to his forehead, the Prime Minister turned to Philip Kerr and said: "Please refresh my memory. Is it Upper or Lower Silesia that we are giving away?" I have always felt that that question completely demonstrated one attitude of mind of the Big Four which alone insured the disaster of Versailles; *they* were to decide what to *give away*—not those to whom the lands belonged.

"What is your own judgment as to what the Germans will do?" asked the Prime Minister. I regretted having to tell him that I did not think that the Germans would refuse to consent to territorial losses. Most of the breakfast hour I gave to describing the general conditions and warning Lloyd George that the German people starved sufficiently would gladly welcome bolshevism—anything in preference to existing conditions. I also acquainted him with the growing feeling of many Germans of property that they would rather have the Allies take over and rule Germany than yield anything except the colonies and Alsace-Lorraine. I further dwelt on the extraordinarily rapid growth of communism in Germany—far more dangerous it was then than when Hitler used it as an excuse to install National Socialism—and told him of some persons of property who had frankly said to me that if the Allies degraded their country they would in preference open their doors to the Russian Bolsheviki.

After breakfast Lloyd George and I looked out of a sitting-room window. Directly across the narrow street we saw Woodrow Wilson walking up and down in a room of his apartment. "A re-

[2] On March 4, 1931, Mr. Lloyd George wrote me: "I am glad to be able to testify that the information you then gave me concerning the gravity of the situation in Germany as a result of the revolution in that country, was of considerable service, not only to myself, but to my colleagues on the Peace Conference."

markable man," said the Prime Minister. "How do you think he will come out in his fight with the Senate?" I hesitated for I was not sure of Wilson's success, yet I felt that I must not weaken the President in my host's eyes. So I said, "I think he will win." "So do I," was Lloyd George's reply. During the rest of the day I got echoes of this breakfast from Henry White who asked how long Lloyd George had kept me and then said: "You must have made a hit with him"; then Thomas Lamont volunteered the information that Lloyd George had told him that I had made a great impression upon him. Finally, in the afternoon as I was standing at the door of the Crillon Hotel a man saw me and literally ran across the pavement to me. It was Colonel House.

"Why, Villard," he exclaimed, "Lloyd George says you gave him a wonderful hour this morning. I didn't realize you had had such a thrilling experience." I reminded him that I had offered to tell him the story and then I asked him if he had conveyed my message to President Wilson. Without hesitation he replied: "Oh, yes, I told him and he told me to tell you that he knows all that you do and a great deal more besides." Here was another revelation of Mr. Wilson's attitude of mind which helped to bring about the defeat of those who aspired at Paris for a better world. Lloyd George was also the head of a great state, and Germany was not only full of British officials and military men but of spies as well. Yet Lloyd George had felt that he could learn from an American reporter who had seen things at first hand, but Mr. Wilson knew it a great deal better than the eyewitness. That was consistency; his conceit and his egotism were ever at hand to betray him. Incredibly ignorant as he was of the European scene and its past history, he none the less was always certain that he knew it better than those who had seen or studied situations at length.

Mr. Lloyd George may have been impressed by my report but it was not until a month later that he rose in Parliament and informed the members that a new and more terrible enemy than the Germans had appeared in Europe—hunger. But he did not tell the members that he, Wilson, Clemenceau, and Orlando were responsible because of those months lost between November and

April when they delayed and wrangled, during which food should have been allowed into all the war-wrecked countries. And not only food. A distinguished American journalist who had just returned to Paris after a tour of Poland, Italy, and Czechoslovakia, observed to me: "What is even more important than food in those countries is the re-establishment of uncensored mail, telegrams, and cables; the through express; the commercial traveler; the breaking down of all the barriers that war erects between states." The sudden surrender of Hungary to Bela Kun and the Communists severely jolted the higher circles but brought about no noteworthy change. Count Karolyi had for weeks in vain been foretelling just what had happened and begging for food to prevent it. Some of the American delegation merely blamed Senator Lodge and the Senate for having amended the Hoover Food Bill so as to prevent the delivery of food to any of the former enemies. Still the Allies would take no warning and let Bavaria finally go communist. On March 26 Hugh Gibson and I lunched with Herbert Hoover in his rooms at the Crillon. Hoover came half an hour late and, without apology, dropped into a chair exhausted. "What day is today?" he asked. "March 26." "Well," said he, "ever since December 4 I have tried to get permission for the little German fishing fleet to go to sea. It took me until Christmas to get English consent and now at last I have the French permission after fighting them again all morning." Thereupon he began to curse with the ease and skill of a coal miner and called the French every kind of a name.

This humane and courageous fight of Hoover's for a sensible policy toward the defeated country and Russia stands out as his finest achievement. Indeed, it seems to me that he was at his best all through the Peace Conference, nearly always standing on the side of justice and decency and speaking right out for his beliefs. That his dreadful fear of bolshevism was one of his most compelling motives is true; that does not detract from the great effort he made to stop the continuance of loss of life in Germany because of semistarvation. What a pity it is that he did not eschew politics, live upon his great war-time renown, and so escape the misfortune of his Presidency and subsequent eclipse! But even Hoover's splendid example did not convince the higher-ups, nor did the sensational refusal of the British soldiers of General Plumer's army in Germany to stand guard over starving women and children without at least sharing their food with them. When I tried to ascertain what would happen if the Germans defied the Allies, the only response I could get was the cold-blooded statement that in that case a complete food blockade would be put on again and tightened.

The ability men had to deceive themselves at that time was beyond belief. The Big Four apparently thought that they could delay the making of the peace and not invite disaster. They really believed that their military success gave them the right to deprive Germany of millions of her people, much of her soil, half of her coal supply, and three-fourths of her iron ore, all of her colonies, all her great steamships, the free use of her railways, and free disposal of her industrial products, and get away with it without paying a dreadful price. In the United States the failure to understand the situation was beyond belief. We in Paris read the *Times*, the *Tribune*, and *The Evening Post*, and tried to understand the utterly different world they brought to us. How, we asked, was it possible for the Secretary of the Navy, Josephus Daniels, to exclaim exultantly that Germany had been rendered impotent for all time to come? In that connection I am reminded of Thomas Lamont's assuring me on my return to Paris that one thing had been accomplished: Germany had been bottled up so that no one could sneak any money or securities out of that country. I listened gravely and politely but with great inward amusement because my little soldier's trunk had never been opened or inspected from the time I left Berlin until I unpacked it in Paris. I knew, if he did not, that at that very moment money and securities were being flown out of Germany into Switzerland, Holland, and Denmark and that this had been steadily going on.

I found when I returned to Paris that the number of wars going on in the world had grown to fourteen. Jesters at the Crillon said that it was entirely fitting to have one war for each of the fourteen discarded Wilson peace terms. One by one they had been abandoned by their originator. "Who," I noted, "hears today in Paris of the freedom of the seas? Who, when he reads of the Saar basin, recalls the fine phrase about 'no punitive damages or annexations'? If there are today four Napoleons setting up new governments and redrawing the map, at least the Great Emperor spared the world the hypocrisy of clothing his acts in language to charm—and to be discarded at will." I found that some of our foremost representatives in Paris had lost all interest in the League of Nations which seemed to me "foredoomed to failure by the insincerity of many of those who have accepted it, by the exclusion from it of the representatives of two-thirds of Europe and all the black races."

The strongest American and British advocates of the League no longer offered any argument for the plan save that it was a half, or a third, of a loaf. "Try it," they said, "and out of it may come something worth while." My indignation was especially aroused by Mr. Wilson's agreeing to join England in giving a permanent guarantee of protection and treaty of alliance to France, for that meant, among other things, our keeping in being a great expeditionary force. "This action," I wrote, "will give the *coup de grâce* to his own creation [the League] and it is no longer worth discussing by serious-minded Americans."

The handling of Russia was one of the most striking evidences of the Big Four's folly and worse. The French policy, voiced by M. Pichon, the French Foreign Minister, was warmly approved even by some Americans, notably Simeon Strunsky, always politically unrealistic in his correspondence for *The Evening Post*. It was to encircle Russia "with a wall of bayonets." That was complete stupidity, if the idea was to prevent the spread of radical doctrines to Europe, for new ideas overleap every materialistic barrier ever erected. It was an excellent plan of Mr. Wilson to dispatch Bullitt and Steffens to Russia, but what did it avail? Their report was completely ignored because it did not picture the situation in Russia as the Big Four wished it portrayed. Furthermore, its existence was even deliberately denied. Of all the many falsehoods of statesmen I have chronicled in forty years, none was more unblushing and flagrant than Lloyd George's evasion in the

House of Commons on April 16, of the fact that he had full knowledge of the Bullitt mission into Russia and had even met Bullitt. I, being then in New York, was able to nail this on the spot by the statement in *The Nation* that Lloyd George not only knew about it but had invited Bullitt to breakfast with him.

When Bullitt arrived in New York he asked if I was a mind reader. "Nobody knew anything about that breakfast," he said. "How did you find it out?" I reminded him that he was to have breakfasted with me on the morning that the Lloyd George meeting took place. To my chagrin I woke up that morning after nine o'clock, already nearly an hour late for my appointment with Bullitt. As I jumped out of bed I noticed a slip of paper under the door. "Sorry I can't breakfast with you," it read, "but I've got to breakfast with L.G.—Bullitt." That was the explanation. I must add that in his testimony before the Senate Committee on Foreign Affairs Bullitt charged Lloyd George with being guilty of "the most egregious case of misleading the public" when he said in Parliament that no approaches or proposals had been made by the Soviet chiefs to the Entente. Soon after Lloyd George's whopper, Bullitt said, Philip Kerr called and apologized for Lloyd George's action, stating that the British Premier had found on his return to England that Lord Northcliffe and others had prepared to oust him if he recommended Soviet recognition!

Wilson flatly refused to see Bullitt, as he had refused to see me, using the old excuse that his mind was a single-track one, that it was then absorbed with Germany and that therefore he could not interest himself in the Russian situation! [3] Nothing more completely revealed Mr. Wilson's inadequacy for his Paris tasks, his mental tergiversations, his habitual refusal to face raw facts, than the treatment of Russia. On January 18, 1918, he had declared that our policy toward Russia would be the "acid test" of our good will. One of the fourteen peace points called for "such a settlement of all questions affecting Russia as will secure the best

[3] Testimony of William C. Bullitt before the Senate Foreign Relations Committee, September 12, 1919.

and freest co-operation of all the nations in the world in obtaining from her an unhampered and unembarrassed determination of her own political development and national policy. . . ." Thereupon Russia was invaded from three directions by American, British, French, and other Allied troops. When the temporary all-Russian government at Omsk begged General Graves not to send American troops further into Siberia, that officer replied that "the policy to be followed by our troops in any country is one to be determined by the Executive." He was quite correct. Congress had yielded its war-making power to the President; the full responsibility for this wanton invasion of a country with which we were at peace will for all time rest squarely upon Mr. Wilson's shoulders and upon his head lies the blood of the Russian and our own soldiers murdered in his private war.[4]

Some time after, when Nansen made his Russian food relief proposal, the Big Four accepted it but made it a cardinal prerequisite that the Soviet government cease fighting! Of course, all the fighting in Russia at that time was being done by Allied and American soldiers, or by counterrevolutionary troops, instigated, financed, and supplied by the Allies as Lloyd George frankly admitted to the House of Commons on April 16—a policy *The Nation* properly characterized as "combined burglary and starvation, coupled with pious phrases." The result of all this horrible blundering and international criminality was the defeat of the Allies and the United States at every point, the establishment on solid ground of the Soviet Republics and their miraculous rise to the position of the world's greatest power next to the United States. Such was the intelligence of the four men who were dominating Europe and by the middle of March were utterly ignoring

[4] In the summer of 1929, when in Nishni-Novgorod, the writer and others unexpectedly entered a classroom in a "People's House" in which some boys and girls were being taught the use of the army rifle. As soon as the instructor noticed that we were Americans he stepped to a large wooden map of Russia and pressed two buttons. Immediately the lines occupied by our American armies in Archangel and Siberia were outlined by tiny electric lights. Russia has not forgotten 1919 if the American public has.

the delegates of all the other nations who were kept in Paris merely in order to sign, like the Germans, on the dotted line!

Among the lesser delegates and diplomats the regret grew hourly that a quick and satisfactory peace, based upon a few principles and the original Wilson terms, was not obtained by January 15 as it easily could have been. Germany would gladly have signed a treaty, which could have been drafted—as Mr. Lansing insisted —in twenty-four hours, to comprise the following points: the League of Nations; cession of Alsace-Lorraine and the German colonies; the surrender of the German fleet; the reduction of the army to a gendarmerie organized only as police to maintain order; the razing of the Rhine fortifications; and a pledge by Germany to pay indemnities, to be determined later, in order to make good the destruction in France and Belgium. With that signed, the blockades could have been lifted and the normal processes of life restored. That was the vital need. Rasped nerves would have been quieted; undernourishment ended; revolutions would have been checked and at the same time the Allies safeguarded. It was all so simple, but too simple to be within the grasp of the four great minds. After such a treaty had been agreed to, the Big Four could have settled down to details and to revising the map if they had to do so.

These are not *post facto* views of mine. I published them all at the time. But what is vastly more important, they were the beliefs of practically all the lesser American officials in Paris. The fight which our ignored Peace Commissioners, and Hoover, Lamont, Baruch, McCormick, Henry P. Davison, and many others and some British officials put up to save Europe seems to me the one bright chapter in the whole dismal story of chicane, intrigue, selfish aggression and naked imperialism which gave the lie to all the pretense of noble aims with which we and the Allies had carried on the war. So keenly was the extent of the betrayal of American ideals recognized in our own official ranks that in May no less than nine attachés of the American Peace Commission resigned in a body in protest. Among these William C. Bullitt was outstanding and his letter of resignation, dated May 26, 1919, was a model of fearless outspokenness. Here are some of the things Mr. Bullitt wrote to Woodrow Wilson in his indictment of his chief:

I am one of the millions who trusted implicitly in your leadership and believed you would take nothing less than "a permanent peace based on unselfish, unbiased justice." But the government has consented now to deliver the suffering peoples of the world to new oppressions, subjections, and dismemberments—a new century of war. . . . Unjust decisions regarding Shantung, Tyrol, Thrace, Hungary, East Prussia, Danzig, and the Saar Valley and abandonment of the principle of freedom of the seas make new international conflicts certain. . . . I am sorry you did not fight our fight to a finish and that you had so little faith in the millions of men like myself in every nation who had faith in you.

He then demanded that our government "refuse to sign this unjust treaty."

After eighteen years this remains a masterly and incontrovertible statement of the facts which time has upheld at every point. It will be, I believe, like Harold Nicolson's analysis of Wilson at Paris, the final verdict of history no matter how paid historians, or official biographers, or sycophantic friends, or supporters of the Woodrow Wilson Foundation, may seek to portray what happened or to palliate the delinquencies of their hero. The English Liberals and Labor leaders were also quick to speak out. The Labor *Daily Herald* in a double-column editorial headed "When There Is No Peace" said on May 18: "President Wilson has been beaten. . . . We do not know what reasons he has had for abandoning 'open covenants openly arrived at' for the sinister secrecy of Paris. What we do know is that from the moment he abandoned the first of his Fourteen Points he, in effect, abandoned all." Philip Snowden wrote in the *Labor Leader* on May 22: "Beyond all other statesmen who are responsible for the Peace Treaty, President Wilson is utterly discredited. He has not insisted upon the observance of a single one of the conditions of peace he has laid down. . . . His intervention in the European war has been disastrous from every point of view. If he had not brought America into the war a decent peace would probably have been secured. His intervention has intensely aggravated the European situation and has left Europe seething with jealousy, hatred, malice, and the certainty of a generation of war and bloodshed. The sooner he gets back to America and ceases to interfere in international politics, for which he has evidently neither the courage nor the knowledge, the better it will be for the peace of the world." A radical change from the mood of the 1917 Club!

As one who at the time approved of Mr. Wilson's going to Paris I have come to realize the fatal mistake it was. What the occasion needed was a much more determined man. He had the whip hand, in fact, every card in the deck. He had the freshest, best-equipped, and only increasing army in France; he had all the money left in the world and controlled the bulk of the food. Without him the Allies could do nothing. Some of the money they owe us was still being poured out to them. A threat to make the separate treaty with Germany which we afterwards did make, a threat to withdraw our army at once and to loan not a dollar more, would have reduced the Allied leaders to pulp. Against this some defenders of Woodrow Wilson protest. It would have been outrageous, they say, thus arrogantly to have dictated the peace. But it would not have been dictation, only a righteous demand that the Allies live up to their pledges made to us and to Germany to make peace on the fourteen peace points. Our failure to insist upon this, whether politely or arrogantly, put us in the position of having broken faith with our enemy, of having tricked them. Can anyone look at the world today and deny that this policy would have been better than to do what we did: help frame a wicked peace which has revived in worse form the German militarism which we set out to destroy, given rise to fascism in Italy and elsewhere, and completely disappointed the hopes and the ambitions of millions everywhere for a better world?

If ever a man was tripped by his faults of character at the supreme moment of his existence, it was Wilson in Paris. His long-cherished belief that there were only four minds in the world equal to his own; the rigidity of his mind which made it impossible for him to deal with the men he confronted, for they were intellectually agile and as foreign to his experience as the natives of Tahiti; his fatal inability to judge men correctly and to accept advice or criticism if he did not like them; his avoidance of facts when they did not please him—all these things contributed to his downfall. But worst of all was his self-deception. On his first return to the United States, February 24, 1919, in the middle of the conference, in a message to the American people he said, at Boston, that the men who were in conference in Paris "realized as keenly as any American can realize that they are not the masters of their people . . . and that no man dare go home from that conference and *report anything less noble than was expected of him.*" On his second return from Paris he solemnly assured his countrymen that he had achieved everything he had set out to achieve, that the conference had lived up to its obligations, and that the peace treaty was just and a proper one to bear the signature of the American Republic.

Two personal aspects of Mr. Wilson in Paris must be touched upon. His decision to leave Tumulty behind him was a great misfortune not merely because he would have been a valuable link to the pressmen as in Washington but because he would not have permitted the ignoring of the three neglected peace commissioners; he never hesitated to tell the President when he thought the latter was wrong and he would have kept the President in touch with American opinion in Paris. The other mistake was the presence in Paris of the second Mrs. Wilson. This is a subject of great delicacy which cannot at present be freely discussed. Her presence certainly added to the strain under which the President labored and did not help him.

At a dinner given by H. H. Johnson, a distinguished Cleveland lawyer, to thirty-six visiting members of the Cleveland Chamber of Commerce who had come to Paris to see what could be done to rehabilitate France and what business could be picked up there, I met General Pershing and General Charles G. Dawes. It was a very large affair, attended by members of the French Cabinet and many distinguished Americans and, as Mr. Johnson had insisted that I be one of the speakers and tell of my experiences in Germany, I was enormously relieved when the list of speakers proved so long—and their speeches likewise—that I was not reached; even then Mr. Johnson insisted upon my speaking to a group in a small room after the adjournment. The dinner was noteworthy for me because it gave me an insight into one side of General Pershing which I was most happy to have. As usual, General Dawes showed his inevitable ability to misbehave. His speech was in the worst possible taste, to the effect that France was a dreadfully back-number country, in great need of modernization, and that American business men would come over and show them how to run their industries and their country. We would put France on its feet just as we had won the war for it. The impression made by this can well be imagined.

It gave General Pershing his opportunity and he rose to it magnificently. When called upon he spoke with the utmost tact and skill, saying that the American army did not feel that it had won the war, only that it had contributed fresh men to that end after the lines had been so magnificently held for years by the Allies; that America would have contributions to make to the restoration of France which would, under its own leadership, find the way to rise to still greater heights of success and usefulness in the years to come. That speech saved the evening and did much to convince me that in Pershing we had an admirable representative at the head of our forces. I am still of the opinion that, with the exception of General Bliss, no other general we had could have done as well or won us as much honor. Perhaps General Pershing did pay too much attention to the detail of men's uniforms, saluting, and other externals, but all the evidence is that in his contact with the Allied generals and statesmen he bore himself with great dignity, with tact, and respect for other people's point of view.

He was right in refusing the Allied demand that we throw our raw troops into the British and French regiments or brigades and give up all idea of a separate army. I am aware that Captain

Liddell Hart, today the ablest commentator on the war, says that while this policy was correct from a national point of view it cost thousands of unnecessarily lost lives. I think he has overlooked important factors, including the effects upon our own men of sudden affiliation with foreign organizations, particularly with the French. Of course, General Pershing was fortunate that, with great sagacity and wisdom, President Wilson and Secretary Baker gave him an absolutely free hand, notably in the matter of selecting and promoting or breaking his generals.

When I met General Pershing he greeted me very warmly and said he wished to see me at once; would I come to his office at eleven the next day? When I was shown in he asked me some questions about the German situation and then said: "I want your help. We are in a very serious situation with the army. Like the Allied forces it is disintegrating rapidly. I am having to dismiss so many officers every day that I can no longer publish the list. Our men are absent without leave all over France, Belgium, and Switzerland. Their homesickness steadily increases. We must have more transports at once. We are having the benefit of some navy ships but all the battleships and heavy cruisers should be sent over with skeleton crews. Will you help by cabling to Washington and publishing statements about the need?" I assured him that I would gladly do anything I could to help but that he was entirely mistaken if he thought that I had any influence in Washington. I felt like asking why he did not go direct to the Commander-in-Chief, since Mr. Wilson was in Paris, but I remembered what Mr. Lansing had said and refrained. Afterwards I thought that if the leaders of the German Republic could have heard General Pershing's statement they might have taken a more manly and determined stand on the signing of the treaty and the war-guilt lie therein.

On April 4, I sailed for home on the *Lafayette* after declining appointment to an important position in Russia and after having been taken over the Argonne battlefields by a young officer, Major Parker C. Kalloch, Jr., who was assigned to me by General Pershing himself to act as guide; a couple of years later it was my good luck to place Major Kalloch with a great American corporation when he decided to resign from the army. I, who am familiar with a number of our Civil War battlefields, marveled that any troops could have achieved such triumphs over so difficult a terrain. On leaving Paris I went to the Crillon and said good-by to Mr. Lansing, Mr. White, and General Bliss. As I got up to leave the General he said: "Villard, if when you get home anyone tries to put the blame for this war upon any one nation, don't let him do it. The trouble in 1914 was that there were too many fellows running around Europe with rifles in their hands. The war was bound to come." I wonder what he would say today as to the conditions in Europe with the maddest armament race in history under way, all Europe dominated by the military power of our "defeated" enemy, and at least a million and a half more men running around with rifles in their hands than in 1914. He would, doubtless, recall his own statement at Paris that that was not peace, but only a truce, and that we were in for a forty years' war.[5] As I left Mr. Lansing he was kind enough to say that if anyone was interested, and I wished to do so, I might state that the commissioners were of the opinion that I had rendered them valuable service. As a journalist I was sorry to leave Paris; as a human being I rejoiced to be out of that dreadful atmosphere of intrigue, deceit, and defeat.

[5] No more magnificent appeal for American disarmament was ever made than that of General Bliss before the *Public Ledger* Forum on December 10, 1920, in which he prophetically said: "Those are mistaken who may think that there can be an enduring and effective association of the nations for the maintenance of peace so long as those nations are armed to the teeth solely against each other." No pacifist ever put the case better at that time.

Chapter XXV. Upstream at Home

THE world I found on landing in New York bore no resemblance whatever to that I had left behind me in Europe. It was then, and for years thereafter, like a different planet. The war hate was still on here although it had subsided to so large a degree in Europe. Many of our returned soldiers were outraged by it. But the public at home was still buoyed up by the self-esteem and self-glorification the war had created. We had again showed our prowess to the world; we had won the war and done what France, England, Italy, and the rest of the Allies could not—we had beaten the Hun. In other words, we were on the top of the world —and without the slightest understanding or real knowledge of what was happening in Paris. The mood of the hour was stronger than ever against those who had dissented or opposed. For all the self-satisfaction and assurance of the bellicose press and leaders, they seemed singularly lacking in a feeling of security. They were even bitterer against the Bolsheviki and anyone whom they dubbed the "Reds." As for the treaty making, they rejoiced that the beaten Germans were being pilloried and fined as they deserved; those who protested were traitorous or pro-Germans.

When the treaty was finally published we denounced it in our next issue in an article headed "The Madness at Versailles." No more powerful or prophetic editorial ever appeared in *The Nation* or, I sometimes think, in any other journal. I can say this because I was not the author of it. It came from the pen of William Mac-Donald and I was proud to give it room. MacDonald rose to that great height of inspiration which few writers ever achieve more than once or twice in a lifetime. His judgment stands today a monument to him and to the correctness of the editorial position assumed at that time by *The Nation*. No historian should write of the Peace Treaty without knowing this article, and no one can justly deny its truth. He called it a peace of "undisguised vengeance" and not of justice, declared that "in the whole history of diplomacy there is no treaty more properly to be regarded as an international crime than the amazing document which the German representatives are now asked to sign," and that it constituted "a peace which openly flouts some of the plainest dictates of reason and humanity . . . flies in the face of accepted principles of law and economics and makes the very name of democracy a reproach. . . . After nearly five years of strenuous effort and high expectancy, the hopes of the people have been destroyed. The progress of democracy as either a theory or practice of social righteousness has been suddenly and forcibly checked." As for Wilson, Mr. MacDonald wrote that: "The one-time idol of democracy stands today discredited and condemned. . . ."

At once several friends called upon me to express their horror at this editorial and begged me to moderate *The Nation's* tone. The war was not yet officially over; they feared that I and my associates might still be jailed. The editorial was denounced by the press as a wild piece of pro-German raving. The Brooklyn *Eagle,* crediting me with the authorship, declared that my judgment had been "affected by prejudices which he cannot overcome and by too close association with and sympathy for the political revolutionaries who imagine they can make civilization over to conform with their own vagaries. Mr. Villard's words will fall upon grateful ears in Germany. . . ." *The Evening Post,* to my great pain, spoke of the treaty as a "voice from Heaven"! The New York *Times* thought it the promised peace of justice, "terribly severe but just" [1] —not until Wall Street found the treaty injurious did the *Times* tell the truth about it. Months were to elapse before Maynard Keynes's *Economic Consequences of the Peace* appeared to uphold us and to convince some respectable circles which had theretofore obediently accepted the treaty at Woodrow Wilson's and the British government's valuation. At the moment the Allies could

---

[1] Cf. Woodrow Wilson at Columbus, Ohio, Sept. 4, 1919: "The terms of the treaty are severe *but not unjust.*"

still do no wrong. Even when the great fight against the ratification of the treaty came, it was not due primarily to blazing indignation at its stupidities or its destructive character but to opposition to the League of Nations.

It was hard for us to oppose the League for all of us had dreamed of a parliament of man, and still harder to find ourselves fighting alongside of Boies Penrose and Henry Cabot Lodge and his satellites, but fight we did and so gave aid and comfort to those whom we opposed at every other point, whose whole influence upon our public life and social and economic progress seemed to us about the most dangerous in our politics. That had happened to us before and happened to us again; one can only stick to the chart one has chosen to sail by and not be diverted by the character of the consorts that may for a brief moment take a parallel course.

Soon after my return my reputation as a very dangerous radical was confirmed for many by an outrageous misrepresentation of a part of the testimony I was asked to give before the New York State Reconstruction Commission. I went reluctantly, in response to repeated urgings. Reading from a carefully prepared manuscript I stated that I was not a Communist. I turned to the reporters and again emphasized this fact; but, I said, as communism had been discussed and urged by some since the days of Christ I felt it was fortunate for all the world that the Russians had taken upon themselves the tough job of trying communism out once and for all. It seemed, I thought, that we ought to watch carefully and without prejudice the Russian experiment and to profit by it if there was anything to be gained. I also stated that the form of the new governments in Bavaria and Russia, namely, the Soviet organization, ought not in itself to prejudice us.

"I am sorry for you," said Allan McCurdy as we left. "There were two reporters from *The Tribune* there with orders to get you." Sure enough, on the front page of the next morning's *Tribune* was the startling announcement that I had "advocated a Soviet form of government for the United States," and this was backed up the next day by an editorial, although my letter of protest was then in the office. A personal protest to Mrs. Ogden Reid was never acknowledged and my brief letter of denial, when printed, was so carefully hidden that few saw it; no word of regret or apology was ever vouchsafed. I could trace the progress of this deliberate falsehood across the continent by the abusive editorials which streamed back to me. The Portland *Oregonian* said that I was greatly in need of some other occupation for my "disordered intellect." The Syracuse *Post-Standard* declared that I was a plain case of "hypochondria." The Philadelphia *Inquirer* felt that I should leave for Russia at once. A Midwestern daily declared that I ought to go back to my ancestral home "where he can exploit his half-baked and asinine theories to his heart's content," and the Springfield *Union* urged the banning of *The Nation* from all schools and colleges. But at least the Brooklyn *Citizen* and the Springfield *Union* later had the decency to apologize; the *Tribune* did not.

My own experiences at the Peace Conference and in Germany, and those at home during the war years, had not made me the dangerous radical that I was said to be, though they had made a profound change in me. Anyone with a brain must have moved during those years to the Left or to the Right, and I had gone moderately to the Left. Unable to embrace either the socialist or the communist doctrines, I still felt that thereafter one must be either for or against the existing political order. I did not wish my children to live in a world managed politically as ours had been during the previous five years. I had lost any hope that the capitalist system would redeem or reform itself, without, however, adopting any hard or fast creed, just clinging to my old-fashioned liberal doctrines, modified by the new facts, the economic revolution. I realized fully the danger of my position—that of falling between two stools.[2] It had become plain to me that all the nations

---

[2] I wrote as to this to Hutchins Hapgood, May 19, 1919: "Perhaps I am too well off and too happily situated in life—perhaps I have not been close enough to the working people. Yet I have had my suffering too, during the last four years and I am still under very heavy social pressure of all kinds, but my suffering has not been due to that; it is due to the sense of spiritual outrage at the injustice and wickedness that we are seeing."

of the world were drifting as steadily as a glacier, and as irresistibly, in the direction of greater control of business and private enterprise which cannot end before they have taken over the public services and the basic industries. I did turn to labor as the one great hope and I trust that I have never since failed in my advocacy of the economic enfranchisement of the working classes, their right to share in the management of industry and to a far greater part of its profits, and, of course, labor's right to organize under leaders of its own choosing. That that leadership will always be wise and just it would be preposterous to assume; I am only sure that it can never be worse than the political and economic leadership of the capitalist countries which I have observed at close range. In short, by 1919, I think that I had been emancipated from any merely smug liberalism and social blindness due to the ease and luxury of my upbringing. Never yet, however, have I been won for a doctrine or a system that requires bloodshed to introduce it or to maintain it once it has been adopted.

In the face of the attacks upon me and *The Nation* its circulation rose so fast that by November, 1919, we were printing 53,000 copies and winning a reader devotion which would have warmed the heart of the most austere editor. To many who had been utterly isolated in their communities, even in their families, who had suffered to their souls because of their conscientious opposition to the war folly and the madness of the peace, the weekly visit of *The Nation* was like a draught from a life-giving spring. From every direction came words of gratitude, even from men in high places, who dared not let their feelings be known. This far more than offset the criticism and denunciations. We were able to laugh in the middle of our indignation when we read in a Denver newspaper of the arrest of a foreign-born worker because the police had found in his room a trunkful of incendiary literature—namely, copies of *The Nation,* as we learned from a front-page illustration. But it was no laughing matter for our poor subscriber who had to face the police third degree as well as utterly unwarranted imprisonment; but his was only one of thousands of cases all over the country of men and women being arrested without warrant, and often through a far more lawless procedure than the offenses with which they were charged. We still had many conservative readers and contributors but the Denver police more nearly represented the popular view of our activities as well as the incredible state of public opinion at the time.

Fear of the Reds, which still lingers in some benighted circles and can always be pulled out of the hat by some cheap and vacant politician, then had a widespread hold and Red-baiting was shamefully practiced—without hindrance from the great Liberal, Woodrow Wilson—by his Department of Justice, or rather Injustice, as we correctly dubbed it. As Lincoln Colcord wrote from Washington: "Wilson and Baker have lost their moral balance in this matter of militarism, the assertion of law and order and the suppression of civil rights and liberties. They are less honest than the Bourbons." [3] The ex-pacifist Baker was now outdoing the generals in his demand for a huge army; he asked Congress for 500,000 men where Pershing wanted 275,000 or 300,000 and even General Wood only 250,000. Always the apologists for Wilson refused to face the facts and sought to excuse him by saying, as they did during the war when the torturing of the conscientious objectors came up, that he was not aware of what was going on, that he was too preoccupied with weightier matters, as if there could be a weightier matter than the daily flouting of the country's Constitution by officials sworn to uphold and obey it. To our retort that if he was not aware of what was happening Mr. Wilson was an inefficient and faithless President, they had no other reply.

Throughout 1919 and 1920 this official lawlessness raged. The Attorney General of the United States, A. Mitchell Palmer, who had Presidential ambitions, set the worst possible example. A brave and outspoken federal judge in Boston, George W. Anderson, condemned Mr. Palmer, his department, and the government itself for the basest deeds to which any government may sink. It was brought out in Judge Anderson's court that under Mr. Palmer's instructions his spies and *agents provocateurs* in the ranks

[3] *The Nation*, November 15, 1919.

of the Communist Party had not only called the meetings on January 2, 1920, which Mr. Palmer's federal agents raided all over the country, but had actually written the *very portions of the Communist platform* upon which the government based its prosecution of the men it duped! In other words, the government manufactured the crime and then sent men to prison for doing what it had induced them to do.

Judge Anderson declared from the bench that "it is perfectly evident to my mind that the government owns and operates at least part of the Communist Party." But his wrath did not stop there. It was proved before him that one man had been arrested on January 2, 1920, on a warrant which was not even issued until January 15 when it was telegraphed from Washington. Judge Anderson declared that the whole procedure of the government "seems to have been carried out on the theory of hang first and try afterwards." When Mr. Palmer's representative tried to defend the action of the government, the Judge replied:

I wish you would show me one case in which the Department of Justice has the authority to arrest persons and hold them two weeks without warrants. A more lawless proceeding is hard to conceive. Talk about Americanization; what we need is Americanization of those who carry on such proceedings. I can hardly sit on the bench as an American citizen and restrain my indignation. I view with horror such proceedings as this.

When Judge Anderson asked Mr. Palmer's representative how he dared arrest a person without warrant, the reply was that he was acting under direct instructions from his superiors in Washington. To this Judge Anderson replied: "Any citizen with a knowledge of Americanism should resign when given such instructions." It was no wonder that *The Nation* exclaimed: "And there at last is the note of real Americanism! Massachusetts has again brought forth a man to voice, under the shadow of Faneuil Hall, the old traditions, the old liberties, the most sacred of our American rights. That there is a Judge Anderson to brand the Department of Justice as it should be is enough to stir the pulses." [4]

---

[4] *The Nation*, May 1, 1920, p. 569.

Between 5,000 and 6,000 people were seized in those January 2, 1920, raids, among them girls of fourteen, sixteen, and seventeen years who were arrested as "criminal anarchists" and women prisoners were poured into Ellis Island until the Commissioner of Immigration protested that it was neither sanitary nor decent to send any more. In Detroit more than one hundred men were kept in a bull pen 24 by 30 feet—a procedure "intolerable in any civilized city" the Mayor of Detroit wired to Washington. Not only were all known Communists arrested but any visitors found in their homes were seized because, said the police, if they were not Communists they would not have gone there! To defend these wholesale arrests, unparalleled in our history, the Department of Justice gave out solemn statements that the Communist and Communist-Labor parties were bent on overthrowing the government by force. It naturally neglected to state that both of those parties had held organizing conventions in Chicago in the previous summer without the slightest interference by the government. Mr. Palmer forgot, of course, to add that advocacy of communism was not a crime unless accompanied by a deliberate attempt to overthrow the government by force.

The authenticated cases of torture, sadism, and crime, committed by agents of the Department of Justice and condoned or encouraged by the department, would take several chapters to recite. They prove that Sinclair Lewis need not have written a book to show that It Can't Happen Here. He need only have cited the Wilson-Palmer record to show that it did happen. Much has occurred under Adolf Hitler in Germany which could be paralleled by official misconduct in this country during this period. One could really believe that the dictators were patterning after us if one were not aware of their sublime ignorance of everything outside the boundaries of their own countries. Mr. Palmer and his officials were denounced in a report signed by Dean Roscoe Pound of the Harvard Law School, five other teachers of law, and six attorneys of high standing. Writing in The Nation, Captain Swinburne Hale stated the case of the committee—that there had been "one thousand and one criminal acts" which had been "intentionally and purposely done to terrorize the foreign working population." He said that he did not refer to the thuggery "which beat Oscar J. Tywerewski to a pulp in the presence of five invited newspaper reporters" and then terrorized them into silence and officially whitewashed the affair; nor to the suffocation nearly to death of three men "in the steam room" of the Hartford jail; nor "to the broken body of fifty-year-old Professor Lavrowski whose crime was teaching algebra in Russian instead of in English"; nor to the forgery of Gaspare Cannone's name to false testimony after filthy words and beatings had not broken him down; nor to the wholesale blackjacking of 300 Russians at once at 133 East 15th Street, New York City; nor did the committee especially dwell on the horrible case of Andrea Salsedo and Roberto Elia, held in eight weeks' secret confinement in the offices of the Department of Justice in the Park Row Building, New York City, and their daily physical and mental torture until Salsedo jumped from a fourteenth-story window and smashed to pieces on the pavement below. Horrible as these things were, what concerned the committee was the criminality of the Department of Justice itself and the fact that these things could happen with the knowledge of Washington and without the punishment of a single wrongdoer.

It is not surprising that on June 12, 1920, we urged the impeachment of Palmer, who, by the way, called himself a Quaker, for misuse of government funds to conduct a personal press campaign against free thought and free speech, for violation of the Constitution in certain deportations, for betrayal of common decency as Alien Property Custodian, and for his failure to check profiteering or other law violations by the trusts. As Custodian alone he was a disgrace to America. Naturally he fathered a sedition law proposal which read that whoever "threatens to commit . . . any act of . . . *hate* . . . against the person or property of any officer . . . of the United States . . . shall be deemed guilty of sedition"! This certainly parallels the present German ruling that any judge may deem any act treason to the State. Of course not even the subservient Congress could stand for this proposal though I am sure Wilson would not have objected.

We had little aid from the press in this fight which was one after my heart since it enabled us to champion the oppressed, the tortured, the innocently convicted.[5] The Associated Press frequently refused to carry the news of what took place and to accept protests against lawless officials. The independent weeklies were as outspoken as we and, of course, the Baltimore *Suns,* the New York *World,* and the St. Louis *Post-Dispatch.* The most powerful newspapers like the New York *Times, Tribune,* and the Chicago *Tribune,* either kept silence or approved. True, when Charles E. Hughes and other conservatives protested against the ousting of five Socialists from the Assembly in New York some of the newspapers followed suit. They had nothing to say about the conviction of twenty Communists in Chicago for the crime of being members of their legal party. When the Sterling Bill was introduced, which would have made impossible the mailing of Lincoln's second inaugural because it contained this sentence: "Whenever they [the people] grow weary of their existing government they can exercise their constitutional right of amending it, or their revolutionary right to dismember or overthrow it," some of the conservatives began to stir uneasily; they even realized that this would make impossible the mailing of the Declaration of Independence. Such was the government-created terror that swept over the land.

We liberal editors were actually denounced with increasing bitterness for fighting for the preservation of our institutions, and so we of *The Nation* set ourselves to printing as able and informative a journal as possible, without regarding the question of cost. I am proud of those fighting issues, whatever their errors.[6] They were not wholly given over to the battle for liberty. Indeed, we

---

[5] In Waterbury, Connecticut, a boy was arrested and sentenced to six months' imprisonment for no other reason than that he said to a customer in a clothing store that Lenin was "the most brainiest man" produced by the war, a sentence some of us succeeded in getting quashed. *The Nation,* April 17, 1920.

[6] In my absence the staff on August 28, 1920, printed a blast that bowled me over when I saw it—an editorial headed: "Take Every Empty House." Because of the great shortage of homes this course was urged upon the mayors of our cities. This leader, I admit, bordered on the hysterical.

printed numerous special issues, devoting one to the railroads with two conservative railroad presidents, Messrs. Lovett and Loree, contributing, and we gave eighteen and one-half pages in one issue to the educational problems of reconstruction; under Carl Van Doren our special book issues were at high-water mark. On July 19, we scored a "beat" by printing a secret government dispatch sent from Tokyo to Colonel House by Arthur Bullard, one of the star reporters in Russia of Mr. Creel's bureau of misinformation. This dispatch told the brutal truth about Kolchak and his unbelievably bloody performances in Siberia—a dispatch which made disgraceful our American support of that monster. Exactly how this and some other dispatches reached me I did not know and do not to this day, for Max Eastman, the intermediary, has never revealed the secret; I found them on my desk one morning. It was at once announced that the Department of Justice would take us in hand but nothing happened beyond the visit of a very dumb sleuth. When Eastman was threatened with arrest—he had read one dispatch at a public meeting—he stopped any further governmental action by giving out a statement that he hoped he would not have to expose other secret documents in his possession beyond those relating to the Siberian adventure. The Wilson crowd did not want any more truths to leak out. I am convinced that the publication of this material compelled the withdrawal of our troops from Siberia.

We devoted much of our editorial space to the fight against the peace treaty and our entering the League of Nations. We gave especial attention to the betrayal of China on the Shantung issue and we "deadly paralleled" Mr. Wilson in issue after issue, giving one whole supplement to citations from his speeches before and after entering the war, not forgetting to print an extraordinary account of Metternich as the predecessor of Woodrow Wilson and recalling the fact that even after his downfall Metternich said: "My mind has never entertained error." To the Progressive senators in Washington we gave aid and counsel. I saw a good deal of Senator Borah at this time and our friendship developed most satisfactorily until it was ended overnight in 1928 when Hoover

was making his first campaign for the White House and I innocently asked Mr. Borah in *The Nation* how he could reconcile two
statements. The first was made in 1919, when he told the Senate
that Herbert Hoover was unfit to be trusted with the expenditure
of $100,000,000 for relief in Russia, and the second, which he had
just made, was his assurance to his countrymen that Herbert
Hoover was the man best fitted in all the United States to be
President—a laughable assertion, indeed, in view of Mr. Hoover's
subsequent record in office. When Washington correspondents took
up my editorial and asked Mr. Borah to answer the question and
reconcile his inconsistency, he frankly said that he could not. He
remains to this day an enigma; gifted with extraordinary talent, a
great fighter in opposition when his indignation is aroused, he
should have been the dominating personality in American political
life and could assuredly have found his way into the White House
had he had stability of purpose, made himself a leader of the
liberal forces, and consistently stuck to his platform.

Naturally we of *The Nation* made much of Woodrow Wilson's
confession in his St. Louis speech of September 5, that: "The real
reason that the war that we have just finished took place was that
Germany was afraid her commercial rivals were going to get the
better of her, and the reasons why some nations went into the war
against Germany was that they thought Germany would get the
commercial advantage of them. The seed of the jealousy, the seed
of the deep-seated hatred was hot, successful commercial and industrial rivalry." This was not only what many had thought from
the beginning but was a confirmation of what Eugene Debs had
said in his speech declaring it to be a capitalist war, for which he
was then in Atlanta Penitentiary, Mr. Wilson refusing, with utmost vindictiveness, to release him despite the fact that Secretaries
Lane, Lansing,[7] and other members of his Cabinet urged that the
great Socialist leader be pardoned.

At this time, too, there came up the question of the secret treaties
which still will not down and was only recently aired again in

[7] Letter of Robert Lansing to the author, Nov. 7, 1919.

connection with the Nye Committee's investigation into the munitions makers. Naturally because of my having printed those treaties in *The Evening Post* I have had a deep interest in this question. As I see the evidence, there is no question whatsoever that Wilson deceived the Senators of the Committee on Foreign Relations who called upon him at the White House on August 19, 1919. In that interview the President stated, in reply to a question from Senator Borah, that his own knowledge of the secret treaties "came after I reached Paris. . . . The whole series of understandings were disclosed to me for the first time then." Senator Borah asked: "Then we had no knowledge of these secret treaties, so far as our government was concerned, until you reached Paris?" The President replied: "Not unless there was information at the State Department of which I knew nothing." Senator Johnson then asked: "Was the United States government officially informed at any time between the rupture of diplomatic relations with Germany and the signing of the Armistice of agreements made by the Allied governments in regard to the settlement of the war?" To this the President replied: "No; not so far as I know." When Senator Johnson asked him whether or not an official investigation had been made by our government to ascertain whether there were "treaties of territorial disposition," Mr. Wilson replied: "There was no such investigation."

Now how was this possible? Not only was *The Evening Post* read daily in the White House but, as I have already stated, the secret treaties were syndicated in nine other daily newspapers as far West as St. Paul and were then reprinted in pamphlet form and put on sale on the newsstands in New York, Boston, Philadelphia, Chicago, and especially in Washington, as well as other cities. More than that, two copies of the treaties were mailed to every Senator and every Congressman, and copies mailed to the White House. The latter, of course, may have been thrown away by mail clerks without an understanding of the seriousness of their import. But it would certainly seem that if there were a vestige of efficiency in the State Department at that time some official would have been sufficiently interested to read and study anything as widely circulated as these treaties. Yet Mr. Lansing had to make the humiliating confession to the Senate on August 11, 1919, that he did not know *until February, 1919,* when the Peace Conference was well under way, of the secret treaties between Japan and the Allies as to the Pacific islands and Shantung, a statement that again gave the lie to Arthur Balfour, who in the House of Commons stated that President Wilson had been kept *fully informed* by the Allies as to what was going on.

But there is further evidence than this. Lincoln Colcord was one of the journalists in the special confidence of Colonel House in the period leading up to the war. Writing in *The Nation* on May 17, 1919, Mr. Colcord said:

Did President Wilson, in the summer of 1917, know about the secret treaties of the Allies? Beyond question, he did. When Mr. Balfour was in America in the early part of that summer, Colonel House requested him, on the score that we were now in the war, and that President Wilson ought to see what we were fighting for, to send copies of all the secret treaties to Washington on his return to England. Mr. Balfour gladly consented. I heard this statement in September *from Colonel House himself.* At that date, Mr. Balfour had submitted no treaties to Washington, and no further request for them had been made at the British Foreign Office.

Again, on September 13, 1919, Mr. Colcord said that in the summer of 1917 he was a member of a group "that had constant access to the highest sources of information. This group at that early date based its conception of American policy in the war upon a knowledge and understanding of the secret treaties. I should be untruthful, indeed, if I did not state that the initiative in the formation of this conception emanated from the Administration." Mr. Colcord then declared that: "On the 28th of June, I think it was, Foreign Secretary Balfour, in answer to interpellations from Liberal members, made his notorious statement on the secret treaties: 'By these treaties we stand—our national honor is bound up in them.' This statement I had the pleasure of bringing to the attention of the *President and Colonel House by letter,* enclosing

the newspaper clippings of the incident and pointing out very fully
its bearings." Mr. Colcord then continued:

> I could multiply the instance by hundreds. Our journalistic group
> was in constant communication with Colonel House; every item of
> news regarding the secret treaties was at the disposal of the Administra-
> tion. I can recall dozens of conversations with Colonel House about the
> secret treaties going back as far as the summer of 1917, and I remem-
> ber how again and again during that season, and during the following
> winter, we urged upon the Administration the danger of the course
> that was being followed by America; the unwisdom of leaving the
> secret treaties unrepudiated. . . .

If the President was really in ignorance of all of this activity
inspired by Colonel House, then he must have lived in an airtight
chamber. Is it conceivable that the Colonel constantly discussed
these treaties with Lincoln Colcord and others of the group, of
whom William C. Bullitt was a member, but failed ever to discuss the matter with the President? Of course he did not. More
than that, Lincoln Colcord assured me at the time that I printed
his article, which he called "Black is White," that he had in his
possession a letter from Colonel House thanking him for two
copies of the secret treaties in the pamphlet form and stating that
he was enclosing those pamphlets "in the private mailbag for the
White House tonight and you know the President alone has the
key to this bag." Yet in the face of all of these printed facts
Senator Carter Glass continues to denounce and to revile anyone
who declares that the President was fully aware of the secret
treaties before he went to Paris. If, however, the defenders of
Wilson are right, they cannot deny that he who held at Paris the
brief for humanity, the greatest brief ever accepted by any man,
failed to take the most important step to win his cause, namely, to
learn his case, to ascertain the background and the facts which
he was to plead before the eyes of the world.[8]

[8] "It does not seem important which of the various versions of President Wilson's acquaintance with those treaties is the correct one—whether he knew their
contents, as did other citizens who bought the ten-cent pamphlet giving their text
in full, and considered them irrelevant; whether he did not know them and there-

Naturally when the end of the treaty fight came and the Senate defeated it we rejoiced wholeheartedly. We felt with Colcord that the "honor of the United States has not been betrayed." We regretted that it was not rejected squarely upon the ground of its inhumanity, of its betrayal of solemn pledges given by the American government during the war, and of its flouting of the great program for world reorganization formulated by Woodrow Wilson in the Fourteen Points. We were sorry, too, that the defeat was largely due to a "group of partisans, most of them narrow nationalists with no adequate vision of the true internationalism which the future holds in store for the world." But we rejoiced that the country had been saved from "acquiescing in a treaty which embodies so gross a breach of faith with the American dead in France and the Americans living everywhere who took at full value and held in honor the assertions of the President that we were in the war to safeguard democracy and advance the cause of human liberty."

To our associate editor, Arthur Warner, came the opportunity to investigate the Boston police strike and to print, as early as December 20, 1919, the facts about Governor Calvin Coolidge's connection with it—facts officially confirmed by James J. Storrow of Lee, Higginson & Company, the conservative head of the Citizens' Committee appointed by Mayor Peters. The truth was that at the crucial time of the strike Calvin Coolidge either refused to face the issue, or disappeared, being "reported to be in the western part of the state." There never was a word of truth in the claim that he ended the strike by the firmness he displayed and by his calling out the state militia—it was actually summoned by Mayor Peters. As the Storrow committee put it: "By Thursday morning order had been generally restored in the city. *On Thursday after-*

fore proceeded in ignorance; or whether he was aware of their existence but brushed them aside without comprehending their significance. The unfortunate fact remains that the secret treaties became the basis of the 1919 peace treaties which the United States was instrumental in enabling the Allies to write, treaties deeply infected with the germs of future wars." Professor Edwin M. Borchard, *Neutrality for the United States*, New Haven, 1937, p. 47.

noon, the Governor assumed control of the situation." Yet Calvin
Coolidge rose to the Presidency because of the absolutely false
press reports of this strike.

I reported the 1920 Republican National Convention at Chicago
and made my contribution to the defeat there of General Leonard
Wood, by publishing his record in *The Nation* of May 29, which
statement was widely circulated in pamphlet form. After the
nomination of Harding by the convention I moved forward on the
journalists' platform and sat among the Massachusetts newspaper
men. When Calvin Coolidge was nominated for Vice-President
they laughed heartily, thinking it a great joke. When the convention adjourned I went to the Congress Hotel. There in the lobby
stood Robert L. O'Brien of the Boston *Herald* and Richard
Hooker of the Springfield *Republican.* The air was blue about
them and they were saying most uncomplimentary things about
Coolidge, O'Brien insisting that Coolidge had never attained any
honor on his merits. He said: "You know, Villard, I have known
all our public men since Grover Cleveland's time. This is the
worst man I ever knew in politics." He then turned to Richard
Hooker, and using the Quaker form, said: "Richard, I will bet
thee a dinner that Harding will die and Coolidge become President."

For us of *The Nation* that campaign soon became "a choice between Debs and dubs." We felt that no self-respecting liberal
could vote for Harding and that what we were witnessing was the
spectacle of the old Republican bosses again in complete control
of a subservient party and defying all aspirations for reform and
progress. Both Cox and Harding were second-rate editors and
speedily showed their intellectual inadequacy for the White House.
Cox himself was of course better than Harding though a graduate
of the politics of the same State; at least it was a cause for thanks-
giving that both Mitchell Palmer and McAdoo were defeated for
the Democratic nomination. Nobody close to Wilson could have
been chosen. Indeed, nobody except Mr. Wilson himself should
have been asked to shoulder the burden of the mistakes, the follies,
the wrongs, perpetrated by the President and his subordinates,

but no Democrat could have won. Franklin Roosevelt made an able campaign for the Vice-Presidency and again and again avowed his lifelong fealty to the League of Nations for which, during his Presidency, he has not been willing to lift a finger.

Soon after the inauguration of President Harding, the "Marionette," I passed through Chicago and as was my wont called upon an old schoolmate of mine who had been in the Ohio Legislature with Harding and the "Ohio gang," and later was a judge until his removal to Chicago. Closing the door of his office, he asked me what I knew of the Harding Cabinet. I told him that I was acquainted only with Hoover, Hughes, and Weeks. He astounded me by telling me that the government had been turned over to a set of third-rate, small-town grafters, that Washington had never fallen so low. He stated that he had played poker night after night with these Ohio men and had repeatedly fought them, and that some of them were open grafters known by everybody as such. It was the first time that I had heard of Jess Smith. Indeed, my friend's horror at what had taken place and what was to come seemed to me so unbridled that I all but dismissed it from my mind and failed to take journalistic advantage of the tip. A couple of years later he was proved correct at every point.

One extremely valuable experience I owe to the temper of those times. I lectured in Cincinnati on January 30, 1921, before the Wise Center and my address attracted no particular attention; it dealt with existing conditions in Europe and what part I thought the United States should play. I returned to repeat the address on February 12 to a joint meeting of the City Club and the Women's City Club. As I stepped off the sleeper from Chicago I was met by two agitated men who, after ascertaining who I was, said: "We must hurry off as fast as we can." That struck me as odd but my attention was arrested by a large group of policemen. "What are they here for?" I asked. "To protect you from being mobbed," was the answer. At the Sinton Hotel I was almost mobbed by a large group of reporters and photographers and found that for the first and only time my name had figured in streamer headlines across the front pages of the morning papers.

For all this I was indebted to Miss Ruth Harrison, the Reverend Frank H. Stevenson, a Presbyterian clergyman, and the Bentley Post of the American Legion. Mr. Stevenson had stated in the pulpit, after citing my record as a Bolshevik, that "an aroused people should be as prompt in muzzling him as they were in stopping the illiterate discourses at the Communist headquarters on Vine Street." Miss Harrison had presented a petition to the clubs bearing one hundred signatures asking that the invitation to me be revoked; eighty-six members resigned from the Women's City Club and twenty-eight from the men's. The Cincinnati *Tribune* declared of me: "He did what he could to make the entrance of the United States into the war a failure abroad and a calamity at home. He still preaches his damnable doctrines," and it added that there were "momentous occasions in a nation's life, where to tolerate other than one universal opinion, conviction, judgment, is to tolerate treason. . . ."

My address was scheduled for immediately after the luncheon hour. I was not allowed to have my lunch with the members. As I stood by the window of an office overlooking the street I saw fine-looking, well-set-up young men entering a music store across the street and then reappearing on the floor above where they crawled on hands and knees to the windows and peeked out. That prepared me for what happened, particularly as I had noticed only two policemen at the door. When I began my lecture I stood on the rostrum facing the entrance to the large room; I could look through it into another room and then through the hallway beyond to the entrance door of the club which had glass panels and was at the head of a flight of stairs from the street. I had been reading my probably rather dull picture of the situation in Europe for about fifteen minutes when the mob came across the street, the two policemen stood aside, and the Legionnaires and others charged up the stairs. A group of club members headed by a courageous American, Guy Mallon, three of whose sons had been in France, threw themselves into the breach, slammed the door, and the fight was on.

The door was forced, the glass broken, and one man badly cut.

The invaders pushed in step by step, finally entering the second room where the fight went on until they were repulsed. All of that put my powers of concentration to a real test, for only the chairman and I could see what was happening. It was a real battle and all my reporter's instincts made me wish to watch it yet I had to go on with my talk; as a pacifist I could not even hesitate. Meanwhile the audience was much disturbed by the noise and confusion and the chairman called down from the balcony behind us asking that a riot call be sent in. In no time at all the police cars were there with their sirens shrieking, which so disturbed the audience that many, among them Adolph S. Ochs of the New York *Times*, who sat in the front row, jumped to their feet and turned around, so that I had to stop. As soon as the police restored order and drove out the mob I asked the audience to sit down and took particular satisfaction in reading every word that I had come to voice. Then we adjourned, the chairman said some pleasant things to me, I found a friend's car waiting for me in a near by street, and I was driven to the home of a relative of my wife's in Wyoming not far away. There I spent the evening until the chief of police, who said that he would not guarantee my life if I tried to take a train from Cincinnati as the Legionnaires were patrolling the streets looking for me, sent an open car with three plain-clothes policemen to drive me to Dayton where I took the sleeper to New York.

With the Legion in the rush into the club were some Covington roughs belonging to a semisecret order of patriots akin to the K.K.K., which was believed to have been responsible for the tarring and feathering of Herbert Bigelow. It was their intention to seize me when I arrived and give me the same treatment; only the fact that no one knew from which direction I was coming saved me from disappearing immediately upon my arrival unless the police had prevented. While the press gave columns and columns to the riot, not one newspaper, so far as I am aware, printed a word of my address or condemned the mob. Ten years later I was again asked to speak in Cincinnati and, being politely applauded when I arose to begin, could not forbear contrasting that friendly greeting with the one in 1921 and lamenting the press's loss of interest in me; I had not even made the first pages. A columnist, "Cincinnatus," writing in the Cincinnati *Post*, said of me: "He returns as a prophet who was despised and now comes to some honor; for the multitudes of prostrate citizens testify to the villainy of the war and of the peace." Not a Legionnaire peeped; the Reverend Mr. Stevenson was dumb, and the Constitution remained inviolate. I am sincere in expressing my gratitude for that riot experience. It was a test that I am glad to have faced, an occurrence I would not have missed.

If this chapter gives a most disheartening picture of our national leaders and the national life in 1920-21, I have only recorded the truth. To such political depths had our republic been reduced in three years as a result of our zeal to slay Huns and make the world safe for democracy! Mr. Wilson insisted to the end that his policies would be upheld; we prophesied the almost unanimous election of Harding "by disgust." Governor Cox was rejected by more than 17,000,000 of his countrymen, of whom 919,799 voted for Mr. Wilson's prisoner, Eugene Debs. The end of a heart-breaking era had come.

Chapter XXVI. Liberty in the Caribbean and Elsewhere

NOT only domestic issues stirred us deeply in those days. When we looked at what was happening in the Caribbean, it was difficult to exercise self-restraint. If Russia was the "acid test" of our unselfishness and benevolent intentions in Europe, Haiti, Santo Domingo, and Nicaragua certainly should have been the "acid test" of our fair play and democracy in the Caribbean. It afforded a genuine opportunity for leadership, good will, and consistency toward the lesser American republics for Woodrow Wilson and his subordinates, William J. Bryan, Josephus Daniels, and Robert Lansing, yet every one of them originated or participated in the most brutal and bloody attacks upon the Haitian Republic without the shadow of a tenable excuse.[1] It was never alleged that a single American had been injured there or a dollar's worth of American property destroyed. The reasons given for this wanton attack upon a helpless little republic were: (1) that there were lawlessness and disorder in Haiti which we could not permit in any country in the neighborhood of the Panama Canal; (2) that unless we rectified internal conditions foreign intervention might result, especially as (3) both France and Germany claimed a special interest in Haiti because of their investments there; and (4) there was a

[1] For the established proofs of this statement see "Conquest of Haiti and San Domingo" by Ernest H. Gruening in New York *Times's Current History Magazine* for March, 1922; "The American Occupation of Haiti," Foreign Policy Association Information Service, Vol. V, No. 19-20, November 27-December 2, 1929; "The Seizure of Haiti by the United States"—a report by twenty-four well-known lawyers, 1922, Foreign Policy Association. Also hearings of the select committee of the Senate on Haiti and the Dominican Republic, October 4, November 16, 1921, Government Printing Office; also the report of Major General George Barnett, October 13, 1920; "Conquest of Haiti" by Herbert Seligmann, *The Nation*, July 10, 1920; Letter of Major General John A. Lejeune, *The Nation*, July 24, 1920.

special danger after the outbreak of the World War that Germany might make Haiti a base for its submarines. The Haitians properly replied that the occupation was plainly illegal for international law conferred no authority upon the United States to intervene as Haiti had injured no Americans, defaulted on no debt, violated no obligation to the United States. There is unhappily plenty of proof that the internal disorders in Haiti were provoked or intensified by the State Department and American citizens in order to advance the interests of the National City Bank and other American enterprises in Haiti.[2]

On December 13, 1914, the government of Woodrow Wilson embarked upon its hypocritical and bloody course. Without warning anyone, American marines landed in the Haitian capital, went to the Haitian National Bank and carried off $500,000 in gold by force, in pursuit of an arrangement entered into by Secretary Bryan and the American directors of the National Bank of Haiti, which bank was owned by the National City Bank of New York. This was surely an extraordinary business for the anti-Wall Street William J. Bryan to engage in! Naturally Haiti protested against this violation of its sovereignty but no answer was ever vouchsafed, doubtless because no defense was possible. The excuse given in Washington was "fear of revolution." The actual pretense for the subsequent intervention was a mob's dragging President Guillaume of the Haitian Republic and General Oscar, commander of the garrison of Port-au-Prince, out of the French legation and cutting them to pieces. The night before these two officials had murdered between one hundred and two hundred Haitians of the better class charged with fomenting revolution, after having lodged them in jail. The mob was determined to have its revenge and had no grievance whatever against the French legation.

This incident was just what Mr. Bryan and Mr. Lansing had been waiting for. A lieutenant and nine men of the French navy

[2] See James Weldon Johnson: "Government Of, By, and For the National City Bank." *The Nation,* September 11, 1920.

having been landed on Haitian soil to guard the legation, this impressive military demonstration was portrayed as an *infraction of the Monroe Doctrine!* The next day a regiment of American marines was put ashore and there began an occupation which did not end for nineteen years and, like interventions elsewhere, did infinite harm to American prestige and our business interests in the Caribbean, Central, and South America. A puppet government—a perfect pattern for the Japanese in Manchukuo—was set up, a constitution favoring the United States forced upon the Haitians, their legislature being dissolved by Colonel Smedley D. Butler, who now freely says that in Haiti he was "doing the dirty work for the National City Bank." Admiral Caperton on September 8 telegraphed to Captain Durrell, commanding at Cap Haitien: ". . . treaty situation looks more favorable than usual. This has been effected by the exercise of *military pressure* [italics mine] at propitious moments in negotiations. Yesterday two members of the Cabinet who have blocked negotiations resigned. . . . Am therefore not yet ready to begin offensive operations at Cap Haitien but will hold them in abeyance as additional pressure." The authorship of this shameless constitution was first credited to Franklin D. Roosevelt, then Assistant Secretary of the Navy. The Associated Press reported on August 18, 1920, that, speaking at Butte, he had said that he "had something to do with the running of a couple of little republics. The fact is I wrote Haiti's constitution myself. . . . Until last week I had two votes in the League Assembly myself." He added that the United States controlled about twelve votes of little American republics in the League of Nations. This report he denied on September 2. Two weeks later Mr. Harding quoted that part of the Associated Press interview relating to Haiti and Santo Domingo which Mr. Roosevelt had not clearly denied. Mr. Roosevelt then telegraphed another denial.[3]

What happened after American control was complete was sub-

---

[3] *The Nation*, October 6, 1920. The A.P. correspondent insisted that he had telegraphed the truth.

sequently told by Major General George Barnett of the Marine
Corps—all honor to him.[4] This officer, who refused to allow his
uniform to keep him from telling the truth, declared that 3,250
Haitians were killed and that he regretted that many of these
deaths were "practically indiscriminate killings." From 1915 on
The Nation almost singlehanded fought the battles for these unfortunate victims of Woodrow Wilson's democracy and Josephus
Daniels' piety. Only three days before the Barnett report appeared
the New York *Times* had attacked Mr. Harding for denouncing
the American policy in Haiti, charging that he "got his information about conditions in Haiti from a weekly paper in this city
which, if not actually bolshevik, is so near it that the distinction
is not visible to the naked eye." When Major General Barnett
told the truth, and confirmed our allegations, the *Times* did not
apologize to us but changed its position and whined that "the
American people have not had the details. They have not known
what was going on"—an interesting admission from the newspaper
which daily boasted, then as now, that it gave "all the news that's
fit to print." Even then it did not bring out the fact that the truth
was suppressed in Haiti by the strictest kind of a censorship
clamped down by the navy.

Some effort was made to break the force of Major General
Barnett's revelations and the previous admission by Major General
John A. Lejeune that "some officers and men have failed, at times
necessitating court-martial and other punishment," by pointing out
that a Lieutenant Brokaw, who was guilty of horrible atrocities,
had been placed in an insane asylum, but Josephus Daniels offset
this by reinstating a captain who had been found guilty by a court
of having given orders to shoot all prisoners.[5] From the moment
in 1920 that I was visited by a committee of the admirable *"Union
Patriotique"* formed to liberate Haiti, the present President Stenio
Vincent being a member of the delegation, we redoubled our ener-
gies. Herbert J. Seligmann, Lewis S. Gannett, James Weldon

[4] The New York *Times*, October 14, 1920.
[5] See *The Nation*, October 20, 1920, p. 436.

Johnson, Ernest H. Gruening, Mrs. Helena Hill Weed, and others went to Haiti for us and brought back the truth or bore the brunt of the fight in the columns of *The Nation*. Doctor Gruening, then managing editor, especially deserves honor; he speedily made himself an authority on Latin-American affairs.

Even the New York *World* failed us in this Haitian fight; it was too closely tied up with the Wilson Administration. Our repeated proofs, our widely circulated pamphlets were ignored by the dailies which believed the gullible—or worse—Josephus Daniels when he declared that "with a few exceptions, the officers and men carried out in letter and spirit the order to set an example in helpfulness and kindness in the discharge of a difficult duty." The character of the slaughter of the Haitians was clearly revealed by the fact that while our marines killed no less than 3,250 men and women—a strange "example of helpfulness and kindness"— the American loss was only *one officer and twelve men*. This was completest proof that it was not war that was waged in Haiti. An illustration of the way error persists was demonstrated at the Williamstown Institute of Politics in August, 1924, when I quoted the figures of Major General Barnett. Two admirals, H. P. Jones and Harry McL. P. Huse, rose and denounced me as a slanderer of the navy and marine corps, Jones saying that it was the "most monstrous and unpatriotic statement" he had ever heard from an American!

Santo Domingo fared somewhat better at Mr. Wilson's tender hands but its government was for a second time deliberately seized by our marines. One week after Haiti had ratified our treaty at pistol point, so that we could have complete military and financial control of Haiti, a similar draft of a treaty was laid before President Jiminez in Santo Domingo—only to be emphatically rejected. Mr. Daniels waited patiently for six months and then his opportunity came. On May 4, 1915, during a revolutionary disturbance, without notification to the Dominican government, marines were landed near Santo Domingo City. On May 13, the American minister told the Dominican government that the subsequent author of the slogan that we went into the World War "for the rights of nations, great and small . . . to choose their way of life and of obedience " [6] was about to land a large force of marines to occupy the capital. The Minister threatened in good Japanese style that these marines would bombard the city and fire upon the natives "without restriction" if there was the slightest opposition. On June 5, the Minister gave formal notice that the American Receiver General of Customs, an official who had been appointed under the treaty of 1907, was to take over all the finances for the government. For five years thereafter the United States—in the name of liberty—held Santo Domingo in "the iron bondage of martial law." Meetings were forbidden, the press completely censored, and protesters against American rule court-martialed; one of them was Fabio Fiallo, a well-known poet, whose imprisonment aroused the anger of intellectuals throughout Central and South America. The Dominicans we killed we called bandits; the Dominicans called them patriot martyrs. It is only fair to say that the marines did a far better job in Santo Domingo than in Haiti, but when they left the Dominicans refused to ratify the acts of our military government, which included loans bearing interest ranging from *9 to 19 per cent!* Our efforts on behalf of these two republics were warmly seconded in Washington by such men as Senator Medill McCormick, who spoke out splendidly in the Senate, Senator Borah, Senator King, Senator Norris, and others—King so effectively that he, a United States Senator, was excluded from Haiti by the marine officers as late as 1927 on the ground that he was an "agent of the *worst elements of disorder*"! [Italics mine.] Senator McCormick headed a commission appointed by the wicked President Harding, which held hearings from May, 1921, to June, 1922, to review the acts of the noble President Wilson. I still stand by my statement to that committee that our intervention in the two republics constituted "the blackest chapter in American history in the Caribbean"—though that was saying a great deal. The commission condemned the forced labor inflicted upon the Haitians by the American occupationary forces and ex-

[6] Woodrow Wilson War Message, April 2, 1917.

pressed "chagrin at the improper or criminal conduct of some members of the Marine Corps." It reported that, besides Lieutenant Brokaw, another guilty officer was dead and a third had been dismissed. It then condemned the efforts of individuals and committees "to bring into general disrepute the whole American naval force in Haiti," instead of pointing out that the fault lay far less with the marines than with the Democratic Administration which placed them in circumstances the bloody outcome of which could be foretold by any person familiar with the history of colonization and imperialism.

President Hoover in 1930 sent a commission to Haiti, headed by W. Cameron Forbes, which included my warm friend, James Kerney, ever benevolent and ever desirous of doing justice. The commission highly praised the then commander of Haiti, Major General Russell, for his "wholehearted and single-minded devotion to the interests of Haiti as he conceived them [*sic*], his unremitting labor, and his patient and painstaking efforts to bring order out of chaos. . . ." But it found: "Race antipathies lie behind many of the difficulties which the United States military and civil forces have met in Haiti. . . . The failure of the occupation to understand the social problems of Haiti, its brusque attempt to plant democracy there by drill and harrow, its determination to set up a middle class however wise and necessary it may seem to Americans—all these explain why, in part, the high hopes of our good works have not been realized." Kerney wrote me on April 10, 1930: "The United States has spent approximately $23,000,000 in Haiti in the last fifteen years and has done nothing to fit the Haitians themselves for handling their affairs." Finally, in August, 1934, the American troops left Haiti and the republic was restored.

I look back upon these crusades on behalf of our Caribbean neighbors with unbounded satisfaction. They alone seem to me to have justified all the time and money I put into *The Nation*. I firmly believe that if we, and the *New Republic*, the Senators I have named, and such public-spirited men as Louis Marshall, George W. Kirchwey, Charles C. Burlingham and Professor

Zechariah Chafee of Harvard, had not appealed to the American conscience the occupation of the sister republics would still be going on. When I visited Haiti for the first time, in 1937, I sought some letters of introduction to people in Haiti only to find to my great surprise on my arrival there that my wife and I were received as guests of the republic and generously entertained by President Vincent. I had supposed that by that time all that *The Nation* had done for Haiti had long since been forgotten—basing my judgment on the length of time the average American remembers with gratitude any favors done him by a newspaper man.

In Nicaragua our military forces were the agents of New York bankers who had invested $15,638,700 in that little republic. We occupied it for the third time in 1912, again giving a false reason for our mission—that we were there to protect our Nicaraguan canal rights. By the time we began to evacuate, in 1932, our protection of the bankers' $15,648,700 had cost us $6,076,000. During all those years we killed hundreds, probably thousands, of the Nicaraguans and lost some precious American lives also—and never caught Sandino any more than Pershing caught Villa in Mexico. It was altogether a disgraceful and utterly uncivilized episode and like our other invasions was bitterly resented throughout Central and South America. *The Nation's* part in the Nicaraguan affair became dramatic when at the beginning of 1928, Carleton Beals, whom I had sent to Nicaragua to report the truth, reached Sandino. He was the first American and also the first bona fide newspaper correspondent to talk with Sandino after he took the field against the marines. Beals underwent considerable risk and hardship to reach Sandino's headquarters as he had to travel overland from Mexico City through Guatemala, San Salvador, and Honduras, and then halfway across Nicaragua. Naturally our marines were furious. They had been unable to locate Sandino but this American interloper held them up to ridicule and laughter by calmly walking into Sandino's camp. As Beals left him Sandino said to him: "Do you still think us bandits?" "You are as much bandits," Beals replied, "as Mr. Coolidge is a Bolshevik." "Tell your people," Sandino flashed back, "there may be bandits in Nicaragua but they are not necessarily Nicaraguans."

Sandino authorized Beals to make public the following terms, upon the acceptance of which he pledged himself to lay down his arms and never take them up again in any domestic struggle and never to accept any public post or salary: First, immediate withdrawal of our marines; second, the appointment of a provisional president, a civilian, who had never been President or a candidate for the Presidency and, third, the supervision of elections by Latin-Americans. These were certainly fair and moderate and just terms, but our marines continued to keep their puppet President in office and to hunt in vain for Sandino as if he were a wild animal. Beals's articles were brilliantly written and gave a most vivid picture of conditions and of the futility of the marines' occupation.

In 1920 *The Nation* undertook another venture which also brought down upon it and its editors a torrent of abuse. Doctor William J. L. M. Maloney, a brilliant young Irishman residing in New York, who had served as a surgeon with the British army and been severely wounded and, for a time crippled, at Gallipoli, suggested the formation of an Irish commission by *The Nation* to call attention to the dreadful situation in Ireland at that time because of the bloody rule of the Black and Tans. The indefensible acts of these hastily recruited British mercenaries had led to similar reprisals by the Sinn Feiners and all who thought the status of Ireland at that time an impossible one. In view of the subsequent establishment of the Irish Republic and the alteration of the relationship of Ireland to the narrow thread which now binds it to Great Britain, without any American protest or excitement, it is hard for me to understand why that Irish commission roused such passionate anger among the ruling classes, especially the "society people" in New York, Boston, and Washington. I suppose that we were then still so near to the war that it seemed an effort to reflect upon the British who were still our dearly beloved Allies. Even from warm British Liberal and Labor friends I received pained and shocked letters at this interference in a purely domestic British affair. To some, who asked me how

Americans would like it if they set up a commission in England to investigate our lynchings, our unconstitutional treatment of our Negroes, our barbaric misrule of our Indians, and our conduct in the Caribbean, I replied that nothing would please me more or help more to alter those grave wrongs committed by my own country.

We were able to start the commission off in a most dramatic way by bringing to the United States the sister and widow of Terence McSweeney, the young Lord Mayor of Cork, who had starved himself to death in a hunger strike in prison as a protest against the British misrule. With marvelous fortitude, super-human endurance, he lived an incredible seventy-four days, suffering tortures beyond purgatory, giving his life for his country as nobly as any soldier who ever wore His Majesty's uniform. For there was no bloodguilt upon him, no stain upon his hands. Once more passive resistance, the most deadly of weapons, triumphed. Once more the whole world was quickened and inspired and glorified by the example of one who placed his cause above his existence, above the happiness of life with his lovely wife and child, which could have been his had he yielded one inch. Muriel McSweeney, the Lord Mayor's widow, turned out to be the ideal person for the role she was called upon to play. No one could have been more charming or more tactful or quicker to understand the situation. Young, slim, pretty, with lovely gray eyes, dressed in deep mourning, she was greeted at the steamer by a committee representing *The Nation* and the commission and escorted by a procession of 10,000 people to the St. Regis Hotel. The police could hardly control the enthusiastic crowds at the pier. Wherever she went she was recognized and followed. When she tried to make purchases in the stores she was all but crushed by the shop-girls and shoppers. Not once did she make a single error of speech or conduct and everywhere she went she aroused the deepest sympathy and respect.[7]

The commission, which comprised Jane Addams, Senator David

[7] For her testimony see *The Nation* of December 22, 1920.

I. Walsh and Senator George W. Norris; L. Hollingsworth Wood, Frederic C. Howe, James H. Maurer, Norman Thomas, and Major Oliver P. Newman, met for weeks in Washington and heard witness after witness. We and they were at once attacked because of the one-sidedness of the inquiry; the British naturally ignored it. In the final report [8] the commission frankly admitted that its inability to obtain pro-English witnesses, and the British government's refusal to allow any of its members to seek pro-English testimony in Ireland or England, had gravely handicapped it. None the less it sought to render as judicial a report as possible and I believe the facts which have now been established by history bear out the commission remarkably. It found that the Irish people had been deprived of the protection of British law and were therefore at the mercy of the imperial British forces which, "acting contrary both to all law and all standards of human conduct have instituted in Ireland a 'terror.' . . ."

The commission recorded that the British government had created a force of 78,000 men, many of them youthful and inexperienced and some of them ex-convicts, and that that force indiscriminately killed innocent men, women, and children (as we did in Haiti), tortured and murdered prisoners and assassinated suspected persons, besides burning houses, villages, and parts of cities. It certified that a campaign had been carried on deliberately to deprive the Irish people of their means of existence by the burning of factories, creameries, crops and farm implements, and the shooting of farm animals, but that all this terror had failed to re-establish imperial British civil government in Ireland. "Throughout the greater part of Ireland," it continued, "British courts have ceased to function; local, county, and city governments refuse to recognize British authority; the British officials fulfill no function of service to the British people. In spite of the British terror the majority of the Irish people, having sanctioned by ballot the Irish Republic, give their allegiance to it; pay taxes to it; and respect the decisions of its courts and of its civil officials."

[8] Printed in full under the title "Evidence on Conditions in Ireland," annotated by Albert Coyle and published by the American Commission in 1920.

On the other hand, while the commission was convinced that
there was a full-fledged revolution on in Ireland, it did not approve the Sinn Fein policies of assassination and reprisal but
"earnestly" deprecated them—the Irish lamentably killed fifteen
British officials in Dublin on one day. We of *The Nation* felt that
the commission could have gone further in attacking the Irish
policy of violence, since that merely gave an excuse to the Black
and Tans to retaliate in kind. But we found that the commission
was quite correct in stating that these outrages on both sides would
cease only when the British troops were withdrawn and we felt
that "there would be peace in Ireland today if Lloyd George could
but have the courage, generosity, and magnanimity to abandon the
policy of trying to crush Ireland by force. The Irish people are
not to be conquered that way." As for the criticism that the commission's work had injured Anglo-Saxon relations, we replied that
it was organized not to hurt but to help those relations, "which must
remain gravely in danger as long as Ireland is bathed in blood by
bankrupt British statesmanship." We cited A. G. Gardiner, the
former editor of the London *Daily News*, who had said that there
were three parties to the Irish revolt, the Irish, the English, and
the American, and John L. Garvin of the *Observer*, who declared:
"It is not a local problem, but is a world problem." [9] The amazingly happy status of Ireland today, with the once so hated Eamon
de Valera the driving force of Eire, is surely the clearest proof of
the correctness of the American commission's view and its complete justification.

In this belief I am upheld by a letter from Doctor Albert Shaw
of October 17, 1938, written after a most careful study of Anglo-
Irish-American relations:

In the concentration of American sentiment upon the outrageous
efforts of the British government to reconquer the Irish people, the
most influential episode was the work of the American Commission on
Conditions in Ireland. This was a difficult undertaking.and, in the end,
it was proved to be a remarkable achievement. . . . There was great

[9] *The Nation*, April 6, 1921.

reluctance in this country to take any steps that were displeasing to the British authorities. They were exceedingly hostile to any American attempts to secure fair play for Ireland, yet, while there was widespread American sympathy for the Irish people, there was also a similarly widespread reluctance to offend the British. Thus, it took rare courage to assume a sponsorship for an organized American inquiry into the conditions prevailing in Ireland. As editor and publisher of *The Nation*, you had long shown your readiness to support causes, however unpopular, when you believed that justice called for vindication.

As I have re-studied the events and circumstances of that period, I have become increasingly convinced that your courage in accepting suggestions that you, personally, and *The Nation*, as an influential journal, should initiate this American Commission, contributed the essential factor that turned the scales. This commission, composed of men and women of great influence, assembled a mass of testimony that could not be refuted. Mr. Lloyd George realized that the time had come for a truce to be followed by an arrangement far more favorable to Ireland than had been proposed in the Home Rule programs of Parnell and Gladstone.

There was precious little liberty in Germany when I revisited it in 1922 and 1923. In the former year I was shocked by the change for the worse and found the Berlin government we are now so prone to denounce for its weakness almost without any freedom of action. Within sixty days the Allied commission which really ruled Germany had sent no less than one hundred demands, orders, and threats to Chancellor Wirth, including an order to change the color of the police uniforms of Berlin at a cost of no less than thirty million marks to that stricken city. At the same time the French off their own bat were lavishly supporting monarchist, communist, and Separatist movements in South Germany—just when they were whining that they could not afford to pay the interest on their American debts. On May 1, I found in the Paris (Royalist) *L'Action Française* the significant words: "It is the destruction of Germany that we want." It looked as if the French were well on their way toward that goal, for suffering and despair were on every hand. I thought that the Russian writer

Remisov put the situation correctly when he said that "Russia is hell but Europe is a waste."

The abortive conference at Genoa I described as "a desert of politics, un-Christian politics, without ideals, without clear-cut aims, with the most vital issues before the world banned in advance; a mess of intrigue carried on chiefly by little men, which may end in utter futility, which may record some slight successes." Utter futility was the outcome and the engineers of the conference were outraged when in the middle of it Germans and Russians signed their Rapallo Treaty and accomplished a most desirable and constructive step forward. Angry as the Allied statesmen were, they were blind to the unprecedented spectacle of four million unemployed in Europe and ten million throughout the world; they were outraged by the suggestion that money be given to the Russians then in the throes of the horrible famine along the Volga. They could not see that something dreadful was bound to come out of the suffering and despair of the German people among whom the groundwork for National Socialism was then being laid—and for the German domination of all Europe. Only one American financier, Frank A. Vanderlip, was enough concerned to go to Genoa. His daily cables to the New York *World* told the truth; but he was a maverick in Wall Street. Why should anyone listen to his prophecies of disaster?

The one person at Genoa who really stood out was Walter Rathenau. True, Lloyd George was there and privately told us journalists that he was then really in earnest in undoing the wrongs of Versailles of which he, Wilson, and Clemenceau were the joint authors, but I rightly did not take him seriously; he had consented to the Boulogne program which had doomed the Genoa conference to futility. Rathenau I had met in Berlin just before his departure for Italy. I had not seen him for twenty-two years when I attended, on April 6, the first reception he gave to journalists in his ministerial capacity. He spoke to us for more than half an hour with profoundly impressive sincerity and earnestness. He seemed crushed by the weight of his official burdens and oppressed by the gravity of his country's plight. He began by quoting Edmund Burke's denial that you can indict a whole people. He disclaimed all desire to propagandize or to alarm unduly but declared solemnly that, if no relief were forthcoming at Genoa or soon thereafter, the government would face violence. "We do not know," he prophetically said, "if it will come from Right or Left but it will come." He told us that hundreds of suicides were being fished out of rivers and canals but "never one yet with under-clothes on" and he spoke sadly of the great number of children unable to go to school for lack of clothing.

When the conference was over I told him who I was. "Are you really," he asked, "the son of my beloved friend, Henry Vil-lard?" He spoke at once of his visits to our home in his appren-tice days in the electrical industry in the United States and begged me to call upon him at Genoa and I did—only to be struck again by the obvious effects upon him of his terrible responsibility and anxiety, by his deep-set, brooding eyes, the plain evidences of marked fatigue, "with all the lightness in his nature crushed out of him." On May 3, in a dull session of the conference, he spoke dully and uninterestingly, in great contrast to a graceful and win-ning speech of thanks he made in excellent Italian to the Italian hosts at the final session. Six weeks later this brilliant business man, who had been the successful head of the great *Allgemeine Elektrische Gesellschaft,* the counterpart and ally of our General Electric Company, this able minister and true patriot, was shot down in the street like a mad dog—because he was a Jew! I still believe that this is one of the innumerable crimes for which the Germany of Hitler will yet pay dearly.

In 1923 the German situation was worse, for the French were in the Ruhr and the inflation brought on by the German govern-ment's printing bank notes to maintain the German workers, who automatically laid down their jobs in passive resistance to the French, was under way. Nothing that could be said against the German domination of Belgium during the war could surpass the brutality of the French occupation of the Ruhr and the Palatinate. Talk about militarists running wild! I saw with my own eyes what went on; how high officials were railroaded to prison merely because of accidents or actions for which they were in nowise responsible. For example, the cultured and able burgomaster of the city in which my father was born, Speyer, was sentenced to *ten years* in prison and locked up for months because a French troop train on entering the city had run over and killed a boy. The French held the mayor guilty because the crossing watchman had refused to serve any longer; the burgomaster, the French said, should have supplied a man to take his place! He spent months sleeping on straw in a cell with two others.

Accompanied by a policeman I visited the brothel in Speyer, instituted contrary to the laws of Bavaria by the French military; the mayor had to recruit the German girls for the use of the black and white troops. It was just across the street from the hospital built by my father. In Zweibruecken I visited the larger and finer brothel the municipality had had to erect at a very heavy cost. I counted sixty Senegalese soldiers standing in line at one of the doors and waiting for their turn and I talked with one of the fifteen inmates, who said that she often had relations with a hundred men on a pay day. All the girls that I talked with assured me that the colored men treated them more kindly than the white French soldiers and declared that they were there voluntarily and had no desire to leave. One of the burgomasters told me, when I commiserated with him on having to recruit women for these houses, that he was constantly receiving letters from out-of-town women who wished these "jobs." Economic necessity drove innumerable women onto the streets. The breakdown of morale during the war continued much longer in Germany than in the victorious countries. In those days Berlin was far more decadent than Paris and homosexuality was shamefully in evidence.

It is hard, indeed, to describe the feelings of people when their medium of exchange varies not only over night but from hour to hour. Nobody thought of saving, only of spending wages as rapidly as they were received, and most conscientious employers tried to pay their workers every day. With those wages the workers rushed to the shops and with what they did not absolutely need for food and clothing they bought anything tangible, pictures that they did not want, books that they could not understand, musical instruments that they could not play—anything solid so that it would not change in value before their eyes. When I left Berlin I did not know how to tip the employees in the hotel. Finally I decided to give each one a dollar bill. I am sure that no Russian grand duke ever received deeper bows. One man almost wept and several of them said they could not thank me enough; that an American bill meant more to them than anything else. My wife stood it in Germany for a couple of weeks and then she was so appalled by the suffering and one's inability to do anything really to help that she returned to France.

Even from the French point of view the invasion of the Ruhr was a horrible blunder. It cost France actually more than they got by it. The burdens that were heaped on Germany may be gathered from the fact that the Rhineland Commission, which, according to the agreement was to consist of four members, comprised in 1922 approximately *thirteen hundred persons* whose maintenance for only eight months cost 178,000,000 gold marks. The furniture in the apartment occupied by one delegate of the commission in charge of a district cost no less than 464,116 gold marks. In Mayence it had cost Germany up to the end of 1921, 3,035,624 gold marks to fit up the castle in which resided the commanding French general. Of course all of these sums rendered the Germans by that much less able to pay reparations. The people were terrorized and tortured in every direction. Expulsions ran into many thousands. From the little town of Gerolstein 2,000 of the 3,000 inhabitants were driven out by the French; often these people were compelled to leave without packing their clothes or safeguarding their furniture. It is no wonder that when on top of this sort of thing the French tried to set up the Separatist governments the Germans took a terrible revenge, in one case in the Palatinate shutting up in a building and burning to death a number of the Separatist traitors. In the old hotel which stands next to my great-grandfather's house in which my father was born, in Speyer, several of the Separatist leaders, as they sat eating dinner in a roomful of people, were murdered in cold blood by patriots who were determined that the Palatinate should continue to be a part of Germany. The bullet marks and a couple of the bullets are still visible in that ancient hostelry in which, including my children, five generations of my family have taken meals and spent nights.

One important thing more: the passive resistance of the Germans, which in some places went so far that not one German man, woman, or child would speak to the French soldiers, very nearly achieved complete success. High French officers admitted that if it had not broken down just when it did the French would have had to leave within two or three weeks; they could not have stood it longer. That this passive resistance failed was a misfortune for the entire world for nothing is as much needed today as proof that there is another way to bring despots and tyrants to book than by resort to force. The passive resistance failed chiefly because of corruption among the Germans, less in Berlin than elsewhere. The money so hastily printed to sustain the resisters stuck to many fingers on the way. Again, the resistance was never planned; it was automatic and spontaneous. No orders were given for it; officials and workers simply stopped working without asking what would happen to them. The government in Berlin was not prepared for this development, did not know what to make of it at first, and when it took hold did so without adequate vision or preparation. Yet for eight months that passive resistance continued until the government itself was compelled to give the signal for its abandonment. There was nothing in this experience to prove that, given proper leadership, this weapon of the spirit cannot be used successfully. At any rate I wrote at the time that some day it might be used again "against that naked brutal force which is today bringing civilization in Europe to its fall"—a prophecy well justified by what is happening in Central Europe as I write.

Chapter XXVII. Harding, Coolidge, and La Follette

ONCE when I lectured before the Women's Club in Waterbury, Connecticut, and spoke of "the corrupt Administration of President Harding, the standstill Administration of Calvin Coolidge, and the do-nothing Administration of Herbert Hoover," at least eighteen of my listeners rose and stalked from the room in wrath, yet it was not an unfair characterization of those three regimes, and certainly entirely true of Harding's. If his administration was not the first in our history in which corruption has reached into the Cabinet, it was surely the only one in which a Cabinet official accepted a $100,000 bribe in the famous "little black bag," in return for the turning over of governmental oil reserves to private individuals. That was on the books when Harding was chosen as Presidential candidate by insiders at an early morning hour in one of the rooms of a Chicago hotel; there is evidence that this robbery was planned well before the convention.

Whether my characterization of these Presidents was right or wrong, no opposition journal could have wished for more shining targets than they. Undoubtedly some good was achieved under each; even Mr. Hoover has something to his credit and Mr. Harding's Conference for the Limitation of Naval Armaments should never be forgotten. The fact remains, however, that the country did stand still or go backward under them. The desire of the New Freedom to rescue the government from the masters of privilege these Presidents wholly ignored because they acknowledged that mastery and served it. Under Coolidge my business friends, especially the bankers, were jubilant. Said they in their shortsightedness: "He is just what the country needs, a quiet, simple, unobtrusive man with no isms and no desire for any reform. The business world needs to be let alone to recover from the war strain and governmental interference in business and control along so many lines." Well did the business world make use of this golden period. The country enjoyed incredible, disaster-creating prosperity—I mean that part of the country which had any prosperity at all. The business men, like Mr. Hoover, were certain that we had forever exorcised the fatal business cycles, that depressions were a thing of the past. *The Nation* insisted during all this period that nothing could be more fatuous. It was the golden hour not to split stocks three to one, not to make huge fortunes overnight on the Stock Exchange, but resolutely to revive the sound ideas of the New Freedom and to bring the national economy and social life in America at least up to the level of the progress, and especially the labor progress, in the really advanced countries.

To say this was crying in vain from the housetops. Nobody wanted anything but to be left alone to make money. Nobody was interested in the fact that, in the midst of unheard-of luxury and unprecedented fortunes, vast numbers of Americans were not only living at or below the subsistence level but were steadily sinking in the economic scale; that millions upon millions of Americans in the South were worse housed and fed than any peasants in Europe. Harding, Coolidge, and Hoover, one after the other, mouthed the sickening old lies about the high American standard of living and prided themselves that we were so far ahead of the rest of the world, Mr. Hoover bringing out his chicken in every pot and two cars in every garage. I have never been able to decide whether this fustian is deliberate deceit or whether it is due to the fact that men like these do not really know how millions of Americans live and starve and somehow survive far below the standards set by the government itself as essential for the decent living of an American family.

I am convinced that if we could have a law requiring every duly elected President to spend his time between election and inauguration not in parceling out offices but among the millions of destitute black and white sharecroppers in the South, whose conditions of life horrify all foreign observers, among the terrorized alien fruit pickers in California, the brutally ill-treated coal miners in Harlan County, Kentucky, or in West Virginia, or in the Negro slums of Harlem and Chicago, or among the shockingly ill-treated Mexicans in Texas and elsewhere, or among child laborers in those of our factories which still employ them, we should have vastly less buncombe and patriotic rodomontade in Washington and much more warmth of heart and efficiency in the White House. Perhaps our future Presidents will read the report published in September, 1938, by the National Resources Committee, in which is shown that the high standard of living in America meant an average family income in 1935-36 of a beggarly *$471 a year!*

Well, at least President Harding had a heart. After the absence of that organ in Mr. Wilson it was a satisfaction to appeal to Mr. Harding as I did with a group of editors in midsummer of 1921, to ask the release of the remaining political prisoners and to receive a most sympathetic hearing from the man who honored himself by willingly releasing Debs from prison—so that Debs might tell great audiences how sorry he was for the vindictive Woodrow Wilson and how sincerely he pitied him. Harding's background *was* democratic.[1] He talked to us about one group of German-Americans whom he had just freed from fearful sentences of thirty-five years and more for having expressed *among themselves*—unaware of the presence of a government spy—some unwise sentiments in regard to Germany after we got into the war. When I thanked him wholeheartedly for his action he said he knew what kind of men they were because on a corner near his home in Marion there lived a German saloon keeper, Jake Schmidt by name, whom he then described with genuine understanding and with real sympathy for the plight many such men found themselves in when war came. Woodrow Wilson might have lived forty years near such a man without knowing of his existence or in any degree understanding him.

[1] He clearly favored justice for the Negro which was the more interesting as he was charged with having Negro blood in his veins.

Harding was extremely handsome and therefore much run after by women. His appearance at the Conference for the Limitation of Naval Armaments in Washington was superb. He read admirably the able speech prepared for him. On his own, however, he was utterly inadequate to the task set him. After his bad break in asserting that the provisions of the Seven-Power Treaty applied to the main Japanese islands when the contrary was the case, he never again answered any question not previously submitted in writing before his press conferences. An idea of his use of the English language and his views on certain important questions may be gathered from the following extracts:

Since freedom impelled and independence inspired and nationality exalted, a world super-government is contrary to everything we cherish and can have no sanction by our Republic. This is not selfishness, it is sanctity.

Reconstruction, readjustment, restoration—all these must follow. I would like to have them.

No one may justly deny the equality of opportunity which made us what we are. We have mistaken unpreparedness to embrace it to be a challenge of the realities, and due concern for making all citizens fit for participation will give added strength of citizenship and magnify our achievement.

There is a luring fallacy in the theory of banished barriers of trade, but preserved American standards require our higher production costs to be reflected in our tariffs on imports.

Our revisions, reformations, and evolutions reflect a deliberate judgment.

These nuggets were all from the President's inaugural. If we really had the sense of humor with which we are credited the Administration would have been doomed in a national roar of laughter then and there. Plainly Harding was a follower of Hosea Biglow, who remarked:

> Nor don't leave no friction-ideas lay'n loose
> For the ign'ant to put to incend'ary use.

Naturally the Senators applauded. Lodge, the literary, called the inaugural "admirable"; New of Indiana, "wonderful"; Kellogg of Minnesota, "remarkable"; Phipps of Colorado, "clever and interesting"; and Ashurst of Arizona, "manly and eloquent."

How much the President was personally involved in the corruption around him we may never know. When there was a Congressional inquiry into the sale of his daily, the Marion *Star*, at a fabulous price, nobody seemed to ask the questions which would have laid any skeleton bare. It is a fact that Harding's letters in his own hand bring tremendous prices—because—so the dealers say—after his death his widow begged or bought every letter of his which several employees could trace and then destroyed them. I am of those who lean to the belief that there was foul play in his death and that here, too, we shall probably never learn the truth. It is, however, an extraordinary coincidence that Brigadier General Sawyer died just as unexpectedly and as suddenly as did the President and under precisely similar circumstances. According to the New York *Times* Mrs. Harding was a visitor in his house at the time.[2]

Harding could not stick to a position—witness the three attitudes he took on the question of American participation in the World Court. Thirty leading Republicans, including Charles E. Hughes and others of his standing, assured the country that Harding's election would be the sure road into the League of Nations. He finished that idea in the words quoted above in regard to a super-government. *The Nation* summarized Mr. Harding's record after he died by saying that "his incumbency of the Presidential office, together with the dominant influence exerted by Messrs. Hughes and Hoover in foreign affairs, has been a dreadful misfortune." Against the records of Hughes, Hoover, and Coolidge must always be the black mark that not one of the three ever uttered one word of protest or regret for the corruption with which they were surrounded during the years which they sat in or with Harding's Cabinet. It seems incredible that they should

[2] See The New York *Times*, September 24, 1924.

not have suspected what was going on; but the habit of resigning from public office—one of the most valuable for honest office-holders—is largely honored in the breach in this country. When Harding died the great captains of industry hastened to subscribe $600,000 for the erection of a magnificent tomb at Marion which thousands visit every year. Enough of the money was saved to give General Sawyer a fine salary as custodian but his term was short. A few months after this money was raised it would probably have been impossible to obtain half of it.

When Coolidge succeeded to the Presidency I wrote: "And now the Presidency sinks low indeed. We doubt if it has ever fallen into the hands of a man so cold, so narrow, so reactionary, so uninspiring, so unenlightened, or who has done less to earn it than Calvin Coolidge. A child of marvelous fortune, he becomes the thirtieth President of the United States because of a newspaper fiction which falsely presented him to the country as a great and vigorous personality who in a dark and troubled hour had saved Boston. . . ." I added that the country's destiny now rested "in the hands of one whose writings and public utterances reveal no spark of originality, no vision, no tolerance, no sympathy with progress and advance. Every reactionary may today rejoice; in Calvin Coolidge he realizes his ideal, and every liberal must be correspondingly downcast." By this I largely stand today, but so undiscriminating is the American public, so prone to hero worship, so ready to assume that whoever becomes President—if he be not a "radical"—is wise, able, just, and a worthy successor to George Washington, that among millions Calvin Coolidge doubtless ranks today as great and good. Fortunately an exactly true sketch of his smallness, laziness, and ineffectiveness as President has been left by Irwin H. (Ike) Hoover who was for many years the day-by-day observer of Presidents as Chief Usher in the White House.[3]

It is easy to imagine with what enthusiasm I threw myself into the Presidential campaign of Robert M. La Follette in 1924, after

[3] *Forty-two Years in the White House*, Boston, 1934. For a more favorable picture, see William Allen White's able and documented *A Puritan in Babylon*, New York, 1938.

having watched day by day the Presidencies of Harding and Coolidge. The Senator reluctantly agreed to become a candidate and did so against the warnings of his physician and his family and thereby he unquestionably shortened his life. We who were eager for him to run could not understand at the time why he delayed his announcement so long and was so slow to take the stump after his nomination; his health was the explanation. This campaign is one of the most remarkable in our history. Although the Senator was promised the support of the American Federation of Labor and $3,000,000 of its funds, actually the total receipts from all sources were only $221,837—I was the assistant national treasurer during the campaign—; the "support" of the A. F. of L. steadily waned as election approached. The New York Labor Council, after having endorsed the Senator, threw him overboard during the last week for reasons that were not too clear. In many States we had no organization whatever. When I toured New York with Senator Burton K. Wheeler, the candidate for Vice-President, acting as curtain raiser for him, in many places we found the merest skeletons of what a fighting political force should be, and in some States we had no organization whatever and could not get on the ballot. None the less La Follette rolled up 4,822,319 votes, without those cast in Louisiana which were not counted. This was more than either Taft or Theodore Roosevelt had polled in 1912 (when, however, there was not woman suffrage), and constituted 17 per cent of the popular vote, while Davis, the Democratic candidate, received 29 per cent. In the Middle West La Follette received more votes than Davis. New York gave him 475,000 but he carried only Wisconsin, the one State in which he controlled a political machine.

This vote proved how great a section of the people desired a Progressive President and how many were as eager as in 1912 for the overthrow of the masters of privilege. I doubt if a more remarkable personal tribute was ever paid to an American citizen than this one to La Follette for it was then only seven years since he had been denounced by President Wilson, burned in effigy in Washington, and even his own State had temporarily turned

against him. His premature death, on June 18, 1925, was a fatal
blow to the third party movement which his sons are now, after
fourteen years, trying to resuscitate. Had he lived I am sure that
he would have run again in 1928. We should by then have built
up a powerful organization; unfortunately there was no one to
take his place. "I don't know how the people will feel toward
me," he said to his son Robert as he lay dying, "but I will take
to my grave my love for them which has sustained me through
life." There never were truer nor more sincere words uttered.
Beyond question he was a politician and in Wisconsin he played
the local political game with the bitter partisanship which he
had learned from his enemies and effectively used the gubernatorial patronage for building up his own machine. But the
people learned in the process to know him; they knew that
deep in his heart he was buttressed by principle, that he had been
absolutely selfless in his fight for them, and that he was genuinely
devoted to their welfare. That and nothing else gave him his hold
upon the people he so thoroughly understood, of whom he was
so proud to be one.

At the La Follette convention in Cleveland which I reported—
it was in extraordinary contrast to the long drawn-out Democratic
struggle in the Madison Square Garden which resulted in the
nomination of John W. Davis—more than four hundred planks
were submitted to the platform committee and some forty-four
accepted, far too many. The Socialists joined forces with La
Follette and that gave the conservatives a point of attack, and so
did a couple of radical planks in the platform, one calling for government ownership of the railroads and the other for the recall of
Supreme Court decisions by Congress by a two-thirds vote, but
only when the Supreme Court had declared an act of Congress
unconstitutional. The Republicans in particular made the welkin
ring with denunciations of this, which today seems a mild enough
remedy for the Court's use of its veto power over legislation. The
heat of the attacks distinctly cooled off when we brought out the
fact that Abraham Lincoln had himself favored the curbing of the
courts. But these planks so excited that refined and high-minded

statesman and patriot, General Charles G. Dawes, that he described
La Follette as "the master demagogue."

That he emphatically was not, as the reader will have gathered.
His range of vision was too narrowly limited by domestic issues;
he was too long ignorant of Europe and Europe's experience. His
platform never seemed thoroughgoing enough to me. "He was
against privilege but he failed to see that the tariff is the greatest
bulwark and creator of privilege; he opposed corruption but he
voted regularly for the tariff system which for generations gave
rise to more political corruption than anything else. He was opposed to war but he was not a pacifist—he could not see that he
who compromises with this evil and refuses to break with it at all
times, under all conditions, merely helps to continue it, helps it
more than does the outright advocate of war. He believed in
co-operation yet lacked the vision to see what enormous benefits
the whole country would derive if it were made of paramount
importance." [4] But he fought against monopoly control of prices
and speculation—never abating his attacks upon the trusts.

That he was constructive in his leadership is demonstrated by
the simple fact that twenty-six out of thirty-one demands that he
and his followers presented to the Republican conventions every
four years from 1908 on had bit by bit become the law of the land
by 1924—nine of them by Republican votes; gradually they all
became part of his party's policies. His Seamen's Bill, long fought
for, when enacted into law became the vital first step in freeing
American seamen from what was a form of chattel slavery. It is
undeniable that he sought to improve our government and institutions piecemeal without deep far-reaching policies embodied in a
comprehensive program. He threw away chance after chance to
advertise himself and advance his fortunes. Charles T. Hallinan
once joined his office force in order to try to set forth the truth
to the public about the Senator but after some months resigned
because he could not get this maligned man sufficiently interested
in himself to make success possible. His causes alone interested

[4] *The Nation*, July 1, 1925.

him. Finally, it can be said of him that he was of that small company who, whatever their mistakes, were inevitably and eternally right. He was a great American.

While Senator George W. Norris has never become a Presidential candidate he, too, bulks large in my story of America as I have known it. For years he has been to my mind the outstanding member of the Senate. No other has to his credit such a long list of constructive achievements in addition to his superb record during the war in remaining true to his oath of office and voting against war as his conscience told him to do. The story of his manly return to Nebraska to report to his constituents, when he had just been denounced by the President, when war passions were at their highest and the flames of controversy and of hatred of him were at their fiercest, is one of the most dramatic in our political records. He took the largest theatre in Lincoln; not a single man would introduce him or sit on the platform with him; he was solemnly warned that his life was in danger. The theatre was packed to the doors and when he finished the audience applauded and applauded him, and he has continued in the Senate ever since— to bring about almost single-handed the change in the date of the inauguration of the President and the meeting of the newly-elected Congress; to save Muscle Shoals and the whole great TVA project for the nation, and to establish in his own State, of his own initiative, and again single-handed, a one-chamber legislature.

One of the happiest moments in my journalistic career was when Mr. Norris told me that in 1923, when he was on the point of declining to stand for re-election, an editorial of mine entitled "Thou Shalt Not Despair" [5] had made him decide to continue in public life. In homely language he had said: "Under the present conditions in Washington and conditions which have existed ever since I came to Congress, it is almost impossible to obtain effective legislation in the interest of the people. I have been bucking this game for twenty years and there is no way of beating it. I have done all I could. Now I am through." He was utterly worn out

[5] *The Nation*, December 26, 1923.

and despairing. He has since been thrice re-elected and will continue to serve the people as modestly, as magnificently, until he dies in harness. Fortunately he is today at seventy-seven still going strong, and he was re-elected the last time on the Independent ticket in the face of the hostility of the Republican machine which in 1930 tried to rob him of his seat by running against him an obscure grocer of the same name—for which this tool of the party under Herbert Hoover later found himself in jail.

The case of Sacco and Vanzetti concerned us deeply during those long drawn-out years of their suffering under the death sentence, and when the horror really took place I vented my feelings in a leader entitled, "Massachusetts The Murderer," described by some as a wild and dangerous outburst. No doubt as to the innocence of these men ever suggested itself to us or to our lawyer friends and advisers, like Charles C. Burlingham and Felix Frankfurter and the many others who did their utmost to save those victims of the post-war anti-Red hysteria. It is of my own knowledge that some of the foremost members of the federal judiciary were with us. Once I thought that I had helped to strike a telling blow for the two men. In 1927, between his Labor administrations, Ramsay MacDonald visited this country. After being entertained at Yale he spent the night at my farm at Watertown, Connecticut, and the next day I drove him to Plymouth so that his daughter, Ishbel, might see where the Pilgrims landed, and then to Boston. On the way we debated how best to approach Governor Fuller so that Mr. MacDonald might speak to him on behalf of Sacco and Vanzetti.

When I telephoned the Governor from the hotel he declared that he would be delighted to receive the former Prime Minister at the State House the next morning, entertain him at dinner in the evening, and ask to it as many people as MacDonald might wish to meet; there was no man he admired more, none whose writings he read more carefully. MacDonald accepted with alacrity upon the condition that no one else should be asked. The Governor invited me. I begged to be excused, saying that I felt sure they would be able to talk more freely if no journalist were present and they were alone—Miss Ishbel had another engagement. The Governor insisted that I come. I went, with the one thought of Sacco and Vanzetti in my mind. How to steer the conversation in that direction kept me preoccupied throughout the greater part of the meal, at which only the Governor and Mrs. Fuller besides ourselves were present—the dinner was in a room hung with superb portraits of the British school purchased out of the Governor's profits as Massachusetts representative of the Packard automobile. Suddenly Mrs. Fuller turned to me and apropos of nothing said: "What do you think of the Sacco and Vanzetti case?" If ever I was ready to kneel and kiss the hem of a woman's gown it was then. "My opinion," I replied, "is of little value but here is a man whose voice is heard around the world. Let us ask Mr. MacDonald what he thinks of the case."

MacDonald was more than ready. In a most impressive way, after disclaiming any desire to mix into American affairs, he told how just before leaving England he had been the guest of the most distinguished law club in London, which embraced, he said, the foremost barristers, solicitors, and judges. The entire evening was given, he declared, to a discussion of the Sacco and Vanzetti trial. In the deepest tones of that beautiful voice he asserted that the unanimous verdict that evening was that, whether guilty or not, men who had been six years under the death sentence should be released at once. Their treatment, he said, was deemed to be not only "cruel and unusual punishment," but so terrible a one that the foremost English legal minds were unanimous in the belief that they had expiated their sins if they were guilty. Unfortunately, Fate, which all through the case seemed bent on destroying these men, played another shabby trick. MacDonald had scarcely begun his statement when the Governor was summoned to the telephone and was gone some minutes. He made the mistake of continuing to talk to Mrs. Fuller so that the Governor lost his impressive climax.

Later when we were in another room viewing some more of that rare collection of portraits, I insisted on MacDonald's repeating to the Governor what he had said to Mrs. Fuller. The retelling under these circumstances was far less impressive and obviously had much less effect upon the Governor than on Mrs. Fuller. I got the impression at the time that the case was beyond the Governor's grasp and that he was relying entirely upon legal advice. It has been a source of special pain to me that it was a classmate of mine, Governor Fuller's legal adviser, who was perhaps more responsible for the carrying out of the sentence than anyone else. When the whole world was seething with the case; when some of our embassies were practically in a state of siege because of foreign protestants against the death sentence; when there was such a tremendous division of opinion among American lawyers and judges; when the whole Massachusetts judicial system as concerned in this case was admittedly archaic, why their sentences were not at least commuted to life imprisonment and time given for the search for additional evidence and for reconsideration in quieter times, I shall never be able to understand.

These men *guilty?* Never.[6] I rejoice to see that William Allen White has now, in 1939, had to revise his former opinion and has gone on record as believing in their innocence; I hope others are likewise seeing the light. "And the gallows, black and hideous, the embodiment of death, the last argument a 'Christian' offers . . . it stands there as a sign of our infamy. . . ." But Sacco and Vanzetti live on in their letters, their aspirations, their martyrdom, whereas the unjust judge will be remembered only because of this case. On August 17, 1927, we said of the following words of Vanzetti to Judge Thayer that they would be the verdict of history and I believe so still. Here they are as voiced when the death sentence was to be fulfilled:

If it had not been for these things, I might have live out my life, talking at street corners to scorning men. I might have die, unmarked, unknown, a failure. Now we are not a failure. This is our career and our triumph. Never in our full life can we hope to do such work for tolerance, for joostice, for men's understanding of man, as now we do

[6] For the latest restatement of the innocence of Sacco and Vanzetti see Louis Stark's "A Case That Rocked the World" in *We Saw It Happen*, by thirteen correspondents of the New York *Times*, New York, 1938.

by an accident. Our words—our lives—our pains—nothing! The taking of our lives—lives of a good shoemaker and a poor fish peddler—
all! That last moment belong to us—that agony is our triumph!

And for how many years did not Tom Mooney, another victim of
hate and passion, languish in jail!

From Boston I conducted MacDonald and his daughter to New
York; they went on to Philadelphia. Few people realize how near
to death MacDonald came at that time. Lillian Wald, Mac-
Donald's most intimate friend in this country, summoned me one
day by telephone to Philadelphia—he was having sinking spells
in any one of which the end might have come—so that I might
be on hand to deal with the press representatives if he should die.
I know there will be many to think that it would have been
better if his career had been terminated then for his own
final standing at the bar of history. We were unfeignedly glad
when medical skill pulled him through and we saw him off to
Europe with profound thankfulness. He was here as the guest and
at the expense of the Jewish *Daily Forward* to celebrate an important anniversary in that remarkable newspaper's history. It was
a dreadful blow to it when he could not appear at the great mass
meeting in the Century Theatre in New York. I escorted Ishbel
MacDonald from Philadelphia to the meeting at which she took
her father's place. It was her first public appearance. Although she
could hardly have known when we left Philadelphia whether she
would see her father again, her self-control was marvelous and
she devoted herself during the trip to memorizing the graceful
and fitting remarks she made, almost without notes, to the great
audience on her father's behalf. I observed her a number of times
in this country and in England and always with admiration for
the manner in which she rose to every responsibility.

Here I must interject the tale of my last contact with Mac-
Donald. I spent the winter of 1930-31 in Germany in order to be
near my son, Oswald, who was at school in Bavaria, and to collect material for a book [7] which is still, I think, a fairly complete

[7] Oswald Garrison Villard, *The German Phoenix*, New York, 1933.

story in English of what was accomplished by the German republic prior to the rise of Hitler. During this period I became convinced that the republic was in the greatest jeopardy and that if aid were not given to Chancellor Bruening disaster was inevitable. I wrote to MacDonald and asked if I might see him—he was then again Prime Minister. In response to a most cordial invitation I went to London, with Sinclair Lewis as a traveling companion, in such haste that I forgot to get a visa; the very courteous official at Folkestone took my word for it that I was in England on the Prime Minister's invitation. MacDonald listened eagerly to my story, agreed to my reasoning that if he were to invite Bruening to London this recognition by the British government would be of great help to the Chancellor—who had not then resorted to the decrees overruling the Constitution which opened the way for Hitler's rise to power—and asked me to go straight from his office to see Snowden next door in Downing Street and Arthur Henderson across the way in the Foreign Office.

The Chancellor of the Exchequer and Mrs. Snowden, who received me at once, were entirely sympathetic. Arthur Henderson was just leaving town for a long week end and so I was turned over to Sir Robert Vansittart, the permanent Under-Secretary for Foreign Affairs. There I found myself face to face with one of the finest representatives of the permanent British Civil Service. He could not accept my arguments that the time had come to invite the German chancellor to visit Great Britain when none had been there since the war. Finally I asked him whether he wished history to record that the German republic had been allowed to go down because Arthur Henderson and Sir Robert Vansittart had not been willing to hold out a helping hand to the German chancellor when he was in dire need of aid to sustain his government. Sir Robert admitted that he did not wish history to record anything of the kind. When I reported to MacDonald Sir Robert's attitude he smiled and said: "Leave the matter to me, spend Sunday with me at Chequers and see Henderson when he gets back from his outing."

I did both. To my astonishment Henderson, the former work-

ingman, was more rigid and bureaucratic than the permanent
Under-Secretary. What I suggested had not been done before. I
could not tell him anything about the conditions in Germany because he had been there recently and knew all that was going on
and he did not think that the situation was as dangerous as I put
it; he thought they were getting on pretty well. "Of course," he
said, "I can't tell the Prime Minister whom he shall and shall not
see or entertain at Chequers which is his private residence but if
he asks me my opinion I shall be against it." None the less, Mac-
Donald took my advice, and after a time Bruening arrived in
London as the Prime Minister's guest.[8] The result, though satisfactory, did not stave off Germany's direful fate—or England's,
either. At least it was an effort in the right direction and the
chancellor acknowledged my mediation by sending me his thanks
and an autographed photograph of himself.

One other pleasant incident of my active connection with *The
Nation* is a source of never-failing wonder. There came to my
office one day Miss Harriet Flagg, who said that she had met me
at my mother's, which fact I could not recall. She then gave me
one of the shocks of my life by stating her quest in these words:
"Will you be my heir?" I had been warned when I went to the
reception room to meet her that she probably wished to ask me to
be her executor for she had already asked Norman Thomas, Scott
Nearing, Roger Baldwin, and perhaps others, and had duly quarreled with them; but I was not prepared for that question. I
replied of course that I was always ready to oblige a lady but that
so far as I could judge from her looks her demise was years off
and that she would probably find someone more worthy to be her
heir. She insisted and I said that if she could find no one else
whom she preferred I would receive the bequest and administer it
for public purposes, as I felt that she would wish me to do. She
promised to leave a letter of instruction and we parted after she
had explained that she had selected me because of her sympathy
with what *The Nation* and I personally stood for.

[8] For Raymond Gram Swing's account of my intermediation see the New
York *Evening Post* for June 7, 1931, p. 1.

I never saw her again but within a few years her executor notified me of her death and informed me that I was her residuary legatee and would receive some thousands of dollars. Actually $100,000 was turned over to me after $50,000 was paid to other heirs—relatives. Other relatives sought to break the will and their lawyer conceived the idea of setting up the plea that I had been guilty of undue influence! When he came to me and asked how long I had known Miss Flagg and how many times we had discussed the matter, and I told him that my sole communion with her had not lasted over twenty-five minutes, he hastily dropped the undue-influence theory but set up a very clever plea, which I have never been able to understand, that somehow or other the will represented an unfulfilled trust. It was carried up to the Supreme Court of Massachusetts and, when I remembered what I had said about that august body in connection with Sacco and Vanzetti, I feared the worst. The court came through nobly and declared that I could use the money for myself or for any purpose that I saw fit but expressed the hope that I would use it for public purposes. This having been my intention from the start I duly incorporated the bequest as The Flagg Fund and have ever since disbursed its income to help liberal causes and needy individuals. From that time on, as the principal in this fairy tale, I have apologized to the writers of those yellow-backed romances of the Gaboriau age, at whom I sniffed when they made their heroines stand on a Seine bridge ready to choose death in preference to the sale of their virtue only to be rescued by a stranger tapping them on the shoulder, and saying: "One moment, young lady; before you jump let me tell you that your great-aunt, Hortense, whom you never saw, has just left you a million francs." No such happening is more wildly improbable than that I should have been the recipient of $100,000 from an able woman who had seen me but once before reaching her decision.

Chapter XXVIII. The Editor Balances
the Account

"IT is certainly curious," Bernard Shaw wrote to me on *The Nation's* sixtieth birthday, "that so outspoken a journal as *The Nation* should have survived sixty years in a country where Truth is tarred and feathered, lynched, imprisoned, clubbed, and expatriated as undesirable three times a week or so. The only encouragement I can offer you is that sixty has a better chance of reaching seventy than fifty of reaching sixty. I have been through both myself and I *know*." Shaw was right, and it is even more curious that the editor of *The Nation* from the years 1918 to 1933 not only survived but came through this period so little scathed.

It is the more remarkable because styles in publications in the United States change without notice and *The Nation* since Shaw wrote that letter has passed its seventieth anniversary and is rapidly nearing its seventy-fifth birthday with a new, but highly experienced, captain at the helm. When *The Nation* was founded, the *Independent*, the *Observer*, and the out-and-out religious weeklies exercised a tremendous influence in the country, and the once extremely powerful weekly editions of the New York dailies, notably that of the *Tribune*, were still alive when I entered journalism. Soon they disappeared, and doubtless *The Nation* and *New Republic*, had it not been for the large means behind them, would have gone the way of the *Independent*, the *Observer*, the *Freeman*, the *New Freeman*, the *Outlook*, the *Review* (founded to combat our heresies and to offer a place of refuge for the seceding readers of *The Nation*), the *Literary Digest*, and numerous others.

As for the dailies themselves, they, too, have shown an alarming mortality. In New York City alone I have witnessed the disappearance of no less than nine dailies—some of which, like the

Herald, the *World,* and Dana's *Sun,* seemed as permanent as the City Hall itself. Although the survivors today print vastly more news from all over the world than did those dailies of 1897, nevertheless there has been decadence in numerous respects. They have been caught, remorselessly, in the drift toward consolidation and monopoly. Every economic influence which affects Big Business affects them, and it is almost impossible to find more than a few which do not reflect the point of view of the great business men and the wealthy and privileged classes. Today the founding of a new daily in a great city is practically impossible—a far cry from that golden age when any young Garrison or Greeley, however poor, who had something in his soul to say to his fellow-citizens, could found his weekly and perhaps watch it grow into an influential daily. This commercialization of the press, together with the creation of chains of dailies, usually controlled from New York with little real interest in the cities in which they appear, have made the few remaining independent dailies and the outspoken weeklies more precious than ever. That any survive is a cause for gratitude.

The Nation and the *New Republic* have, however, been preserved not merely because ownership wealth or friendly aid met their deficits. They have also survived because they are interesting, constantly print facts not to be found in the dailies, and are vital and alive. They have held deep and earnest opinions; they are sincere and enthusiastic in their championship of their causes. The journals of conformity, for all their sedative and supine acquiescence in everything said and done by authority, for all their defense of the *status quo,* have died one after the other because of dullness and lack of fire and of leadership. In their places have appeared far more successful and more widely circulated types of weeklies, such as the digests and the weekly recorders of news events, which will in time yield to still others. Lord Morley once wrote, in the exquisite introduction to his *Recollections:* "The oracle of today drops from his tripod on the morrow. In common lines of human thought and act, as in the business of the elements, winds shift, tides ebb and flow, the boat swings, only let the anchor hold." To no other form of activity than to our press do these words apply better. I am old-fashioned enough still to believe, and with all my heart, that to survive, with or without large means, a journal must be anchored by ability, character, leadership, and genuine skill in the presentation of facts and opinions.

Long ago it was said: "One who molds the people's beliefs ought to have the wisdom of a sage and the inspiration of a prophet and the selflessness of a martyr." Still more is asked of the editor of today. In addition to the economic pressure upon him, his lot is made extraordinarily difficult because never in the history of the press has such all-embracing knowledge, such rapidity of judgment, such surety of vision been demanded of leader writers. From every corner of the world comes news, often of extreme significance in its bearing upon events fifteen thousand miles away. There is little or no time for careful consideration. When I joined *The Evening Post* we often found ourselves hard put to it in summer to discover subjects enough to fill the daily editorial page. Today, politics having become economics and economics politics, and the world standing on its head, a journal needs a large staff of specialists and expert legal advice to be had for the telephonic asking. Fortunate indeed were the Abolitionists and other early reformers, for their causes were simple and understandable of all men. Slavery presented a plain issue and yet that was threefold: it was an economic problem, a vital political problem, and, most important of all, a burning human problem. It has often seemed to me that one of the foremost reasons for the failure of nations to progress faster, and of the intelligent peace-loving minorities in all countries to make themselves potent, is that the multiplicity of reforms, of issues, and of news events the world over, bewilders the multitudes, just as it often dries up the sympathies and paralyzes the enthusiasms of the reading public. The human mind cannot react simultaneously to horrors in Ethiopia, slaughtering in Spain, and indescribable massacres in China. The wellsprings of human emotion are inevitably sucked dry.

Although the demands upon the editor are beyond any one man's powers today, the rewards of a free journalist remain of the greatest. We now know well what happens when the editors of a country all lose their freedom under government control. Of all the prostitutes in the world such editors are the most contemptible because they deliberately and knowingly lend themselves to misleading and poisoning the identical people their newspapers were meant to enlighten and inform. Under freedom, the education of the unchained editor never stops. He acquires knowledge every day, whether he wishes to do so or not. The very studying with expert eye of the day's dispatches adds to his store of facts, gives him a deeper background, and—if he has within him the possibility of growth—a wider and wiser perspective. That is one of the chief attractions and one of the great rewards of the profession— the joy of intense intellectual absorption in stimulating and exciting tasks which put the editor behind the scenes of politics and in touch with the men who work the governmental machinery.

I have repeatedly asserted that one who has had the joy of saying in print just what he thinks and feels, of breaking a lance on behalf of any cause in which his heart was enlisted, never relinquishes this privilege happily but always with deep regret. That privilege has been the great boon which inherited means bestowed upon me. They gave me the opportunity to be my own master; they enabled me to write as I pleased without ever having to wait upon another to get his orders. The ability to roam the world in order to see for myself the kinship of all peoples; the power to aid in some slight degree the suffering, the oppressed, the victims of prejudice, of injustice, and of cruelty everywhere; above all, the freedom to say one's soul is one's own: these are the sole justifications of wealth that I have been able to discover. In darkest days friends have asked me how I could still be optimistic—undaunted. I have replied: "Being one of the most fortunate of men I have no right to be other than one of the happiest."

Still it has been far from easy to retain one's courage when bitterness, hatred, and medieval cruelty have entered into men's hearts and brute force at this writing rules the world. Much of the great promise of my youth has been dispelled. All that hope and belief that we, in a country of unlimited riches and inexhaustible lands, were destined to be a tranquil, happy, uniquely prosperous people safe from all the quarrels and embroilments of the Old World, have vanished. Our social problems have become those of the old countries—by our own folly and shortsightedness. We have wasted our natural resources, deliberately and needlessly invited class strife engendered by special privilege, by unequal economic conditions, by unfair governmental favoritism. We actually face real danger to the Republic that, until 1917, no one believed could again be put in jeopardy. We confront the pressing danger that economic stupidity, fostered by crass nationalism, the armament race, and war, will end not only the creation of the American Revolution, but will destroy all democracy, and civilization itself —a condition none the easier to bear because it has been due primarily to the lack of fidelity and vision, the obtuseness and selfishness of those who have conducted governments here and abroad.

How can one keep one's faith? How present a cheerful mien to those coming after? For one thing, the causes which *The Nation* has championed since 1865 can never be wholly defeated unless humanity is to destroy itself. The ideals which we have professed will never perish even if we face another dark age. They have been the goals which for centuries have beckoned men onward—the desire for justice, for equality, for complete freedom, for the happiness which comes from social security and peace—and they will never perish. No dictator, for all his boasted efficiency and masterfulness, has anything similar to offer. We have not lost those ideals, nor have we individually been defeated. I refuse to admit discouragement save for the immediate future. That is, I think, not just a matter of inborn temperament. It is merely due to the rightful consciousness that the angels have fought with us—and that we ask of no one what we are not willing to concede ourselves. We have much with which to reproach ourselves in the frequent failure of our leadership, our own weaknesses, but not as to our aims. Victory always—that is impossible. As Robert E. Lee said at Gettysburg to his retreating soldiers, after admitting his personal responsibility for the disaster of Pickett's charge: "We cannot win all the time." The independent, liberal, internationally-minded journalist is content if he can win part of the time.

That we of *The Nation* have done—we *have* won from time to time as everyone must who fights long against cowardice, hypocrisy, greed and human stupidity. More than that, if we wished to offset the demnition total of our errors of judgment, it would be easy to show case after case, year in, year out, in which we have warned the masters and rulers of America what the inevitable results of given policies would be and then, when those results appeared, have been able to say: "We told you so." There is where we have drawn unending confidence and courage—the demonstration, in defeat, that our principles were right, our deductions correct. We have seen Time again and again catch up with some of the Lord's anointed in a way to amaze, and to hearten us no end. In the face of Hitler and the triumph of militarism at home and abroad, we recall Mr. Wilson's statement to the American Federation of Labor on March 12, 1917: "What I am opposed to is not the feeling of the pacifists, but their stupidity. My heart is with them, but my mind has a contempt for them. I want peace, *but I know how to get it and they do not.*" When in all history was there an idler boast? Never has the falsity of solemnly spoken words been more clearly demonstrated and in so short a time—and the utter fallibility of the man who voiced them.

It was he, too, who amid the plaudits of a victorious people declared on the first Armistice Day, November 11, 1918, to the assembled Congress in Washington: "Armed imperialism such as the men conceived who were but yesterday the masters of Germany is at an end, its illicit ambitions engulfed in black disaster. Who will now seek to revive it?" Yet at the very moment that he uttered these words there was an obscure lance-corporal, still in his tattered field-gray, who in the incredibly short space of time of less than twenty years, was to give a complete reply to Mr. Wilson's rhetorical questions and to win the World War without the firing of a shot. Discouraged by the Munich disaster, the hideous, unforgivable cruelties to the Jews of Germany, the subjugation of a great people to the will of a conscienceless, murdering fanatic?

Yes, indeed; it makes facing the day-by-day world almost a trial as by fire.

But a vital sustaining fact is that the world is witnessing the greatest, the most overwhelming, proof of the futility of force in the settlement of national and international problems and that fact millions are admitting. Never did it occur to me in 1917 that within twenty years the bulk of our countrymen would agree with us who declared that we could not win the war and that our entry into it was the greatest blunder in American history. But there the fact is; poll after poll tells the tale. Never could there be under heaven a more complete demonstration that you cannot shoot virtue or democracy into human beings nor kill sufficient to make the survivors forswear militarism and mass destruction. It is not because we can say with undeniable truth in 1939: "We told you in 1914-1918 what would be the exact outcome of the World War," that our spirits remain steadfast, but because of the proof that the principles of human conduct, the ethics, derived from Christ himself, which we championed, for which some of us were martyred in prison, have been completely justified.

We see that the prophecy that they who take up the sword shall perish by it may yet come true of the nations which sought in 1914-1918 to establish peace on earth by unparalleled human destruction. We are of the opinion that the present armament race, if it does not result in war, will do almost as much injury to the economies of the nations taking part in it as war itself; that the devoting of such large portions of a nation's revenues to the making of munitions opens a direct way to the regimented, totalitarian State. We believe that if the democracies seek to maintain themselves by war they will inevitably emerge from it as fascist States. But we think in all sincerity that sooner or later the madness of the present hour will pass and the nations realize that armaments offer no security whatever, but the reverse; that the road they are now following leads not to safety, nor glory, but to despair.

The list of our successful causes we are prone to forget because the unsuccessful press us on every side—yet it is there. We have seen kings and kaisers, who seemed beyond question enthroned, fall overnight. We have witnessed the disappearance of one prejudice after another, the breaking of social chain after chain, the removal of injustice after injustice. We have seen caste lose its hold even under the dictators. We have beheld the complete change in the status of women; a Hitler has tried in vain to restrict them to *Kinder* and *Küche*, though not to the church. Women can and do conquer as much of the industrial world as they desire and they have penetrated deeply into the professions in all enlightened countries. They have captured advanced positions in their assaults upon the archaic laws which have held them in bondage—with some redoubts still to be taken. Woman now knows that her body *is*, or should be, her own; that she has rights as to her children and, in some countries at least, owns her own property free from the control of her husband. The establishment of her right to vote, and to participate in government in as many countries as have yielded it, insures the inevitable spread of her political power when the present period of darkness has passed. Even in Turkey the veil, which had seemed perpetual, was abolished, with the fez, by one stroke of the dictator's pen; Turkish women have literally overleaped centuries in twenty years, and now find themselves almost in the status of their sex in progressive countries of the giaour.

Best of all has been the marvelous alteration in the relations of men and women, their having been freed, even in Germany, from the incredibly degrading assumption that if a young man and woman found themselves together they could have but one thought and aim—a relic of the age-old theory that the woman existed solely for the gratification of the man. With this has come the growing recognition, especially in the Anglo-Saxon countries where it was particularly needed, that in this field, as in relation to the liquor traffic, individuals cannot be made moral by law. We see on every hand the new understanding that the private lives of individuals, where they do not affect public order or exploit victims of our capitalistic system, are their own affair; that morals and personal standards do change and change for the better; that individuals are not to be gravely punished and ostracized for life if they transgress what hoary tradition, selfish privilege, and hypocritical religionists declare to be the immovable *mores* of the hour. The first editor of *The Nation*, Mr. Godkin, declared and believed that any divorced woman—divorced "for cause"—should be driven out of decent society. I, the sixth editor, have seen the full acceptance in all circles of women known to have had children by men to whom they were not married, whom they never had any intention of marrying. Nor were they famous actresses of "loose morals" such as even Mr. Godkin respected because of their talents, and deemed exceptions to his rule.

To me this revolution means not license and debauchery but the emancipation of society from unbearably degrading chains of falsity, sanctimonious hypocrisy, stupid prudery, and deliberate disregard of truth and the realities of life—sins far worse than that which was to have been curbed not only by monogamy but by divorceless marriage. In the generations to come, I believe, nothing will seem more incredible to historians of our time than that women should have been for centuries chained by law to human brutes whose very aspect was loathsome to them, whom they could not divorce, who would not divorce them, who made their lives a daily hell, indescribable in the refinements of its cruelty; nothing will seem more tragic perhaps than that those martyred women could not leave their husbands to fend for themselves because there were almost no decent economic opportunities for them to earn a livelihood. If there ever has been an advance it lies in the discovery that even youth may freely discuss the problems of sex not only without injury but on the whole immensely to its own benefit. In other words, frankness, honesty, openness, intelligent knowledge of any problem are vastly preferable to concealment, evasion, misrepresentation, deceit, humbug, hypocrisy, the refusal to look facts in the face, the intolerant persistence in pretending that the most important factor in life is not what it is. Because of this belief—shared by all my associates— *The Nation* under me fought just as staunchly against every form of censorship of art, books and plays as it did for the other forms of human liberty.

During its long life its editors have witnessed the spread of knowledge the world over. It has not made men free nor saved whole countries from enslavement by the new and direful propaganda of governments made possible by some of the latest and greatest inventions. The system of free public education in this country has never equaled in efficiency that of pre-World War Germany, despite the hundreds of millions of dollars lavished on bricks and mortar. It was Montaigne who declared that he was "very fond of peasants—they are not educated enough to reason incorrectly." I have recorded my belief that I would rather trust the innate good sense and the judgments of five hundred Americans of the farms and villages than a similar number of more or less class-conscious college graduates. This is no pose but the absolute truth. It has been a result of my journalistic education that I have acquired faith in the plain people whom Lincoln trusted so completely, provided—and this is a large "if" indeed—the facts can be laid before them; Lincoln himself might tremble in the face of a governmental control of all organs of opinion and all means of communication!

This faith does not permit me to believe that the votes of any very large number of Americans have been bought by the lavish expenditure of government moneys since 1932, nor to entertain any doubt that if the mass of the people were convinced that the New Deal has become something else than what they desire in concept and execution they would vote Franklin Roosevelt out of political life as emphatically as they did Herbert Hoover. Proof that the plain people have been deceived repeatedly by false leaders is scattered all through this book. But the public has risen to the three men who at one time or another have asserted that they sought to free the America of today. The slogans "Square Deal," "New Freedom," and "New Deal" may have meant little or nothing in the Park Avenues and Wall Streets of our cities; they have meant much to those whom Woodrow Wilson had in mind when he said: "The government, which was designed for the people, has got into the hands of bosses and their employers the special interests. An invisible empire has been set above the forms of democracy." And again: "Our government has been for the past few years under the control of heads of great allied corporations, the special interests. . . . As a result there have grown up vicious systems and schemes of governmental favoritism (the most obvious being the extravagant tariff), far-reaching in effect upon the whole fabric of life, touching to his injury every inhabitant of the land, laying unfair and impossible handicaps upon competitors, imposing taxes in every direction, stifling everywhere the free spirit of American enterprise." [1]

Not Woodrow Wilson nor Franklin Roosevelt has unchained the people, but the story of our political life covered by this volume is proof that however faulty, incompetent, deliberately recreant, or heavily handicapped the leaders, the fight for a better America has gone on somewhere in our country all the time. It has had different names and has flown different banners, but whether in Wisconsin or Minnesota or New Hampshire or California, there is ever a striving for popular control of the public's affairs which neither treason, nor economic and social stupidity, nor the making of war have been able to destroy. One need only cite as proof of this the extraordinary vote in the House of Representatives in the winter of 1938, when, despite tremendous Presidential pressure, that body came within twenty-one votes of the first step to take the war-making power out of the President's hands and to place it where it belongs, not in those of Congress, where it ostensibly inheres, but in those of the people who are asked to make the sacrifices and to give their sons.

As the reader has seen, forty-one years of responsible journalism have given me little respect for most of the men in high office in any country. Often I have said to myself: "Would that mine enemy could become President or Prime Minister." Nothing in my life has been more disheartening than the discovery of how high officeholding eats into the characters and souls of human beings—again with rare exceptions. I speak here not of legislators but of men in powerful executive positions controlling the destinies

[1] Wilson; *op. cit.*, p. 25.

of great masses of their fellow human beings, the Wilsons, Roosevelts, Hoovers, Clemenceaus, MacDonalds, Lloyd Georges, not to speak of dictators, who seem to feel when they take office that they are, first, indispensable to their respective countries; second, no longer bound by the rules of ordinary morality and so free to misrepresent and to lie, to grasp power, to break faith; and, third, that they are blessed with absolute infallibility. So they change all their viewpoints by processes of self-delusion and rationalization until they convince themselves that they are as consistent as they are righteous, as true to themselves and to their beliefs as they are just.

Most menacing to humanity is the ability of such men to order others to their deaths—by millions—without any real sense of responsibility or human feeling. So Lansing and McAdoo were ready to plunge this country into the World War without really caring what the cost would be in lives, merely because they felt that if the Allies were to lose the war our base blood-money prosperity would collapse over night. So Wilson was ready to make war upon Mexico and Haiti and Nicaragua to have his way with those countries, with whose governments and fates he was never charged. Of the Prime Ministers few have hesitated at undertaking any kind of political chicanery to achieve their ends, not only in war but in peace. Sometimes I feel that the Hitlers and Mussolinis are just Wilsons and Lloyd Georges who have risen to power merely because they were more ruthless than these Anglo-Saxons, more ardent and brutal in fighting for their beliefs, besides being vastly abler executives and more dominating leaders.

I have no doubts about one thing: the business of governing, as I have observed it, is no unfathomable mystery, no impossibly difficult task even in these times, if only the men in highest offices would forswear their selfish politics, forget their parties and their own ambitions, and really accept their offices as a public trust. There is nothing stranger than that your practical politician cannot see that the straightest course becomes the most direct and certain road to popular favor. Nothing concerning them is more offensive than their skulking one moment behind what they call public opinion, when they do not wish to do something, and then refusing to pay the slightest attention to the public will when they wish to go ahead and have their own way; especially has this been true in the making of war. Of all the Presidents I have known and studied, Grover Cleveland seems to me the best, the bravest, the most honest, and the truest. He was a politician and he leaned toward conservatism. He did not always have the vision we need today; he was mistaken in his labor policies and perhaps in handling bond issues; he made one gross error in foreign policy. Yet he was free from inordinate ambition; he was not constantly thinking about his own advancement; he stood foursquare to the winds; he was unpurchasable; he was stubborn in holding to a principle to the verge of a dangerous obstinacy. Looking back, however, those seem halcyon years—when there was a man in the White House who was a very great administrator, who stood on Monday where you had left him on Saturday, and believed in principles in 1894 in which he had believed in 1884.

To my mind the high-water mark of personal virtue and patriotic service in the White House in my lifetime was that scene when, in 1888, Mr. Cleveland called in his chief political advisers and lieutenants to talk to them about the coming presidential campaign. He did not ask them what he should do so far as his own fortunes were concerned; he did not ask them what political issues he should espouse. When they had assembled he told them that he had determined to stand for re-election and on the issue of a tariff for revenue only. Promptly every man in the room protested and told him that if he asked for re-election on that issue he would be defeated. "Well then, gentlemen," said Grover Cleveland, "I *shall* be defeated"—and he was. It is strange that it is necessary to portray this simple, and normal, and conscientious stand as the greatest act of moral courage by a President in fifty years—but that it is. Not one of his successors would, in my judgment, have been capable of a similar greatness—certainly not his first Democratic successor, Woodrow Wilson.

It is hardly any wonder that the American people rose so remarkably, almost unitedly, to Franklin Roosevelt immediately after his taking office, when the country was in the midst of a dire economic catastrophe. For then it appeared as "if he had ideas, determination, a program which he was prepared to carry through with unfailing courage and most heartening cheerfulness, the latter conveyed to all his countrymen in beautiful English by a captivating voice. The promise of those years has not been wholly lost. Side by side with disheartening blunders, with administrative inefficiency as striking as was the extraordinary executive ability of Grover Cleveland, we have gained more for labor and more social security under his Administrations than under those of all the other Presidents put together. I hold no great brief for Mr. Roosevelt despite my lifelong friendship with him; despite the fact that, in 1910, when he had just won his first office, a seat in the Senate of New York State, I introduced him to a City Club audience as the young man who, in my judgment, had the greatest political future before him of anyone of his generation; despite my writing in 1928, in *The Nation*, that, if his health should be completely restored, he would be nominated some day for a still higher office than that of governor. I have cited him here not, of course, for these reasons but because he, too, affords clear proof of my thesis that the American people want nothing so much as leadership of the type that they thought Theodore Roosevelt and Woodrow Wilson were giving to them and that Franklin Roosevelt certainly offered in those days in which everybody sang his praises, even the "economic royalists" who now revile him from sunrise to sunset and circulate disgusting stories about his personal character.

To pass complete judgment upon him is not possible at this time; we cannot yet tell how events on the other side of the world will affect our destiny, nor can we yet measure the extent and dangers of his obvious weakening, his blunders, his unstable leadership, his lack of sound economic beliefs, his insistence on playing the political game. We do know that he has led this country into a most dangerous militarism which, because of inadequate forethought and lack of planning or definition of what we are to defend, repeats the worst blunders and follies of the statesmen of Europe and other countries. Under him we have joined in that

deadly race for preparedness and more preparedness which, even
Mr. Roosevelt admitted, in Buenos Aires December 1, 1936, spells
bankruptcy and the lowering of the standard of life for vast multitudes, and the destruction of a country's economic system and
war.

Here we have again proof how little statesmen have learned;
how they are bound by conventions; how they imitate one another
in folly and wrongdoing; how they actually set their feet upon
paths which they admit lead but to destruction. So, in the economic
field, they pattern after one another. If one puts up a tariff the
other raises it, too; if one seeks colonies, another demands them as
his right, without the slightest consideration of what his having
colonies before meant to his country, without inquiring whether a
single dollar is to be gained by the subjugation of foreign peoples.
Not one of the leaders is willing to try methods short of war although they know that it is no longer possible to win any victory
when war comes—only to reap a harvest of wholesale murder, of
immeasurable misery, of economic disaster.

Franklin K. Lane was right when he upheld the *gaudium
certaminis* even when battling against the greatest possible odds.
Said he but a short time before he crossed the Great Divide: [2]
"There is no way to make the fight excepting to believe the fight's
the thing, the one and only thing—the one, only, greatest thing.
(To deny this is to leave all in a welter and drift into purposeless
cynicism—blackness.) To determine that this is the way, the truth
and the light, is to get serenity. Then the winds may howl and the
seas roll, but there can be no wreck." It is the spiritual fight to
better human conditions which brings serenity and peace within.
To such a battle the response is instant. On the tenth anniversary
of my editorship messages of good will, friendship, and solidarity,
and appreciation of the battle we were waging reached *The Nation*
from all the European and South American countries, from Russia,
New Zealand, Madagascar, China, even Tahiti. They touched me
deeply because they came from protestants against the folly of the

[2] *The Letters of Franklin K. Lane*, Boston, 1922, p. 393.

age, from fighters, too; I was far too conscious of my debts to my fellow-workers to apply these words of gratitude and encouragement to myself alone. Until my retirement in 1933, after fifteen years in the editor's chair, these many evidences of good will continued. In addition, whenever needed, there came generous financial aid, reinforcing my own gifts, from a small group of friends and adherents.

Finally, in this hour of diabolical, unChristian, psychopathic, anti-Semitic barbarism, I must state the simple truth that if I had not had the support and encouragement of many Jews I could not have carried on in the measure that I did. Their idealism, their liberalism, their patriotism, their devotion to the cause of reform in the time-honored American way, heartened me in the hardest hours. I have been wholly unable to discover the slightest difference between their support and that of Gentiles, except that they responded more quickly, often more generously. I have never appealed to them for aid for the Negro, for the sick, the poor, the distressed, or for any philanthropy and been rebuffed. And never once have the Jews who aided my causes and responded to my appeals for others sought to capitalize upon this, to ask favors, to presume that their responses entitled them to rewards at my hands. My pen may have some skill, but I could not begin to measure the debt that this country owes to its Jews and to millions of its foreign-born citizens, first for a jealous guarding of American rights and liberties to which the native-born have too often been indifferent; second, for preserving at all times a great reservoir of idealism and liberalism, and, thirdly, for keeping alive a passionate desire for knowledge in every field, which has steadily quickened American life and notably in its colleges.

That this editor's mistakes have been numberless during his editorial career, his failures egregious, must be perfectly plain to the reader. Perhaps, however, it can be said of him in retrospect that he did know how to fight and cared enough about the struggle to put into it all that he had to give during his fighting years— as his life's contribution to the country which he has sought to serve and the democracy for which he will never cease to strive.

Index